Good Music, Sacred Music, and Silence

Written or Edited by the Same Author

Good Music, Sacred Music, and Silence

Three Gifts of God for Liturgy and for Life

PETER A. KWASNIEWSKI

Foreword by
Fr. John A. Perricone

TAN Books
Gastonia, North Carolina

Scripture quotations are taken from the Douay Rheims Bible, in the public domain, as well as *The Revised Standard Version of the Bible—Second Catholic Edition* (Ignatius Edition), copyright © 2006 National Council of the Churches of Christ in the United States of America, used by permission, all rights reserved; and *The New Jerusalem Bible*, published and copyright 1985 by Darton, Longman & Todd Ltd and Les Editions du Cerf, and used by permission of the publishers.

Magisterial documents are cited from the Vatican website unless otherwise noted.

Cover design by Andrew Schmalen

Cover image: *Christus met zingende en musicerende engelen*, Hans Memling, (1483–1494)

Library of Congress Control Number: 2022952441

ISBN: 978-1-5051-2228-2
Kindle ISBN:978-1-5051-2229-9
ePUB ISBN:978-1-5051-2230-5

Published in the United States by
TAN Books
PO Box 269
Gastonia, NC 28053
www.TANBooks.com

Printed in the United States of America

*In thanksgiving for those who have shared the gift of music with me,
especially these teachers and friends:*

Roy Horton†

Fr. Germain Fritz, OSB†

Lawrence Kay

Stephen Grimm

Timothy Fortin

Don Reto Nay

Michael Waldstein

Timothy Woods

Rick Wheeler

Nicholas Lemme

Music lays bare man's inner existential condition, removing veil and façade (and it *cannot* be otherwise), while this same inner condition receives from music the most direct impulses, for better or worse.

—Josef Pieper

It is necessary that one who takes delight in things becomes then similar to the things he takes delight in. . . . If someone makes a mistake in regard to music, he becomes well disposed toward wicked characters and he suffers the greatest harm.

—Plato

Inasmuch as this kind of pleasure [in singing] is thoroughly innate to our mind, and lest demons introducing lascivious songs should overthrow everything, God established the psalms so that singing might be both a pleasure and a help. From strange songs are brought in harm, ruin, and many grievous matters, for lascivious and vicious things in these songs take up residence in parts of the soul, making it softer and weaker; whereas from the spiritual psalms proceed plenty of profit, the greatest benefit, eminent sanctity, and every inducement to philosophy, for the words purify the soul and the Holy Spirit descends swiftly upon the singer's mind. . . . And just as swine throng together where there is mire, but where there is incense and fragrance there bees abide, so demons congregate where there are licentious songs, but where there are spiritual songs there the grace of the Spirit descends, sanctifying mouth and mind.

—Saint John Chrysostom

At the beginning of great sacred music there is of necessity awe, receptivity, and a humility that is prepared to serve by participating in the greatness which has already gone forth. . . . One recognizes right liturgy by the fact that it liberates us from ordinary, everyday activity and returns to us once more the depths and the heights, silence and song.

—Joseph Ratzinger

Be silent before the face of the Lord God: for the day of the Lord is near, for the Lord hath prepared a victim, he hath sanctified his guests.

—Zephaniah 1:7

Contents

PART III
Giving Way to Silence

Foreword

ONLY THE MOST myopic would deny that a kind of mushroom cloud has covered the Catholic Church for the past half-century. A small, but quite significant, part of that spiritual nuclear winter has been the profound collapse of sacred music. Votaries of the "spirit of Vatican II" (in today's *au courant* vernacular, "the New Paradigm") knew well the power of music in liturgy. If their "reimagining" of Christianity was to settle its roots deeply in the souls of Catholics, music was the key.

They learned well the perennial wisdom of Plato when he wrote in *The Republic*: "Musical training is a more potent instrument than any other, because rhythm and harmony find their way into the inward places of the soul." Or the wisdom of Aristotle, whose view in *The Politics* is ably summarized by Goldsworthy Lowes Dickinson: "Emotions of any kind are produced by melody and rhythm; therefore, by music a man becomes accustomed to feeling the right emotions. Music has thus the power to form character, and various kinds of music, based on the various modes, may be distinguished by their effects on character—one, for example, working in the direction of melancholy, another of effeminacy; one encouraging abandonment, another self-control, another enthusiasm, and so on through the series."

Almost eight hundred years later, Boethius echoed these great giants of natural wisdom when he wrote, "Music can both establish and destroy morality. For no path is more open to the soul for the formation thereof than through the ears."

Added to these, they observed the great success that Arius enjoyed in winning the masses by composing hymns. Whole populations found themselves praising the Arian Christ, no longer God, but only *like* God. Stevedores sang these Arian hymns as they loaded cargo on ships anchored in the harbors of Alexandria, Carthage, or Thessalonica. In this way, Arius's poisonous heresy swept over fourth-century Catholicism like a mighty tidal wave. So swift was this heretical deluge that it prompted the now famous, albeit terrifying, lament of Saint Jerome, "The whole world groaned, and was astonished to find itself Arian."

For all these reasons, we could justifiably add to the venerable theological axiom *lex orandi, lex credendi* a new one: *lex cantandi, lex credendi.* Or, more idiomatically, "We begin to believe, the way that we sing." When Catholics in a typical parish are served lounge music instead of sacred music, their souls suffer a kind of dry rot. They experience not the "fear and trembling" of Calvary but only the wispy breezes of the musical theater. This is no longer religion but vaudeville. Worse still, when the music descends to mimicking the rock concert, the soul undergoes a proportionate excitation. And not to divine things.

If a Catholic, denied traditional music, is not allowed to be struck to the depths by the likes of "Let All Mortal Flesh Keep Silence" or Byrd's "Ave Verum Corpus," then he is left to be drowned beneath the indulgent waves of sentimentality. The former hymns steel the soul for supernatural contest, the latter for mindless self-absorption. Sacred music is the indispensable instrument of the Holy Spirit in leading souls in their march toward heaven: it is gravity and solemnity wrapped in the stunning beauty that only music can offer.

Looking at music in general, or sacred music more particularly, we see two principles at work. One has to do with simply being human, the other with being a Catholic. Both reasons go directly to the soul of man and his civilization. For those who think narrowly, music in Church is a kind of mood-setter, cute but irrelevant. An ampler mind recognizes that music acts like an earthquake upon the soul, unleashing powerful forces for good or ill.

On a purely natural level, music is the sheen that glistens over life's quotidian dreariness. It is an art of beauty. Without beauty, man's life becomes flat and self-absorbed. Music lifts man's soul out of its prosaic circumstances and sends it soaring to heights it would not know without it. Or depths. Music's power is so potent that it can arouse passions driving toward heroic actions or debased ones.

Almost twenty years ago, the Port Authority of New York and New Jersey decided to play only soft classical music throughout its Manhattan Bus Depot because psychologists had proven it would lower crime. On the other hand, nightclub owners know to play loud, percussive music, piquing the passions and producing the emotional abandon that sells liquor and facilitates sexual license. No human heart is exempt from racing to the stanzas of "The Battle Hymn of the Republic" or any march of John Philip Sousa. Music has its own grammar and vocabulary. Differences of language, age, and race cannot impede its impact.

Once again, such an impact was duly noted by Plato. In *The Republic*, he teaches, "No change can be made in styles of music without affecting the most important conventions of society." It was exactly for this reason that he forbade certain kinds of music in his envisioned city. Plato spoke brilliantly to this subject when he taught that "music does not merely *depict* qualities and emotional states but *embodies* them." A performer singing (or a hearer listening) "about the rage of Achilles, for instance, would not only be depicting the emotional states of anger and violence and the personal qualities of Homer's hero, but he would be experiencing those things himself."[1]

In 1570, France's Charles IX created the Académie de Poésie et de Musique. In his *lettres patents*, the king declared, "It is of great importance for the morals of the citizens of a town that the music current in the country should be kept under certain laws, all the more so because men conform themselves to music and regulate their behavior accordingly, so that whenever music is disordered, morals are also depraved and whenever it is well ordered, men are well-tutored."

Not only is music integral to a full human life, it possesses the power to *shape* human life. Though Plato expresses it with philosophical brio, each one of us already knows this truth. One need only consult one's own experience. Victor Hugo once remarked that a man has the power to make of his soul a sewer or a sanctuary. Music, too, has that power over the soul, and that is why we must be vigilant.

Sacred music builds civilization and ennobles character. It does, however, even more. When music is composed to honor the Blessed Trinity at Holy Mass, it is called *sacred*. Under that purpose, music consummates its highest end. It not only brings man to the heights of beauty; it brings man to Beauty Itself, Almighty God. Man is never so enraptured as when he is surrounded by sacred music. This music transforms him and pierces his soul to the core of his being. Often, it produces a contrition so profound that a man's life can take a wholly different course. Saint Augustine attests to this in Book IX of *The Confessions*: "How I wept to hear your hymns and songs, deeply moved

---

[1]   See Michael Linton, "The Mozart Effect," *First Things*, March 1999, online at www .firstthings.com/article/1999/03/the-mozart-effect.

by the voices of your sweetly singing Church! Their voices penetrated my ears, and with them, truth found its way into my heart; my frozen feeling for God began to thaw, tears flowed and I experienced joy and relief."

On these grounds, Mother Church has encouraged the most exquisite sacred music known to man. Not only that, she has felt it her grave obligation to *protect* it. The stakes could not be higher. Man's soul hangs in the balance. If the music is wrong, the teaching absorbed from it will be wrong, and men will go wrong. So it is that in this century the popes have devoted such energy to defining and carefully regulating the conduct of sacred music. They also appreciated the corrupting forces in the last hundred years militating against dogmatic truth and trumpeting sentimentalized subjectivism.

It was this awareness that clearly inspired Pope Saint Pius X to promulgate his masterpiece on sacred music: *Tra le Sollecitudini,* whose one-hundredth anniversary Pope John Paul II honored with an appropriate tribute. In that document, Pius X taught that the three properties of sacred music are *universality, goodness of form,* and *holiness.* He declared that those properties are perfectly fulfilled in the Church's Gregorian chant, which thereby also becomes the paradigm of all sacred music. Such properties raise it above the idiosyncratic in cultural forms (universality), possess the high marks of the grand music of the ages (goodness of form), and excite in souls a hunger for God (holiness).

Pope Pius X teaches: "The Church has constantly condemned everything frivolous, vulgar, trivial and ridiculous in sacred music—everything profane and theatrical both in the form of the compositions and in the manner in which they are executed by the musicians. *Sancta sancte,* holy things in a holy manner" (*Tra le Sollecitudini* 13). The Church's sacred music is part of the Dove's Pentecostal descent, carrying Christ into man's soul on wings of reverential beauty. Remember: when you hear choirs singing the jewels of the Church's treasury of sacred music, you are witness to a great moment. Culture is being changed, and starved souls are being filled with God.

Dr. Peter Kwasniewski, to whom we owe so much when it comes to the illumination and defense of the Catholic Church's rich liturgical heritage, has given us in this book a thorough, lucid, and persuasive guide to the hard-won truths about the art of music bequeathed to the West by ancient philosophy, the inspired Scriptures, the High Middle Ages's lofty theology, and more recent sources of insight, including the modern ecclesiastical magisterium. The author delves deeply into the themes I have touched on above with his telltale combination of scholarly calm and polemical dash. In this work, one senses above all the fruit of decades of listening, singing, playing, praying, composing, conducting, thinking, and writing about music. He knows whereof he speaks.

The title exactly matches the content. Part I expounds "good music"—that is, the music of the great Western musical tradition that spans the centuries, from religious chant to the classical masters to such modern composers as Arvo Pärt (and not excluding authentic folk genres)—and explains why today's mass-produced pop music is cultural junk, ethical ennervation, and spiritual poison. Here the author does not remain in the clouds but offers ample and specific recommendations of good music to listen to. Part II, on sacred music, not only articulates with uncommon clarity why chant and polyphony are ideally suited to the liturgy but critiques the false inculturation represented by "praise & worship" and the all-too-common use of guitars and pianos in churches. He offers very concrete pastoral advice, even providing a model circular letter a reforming bishop could send around to his presbyterate to correct musical abuses and reinstate traditional sacred music! Part III, on silence, reminds us that there is an important place for that which goes beyond what we can express in words and melodies and harmonies: it is a mistake, Kwasniewski says, to fill every nook and cranny of the liturgy (or of life) with sound, because our souls need silence too, the expectant "open space" that makes meaningful conversation and art possible.

In short, the book you hold in your hands is an ideal introduction to the philosophy, theology, and spirituality of music from a Catholic point of view. It comes at the right time—a time when many clergy, religious, and laity are rediscovering the treasury of tradition that had been foolishly locked up after the Second Vatican Council, to the immense imperilment of the Church's doxologizing and evangelizing mission. But tradition, being a gift of Divine Providence, shares in His immortal vitality and cannot be extinguished or entirely forgotten. Its roots will put forth green shoots and the tree will bloom again. In these pages, Dr. Kwasniewski eloquently makes the case for good music, sacred music, and silence—"three gifts of God for liturgy and for life." May we rediscover and embrace these gifts to the fullest!

Fr. John A. Perricone
November 22, 2022
Feast of Saint Cecilia

Preface

THIS BOOK EXPLORES the fine art of music and its loftiest category, sacred music for the liturgy of the Catholic Church.

I entered into church music at an early age by singing in the choirs at my local parish. In retrospect, I came to realize that only a small portion of what we sang could be categorized as *sacred* music, but nevertheless, I learned how to read music, how to sing in parts, and how to be punctual for rehearsals and warm-ups. In high school I studied composition and conducting with a teacher who had been trained at the Eastman School of Music; I sang in the boys' schola he led, which performed chant and polyphony, and took voice lessons with his wife, an opera singer. It was at the end of high school that I began to compose my own musical works.[2]

My introduction to Gregorian chant came through listening to recordings;[3] it was something I had never encountered in church. At about the same time, I was invited to a charismatic prayer group, which awakened my prayer life and led to good friendships. I even attended a Steubenville "Big Tent" meeting and wrote a peppy guitar song! That phase lasted for about two years.

By the time I went to Thomas Aquinas College in California in the fall of 1990, I had already fallen in love with great classical music and chant, and it was an enormous joy for me to be in the polyphonic choir and the men's chant schola. In the former, I learned how to run rehearsals to assist the director, and in the latter, I learned how to read square notes, count the rhythm, sing with solfège, and perform the Ordinary and Propers at a Novus Ordo Mass

---

[2] A discipline I have continued ever since, at varying levels of intensity depending on the demands of my primary career—the primary career being either teaching or writing or some combination thereof. To date, I have composed about 150 pieces of music, nearly all of them sacred choral works. Recordings of many pieces will be found at www.youtube.com/@DrKwasniewski.

[3] In particular, of the Choralschola der Wiener Hofburgkapelle under the direction of Pater Hubert Dopf, SJ.

in Latin.[4] I first encountered the Tridentine Mass at TAC, and to say that it piqued my curiosity would be an understatement.

In graduate school at the Catholic University of America, I attended the traditional Latin Mass more and more frequently, both at Old Saint Mary's in Chinatown and at Old Saint John's in Silver Spring. I directed the Gregorian scholas at both places (though not simultaneously). While immersing myself in the classical Roman rite, with its contemplative, almost monastic atmosphere, I finally understood where chant came from, how it fit into and complemented and completed the liturgy. The connection between chant and the Novus Ordo liturgy was less clear because the latter had been designed along entirely different lines—modular, efficient, and activity-oriented, with immediate rational comprehension as its primary aim. At my first place of employment, the International Theological Institute (then in Gaming, Austria), I continued singing and leading chant, hymnody, and polyphony at celebrations of the Mass according to both the traditional and modern missals. Crucially, I also immersed myself for the first time in the Byzantine liturgy, which I learned how to cantor more or less by osmosis. The Eastern rites, sung in a variety of languages, continued my education about what makes a liturgy traditional and how its customary music is part of its essence.[5]

In 2006, I helped establish Wyoming Catholic College in the town of Lander, adjacent to the Wind River Range, in cowboy country—a very long distance, both geographically and culturally, from the heart of Europe. From the start, and with the co-founding bishop's encouragement, we had a mixed SATB (soprano, alto, tenor, and bass) choir and a men's schola, singing for both "forms" of the Mass (indeed, Benedict XVI's *Summorum Pontificum* had been released only weeks before the first freshmen arrived on campus). Throughout my twelve years at the college, I led the music for the Tridentine Mass and the Novus Ordo, the latter featuring chant not only on Sundays but also on weekdays. The choir sang a rich repertoire of chant, polyphony, and hymnody; all students were required to take a year of introductory music theory, history, and appreciation, in the course of which we studied what the magisterium teaches about sacred music, and, for fun,

---

[4]   For a defense of the allowability of this terminology, see my article "Are We Justified in Calling Paul VI's Creation the 'Novus Ordo [Missae]'?" Full information about all sources cited in short form in the footnotes will be found in the bibliography at the end.
[5]   See Kwasniewski, *The Once and Future Roman Rite*, 278–311.

sang rounds, folksongs, and partsongs. It was about as close to a "Benedictine" musical ideal as one could have wished.

At the collegiate Novus Ordo Mass, I was able, to a large extent, to "lose myself" in the chant as a child might play for hours in the woods behind his house, thereby not noticing that the house itself is perhaps falling apart or the neighborhood is derelict. Nevertheless, the nagging sense remained that the chant and polyphony did not harmonize as well with the so-called "Ordinary Form" as they did with the "Extraordinary Form."[6] To be sure, the traditional music *can* be used with the liturgical books of Paul VI, not only for the Mass but also for the Divine Office and so forth; and yet it remains a difficult relationship to navigate. Moreover, during these years, I studied the "liturgical question" more and more intensively, reading authors from many centuries and especially from the decades on either side of the post-Vatican II reforms. Through study and experience, I arrived at the realization that the rites promulgated by Paul VI were in fact deformations of the Roman heritage, inconsistent assemblages of decontextualized and modified ancient material and whole-cloth innovations based on pastoral utilitarianism and, at times, progressivist theological concepts. The bare validity of the rites has never been in serious question, but their authenticity as liturgical forms and their fittingness for divine worship can and must, sadly, be questioned.[7]

I eventually concluded that I must commit myself to a liturgically coherent life. A series of events and opportunities that led to my departure from Wyoming Catholic College initiated this liturgical change. At the time of writing this preface, I have attended only the traditional Mass for the past four years. I sing in a men's schola every Sunday and most holy days, and look forward—if anything, even more than I did before—to the joy of singing these incomparable ancient melodies, so perfectly suited for the rites to which they give musical utterance and shape. Their beauty elevates my mind to God; their tranquility comforts my heart.

---

6   On this terminology, see Kwasniewski, "Beyond *Summorum Pontificum.*"

7   The liturgical question as such is too large and complex for a book dedicated to the subject of music to tackle and, besides, has been the subject of numerous books, including several of my own, to which the notes and bibliography will make reference. In order to keep within bounds and maintain focus, the last century's liturgical reforms are here addressed only to the extent required by the subject matter.

I do not write this short account of my journey to discourage musicians from doing their best in the circumstances within which they wish to work or must work. Not everyone has access to the traditional rites of the Church, and not everyone prefers them. I tell my story to let my readers know where I am coming from and that I can relate to them. In my meandering journey from a liberal parish and a contemporary youth group to a charismatic prayer group to a Latin Novus Ordo with a chant schola to immersion in the Byzantine liturgy to a mixed old-and-new-Mass chaplaincy to parishes run by the Institute of Christ the King Sovereign Priest and the Priestly Fraternity of Saint Peter, it is highly likely that I have been, for some portion of my life, in a situation similar to that in which *any* Catholic musician, music director, or music lover may find himself right now.

Dear reader, I believe that I understand you, and I do not despise where you are at or what you are trying to do, even if I may no longer serve at such a post and have taken up my abode elsewhere. I agree with the saying recounted by Father Zuhlsdorf: "A rising tide lifts all boats." I would like great music and the finest sacred music to flourish everywhere, in every situation, to the fullest extent possible. That is why I even include herein some "Reform of the Reform" ideas, giving voice to a perspective that I no longer share. It will be easy for the attentive reader to distinguish between what I am putting forward in my own name and what I am raising as a possible approach, a hypothetical scenario.

In the first part, "Music Fit for Kings: The Role of Good Music in the Christian's Life," I explain why the great "classical" music of Western civilization is morally and intellectually good for us, and that more is at stake in what we listen to than most people are aware. In the second part, "Music Fit for the King of Kings: The Role of Sacred Music in the Church's Life," I explain why the admired sacred music of the Latin-rite Catholic Church, especially her Gregorian chant, is well-suited to divine worship and should be retained or reintroduced for theological and spiritual reasons. In the third and final part, "Giving Way to Silence," I explain why silence is, in its own right, as valuable as, and at times more valuable than, even this great music—precisely because music itself intimates or opens the way to a reality that is ineffable, transcending all that we can say or sing.

In this book, there is no attempt at offering a grand all-encompassing theory of music. For that, one will need to look to such authors as Victor

Zuckerkandl and Roger Scruton.[8] Nor is it meant as a history of, or a guide to, classical and sacred music, or a detailed account of the function of different types of chants or motets within the liturgical rites—tasks, once again, that have been accomplished by those better qualified to do it, such as William Mahrt, Joseph Swain, Edward Schaefer, and Susan Treacy.[9] You will find here a medley of meditations and an arsenal of arguments from my decades of experience as a singer, composer, director, and liturgical scholar and culminating in the conviction—presented in these pages under many vantages and without the slightest hedging or apologizing—that our traditional music is the loftiest of God's gifts to us in the natural order, the greatest artistic treasure the world has ever known, and, in its specifically liturgical manifestations, a vital, indispensable bearer of the theology, spirituality, meaning, and identity of the Catholic religion. We cannot live well without it; we will not pray well without it. Music is the language of the soul, its most intimate and exalted expression. Sacred music is the liturgy's blood and bone, the carrier of its organic life, the architecture of its prayer. If something goes wrong with music, as Plato saw long ago, the culture is lost; if something goes wrong with liturgical music, as Ratzinger saw so clearly, the *cultus* is depressed and devalued. In short: Divine Providence knew what it was doing, as did the great artists in their own capacity. We must become again as little children who receive eagerly the marvels offered to them.

Progressives reading this book may take offense at my musical traditionalism; traditionalists reading this book may be offended by my citations from recent magisterial documents (although there are plenty of older sources too);[10] and conservatives may be offended by my intransigent traditionalist sympathies and sentiments. But keep reading anyhow. Of music and of silence, there is much to learn, much to rejoice in, much to love—and, I believe, much that can unite us. May these good gifts coming down

---

[8] Zuckerkandl, *Man the Musician*; Scruton, *The Aesthetics of Music*.

[9] Mahrt, *The Musical Shape of the Liturgy*; Swain, *Sacred Treasure*; Schaefer, *Catholic Music Through the Ages*; Treacy, *The Music of Christendom*.

[10] Thus, I will quote from the Constitution on the Sacred Liturgy *Sacrosanctum Concilium* of the Second Vatican Council when it is in manifest continuity with the preceding tradition and also because it is rhetorically opportune for those who wish to promote authentic sacred music to know how to defend their goals on the basis of clear texts from the most recent ecumenical council. Nevertheless, I am certainly not unaware of the problematic aspects of the Council.

from the Father of lights be for you and for me a foretaste of the joy that awaits us in heaven.

The chapters herein began as articles at *New Liturgical Movement, OnePeterFive, LifeSiteNews, Homiletic & Pastoral Review, Rorate Caeli,* and *Views from the Choir Loft* of Corpus Christi Watershed. Chapter 21 appeared in the journal *Sacred Music* under the title "Blessed Silence." Chapter 8 was developed from a lecture given at a number of places, until it was given in its final form at the Sacred Liturgy Conference in Spokane in May of 2019. I am grateful to the editors, publishers, and organizers for giving me the opportunity to research and express the ideas that have coalesced into this book. I also thank the editors at TAN for their persistence in seeking this book from me.

Sources of the epigraphs: Josef Pieper, *Only the Lover Sings,* 50; Plato, *Laws,* 656b and 669c; Saint John Chrysostom, *Commentary on Psalm 41,* modifying Strunk's translation with reference to the Latin in *PG* 55:157; Joseph Ratzinger, *A New Song for the Lord,* 158.

Peter A. Kwasniewski
September 14, 2022
Exaltation of the Holy Cross

Abbreviations and Conventions

GIRM	*General Instruction of the Roman Missal*
NLM	*New Liturgical Movement* website
SC	*Sacrosanctum Concilium*
ST	*Summa theologiae*

Psalms are referred to by their Septuagint/Vulgate numbering.

To avoid clutter in the notes, hyperlinks have generally been avoided; instead, the author and title are listed; the site and date are listed in the bibliography, which are sufficient for locating the piece. All internet citations were verified as of August 22, 2022. Full information about *all* sources cited in short form in the footnotes will be found in the bibliography at the end.

The *Summa theologiae* is quoted from the bilingual edition prepared by The Aquinas Institute and co-published with Emmaus Academic.

PART I

Music Fit for Kings

The Role of Good Music
in the Christian's Life

1

Music as a Character-Forming Force

IN THE FIRST part of this book, I will argue that Christians, inasmuch as we are "priests, prophets, *and kings*" by our baptism into Christ the High Priest, Word of God, and King of kings, deserve and require a diet of the most artistically beautiful, most emotionally satisfying, most intellectually stimulating, and most spiritually beneficial music. We need, in short, music that is both *good* and *great*.

Music never lies

In a Christopher Nupen documentary on the acclaimed cellist Jacqueline du Pré,[11] one of her close friends says, "Music never lies." How true this is! People can lie, the lyrics of songs can lie, but *the music itself can never lie*. It contains and conveys, perfectly and purely, the spirit embodied in its rhythms, melodies, and harmonies. We cannot translate this spirit into a sequence of descriptive words; could we do so, music would cease to be music; it would be a vaguer form of poetry. But that indefinable message of the soul contained in every piece of music, great or small, is still present, communicative, formative.

Jacqueline du Pré herself demonstrated the specific and irreducible truth proper to music in the remarkable depth and intensity of her performances. Listening to her play in Beethoven's "Ghost" Trio or a Brahms cello sonata is a revelation of intuitions, feelings, memories, discernments, opportunities, interventions, choices, fates—of all that is distinctively human, yearning for empathy and straining towards immortality. She is described at one point as a person "always striving for beauty, for the most distant horizon." This, indeed, is the noblest measure of man, the animal that can *see and hear beauty*, and not merely see colors and hear noises; the animal that,

---

[11] *Remembering Jacqueline du Pré* (Allegro Films, 1994).

perceiving the ground, the expanse ahead, and the vault of heaven, knows what a horizon is and then transforms these perceptions into metaphors of its own intentionality.

"Nature and music have the same grandeur," says another person interviewed. They do, because they both speak of the eternal and the infinite to the human heart, which has *the capacity for grandeur.* The human heart has also *the capacity for giving and for suffering.* "Music does not speak of things, but tells of weal and woe": of giving in love, of trials and pains, of a grandeur once beheld but now past, nostalgia for what has been, hope against hope for what might still be, and of a grandeur not of this world, more real than this world, glimpsed like a sliver of sun through the clouds, drawing us on and dispelling our despair.[12] Is it not a miracle that music speaks of all this? Music influences plants only physically; it can sway animals to a degree, but their field of perception comprises no more than the immediate surroundings. But man is finely equipped to perceive the message contained in both nature and music, and resonates with it when he encounters it with a properly attuned ear.

In the same documentary, another person remarks, "Sound comes from our being." What is this mysterious thing called "sound"? Aristotle analyzed well its physico-psychical aspects in his treatise *On the Soul,* but he did not attempt to explain the mystery of *meaningful* sound, which only the higher animals produce, nor the far greater mystery of rational language and the suprarational discourse of the fine arts.[13] The sound that is properly language comes from our unique mode of being in this world—as being *in* the world, due to our physicality, but not *of* it, due to our being made in the image and likeness of God. The sound that is music is the finest flowering of language; no wonder it is the province of worship, loss and lamentation, exultation and joy. For it is a wonder past all other wonders that proceed from the heart of man. In the words of a medieval commentator, Bernard Silvestris:

> Music rules over us, given that we are held together through it.
> When nature catches in voices what she feels innate within her,
> she is moved with a deep, wondrous affection, since like rejoices
> in like. Music endows voices, removes anger, suggests clemency; it

---

[12] The quotation is from Schopenhauer, commented on by Josef Pieper, "Thoughts about Music," in *Only the Lover Sings,* 39–51; for Schopenhauer's formulation, p. 42.
[13] See Aristotle, *De Anima* II.8; cf. *On Sense and the Sensible* I; *History of Animals* IV.9.

persuades. And every age, every sex, and the nature of almost all living creatures is moved at the whim of music. For what compels the thrushes, swans, nightingales, and other sweet-songed living things to utter their loquacious comfort? Just as they breathe without labor, so too do they sing. This is a sign that music is innate in souls, since those things which have no free will with which to deliberate, produce (led by nature alone) harmonious voices, or rejoice at [others] doing so. Through the comfort of music the Theban Ismenia used to heal the maladies of the Thebans. And so too did David with the royal madness [of King Saul]. And we even read that Empedocles with a swaying mode calmed the youth who was rushing at his host, since he had accused his father. The Pythagoreans, also by song, caused a light and pleasant sleep to waft over themselves; just as by other modes they used to shake off the stupor of sleep once they awoke. What shall we say about how such a diversity of souls are pleased by a variety of modes?[14]

A character-forming force

The philosopher Roger Scruton observes, "Nobody who understands the experiences of melody, harmony, and rhythm will doubt their value. Not only are they the distillation of centuries of social life: they are also forms of knowledge, providing the competence to reach *out* of ourselves through music. Through melody, harmony, and rhythm, we enter a world where others exist besides the self, a world that is full of feeling but also ordered, disciplined but free. That is why music is a character-forming force, and the decline of musical taste a decline in morals."[15]

In Aristotle's ethical theory, we find this cardinal principle: "According to the character of a man so does the end [i.e., the good] appear to him."[16] Our ability to perceive the good, the true, the beautiful, to *recognize* it

---

[14] Silvestris, *The Commentary on Martianus Capella's* De Nuptiis Philologiae et Mercurii, 53–54. I thank Jason Baxter for introducing me to this text.

[15] Scruton, *Aesthetics of Music*, 502. On the relationship between music, personal character, morality, cultural change, and social order, see Scruton, *Music as an Art*.

[16] Or, in another translation, "It is by our being the kind of people that we are that we assume such and such as our end." See Aristotle, *Nicomachean Ethics* III.5, 1114b24; cf. Aquinas, *On Evil*, Q. 6, corp., p. 242.

when we meet it, hinges on the formation our powers have undergone. As a Protestant author, Frank Gaebelein, admits, "The key to better things in Christian music is the habitual hearing of greatness in music not only in school, not only in college and Bible Institute, but in Sunday school also. For the music that younger children hear exercises a formative influence on their taste. Not even the smallest child may safely be fed a diet of musical trash."[17]

A Christian's spiritual maturity is not disconnected from his familiarity with and appreciation for the fine arts. Learning to distinguish between the beautiful or worthy and the ugly or trite is as much an acquired habit as is learning to obey one's parents, being responsible for one's actions, or treating one's siblings well. It is as much a habit as temperance, bravery, justice, and prudence. To think that children will *automatically* mature into adults who have a sense of what is and is not fitting, appropriate, noble, or beautiful is as naïve as thinking that they would behave morally or turn to God in prayer with no discipline and no religious education.

When asked the question "What is the best guardian?" Socrates says, "Argument mixed with music. It alone, when it is present, dwells within the one possessing it as a savior of virtue throughout life."[18] Argument mixed with music: this sounds to me like a description of Gregorian chant, which artfully combines the Word of God, the *Logos*, with the music of the angels. It can dwell within our souls as a savior of the theological virtues, expressing faith, spurring on hope, fueling charity.

Our human potential for the beautiful is vast. In the realm of music alone, consider the stunning masterpieces left to us by the likes of Giovanni Pierluigi da Palestrina, Tómas Luis de Victoria, Johann Sebastian Bach, Georg Frideric Handel, Wolfgang Amadeus Mozart, Ludwig van Beethoven, and to race ahead to our own day, Arvo Pärt. Apart from rare circles, this human potential is nowadays vastly underestimated and underdeveloped. Young Americans are not even *aware* of the artistic potential of their souls, either as makers or as recipients of the gift of art.

---

[17] Gaebelein, *The Christian, the Arts, and Truth*, 171.
[18] *Republic* 549b, in *The Republic of Plato*, 226; or, as Paul Shorey renders it: "Reason blended with culture, which is the only indwelling preserver of virtue throughout life in the soul that possesses it." *The Collected Dialogues of Plato*, 777.

Let me offer an example of the power of music as well as of the subtlety human beings are capable of when high culture prevails. One of Blessed Columba Marmion's numerous epistolary disciples was a Benedictine monk named Dom Pius de Hemptinne, a selection of whose writings were published in 1935. They make for fascinating reading for all sorts of reasons. In any case, I was struck by a passage Dom Pius cites from the memoirs of his grandmother:

> During the Easter holidays of 1864, fearing lest the light music so fashionable then should be harmful to my dear children, I asked them to limit themselves in the future to music of a style fitted to elevate their souls, as religious music does, instead of such as softens and enervates them. To dear M. this was a real trial. She loved music, and could not make up her mind to part with a number of operatic pieces which I regretted having ever allowed her to play. She protested, and, for the first time was unwilling to do as I wished. I was heart-broken at giving her so much pain, and would gladly have endured far more myself to spare her; but I felt it my duty to insist, and nothing could dissuade me. In a few hours the dear child had calmed down, and she said no more about it. I comforted her as well as I could by undertaking to pay for the lodging of a poor girl whom M. visited and was interested in. This offer on my part made her quite happy again.[19]

The author of the biographical sketch goes on to comment, "It was in this way [that] the supernatural joy of a good deed obliterated the sensuous charms of worldly music in a young girl of eighteen."[20]

This is an amazing passage to analyze. We see a mother who bitterly regrets having allowed her daughter to play at the piano *operatic arias*—light and frivolous music, no doubt, but hardly disordered, at least as far as music goes. (Note, too, the talent taken for granted—it is no easy feat to play the accompaniment to an aria.) What sensitivity of soul must this generation of Christians have had! They could perceive how the frivolity and superficial

---

[19] de Hemptinne, *A Benedictine Soul*, 7.
[20] de Hemptinne, 7.

sensuality of worldly music would, over time, weaken or undermine the moral fiber of youths, how it would confuse their moral compass.

And what is the daughter's reaction? A girl of eighteen was unwilling *for the first time* to do what her mother asked her to do. The beauty of obedience shines here, but also the immense power of music over the soul. Music works from within, pulling one's character to itself, and shaping the soul until one feels pleasure only in its embrace and sharp pain in being severed from it. Music alone was the veiled enemy that broke into the girl's gate and began to sap her wonted deference to the will of her parent. This, and more, can music do, and in a way that is scarcely noticed by its votaries. The daughter's mother offers to do a work of charity for a poor friend of hers, and the trauma yields to joy. This vignette offers us a window into a different time, when parent-child relations were healthier, when souls were far more sensitive to the ethical power of music, when a kind of "aesthetic asceticism" was practiced for the sake of virtue, and when works of charity for the poor were a cause of sincere joy. We might consider whether all of this goes together somehow, like a package deal.

The inescapable reality is that we *internalize* the music we sing and listen to—it becomes a part of us, it shapes us in its image. You are what you listen to and look at, more than you are what you eat. What we take into our souls is the food and drink of our souls, and we will be healthy or unhealthy depending on the quality of that food and drink. If our music is that of the Holy Spirit, we will be eating and drinking the spirit of truth, the love of the Father and the Son. If our music is that of the world or the prince of this world, we will be eating and drinking the spirit of worldliness. We cannot be too careful about this dietary discernment.[21]

---

[21] Kevin Vost shares a bit of ancient Stoic wisdom: "He [Seneca] praises Lucilius for seeking out what is truly noble and best while trampling under his feet the petty, vulgar things that popular crowds deem good, and warns him of the need to ignore the enchanting voices of the crowd. . . . He warns that while the song Odysseus heard was alluring, it did not come at him from every side. This rings even truer for us in the 21st century as we are constantly bombarded by popular culture from ever newer and more pervasive forms of media. If we are to become what we truly are at our best, we'll need to carefully monitor which voices from the crowd we allow into ears and our souls every day." *Memorize the Stoics!*, 149–50.

What is the depth and breadth of the music you listen to? How deeply does this music delve into your immortal soul and into the reality of God? How well does it encompass and echo the grandeur of the world around us?

The link between art and morality

Surprising as it may seem in light of the foregoing pages, Saint Thomas Aquinas defends the thesis that there is not an *immediate and necessary* connection between good art and good morals. In other words, a morally good person does not, by that fact alone, generate beautiful art, nor must a bad man produce bad art. All the same, as we will see, Aquinas also proves that there *will* be a connection, albeit in a roundabout way: in the larger picture of human life.[22]

In holding this position, he differs from some contemporary conservative critics, like E. Michael Jones, who maintain that bad morals necessitate or result in bad art, or, vice versa, that bad art indicates bad morals. The history of the fine arts clearly disproves that position, which is founded upon a simplistic psychology of the human faculties and the habits that perfect them. In the Renaissance, for example, one can find truly outstanding artists who led morally disordered lives—for example, the painter Caravaggio, who produced spectacular paintings, with true spiritual depth; the composer Carlo Gesualdo, who wrote sublime music, although he had murdered his wife and her adulterous lover in a fit of rage. Similarly, while Wagner was an adulterer and a notorious anti-Semite, his giftedness as a composer is past all doubt: just listen to the *Siegfried Idyll*, the *Meistersinger* overture, or the *Ring* cycle (if you can stifle your distaste at the vapid storyline and pompous libretto). The same holds for Schubert and Brahms—whether they visited prostitutes, as some of their biographers say they did, or not.

The lack of an immediate connection between art and morality is not bothersome provided we understand the kind of intellectual perfection art refers to. Art is a habit of applying reason to artistic materials in an orderly way to produce a definite effect, and an artist who is talented to begin with,

---

[22] See *ST* I-II, Q. 57, arts. 3–4 and art. 5, ad 1; Q. 58, art. 5. For a full exposition, see Maritain, *Art and Scholasticism and The Frontiers of Poetry.*

and well trained, can develop a high level of perfection in the exercise of this habit, in spite of personal failings.

That being said, many connections exist between the practice of art and the quality of morals *in real life*. An artist who lets his daily life become very disordered cannot be expected to retain the discipline, self-mastery, and concentration required to produce masterpieces—or, in the worst case scenario, to acquire the technical skills in the first place. Picasso is a conspicuous example of a talented artist who fell so much under the sway of his lechery that he could no longer produce great art. He sacrificed his intellect to his libido, and that is why his works are so lacking in intelligibility and beauty. They seem to be efforts, increasingly childish and embarrassing, to represent appetite or feeling divorced from reason—the very principle of form, order, communication.

The openness to "inspiration" that characterizes genius runs the danger of being more or less closed off by licentiousness, by immersion in dissipating and distracting pleasures.[23] To be open to inspiration requires a certain peace of soul and delicacy of sentiment—an ability to *listen and receive*, to await ideas and cultivate them patiently and with self-denying labor. Prudence is the "eye of love," and since the moral virtues are connected through prudence, the artist who lacks self-control lacks the *capacity to see* which is indispensable to conceiving and executing great works.[24]

It seems to me that the otherwise underground link between morals and art comes right to the surface in pop music and modern art in general. Modern art has often been art of unrestrained sensuality or bleak despair, and this is strikingly captured in the two extremes into which it has fallen: pornography and sexual excess on the one side, atonality and abstraction on the other. Men whose minds are in the gutter will transfer that gutter to the canvas, the photograph, the lyrics, or the rhythm, while men whose minds are cut off from nature and its beauty will represent their cold and empty soul-world in a chill abstraction from form or shape, from tonality or controlled and orderly rhythm. We will see a womanizing Picasso painting

---

[23] The history of art affords many sad examples of how promising artistic careers were derailed by alcohol or drug addictions.

[24] See Josef Pieper's illuminating discussion of prudence in *The Four Cardinal Virtues*, 3–40.

prostitutes or a suicidal Pollock splattering paint at random; we will hear Ravel's stupefying *Bolero* or Schoenberg's chilly *Pierrot Lunaire.*

So, it is important to see on the one hand that art, as a virtue of applying reason to materials, is distinct from the moral life, and on the other hand that a man's life, which dictates *goals* for art, necessarily impinges on his products, since he cannot but identify himself with a certain way of life and the pleasures associated with it. In this way, we will understand how it is possible for artists fortunate to be born into a Catholic or Christian culture to produce marvelous works of art in spite of their personal failings, because they received a sound training and adhered, to some extent, to the larger Christian goals of their society, whereas the artists whom modernity has permitted or encouraged to be truly perverse end up producing the most perverse art.

Thus, while art and ethics are distinct, they cannot help influencing one another over time. Hence we should be vigilant, even scrupulous, about the influences we allow into our souls. This would always have been true and will always be true: no matter how "different" modern man may be, he still has a soul to save, and that soul will be saved through the same virtues, the same harmony of faith and reason, reason and passions, as that of pre-modern man, post-modern man, and any other man there may ever be.

These observations are not limited to certain contemporary genres but extend over the whole history of music in all cultures. There have *always* been deviations in the fine arts, just as there have always been clothing, dances, and language of questionable modesty. Due to the profound influence of Catholicism, a sense of order, decency, and gracefulness generally prevailed for many centuries in Western fine art, and this cultural force was strong enough to carry into the twentieth century, although it was already weakening considerably in the nineteenth. There are hopeful signs of rebirth and renewal in the twenty-first, as Catholic and Christian artists are leaving behind the stale conventions of modernism and the low horizons of populism to seek once again that cosmic and divine grandeur that is the essence of great art.

2

Nourishing Our Souls on Beauty

IF A NATURAL *rational* perfection is attainable, then it is a moral fault not to strive for it as much as possible; if one has achieved such a perfection, it is a moral fault not to strive to maintain it and to augment it, if possible.

This is true of any *essential* rational perfection—that is, not of tulip collecting or astrophysics, which are specialized knowledge and therefore not for everyone, but of such things as the correct use of the faculties of thinking and speaking, and some understanding of the orderliness of reality. Our forebears called these rational perfections the *artes liberales* or liberal arts, comprised of the "trivium" (grammar, logic, and rhetoric) and the "quadrivium" (arithmetic, geometry, astronomy, and music). To the extent that one can attain such essential rational perfections, one should strive to attain them, and a failure to do so, owing not to unavoidable circumstances or pressing obligations but to laziness or distraction or disordered appetites, would be a regrettable failing.

A fortiori, this imperative would not include physical perfection, such as weight lifting or triathlon competency. All that is morally required of us in regard to our bodily nature is a diet and daily regimen adequate to sustaining the higher activities of reason and will. Indeed, if physical exercise were actually to take up so much time and attention that they rendered impossible a life of thoughtful leisure, art appreciation and the making of art, and Christian prayer, this would be a manifest imperfection, not a perfection.[25]

Let us apply this principle to music. If one *knows* that Palestrina or Bach or Handel or Mozart or Beethoven wrote superior music, then choosing consistently to listen to less excellent music would be a moral fault. One could even

---

[25] By the "making of art" I mean everything from playing instruments to singing folk songs to composing music to painting, sketching, sculpting, writing verse, or writing stories—in short, any activity that produces a beautiful work.

stray into mortal sin, depending on the matter and the intention; for example, listening to Satanic heavy metal or songs that celebrate sexual perversion or licentious behavior would be mortally sinful. However, since we must strive to flee even venial sins lest they prepare the way for mortal sin, it is better to assume that popular music produced by hedonists who sing about sins is a slippery slope leading to some kind of intellectual pollution and consent of will.

I have often heard people make a distinction between listening to music for its entertainment value and listening to it because it is beautiful art. They are trying to find a way to defend their practice of listening to Handel's *Messiah* or Mozart's *Clarinet Concerto* one day and their favorite rock band the next day. To a virtuous person, however, that which is most beautiful and noble in its qualities is that which is most pleasing to his taste and compelling for his attention.

For a person attracted by the goodness inherent in art, there can be no divide between entertainment and profundity or worthiness. We should *want* to listen only to that which is beautiful; to settle consciously for something less is a lessening of our humanity, of our rationality. It would be like saying that only a church needs to be holy, while a home can be profane. No, the home itself must be made holy, it must be a "domestic church," a sort of monastic enclosure for the bringing up of saints.[26] The divide between entertainment and fine art is a form of dualism, seen as well in the all-too-common divide between worldly events or occasions and religious ones (e.g., when Americans celebrate purely political holidays with no connection to the true religion revealed by God, and celebrate their religious holy days with no connection to their civic life and identity).

If we can, we should elevate our souls to the point where what is intrinsically best or most beautiful *is* what gives us the greatest pleasure and restfulness. In other words, we should aim at a condition where anything we choose to do—whether for relaxation, leisure, or work—is noble, excellent, and praiseworthy. When I am in a serious mood, I should sing, play, or listen to Bach (or any other great composer); when I am in a light mood or in need of relaxation, Bach (or any other great composer) would still be no less appropriate.[27]

---

[26] See St. John Chrysostom, *On Marriage and Family Life.*

[27] As one becomes familiar with a great composer like Bach, one discovers music of

As rational animals, and even more, as Christians who worship the crucified and risen Logos, the incarnate Word of God, we ought to nourish our souls, to the extent possible, on the *best* of the fine arts, giving less room to what is mediocre or shallow, and none at all to what is base. There is a kind of moral imperative to pursue excellence in all aspects of life, including our leisure and recreational activities.

One might imagine the following objection: "Hmm . . . something's not quite right with your argument. By your assessment we will never listen to what is less perfect (however we are to determine that!). So is it always Bach, even at a barn dance? And there are levels of perfection too. 'Tea for Two' is not Gerard Manley Hopkins, but its delightful rhymes and cadences do bring joy. And when I'm stuck in traffic I can belt out 'Chattanooga Choo Choo' all by myself, but Beethoven's Ninth Symphony would need some help. Yes, one should stop one's ears to the perverse and the subversive, but one should also be attentive to the beautiful wherever it resides."

This objection gives me a welcome opportunity to clarify my position.

We have a duty to pursue excellence in every circumstance. In keeping with traditional ethics, we know that as circumstances themselves vary, we must vary what we are doing and how we are doing it in order to be virtuous. Square dancing music is appropriate for square dancing, a folk song or a lullaby for the family circle, a campfire song for singing around the campfire, and a moody soundtrack for a movie. All of those genres can be done well or badly, in a way that accords with our rational dignity or not. And it would be better to have a well written and well performed square dance than one that is poorly written and poorly performed. One may indeed sing, perform, or listen to something that is less than the best, simply speaking, as long as it embodies good principles and therefore is in a line of continuity with the best. I agree with the Arts and Crafts movement that the whole of life should be beautiful, a work of art, all the way down to forks and knives and spoons.

---

every mood and manner, earnest and frolicsome, elaborate and simple, sacred and secular, vocal and instrumental, and so forth. Multiply this harvest by hundreds of great composers and thousands of minor composers, and one would have enough to listen to on any occasion for a dozen lifetimes.

Another objection might be that my argument commits the fallacy of equating the good with the perfect. My response is that we should espouse the search for excellence in every domain of human life, in all the appropriate media and venues and registers, and that the good of rational human nature compels us towards perfection. My great concern is with our culture's seemingly irreversible slide into mediocrity, banality, ugliness, violence, sensuality, and (fill in the blank with any other negative concept). This slide has threatened to destroy high culture and authentic folk culture, both of which are beautiful in their distinctive ways.

Seven theses for evaluating music

Our mental and spiritual health depends radically and essentially on listening to and producing beautiful music—music that is in continuity either with the rich Western tradition of folk music or with the even richer "classical" or high cultural music of great composers from the Middle Ages to the present day ("from Perotin to Pärt," one might say). Distinct aspects of this view may be formulated as follows.

Thesis #1. Music is the most telling expression of cultural health and spiritual vigor. By taking its pulse, one evaluates an entire age and people.

Thesis #2. Genuine folk music—that is, music produced live by amateurs on natural instruments, in continuity with local tradition, and in connection with real human events of communal importance—is intrinsically superior to technologically produced and mass-marketed music, even if the latter claims to be folk or folk-inspired.

Thesis #3. Johann Sebastian Bach's music is generally superior to that of his German contemporaries, for all of their undoubted excellence; Mozart's to Salieri's; Brahms's to Rheinberger's, Busoni's, or Rubinstein's. Such examples could be multiplied for all of the fine arts, but the point is clear: there exists a real hierarchy of genius, of mastery and merit, of universal appeal, in the artistic world. It is not purely by chance that certain composers' works have stood the test of time and continue to be enjoyed centuries later.

Thesis #4. The great European composers wrote the noblest and most beautiful music the world has ever known, and their greatness had everything to do with the phenomenon of Christianity and, more specifically, the Catholic Church, in its cultural ramifications. There is a fertility and richness, a capacious scope and elevated quality in the output of these composers that points to a heaven-bestowed genius.[28]

Thesis #5. Periods of cultural vitality, intellectual acuity, and spiritual depth produce correspondingly vital, profound, and complex music. Think of Renaissance polyphony, Baroque oratorios, Classical string quartets, Romantic symphonies. Periods of cultural stagnation and retrogression, intellectual morbidity, and spiritual anguish produce the extremes of trite garbage and the earnest, sublime, at times difficult music of searching souls. One might think in this connection of Gustav Mahler or Arvo Pärt. In confusing periods, some composers, such as John Cage, cannot make up their minds between the genuine musical impulse and trendy popularity or avant-garde exhibitionism.

Thesis #6. Each major historical period's music is not susceptible to a judgment that is altogether outside all periods and therefore capable of claiming absolute objectivity. Rather, the organically evolved and artistically adept music of each period is incommensurable with that of any other; *each* period can therefore manifest "the greatest works," the best music ever written with *its* musical language and *its* distinctive purposes. It can never make sense to say, "Which is greater: a Byrd piece for viol consort or a Beethoven string quartet?" They are incommensurably different. To the question "Who is your favorite composer?" an entirely appropriate response would be: "Of which period? And in which genre?" Unlike the goodness of the God who is simple, greatness among creatures is greatly multiplied and varied, as, indeed, are mediocrity and triviality.

---

[28] The hänssler CLASSIC's *Complete Works of Bach* numbers 172 compact discs and the Brilliant Classics *Mozart Edition* numbers 170. Let the sheer magnitude of this accomplishment sink in: Mozart composed 170 full-length discs' worth of great music, Bach 172 discs' worth. Just about any one of Bach's or Mozart's thousands of pieces chosen at random evinces more technical skill and musical inventiveness than the life's work of any modern pop star. Mozart died at the age of thirty-five, and although Bach was sixty-five at his death, he had also been building organs, hiring and firing orchestras, teaching choir boys, giving music lessons, and spending an inordinate amount of time dealing with the obtuse town council and church board in Leipzig (not to mention attending to the needs of his large family). Such monumental artistic accomplishments are what *genius* actually means, and they back up the conviction that there is something bordering on the miraculous, and certainly divinely bestowed, in these towering figures—all the more reason to get to know their music.

Thesis #7. It is a matter of immediate and certain intuition based on edu-cated sense-experience that the music of Byrd, Bach, Beethoven, Bruckner, or Brahms (just to stick with B's) is incomparably more beautiful, skill-ful, and rewarding, not to mention perfective of the spiritual soul, than any atonal noise or so-called popular music. For this reason, in our times of leisure and recreation we would be foolish not to prefer, as a general rule, music that is more beautiful, skillful, and rewarding. There is only so much time in one's life—barely enough to become familiar with the greatest works of art in any domain or from any period, let alone all of them.

Let us take up the best and make it the exemplar, the teacher, the inspi-ration, and the consolation of our interior life as aesthetic beings. We need not condemn the less worthy when it has a due place in our recreations, but we should avoid what is shoddy, shallow, frivolous, morose, or ugly. As for what glamorizes or wallows in sin, let it not so much as be *mentioned* among us (cf. Eph 5:3).

On the objectivity of the beautiful

Now, it is easier to see the obvious ends of the spectrum or hierarchy (Mozart = good, metal = bad) than it is to sort out a ranking in between, especially as one descends further into details. Is Beethoven greater than Bartók? Undoubtedly; but Bartók was a genius too, and his music is worthy of our time and effort. Is Bartók greater than Babbitt? Absolutely—there's not even a competition there. What about certain styles of popular music? They are as inferior to the great composers (of our age and of every age) as the crude singing of a rock star or the vulgar monotony of a rapper is to the prayerful chanting of a monk, the loftiest use of the God-given instrument of the voice, or the sublime vocalizations of a diva, the apogee of human vocal development. We should not be relativists or subjectivists about artis-tic truth any more than we are about the objective reality of human nature and the natural law. Anyone who is consistent will see that the beautiful, like its companions, the good and the true, is not reducible to subjective whim but is based on objective criteria that already point towards the divine.[29]

---

[29] A claim defended at length in James Matthew Wilson's *The Vision of the Soul.*

My wife is a painter and iconographer, and I have enjoyed looking at her library of books, both about the works of great artists and by artists themselves teaching how to paint, and listening to her discerning comments. There exist concrete qualities that make a painting great, from the combinations of colors and textures to the hard or soft edges of shapes to the overall arrangement (e.g., centered vs. off-center, or the use of geometrical ratios), to the placement and handling of the vanishing point, and so on and so forth. Something exactly like this is true for *all* of the arts, including music.[30] Palestrina and Bach are great not because they just happened to cough up inspired music, as if by an irrational spasm, but because their minds and hearts were beautifully attuned to the microcosmic and macrocosmic principles of harmony and rhythm. A lot of different styles of beautiful music can emerge from these principles, but the principles are real and not created by man—they are discovered, internalized, embraced, and made fruitful.

The "beautiful" is largely distinguished by the degree to which the beautiful "thing" is *in accord with nature*. As nature in itself and untouched by man—God's direct creation—is simply beautiful, so then is fine art and human life beautiful insofar as it is in "accord with nature," meaning, the metaphysical laws that run throughout creation and the natural moral law that specially abides in man.[31]

The ancient Pythagoreans discovered that nature gives us the natural harmonic series through *melody and harmony*. The further harmony deviates from the concord of these natural vibrations, the less beautiful it is. In *rhythm and meter*, nature gives us the gentle flowing of water or of human speech, the steady beating of the heart and cycle of respiration, as well as the vigor of the wind and of fleet-footed animals, and so we find beauty in Gregorian chant as well as in the "Ride of the Valkyries." In *timbre*, nature gives us the songs of birds, the whistling of the wind, the roaring depths of canyons, the nearly-angelic human voice. The choirs and orchestras of the

---

[30] See David Clayton's writings, starting with *The Way of Beauty*.
[31] One of the best modern writers on the simultaneously physical, metaphysical, cosmic, ethical, and spiritual nature of music is Peter Kalkavage. See his numerous lectures published at *The Imaginative Conservative*, especially "Music: Giving the World a Rhythmic Sway," "Music and the Idea of a World," and "The Neglected Muse: Why Music Is An Essential Liberal Art."

world bring us man's best attempts to reflect nature's awesome beauty. The electrified, noisy chaos of Western modernity stands out in stark contrast.

One might think here of the older usages of the terms "monster," "monstrosity," or even "freak of nature." Things called by these names in the past, owing to their departure from the natural forms, have practically become glorified in our time, in every part of human activity. Ugly paintings, ugly buildings, ugly music, ugly literature, and even literal monsters in movies fill our senses with so much anti-beauty that the very lives of people forced to live in this environment can become unnatural and ugly. Interestingly, this decay appears directly proportional to the extent to which any given society has succumbed to Western modernization, which translates roughly to abandoning the spiritual life and the rural life for a high-tech consumerist urban life.

Wherever we find people trying to classify ugly music as "beautiful," or secular music as "sacred," we also find manipulative *agendas*. Whether it be self-aggrandizement or making a killing on the market or still more infernal things, the encroachment of the ugly and the un-sacred always has the feeling of something forced or violent (which is, almost by definition, un-natural),[32] and it always seems to be appreciated and supported either by those who share the agenda or by passive consumers lacking the power of discrimination.

An age governed by the dictatorship of relativism will readily subjectivize the arts altogether, as if artistic excellence were nothing more than a matter of taste. What's at stake in the debate over music is nothing less than our need to undergo a radical conversion of intellect and will towards the beautiful, which is a constitutive element of our holistic salvation, and maybe even a precondition for it (and certainly a result of it—in different senses). Far from being a matter solely of individual taste or cultural conditioning, the nobility of works of fine art is an attribute *they* possess, a reflection of the Divine, and a privileged path that leads man to God. Conversely, bad art, art unworthy of its vocation, mediocre and crass art, leads men away from God and even from the dignity of their own nature.

So, there is a *lot* at stake. That is why I stir up a debate: to cause people to *think* about the relationship between music and their immortal souls; to make them reconsider what they are listening to habitually; to encourage

---

[32] See Aristotle, *Physics* IV.8; V.6; VIII.4.

them to strike out in new directions with the adventurous spirit of explorers seeking new continents.

I have a large collection of music scores and recordings and enjoy the work of many, many composers (including not a few "minor" ones). Obviously if I thought that only Bach's or Mozart's music had worth, I wouldn't lift a pen to attempt to compose my own music. But when I do write a piece, as unworthy as I am of this great tradition, I nevertheless strive to say something in continuity with it, inspired by it, and almost as an offering to it as well as to God and His people. And I see the same to be true of the mentality of most of the great composers—they know themselves to be within a tradition and they defer to it and trust it, even while they innovate. The loss of a profound sense of belonging, imitation, and gratitude is a kind of "mortal sin" in fine art, and I think it has much to do with the rampant relativism of judgment that surfaces the moment anyone dares to suggest that there is something in the music of (say) J. S. Bach that transcends time and establishes a notable measure of the greatness of all subsequent music.

I don't think there can be any argument, any meaningful conversation, with a person who holds that all beauty (or all judgment of beauty) is merely subjective, any more than there can be with a person who maintains there is no truth, or that the good is solely determined by my wishes. As Aristotle says in Book IV of the *Metaphysics*, arguing with such a person is like trying to argue with a vegetable—no progress can be made, because the first principles of reasoning are being denied.[33] Like his master Plato, Aristotle argued with the sophists of their day who denied that there was truth at all or that truth could be known and spoken. In our day, the problem has become graver still: people often suffer from an acute, almost innate anti-philosophical bias, an irrationalism that cannot abide patient argument and disputation.

A basic and essential food of the soul

All great art is straining and pointing towards transcendence and ineffability. This is why I so love the music of Jean Sibelius and Arvo Pärt, as different as these composers are: each is, as it were, a prophet of the Absolute, a

---

[33]   See Aristotle, *Metaphysics* IV.4, 1006a12–15 and 1008b10–12.

pilgrim of the yonder, whose utterance borders the unutterable. As a result, the principles that make art great cannot be reduced to a handful of finite formulas; one cannot merely "connect the dots" to generate a masterpiece. But this in no way cancels out the reality of objective principles that stand behind the works of fine art and serve as criteria for judgment. Perhaps it's the word "objective" that offends, suggesting as it may a kind of detached and disembodied perspective; but granting the inadequacy of our existential situation and the non-ultimacy of our judgments, we *do* have potent intellectual equipment for this work of discrimination and valuation, which we first learn by sitting as pupils at the feet of great artists and soaking in the beauty they have revealed to us.

The best and most beautiful things God has permitted man to produce contain an almost infinite wealth that can be tapped into throughout all the vicissitudes of life. Good music speaks to all the emotions, all the phases of our human journey, all the daily and weekly junctures. If one needs to unwind and wishes to do so with music, one might put on lute pieces by Dowland or a pleasant Haydn symphony; better yet, one can take up an instrument and relax with it. For working intensely on a certain project, some surging Bach or bracing Beethoven will assist; for elevating the soul to thoughts of God, a Mass of Palestrina or a work by Maurice Duruflé might be chosen. There is no room for "pop" music in a soul that is thoroughly attached to and captivated by the beautiful, the noble, the elegant, the profound. In fact, such a soul will hate the ugliness and triviality of such music, which does not deserve to be honored by the name of the Muses.

We have a God-given duty to sanctify our lives in every respect, including our leisure pursuits, our recreations and entertainments. Only that which, due to its inherent soundness of form, *can* be sanctified is worthy of a Christian's choice and favor. Just as we cannot be holy bank robbers, we cannot be holy rock musicians or holy consumers of unholy music, because such music is morally tainted, intellectually inferior, and culturally decadent.

Saint John Henry Newman once said that going to church is our greatest privilege and should be our central desire.[34] Our entire life should be

---

[34] Newman says something like this in many of the *Parochial and Plain Sermons*, for example: "Stated and continual prayer, then, and especially united prayer, is plainly the duty of Christians. And if we ask how often we are to pray, I reply, that we ought to

permeated with the sacred, with order, beauty, purity, light—not excluding at the same time the emotional power and depth that always accompany true greatness. In the most sublime moments of the string quartets of Beethoven or the symphonies of Bruckner or Mahler, it is as if the veil between time and eternity is lifted, the abyss between creation and the uncreated spanned. It is our highest privilege as artistic beings to listen to music that is religious or finely crafted or sublime (or all three, as in the cantatas of Bach); and if we are listening to music for "relaxation," it should still be of high quality. Because the primary thing in man is his spiritual nature, music should contribute to his spiritual well-being. It is indeed meant to entertain, but it should do so while enriching the heart and elevating the mind. Music that does not take the whole man into account, according to the anthropological hierarchy within him, is music that inculcates a lie, promoting a false self-understanding and inhibiting self-knowledge.

Everything comes down to the question of beauty. Beautiful music is intrinsically worth listening to at *any* time when music is appropriate. Today we have easy access to the greatest music the human heart has ever poured forth, a limitless harvest of centuries of art. There can be no possible excuse for debasing oneself with trash, for lowering oneself to the level of the masses who have no taste, no ear, no musical intuition, no discrimination. The masses listen to the music of techno-barbarians, with no other effect than the fueling of the basest passions and the retarding of cultural or mental advancement.

---

consider prayer as a plain privilege, directly we know that it is a duty, and therefore that the question is out of place. . . . I do not tell men that they must come to Church, so much as declare the glad tidings that they may. This surely is enough for those who 'hunger and thirst after righteousness,' and humbly desire to see the face of God" (vol. 3, serm. 21, The Daily Service). "Prayer, praise, thanksgiving, contemplation, are the peculiar privilege and duty of a Christian, and that for their own sakes, from the exceeding comfort and satisfaction they afford him, and without reference to any definite results to which prayer tends, without reference to the answers which are promised to it, from a general sense of the blessedness of being under the shadow of God's throne" (vol. 4, serm. 15, Moral Effects of Communion with God). "It is then the duty and the privilege of all disciples of our glorified Saviour, to be exalted and transfigured with Him; to live in heaven in their thoughts, motives, aims, desires, likings, prayers, praises, intercessions, even while they are in the flesh" (vol. 6, serm. 15, Rising with Christ).

The soul's emotional range is vast, far more vast than rock (or, for that matter, jazz, pop, or rap) allows for. Rock music is about angst and anger, lust and cupidity; traditional music is about so much more—all the subtle colors of our inner life and the ultimate things to which we are directed: about devotion, loyalty, betrayal, courage, glory, nostalgia, sweetness, bitterness, sorrow, loss, discovery, renewal. Because of rock and pop music, the soul's capacity for feeling has been anaesthetized, stifled, crimped, the pinion clipped, the tongue muted; the depth is dormant, everything is surface squalls. Do we not need to ennoble the senses and the sense appetites, lest we be dragged down by them? Would it not be strange to say that our intellects need truth, our hearts love, our bodies good nutrition, but that our senses, imagination, and memory do not need beauty?

Music is a basic and essential food of the soul. Just as the body can only be as healthy as the quality of the food ingested, so the soul can only be as healthy as the quality of the sensible goods it takes in. We must resolve to nourish our souls on the health-giving food of the beautiful—on music that is profound, rich, subtle, varied, and splendid, and in all these ways, worthy of the image of God that resides in our rational nature.

3

Problems with Rock Music
and Its Offshoots

THE FUNDAMENTAL PROBLEM with rock music, many of its antecedents, and nearly all of its offshoots, can be summed up quite simply: its rhythm is unnatural and morally tainted. There are other intellectual and moral problems with it, such as dumb or lurid or violent lyrics, insipid and monotonous melodies, sloppy singing, distorted instrumental timbres, and the lack of a well-structured progress from beginning to middle to end,[35] but the rhythm is the essence of the music and the pith of the problem.

The normal pattern for almost all music in the world, from all periods of history, whether genuine folk music or the art music of high cultures, accentuates the odd beats—that is, the downbeat (the first) and, to a lesser extent, the third (if one is speaking of a four-beat rhythm), like this:

ONE-two, ONE-two (as in a march);

ONE-two-*three*-four, ONE-two-*three*-four (as in common time);

ONE-two-three, ONE-two-three (as in a waltz).

---

[35] As a modern Aristotelian philosopher noted: "Most of the rock music I have heard seems to aim at a kind of irrational excitement, pursued, in a way, for its own sake. In such music, you find no resolution, but only exhaustion. It is like a binge or an orgy; it stops when people are tired out. It has no natural term. One is reminded of the story about some Victorian drinking parties, which were over once every guest had slipped under the table. Such celebrations do not have any internal structure to them, they do not have a beginning, middle, and end, they only go on until they stop. Isn't there a popular song, or one of those rock songs, that says 'I can't get no satisfaction'? Well, if what this music aims at is a sort of permanent emotional high, which is against the very nature of the emotions insofar as they are something of nature (and therefore the work of divine reason), if one tries to stay 'up there' forever, then of course one doesn't get any satisfaction. The emotions should be finite movements that have beginnings, middles, and ends." Berquist, "Good Music and Bad," in *Learning and Discipleship*, 233.

Rock music, on the other hand, generally uses a constantly syncopated or *off*-rhythm, accentuating the even beats instead of the odd:

one-TWO-three-FOUR, one-TWO-three-FOUR.

One can hear this off-rhythm particularly clearly when drum sets are employed: the bass drum followed by the snare.

It is hardly surprising that, terminologically, "rock 'n' roll" and "jazz" were both euphemisms for sexual intercourse, or, more accurately in their historical context, fornication: the rhythm is suggestive of the pelvic thrust. People who dance (if it can be called that) to rock music often perform this kind of motion instinctively—think of Elvis Presley, one of the first to gyrate his hips in an explicitly sexual way, in accord with the rhythm of his music. The Ed Sullivan Show televised Elvis performing but would not televise his suggestive hip motions.[36]

It is not as if Catholic authors have failed to come to the defense of rock music, as witness Peter Mirus and Jeff Mirus.[37] But their defenses are weak. There is no escaping from the sensuality and sexual innuendos intended by the pioneers and protagonists of rock music. I don't mean merely that they themselves led lives plagued by promiscuity, alcoholism, drug use, and even violent crime, but rather, and more importantly, that their *music* is intentionally and recognizably an expression of and a moving appeal to the same Dionysian behavior. Joseph Ratzinger describes the character of pop and rock music as follows:

> The music of the masses has broken loose from this [classical music culture] and treads a very different path. On the one hand, there is pop music, which is certainly no longer supported by the people in the ancient sense (*populus*) [i.e., it isn't real music "of the people"]. It is aimed at the phenomenon of the masses, is industrially produced, and ultimately has to be described as a cult of the banal. "Rock," on the other hand, is the expression of elemental passion,

---

[36] See the detailed account given in "Why Elvis Presley was censored on The Ed Sullivan Show," https://elvisbiography.net/2020/09/09/why-elvis-presley-was-censored-on-the-ed-sullivan-show.
[37] See Peter Mirus, "Hear No Evil—My Perspective on Rock Music"; Jeff Mirus, "So What's Wrong with Rock Music?"

and at rock festivals it assumes a cultic character, a form of worship, in fact, in opposition to Christian worship. People are, so to speak, released from themselves by the experience of being part of a crowd and by the emotional shock of rhythm, noise, and special lighting effects. However, in the ecstasy of having all their defenses torn down, the participants sink, as it were, beneath the elemental force of the universe. The music of the Holy Spirit's sober inebriation seems to have little chance when self has become a prison, the mind is a shackle, and breaking out from both appears as a true promise of redemption that can be tasted at least for a few moments.[38]

The only reason why some today may no longer feel the connection between the music and the moral attitude it embodies is that our entire society has broadly accepted the sexual revolution along with the rock music that heralded it, and therefore both the permissiveness and its music are in the very air we breathe: we have no other cultural consciousness against which to compare the music *or* the morality. Back when Elvis and the Beatles first came around, there were plenty of people familiar with the older styles of music (classical and popular) that preceded such performers, as well as plenty of people formed by Christian notions of modesty and chastity. To such observers, the aesthetic and moral contrasts were obvious and shocking, even while fans celebrated the overthrow of "bourgeois" styles of music and the undermining of "conventional" morals.

Rock music was the music of youthful rebellion in the 1950s, '60s, and '70s: it gave expression to the desire for erotic liberation, which more often than not took the form of "rocking and rolling" in the backseat of the Chevy. The bourgeois conservative social restraints, themselves already unhealthy because no longer psychologically and religiously integrated, were thrown off in the euphoria of fornication, or at least in the sensuality and stimulation that lead up to it. Rock represents, at any rate, the total dissociation of the concupiscible appetite from the rule of reason, the subordination of reason and will to concupiscence or the desire for sense-pleasure. A later phase of rock music performed the same disservice to human nature by indulging wantonly in the irascible passions of anger and despair.

---

[38] Ratzinger, *The Spirit of the Liturgy*, 148; in the commemorative edition that also includes Guardini's work of the same name, 161–62; in *Theology of the Liturgy*, 92.

Students of theology will recognize in these facts a reproduction of one of the many results of the fall of our first parents: the insubordination of the powers of the human soul as a punishment for the insubordination of man to God.[39] God is Divine Reason, so to speak, and just as human reason is meant to be submitted to Divine Reason, so human appetites are meant to be submitted to and elevated by human reason, and the body, as such, to and by the soul. Rock music encourages and glorifies the revolt of the appetites against the order of reason, and by undermining the grounds of thinking and willing in accord with natural law or Divine Reason, it actually *embodies*, even as it renews and deepens, the rebellion of Adam against God.

It also takes little familiarity with the biographies and lyrics of early rock musicians to know that the constantly syncopated sensual rhythm and the other features of the style heralded a rejection of the Western musical tradition that preceded it. Notice, quite apart from the sexual innuendo, how unnatural it is to start a measure (the unit one, the beginning) not as a dominant but as a weak beat: instead of "*down* up up up," you have "up *down* up *down*." The rhythm does violence to the natural prominence of the beginning of the measure. It is like gently lifting up a baby rabbit by the ears and then smashing it down, lifting it up, smashing it down. The traditional rhythm has a certain lightness to it, there is a buoyancy to the weaker beats which leads elegantly back to the dominant beat, like a dancer taking a decisive step and then two or three short, graceful steps, before the next decisive step. One really has to see the dancing to see the difference. It is impossible to dance gracefully to the impulsive and violent "x X x X" beat.[40]

---

[39] As Saint Thomas puts it in the *Compendium theologiae*, I.192: "The harmonious integrity of the original state depended entirely on the submission of man's will to God. Consequently, as soon as the human will threw off the yoke of subjection to God, the perfect subjection of the lower powers to reason and of the body to the soul likewise disintegrated. As a result, man experienced in his lower, sensitive appetite the inordinate stirrings of concupiscence, anger, and all the other passions. These movements no longer followed the order set by reason but rather resisted reason, frequently darkening the mind and, so to speak, throwing it into confusion. This is that rebellion of the flesh against the spirit which Scripture mentions."

[40] For a thorough exposition of the relationship between music, dancing, ethics, and society, see Platt, "A Different Drummer."

When rock 'n' roll started, the youths swaying and gyrating to its strains knew what it meant, or if they did not know intellectually, still they felt the meaning in their blood: the unshackling of the libido, "letting go," letting passions be stirred up. If additional proof is needed, one can look at the lyrics and the behavior of those who perform it and those who listen to it. A disproportionate number of songs, especially after a certain point when societal conventions broke down, are about (sooner or later) getting into bed—quite without the humor, cleverness, ardor, or refinement of traditional erotic poetry, such as that of the ancient Greek poets or the medieval troubadours and trouvères. As for the moral behavior of rock stars and their groupies, that is a witness that speaks for itself.

Rock music and pop styles in general are therefore a definite statement, an open manifesto against chastity and purity and self-control, against marriage and the reasonable use of the generative faculties, and, more broadly, against the hierarchical order of the cosmos represented by the natural rhythm. Pop music is defiantly carnal. This descent into licentiousness is what its exponents and first practitioners exhibited in their lives and said they *meant* by their music; this is exactly what the first opponents of rock music immediately picked up on and protested against; decades later, this is now the assumed and "institutionalized" way of living for modern youths. Although overlooked nowadays, there is a real connection between the music young people listen to and the way of life they lead, as well as the worldview that sustains and justifies it.

To summarize: rock music is tainted because of its unnatural rhythm, which is a musical representation of sexual concupiscence, an invitation to irrational excess, and a major contributing factor in the hypersexualization of today's popular culture. One may say more generally that rock music is intended to stir up the passions excessively, whether concupiscible or irascible, against the measure of reason and without regard to the beauty apprehended by the mind. It treats man as an irrational animal, and in this way abuses the art of music, which is a rational art for spiritual perfection. Styles that derive historically from rock frequently have the same qualities; sometimes they are even more exaggerated. Techno music, for instance, accentuates all four beats, in a hammering rhythm that induces animalistic excitement and a stupor of consciousness.

Objections and replies

If my reader has been patient enough to read this far, he or she may be happy to hear that I shall now offer some nuances and respond to some objections.

First, a condemnation of unnatural rhythm does not equate to a condemnation of all popular music and its performers, because not every piece of popular music follows this kind of syncopated off-rhythm. Sometimes a particular band has deep enough roots in the folk or classical tradition to produce a song that follows a traditional rhythm. So-called folk singers often do just this: think of Simon and Garfunkel's "Scarborough Fair." When a band performs a more traditional song, one may not be able to criticize it from *this* point of view, even if there are other respects in which it is likely to be wanting, such as the crude vocal technique, far from the perfection of the trained human voice.

Generally speaking, folk music—*real* folk music, such as people have sung for centuries everywhere in the West—is almost never a problem, ethically or spiritually, for several reasons. First, the music is melody-driven. The rhythm is of course present, but the melody is king. Only barbaric music emphasizes the rhythm as the main thing or as equal to the other elements. Second, it is mostly meant for group singing, not for soloistic showing off. The instrumental accompaniment might have a single drum modestly keeping time, but it will usually consist of bowed, plucked, or hammered string instruments, flutes, accordions, and other instruments powered by hand or breath. Third, the rhythm itself is natural; that is, it emphasizes the strong odd beats (in common or 4/4 time, beats 1 and 3) or accentuates weak beats in a gentle way subordinated to melody and harmony (think of the toe-tapping rhythm of bluegrass, which it is impossible to conflate with rock). Folk music uses a variety of meters as well, including triple time. Unfortunately, today a lot of folk material is "rockified" with a back-beat and amped-up instruments because that's the sugar-candy the modern taste craves. This perverts its nature. In short, *authentic* folk music grows from local communities and follows good musical principles.[41]

---

[41] For a list of recommended folk music groups, see the description given for my lecture "Prayer, Music, Dating—Advice for Young Catholics" on YouTube.

Rock rhythm is not the only kind that makes a disordered appeal to raw concupiscence. One need only think of the tango rhythm and the dance it serves. The tango originated in the bordellos of South America, and again, the connection is not hard to see: its rhythm is an unremitting assault on the senses so as to bring about a state of hyperactive concupiscible excitement. The sensuality of the dance, in which the partners are together as closely as a man and a woman can be while still having clothes on, is well served by the insistent beat which makes it easier to lose control and forget oneself, plunging into the realm of the flesh.

"Wait a minute," someone objects. "According to John Paul II's theology of the body, sexual intercourse is a good and natural thing and it can be supernaturally good too. It sounds like you're just condemning sexuality."

But of course sexuality is part of the good human nature that God created and redeemed and sanctifies through the sacraments! Sexuality, like everything else, is good precisely when it is in accord with right reason, divine faith, and personal dignity—not to mention the requirements of intimacy and modesty.[42] Excessive kindling of concupiscence and going public with the pubic, as it were, is the problem in our post-1960s society and its popular art forms (think of television and movies). Music, for its part, should purify and sublimate the passions of desire and anger, not celebrate them or urge them on. Our fallen nature needs restraint and elevation, not rowdy encouragement and self-indulgence. This was one of the key lessons that the Christian religion brought into the fallen world. According to Anthony M. Coniaris, the ancient pagans "deified their passions. They worshipped the animals within themselves. They bowed down before the passions of their own natures, which they could not control or understand. Bacchus was the deification of appetite. Aphrodite was the deification of the passion of lust. Jupiter the deification of war." Christ came to liberate us from this inversion and perversion of worship.[43]

---

[42] See Kwasniewski, *Treasuring the Goods of Marriage in a Throwaway Society*.

[43] Anthony M. Coniaris, *Philokalia: The Bible of Orthodox Spirituality* (Minneapolis: Light & Life, 1998), 150, cited in Clark, *Can We Believe in People?*, 13. Our art forms should elevate and ennoble us: "Statues, stories, music represent a dream—of justice, majesty, generosity and other virtues. We make these [artworks] up, individually and collectively, and live among them, drawing inspiration rather than explanation from them all" (Clark, 59). Libby Purves writes, "Sculpture, like music, has a peculiar power

Another objection comes fast and furious: "Even classical music now-adays is sold by displaying on the CD booklet cover a sexy violin player or an operatic heroine dressed in seductive garb. Sex is just a tool used by marketers and performers, not something intrinsic to any style of music." It's true that capitalists have known for decades that "sex sells," and so, this combination of avarice and lust has pervaded every aspect of our con-sumer culture. If the appeal to sexual concupiscence is wholly extrinsic to the music, there is no reason *in principle* why it should be associated more with rock than with classical. Yet this is manifestly false in practice: classical music has nothing like the hyper-sexualized culture that enmeshes rock. To take a more concrete example, Peter Mirus claims that Elvis "hyped [his] own music and image by marketing and glorifying sexuality." Well, then, why doesn't the concert violinist or the lyric soprano try to hype classical music by similar behavior *during a performance?* Everyone would find this laughable precisely because of the manifest incongruity between the behav-ior and the music. In other words, an argument like Mirus's hinges on the claim that musical-cultural associations that happen always or for the most part are essentially by chance. As Aristotle pointed out long ago, however, that which happens always or for the most part cannot be by chance.[44]

The next person might accuse me of insulting people's intelligence and casting aspersions on their moral character: "How dare you say that those who listen to [fill in the blank] are not living fully in accord with their ratio-nal dignity and its moral demands? Are you suggesting we are bad people because of the music we prefer?"

A discussion of aesthetic sensibilities necessarily deals with generalities, and at this level, one *can* examine whether musical tastes are well-founded and well-formed or not. Lacking further evidence, however, one cannot then call into question people's *moral character*, which has to do with particulars. Character is formed by a thousand influences, and it is *possible* for a person who listens to Bach and Mozart to be a complete hedonist (as are many professional musi-cians) and for a person who performs or listens to rock or atonal music to be

---

to start communicating at the place where logic and experience have to stop. Great statues, like music, speak to small children with a directness not to be underestimated" (cited in Clark, 59).
[44] See Aristotle, *Physics* II.4–6.

morally upright. I do think some kinds of music are spiritually dangerous while others are spiritually beneficial, but music is obviously only one of many elements that make up a human being's moral, intellectual, and spiritual identity.

An aficionado might try this more sophisticated counterargument: "In the Romantic period, one can find great composers such as Beethoven, Sibelius, Smetana, or Brahms using repeated syncopation in certain works—for instance, Beethoven in the third movement of his String Quartet no. 12. The unnatural rhythm you're criticizing, then, is already found in 'classical' music."

These composers use syncopation like an exotic spice, not even for an entire movement but only for a few measures at a time. Within that context, the effect, while strange and interesting, carries none of the social and psychological message of rock 'n' roll, where syncopation takes over as the baseline. One feels that the Romantic composers are looking to startle jaded listeners with a brief clever move; one fears that they are straining for a novel effect, which is part of the eventual downfall of romanticism—its dissipation into cheap novelty, into dazzling but depthless effects.

The reason traditional music emphasizes the downbeat is that, as Aristotle observes, one is not a number but the principle of all number, with two being the first number. So there is a natural primacy to unity and the first in a series, as Nicomachus, Plato, and Euclid also taught. Moreover, in a repeated series of groups of beats, the first is the "home" beat, just as the home key of a piece is what we expect it to cadence to. In a waltz, the 1-2-3, 1-2-3 groups begin with 1 and return to 1, making a satisfying rhythmic whole. When the off-beats are accentuated, the natural primacy of the first is frustrated or thwarted. Used sparingly, as in Beethoven, this syncopation comes as a surprise and stirs up feelings of excitement. When used constantly, however, it is like a heart suffering from arrhythmia, a chronic condition of awkwardness, a sort of twitching or punching rather than a noble movement.

A last objector might try to defend jazz as an artistically superior ancestor of and an alternative to later popular styles. Yet leaving aside its key role in the eventual emergence of rock, jazz has problems peculiar to itself. In the 1920s, jazz was stigmatized, not without reason, as "the devil's music" for its musical style, lyrics, and performance practices.[45] Although it bears melodic

---

[45] See "The Devil's Music: 1920s Jazz," www.pbs.org/wgbh/cultureshock/beyond/jazz.html.

and harmonic interest, jazz could be described as music that "fools around"; it is almost a parody or satire of the art of music—music reduced to "having fun."[46] We *should* have fun, but in a way consistent with our rational dignity. Jazz lacks the orderedness of folk and classical; it has little definite to say (it is the quintessential "background music" for fancy nightclubs) and shows off in a superficial manner (the passing around of flashy solos). While there are elements of improvisation in Baroque music, it is wonderfully ordered in every respect, and spontaneity is not the main point, but beauty of sound and depth of emotion. The individual performers take a back seat to the ensemble and its overall sound. In jazz, on the other hand, the improvisation becomes the central element, and this brings about a focus on the performers quite as much as on the music itself.[47]

Animal emotion versus elevated emotion

One often hears a false claim: today's popular music is "more emotional," while traditional music is "less emotional."

In reality, the emotions evoked in today's popular music are more crude and monotonous. The emotions elicited by the music of a Palestrina, Bach, or Mozart are more profound and pure—therefore, more variegated, subtle, and rich. There is no expression of joy or sorrow as intense as what one finds in Victoria's Passiontide motets, Bach's cantatas, Mozart's piano concertos, or Beethoven's quartets. Intellectual pleasures are the highest pleasures, as Aristotle notes,[48] but *awareness* of them requires a certain process of maturation, which must be accompanied by a purifying of the passions. Nevertheless, the final result of this journey is the ability to experience passions that are more subtle, more all-encompassing, more fully what passions are supposed to be. In that sense, the best music is also the most emotionally satisfying.

Consider the difference between *a great expression of emotion* and the *expression of great emotion*. The former is an intellectually refined or purified expression, one might say emotion spiritualized or conformed to *logos*, while

---

[46] It is no coincidence that the first major wave of modern contraceptive use coincided with the loosening morals of the "roaring '20s."
[47] In this regard, traditional liturgical rites are like Baroque music, while the modern rite of Paul VI, with its plethora of options and its focus on the performer(s), is like jazz.
[48] Aristotle, *Nicomachean Ethics* X.7.

the latter is a raw outburst, a sort of exhibition of animal vitality. The question is: Which is most proper to man as man, to man as *imago Dei*, to man as redeemed by the Blood of the *Logos* and sanctified by the indwelling Trinity?

A sign of the difference can be seen by comparing real dancing with the aerobic flailing that passes for dancing in the youth anti-culture—a difference traceable to the styles of music that accompany these activities. The Baroque gavotte, the Classical minuet, even a Strauss waltz, are embodiments of order, pattern, symmetry, and gracefulness, examples of disciplined motion that is more human, more social, and more aesthetically pleasing than individualistic gyrating. Which of these exercises is more truly *dancing*? Ballet, when all is said and done, is more beautiful, requires more strength, exhibits more fully the inner potentiality of man and woman, than rock or pop "dancing." Being a more rational and more unified activity, it is more fully the perfection of the activity itself and of the human person who performs it. Needless to say, we can learn a lot about the nature of music by observing the human excellences it supports or the abominations it encourages.

We've come a long way since Elvis and the Beatles. Popular music has gone in various directions, including some that are far worse than the first wave of rock music. Rap, hip-hop, and techno strains are even more narrowly focused on the insistent, inescapable, infernal beat, abandoning melody and nuanced harmony as if to reduce sound to rhythmic machinery, an inhuman trance of sensual repetition, a pumping exploitative energy with no soul. Vincent Clarke offers a memorable description:

> Contemporary rap and hip-hop music . . . are designed to degrade. Whereas earlier iterations mixed upbeat rhythms with degrading lyrical content, contemporary iterations drop the upbeat rhythms in favor of dreary and repetitive beats. One of the most popular songs in this new genre is 'Gucci Gang' by Lil Pump (1 billion views on YouTube!). . . . There is no point in highlighting here the infantile simplicity of its lyrics or its borderline self-parody of crude consumerism. What is fascinating is that it performs a sort of *reductio ad absurdum* on pop music itself. Pop music, of course, relies on crude hooks to catch the attention of listeners. Trap music pushes

this to the next step where it inserts strange vocal utterances that sound like they are from a child's cartoon. . . . But this "gagagoogoo" is presented against a dark and bleak backdrop, where the music sounds like it is pulling the listener into a depressive spiral. This is not the melancholy of Schubert's "Der Doppelgänger"—and, take caution, even such Romantic excesses are (at least in the opinion of this writer) dangerous for the soul—no, this is degradation pure and simple. This is not the melancholy of the frustrated lover; this is the suicidal nihilism of the opium-eater, mixed with the morality of the mugger.[49]

About heavy metal we should say nothing: for, according to Saint Paul, there are certain things that should hardly even be mentioned (cf. Eph 5:3– 4). Then there is a genre loosely called "post-rock," whose practitioners, as if responding to a call to transcendence, have moved away from the hege- mony of the beat into a more complex world of sound, veined with existen- tial angst and questionings; yet they have not overcome their psychological alienation from ancient and Christian wisdom, which dooms them to artis- tic inferiority to the great Western musical tradition.

Fortunately, although often unrecognized and unrewarded, there has always been, right through the twentieth century and into the twenty-first, a "classical" tradition of composers who recognize the artistic primacy of

---

[49] Clarke, "The Need for an Integral Approach to Music." Jason Baxter has similarly negative things to say about pop hits, with their "pounding rhythm and monotonous melody": "We are a market with a predisposed taste for the mechanistically reductive, a music that mechanically hammers home a simplistic lyric. If you're building a machine, you want as few parts as possible to accomplish as many cycles of production in as little time as possible. That's become the paradigm for songs, too. . . . In other words, while [Calvin] Harris intentionally aspires to the sound of machines, and chooses the female voice because it better blends into his machinescape, Mendelssohn [in the *Hebrides Overture*] has aimed to create an art which resembles the complexity of the natural world. . . . Mendelssohn's music better resembles the ecological diversity of untended nature, whose range is infinitely richer than the mechanized. It's strange, then, that we find classical music flat and boring. But I'm beginning to wonder if that is in part due to the restriction of our emotional vocabularies, which is due in part to the mechaniza- tion of our music. If we're going to be uploaded into digital utopia, do we first have to be pared down to kilobytes?" Baxter, "The Shrinking, Post-human Vocabulary of Our Tone-deaf Culture."

melody and harmony and who seek an incarnation of spirit in the flesh of their music—such composers as Henryk Górecki, John Tavener, Pēteris Vasks, and Arvo Pärt.[50] No less worthy of praise are the many practitioners of early music and authentic folk music, such as Jordi Savall and Hespèrion XXI, who have reintroduced into contemporary musical culture many noble and emotionally satisfying works from earlier centuries, including the folk music of various cultures, embellishing them with skillful improvisation. Composers and musicians like these are following the essentially human and Christian principle of tradition—namely, that we cherish with love what we inherit with humble gratitude, and we develop organically what we cherish. Such music and musicians can indeed guide us into a future dominated by the uplifting lyricism of the Divine Logos.

Orientation from the Word of God

That brings us squarely to the spiritual dimension of this whole question. Is there any evidence that Christians have a moral imperative to pursue an all-embracing excellence in the fine arts and to avoid the contamination of worldliness, whether it be in lyrics, themes, genres, or lifestyles? I believe the answer is a resounding YES. Although part of my explanation will come in the next chapter, for the time being let us consider the following verses from Sacred Scripture:

> Now we have received not the spirit of the world, but the Spirit which is from God, that we might understand the gifts bestowed on us by God. (1 Cor 2:12)

> For the grace of God has appeared for the salvation of all men, training us to renounce irreligion and worldly passions, and to live sober, upright, and godly lives in this world, awaiting our blessed hope, the appearing of the glory of our great God and Savior Jesus Christ, who gave himself for us to redeem us from all iniquity and to purify for himself a people of his own who are zealous for good deeds. (Ti 2:11–14)

---

[50] See Reilly, *Surprised by Beauty*, and chapter 5 below.

Unfaithful creatures! Do you not know that friendship with the world is enmity with God? Therefore whoever wishes to be a friend of the world makes himself an enemy of God. Or do you suppose it is in vain that the scripture says, "He yearns jealously over the spirit which he has made to dwell in us"? (Jas 4:4–5)

The Lord knows how to rescue the godly from trial, and to keep the unrighteous under punishment until the day of judgment, and especially those who indulge in the lust of defiling passion and despise authority.

But these, like irrational animals, creatures of instinct, born to be caught and killed, reviling in matters of which they are ignorant, will be destroyed in the same destruction with them, suffering wrong for their wrongdoing. They count it pleasure to revel in the daytime. They are blots and blemishes, reveling in their dissipation, carousing with you. They have eyes full of adultery, insatiable for sin. They entice unsteady souls. They have hearts trained in greed....

For, uttering loud boasts of folly, they entice with licentious passions of the flesh men who have barely escaped from those who live in error. They promise them freedom, but they themselves are slaves of corruption; for whatever overcomes a man, to that he is enslaved. For if, after they have escaped the defilements of the world through the knowledge of our Lord and Savior Jesus Christ, they are again entangled in them and overpowered, the last state has become worse for them than the first. (2 Pt 2:9–20)

Do not love the world or the things in the world. If any one loves the world, love for the Father is not in him. For all that is in the world, the lust of the flesh and the lust of the eyes and the pride of life, is not of the Father but is of the world. (1 Jn 2:15–16)

The world of rock music, and, more broadly, the world of contemporary entertainment, is permeated with "the lust of the flesh and the lust of the eyes and the pride of life." *Not all of it,* thanks be to God, but far more of it than the sophisticated defenders of popular culture have persuaded themselves to believe. The human person seeking moral virtue, wisdom, and fine art, the Christian seeking holiness, contemplation, and beatitude, would do well to be supremely vigilant, keenly discriminating, and ready to avoid or repudiate all that is not true, honorable, just, pure, lovely, and gracious (cf. Phil 4:8). Such behavior, far from showing a pusillanimous fear of the world or a failure of apostolic engagement, manifests a righteous fear of the living God and an intense love of His beauty.[51] This beauty must permeate our whole lives, from *logos* to *pathos*—from the pinnacle of reason to the depths of emotion.

Let heaven enter

In 1858, Saint John Henry Newman published a magnificent essay called "The Mission of St. Benedict."[52] In it there are many colorful passages about different figures in the Benedictine tradition. At one point, Newman says of Saint Dunstan:

> He had a taste for the arts generally, especially music. He painted and embroidered; his skill in smith's work is recorded in the well-known legend of his combat with the evil one. And, as the monks of Hilarion joined gardening with psalmody, and Bernard and his Cistercians joined field work with meditation, so did St. Dunstan use music and painting as directly expressive or suggestive of devotion. "He excelled in writing, painting, moulding in wax, carving in wood and bone, and in work in gold, silver, iron, and brass," says the writer of his life in Surius. "And he used his skill in musical instruments to charm away from himself and others their secular annoyances, and to rouse them to the thought of heavenly harmony, both by the sweet words with which he accompanied his airs, and by the concord of those airs themselves."

Ponder what is being said here. Newman is praising Dunstan not just for the quality of his sacred music but rather for his use of the art of music simply speaking. The saint "use[d] music and painting *as directly expressive or suggestive of devotion*." This sentence makes quite a striking claim: the

---

[51] See Kalinowska, "The Art of Dress—Problems with Normalcy."
[52] See Newman, *A Benedictine Education*, 41–42.

fine arts, of their very nature, are capable of expressing or suggesting to the soul the right attitude or relationship it should have with God. Naturally, this also means that they are capable of doing the opposite; and it is not at all clear to me that they are capable of being neutral, neither favoring nor hindering devotion.

Moreover, his biographer tells us that Dunstan used his *skill* in *musical instruments*—here, again, we are not in the world of unaccompanied plainchant for Mass or the Divine Office but rather looking to the effect of instruments played recreationally—to do two things, one negative and one positive. First, by his music he would "charm away from himself and others their secular annoyances." Let us be honest with ourselves. Is not much of our life an annoyance to the spirit? We are constantly fighting the world, the flesh, the devil; it is hard going, an uphill battle, a steep climb, an unremitting campaign. Our path to heaven is strewn with obstacles, beginning with our own besetting sins, and the temptations thrown at us to indulge in them. From time to time, we need the refreshment of losing ourselves in something peaceful and pacifying, beautiful and beautifying—something that exists for its own sake, just because it is good, like God. The world will always be with us while we draw breath, but its annoyances can be chased away for a blessed moment by the power of music.

That is not all; the best is yet to come. By his music, Saint Dunstan would "rouse them to the thought of heavenly harmony." Ah, the thought of heaven and its eternal harmony, where God's will is ever done, and, for that very reason, every saint and angel is profoundly happy, resting in His ineffable sweetness, beauty, and glory! That goal should be the Christian's mainstay in this valley of tears. We are told that Dunstan's music actually contained something of that goal in its "sweet words" and the "concord" of the airs or melodies. It is as if a piece of heaven were present in his music, the way a man is already present when you hear his voice from a distance, even if he himself is not yet on hand.

We see here a lofty saintly standard for all of our music. We learn about the true vocation of the musician, which is to elevate our listless, wounded, earthbound minds to sempiternal vistas of light, and even to set what is dark and difficult in the radiance of the light. Music, for a Christian, should serve the same purpose as everything else in life: weaning us from excessive attachment to this world and lifting our souls heavenward. If Newman is right, the message poses a challenge for each of us. Is the music we create, listen to, and take delight in, whether it be sacred or secular, music that will fit us to be better Christians and more noble human beings? Is this even a question we are asking ourselves?

4

Why I Threw Away My Rock and Rap Cassettes in High School

In my high school days, I used to listen to a wide range of rock music—bands like The Beatles, The Police, The Doors, U2, Rush, Van Halen, Yes, Genesis, King Crimson, Gentle Giant, ELP, Steely Dan—and rap was part of the mix too.

At a certain point, thanks to a charismatic prayer group at church, I started taking my Catholic faith more seriously. For the first time, I was choosing to attend Mass on weekdays and reading the Bible on my own. I began to pay attention to the lyrics of the music I was listening to and noticed how vulgar and stupid they often were. It was not difficult to see that the musicians, too, at closer look, were anything but models of virtue.[53]

At about the same time, thanks to a required music appreciation class in which the teacher regaled us with Vivaldi's *Four Seasons*, Mozart's *Eine Kleine Nachtmusik*, and other renowned classics, I slowly grew in awareness of how the music of the great composers was more complex, interesting, and beautiful in its melodies, harmonies, and rhythms—and in its words too, if words happened to be present (songs, choruses, oratorios, and the like). It spoke to many levels of my being—not just stirring up lower

---

[53] There were some "bad boys" in the history of artistically serious music too, but the difference between them and our present-day musicians is that the former generally had to dissimulate their vices, whereas the latter openly celebrate them. Along these lines, Bob Larson's trio of books about the satanic origins of and influences on rock music, which I discovered thanks to Joseph Ratzinger's recommendation, makes for eye-opening reading. See Ratzinger, "The Image of the World and of Human Beings in the Liturgy and Its Expression in Church Music," in *A New Song for the Lord*, 111–27, at 123.

passions, making the toes tap or the hips gyrate, but appealing to mind and heart as well.

At first, I'll admit, it was an uphill climb. One does not make an instantaneous transition from one set of listening habits to another. But over time, this great music started making sense. I became aware, bit by bit, of the vastness of the musical cosmos from which my music teacher had selected these pieces. When he sensed my curiosity, he encouraged me to explore a huge record collection upstairs in the fine arts building. Nearly all of it was what people call "classical music,"[54] ranging from Gregorian chant to the latest atonal and aleatory experiments. I felt awed, dwarfed, provoked, and fascinated. It is as if the music, in all of these diverse periods, styles, and messages, were quietly inviting me to a new realm, a kind of Narnia, to which the culture of my adolescence had been barring my entrance. It wasn't long before I gave up on the weirder contemporary composers and settled into a steady diet of music from the Renaissance, the Baroque, the Classical, and the Romantic eras, along with some of the more "conservative" modern composers like Vaughan Williams, Stravinsky, Sibelius, and Poulenc.

At a certain point, it occurred to me that I no longer wanted to give the rock and pop "artists" my time, my money, or, most importantly, access to my soul, and that (fortunately!) there was a wider, deeper musical world out there. I decided to quit listening to the pop and rock stuff. In fact, at a certain point, I took all of my cassettes—we used cassettes back then—and threw them in the garbage can. I've never regretted that decision, or my turn to more serious and more artistically worthy music. Here I will attempt to explain why.

---

[54] People nowadays use the term "classical" to refer to any music other than the so-called "popular" genres such as folk, jazz, or rock. As handy a term as it may be, it is terribly inaccurate. "Classical" refers to a particular period, ca. 1770 to 1828, epitomized in the music of Haydn, Mozart, Beethoven, and Schubert. Other periods of music prior to this one (i.e., Medieval, Renaissance, Baroque) and subsequent to it (i.e., Romantic and Modern) sound very different. Second, there is plenty of "serious" or "art" music still being composed, but it usually has little in common with the style of the aforementioned classical masters. To group such disparate composers as Perotin, Josquin, Byrd, Monteverdi, Corelli, Haydn, Wagner, Chopin, Debussy, Webern, Messiaen, Stravinsky, and Pärt into a single category is lunacy.

Seeking and striving for greatness

"Why should it make a difference whether we listen to geniuses like Bach and Beethoven or whatever three-minute pop song happens to be on the radio? I don't have time for these long, complicated pieces, and I need to get pumped up for my gym workout."

We are the beneficiaries of over one thousand years of glorious Western music, a heritage that has no parallel in any other human civilization or culture. This is *our* heritage—something that has been passed down to us. Each one of us, as a rational animal, as a citizen of the West, and as a Christian, should take hold of it and take advantage of it. As men, as believers, we should be striving for intellectual, cultural, moral, and spiritual excellence.[55]

Our life is not bifurcated into two hermetically sealed compartments—namely, inside the church and outside the church. *It is one single life.* As Saint John Chrysostom preached to his flock: "Some people make their houses a theater; you should make your home a church."[56] He did not mean that we should always wear our Sunday best and listen only to plainchant or Palestrina but rather that we should conscientiously pursue in our homes what is good, gracious, beautiful, and life-giving, as the Apostle instructs us to do: "Brethren, whatever is true, whatever is honorable, whatever is just, whatever is pure, whatever is lovely, whatever is gracious, if there is any excellence, if there is anything worthy of praise, think about these things" (Phil 4:8). We are not supposed to make ourselves a battleground between two opposed worldviews. Music outside of church, while it need not be sacred, should still

---

[55] Music is one of the most obvious concentrations and carriers of a people's cultural identity. It can escape no one's notice that, as pop music floods the globe, the youth are torn away from their own cultures, histories, traditions, ultimately their nations. Culture and spirituality are nipped in the earbud.

[56] The full quotation: "As those who bring comedians, dancers, and harlots into their feasts [sounds like a lot of today's Hollywood movies, half-time entertainments, etc.!] call in demons and Satan himself and fill their homes with innumerable contentions (among them jealousy, adultery, debauchery, and countless evils); so those who invoke David with his lyre [i.e., who pray the psalms] call inwardly on Christ. Where Christ is, let no demon enter; let him not even dare to look in in passing. Peace, delight, and all good things flow here as from fountains. Those make their home a theatre; make yours a church. For where there are psalms, and prayers, and the dance of the prophets, and singers with pious intentions, no one will err if he call the assembly a church." *Exposition of Psalm XLI*, in Strunk, ed., *Source Readings in Music History*, 69.

be in *harmony* with the music proper to church. They ought to be consistent with one another: two areas of a single coherent Christian life.

This apostolic teaching does not mean we must do what is objectively best all the time, whether in cultural pursuits or in life in general—assuming we could even know with certainty what is objectively best. That would hardly be possible for us mortals.[57] Saint Paul is urging us to aspire to what is better, more nourishing, more sanctifying, more proper for rational beings made in God's image and likeness. On judgment day, the Lord will ask us to give an account of how we used our time, our mental energy, our passions, our divine capacity for beauty and wonder, nobility and courtesy. We will have to explain why, when we learned that there was a greater beauty and wonder, nobility and courtesy, we failed to make it part of our lives. The same Apostle exhorts us, "I appeal to you therefore, brethren, by the mercies of God, to present your bodies as a living sacrifice, holy and acceptable to God, which is your spiritual worship. Do not be conformed to this world but be transformed by the renewal of your mind, that you may prove what is the will of God, what is good and acceptable and perfect" (Rom 12:1–2).

We do, therefore, have an obligation *not* to be conformed to the secular world and its values when these are opposed to what is sacred and supernatural. We have a duty to seek interior transformation by putting on the mind of Christ. We are called to offer our bodies as a holy sacrifice by which the flesh is subordinated to the spirit, the lower powers to the higher powers, and our intellect and will to God. This is how we will fulfil Our Lord's injunction: "Be perfect, as your heavenly Father is perfect" (Mt 5:48).

Music shapes our souls for better or for worse

"But isn't the music we listen to a matter of indifference? Surely, it's just superficial entertainment."[58]

---

[57] When it comes to our state in life, for example, and the activities connected with it, we are not required always to choose the best—otherwise every baptized Christian would be obliged to choose consecrated virginity or celibacy and the contemplative life. See Kwasniewski, "On Discerning Vocations: How to Think about 'States of Life.'"

[58] Scruton observes, "The *anomie* of Nirvana and REM is the *anomie* of its listeners. To withhold all judgement, as though a taste in music were on a par with a taste in ice-cream, is precisely not to understand the power of music." *Aesthetics of Music*, 502.

Such may be a common point of view in the modern democratic Western world, but it is a minority opinion in the history of human thought—and I'm not quite sure that anyone really believes it anyway.[59] That music has a profound effect on the formation and development of our human potentialities and moral character is the teaching of Plato, Aristotle, Augustine, Aquinas, Schopenhauer, Nietzsche, Pieper, Ratzinger, and Scruton, among other heavyweights—and surely, when thinkers opposed on so much else agree on this major point, their agreement should give us pause. If what these thinkers hold is true, music cannot but affect our lives as Christians and our eternal destiny.

According to the two greatest philosophers of antiquity, Plato and Aristotle, whenever we listen to music, we are allowing it to come inside and make its home in our souls. We are saying: *Shape* me; make me like yourself. We wouldn't sleep with just anyone, or entrust our education (or that of our offspring) to just any teacher—yet we often allow sordid characters and their cheap goods to enter the doors and windows of our body and live inside our minds and hearts! Plato in particular argues that what we really believe, what we *are*, is most of all revealed by that in which we take pleasure.[60] If our tastes in music or movies are the same as those of modern American atheistic hedonists, what does that say about the strength of our faith or the vitality of our intellectual life?

The *Logos*, the Word of God, should permeate our thinking, our feeling, our loves and hates, our way of being human. This is what it means to live a life of virtue and to be a son of God. We become beacons of light, keeping alive the memory of the beautiful and attracting others to a nobler way of thinking, living, *being*. That we are supposed to care very much about the reformation of our interior life, especially by turning away from corrupt passions, is impressed on us by Saint Peter: "His divine power has granted to us all things that pertain to life and godliness, through the knowledge of him who called us to his own glory and excellence, by which he has granted to us his precious and very great promises, that through these you may escape from the corruption that is in the world because of passion, and become partakers of the divine nature" (2 Pt 1:3–4).

---

[59] This becomes quickly apparent in the passions stirred up if someone dares to challenge another's taste in music or questions whether it's good for him!

[60] See Plato, *Laws* II.

What's wrong with today's "popular music"

"So far, so good. But all of the above is too general—painting with a broad brush. Can you be more specific about what's wrong with the music you threw away in high school, and what, in contrast, is so good about the more artistically refined music?"

Rhythm is the most basic element of music, the most primitive. This is why the music of some primitive cultures consists mostly of drumming. More advanced cultures, presupposing the framework of rhythm, develop beautiful melodies above it. The most advanced, presupposing both rhythm and melody, develop a system of harmony. When you listen to a piece by (e.g.) Palestrina, Bach, Mozart, Tchaikovsky, or Pärt, the rhythm, although discernible, is subordinated to the melody and harmony, which take "center stage."

Pop, rock, rap, metal, and other such "popular" styles are unhealthy for the soul because they invert this rational hierarchy of rhythm, melody, and harmony. They accentuate the beat, strip the harmonic framework to a bare minimum, and employ repetitious, unlyrical "melodies" (if they can even be called that) in order to stimulate the concupiscible and irascible sense-appetites in a disordered manner. We are dealing here with music deliberately primitive and passionate, simplistic and sensual.[61]

It is one thing for such music to proceed from genuine savages who know no better, but it is quite another for it to proceed from the descendants of a rich folk culture and a resplendent high culture. In the latter case, it is a rejection of their own inheritance, a symbolic statement of repudiation and revolution. We may compare it to the difference between naïve pagans who do not yet know the Gospel and nihilistic neo-pagans who hold it in contempt—so much so that they do not even bother to find out whether or not they understand what they are rejecting.

We can see the simplism and sensualism of many "popular" forms of music if we look at the rhythmic underpinning. All traditional Western

---

[61] It can bring about this submersion into sensuality in different ways, from slow and seductive to fast and furious. The point is not the tempo or the loudness but the overall *manner* in which the musical elements achieve their impact. That popular styles are simplistic is a claim many people bristle at, but the sum total of today's pop music could not vie with, let alone equal, the artistic qualities of a single page of Mozart or of any other great composer.

musical styles follow the principle of the downbeat, where the first beat in a measure of 3 or 4 beats is the most accentuated, as is quite natural. Syncopation—the practice of accentuating an "off" beat—is used by great composers as "spice," but pop styles lean on it relentlessly, monotonously, to induce a kind of false ecstasy. Rock music in particular is *defined* by the continual accentuation of the weak beats (2 and 4) rather than the downbeat and its partner (1 and 3). This accentuation is unnatural: it is the MSG of the music world.

The rarity of triple time (3/4, 6/8) in pop culture is also indicative: it bespeaks a loss of the art of dance. Dances in triple time are notable for their lilting, gentle, noble, or debonair attitude. In the pulsating, gyrating, pumping, aerobic-type exercise that many nowadays call "dancing," such triple-time dances of the past, which were numerous, widespread, and beautiful, are gone. If ever there was a manifest sign of cultural degeneration, it would have to be the descent from minuet to waltz to swing to disco to deafening nightclub mixes of throbbing monotony. With each step in the descent, we see a lessening of the social and communal dimension of dance, which is supposed to be an imitation of the orderly cosmos and the relations of the sexes within it; with each step, we see a decrease of formal beauty, a lapse of dignity, a loosening of morals, a growing contempt for order, symmetry, coordination of partners.[62]

What can we say, then? Today's popular music is largely unhealthy for its imbibers, in a way that is not dissimilar to the way in which

- ✦ eating junk food or doing drugs is bad for your body;
- ✦ playing videogames is bad for your psyche;
- ✦ seeking sexual pleasure for its own sake or looking at pornography is bad for your soul.

It can also be bad for you in the way in which reading only comic books when you could be reading great literature is bad, or dressing sloppily or immodestly when you could dress well.

With much of the bad music out there, we are not dealing with something *intrinsically* evil, such that the mere listening to it constitutes a mortal

---

[62] See Platt, "Different Drummer."

sin. Rather, we are dealing with something *relatively* evil: something that indicates and fosters moral imperfection, which, if unresisted, may lead to mortal sin. Saint Thomas Aquinas argues that venial sin is bad not only because of the offense in itself, light though it may be, but also because repeated venial sins are a slippery slope to mortal sin.[63]

By listening to rock or pop or rap, one is stunting one's moral growth, depriving oneself of intellectual perfection, and impeding or clouding one's spiritual life.

A musical examination of conscience

"But are you saying that popular music always has to be bad? That the only good music is that of a cultural elite? Are all of us supposed to become snobs?"

No, not at all. I mean, it wouldn't hurt to develop some aesthetic sophistication; after all, it's a rational perfection, as argued above. Yet the point is not sophistication for its own sake, or to show off or think poorly of others (*that* would be snobbery). The point is to develop an ear for what is beautiful and what is fitting for every occasion, with all the diversity that occasions allow and encourage. At a square dance, one should have good old-fashioned square dance music. When sitting around a campfire, one should sing the classic folk songs of one's people or nation (and woe to that people or nation that has no such songs, or never learns them). At a wedding reception, one might showcase waltzes, swings, and country dances.[64] Every normal human occasion has well-crafted music that suits it. In traditional cultures, even funerals were graced with special mourning music, a genre that has completely died out among modern Westerners.

---

[63] See *ST* I-II, Q. 88, art. 3.

[64] This may sound unbelievable to people living in mainstream culture, but I have been to weddings of alumni from Thomas Aquinas College and Wyoming Catholic College where the selection of music at the reception was tasteful and where real dances were done by adventurous young people. I suspect it is somewhat like the traditional Latin Mass: the young take to it readily, while some older folks frown at the freakish behavior. The oldest of all, however, are overjoyed to see the "youngsters" doing something orderly and fun, as it reminds them of a world they might have considered extinct.

Popular music does not have to be bad. The popular music of a healthy age, like the Catholic Middle Ages, is beautiful through and through: to borrow a saying of John Paul II, its makers and listeners are soaring on the wings of faith and reason. Music from the Middle Ages, whether it be the pilgrim songs of the *Llibre Vermell de Montserrat*[65] or the rollicking ballads of the troubadours,[66] shows us that music can be lusty but not lustful, toe-tapping but not Dionysian, vivacious but not disordered.[67]

This illustrates an important truth: music, to be good, does not have to be "boring" and straight-laced or super-refined and intricate.[68] Medieval music displays immediacy, spontaneity, innocence; its inventive melodies, harmonic freshness, and powerful rhythmic drive are compelling and captivating. In this way, it passes with flying colors what I call "the Quintuple Challenge":

1. Is the *rhythm* natural and orderly, balanced with and subordinated to the other elements?
2. Is the *melody* lyrical, interesting, and supportive of good vocal technique?
3. Is the *harmony* well integrated with the melody and rhythm, showing skillful use of consonance and dissonance, with sufficient variety?
4. Are the *lyrics* (if there are lyrics) expressive of or compatible with a Catholic worldview, with natural law and divine law?

---

[65] Searching on YouTube/Spotify for "Llibre Vermell Savall" will turn up many pieces from a live Hespèrion XXI concert. These were all-time favorites of my college students when I shared them in music class.

[66] Search on YouTube/Spotify for "Martin Best Mediaeval."

[67] Clarke's "The Need for an Integral Approach to Music" discusses the cultural conditions that militate for and against the development of artful popular music.

[68] There is, of course, something to be said for refined and subtle music, especially for the well-educated listener and for the well-catechized, practicing Catholic; one's music should match one's general level of intellectual and religious culture. It would be strange for those who derive literary enjoyment from great poets, playwrights, and novelists or who participate in the sublime sacrifice that unites heaven and earth to subsist on the musical equivalent of hot dogs, Twinkies, and soda pop. The larger problem, then, is that modern Christians have—usually through no fault of their own—such low cultural literacy and expectations that they do not perceive the massive disjunct. Individual Christians need to address this problem in their own lives, to the extent that they become aware of it.

5. Does the music arise from and give expression to a vigorous and healthy culture? (Here is where one can reasonably look to the lifestyles, avowed intentions, and assumptions of the composers and performers, which is not an infallible sign but often a telling one.)

Note that I have listed lyrics fourth. For many conservative critics, the lyrics are the only thing or the main thing objected to. That is to give short shrift to the greater power exercised by the music itself. Nevertheless, bad lyrics are prevalent throughout today's music. Sometimes the lyrics are just plain repulsive—vulgar, obscene, violent, satanic, et cetera. There can never be an excuse for listening to pieces with lyrics of that sort. However, the larger problem is the death of worthwhile poetry. Lovers of popular music protest bitterly when I attack the lyrics of their favorite genres, but it's difficult to take seriously lyrics that barely ascend above pubescent preoccupations conveyed in high school vocabulary that barely rhymes and almost never respects meter—that is, crummy poetry. Catholics, above all, should have no difficulty admitting that there are objective standards in the fine arts; that poetry, like any other art, has its rules and ideals; and that we should care enough to seek out good poetry in music, since we will be giving it a permanent place in our souls. The difference between rock, pop, or rap lyrics on the one hand and medieval popular songs or European lyric poetry on the other is starker than the difference between night and day. A sign of this is what happens when you try to recite it aloud, apart from the musical setting. Can it stand on its own two feet (or however many feet it has)? In its diction, use of metaphor, meter, and rhyme, and conceptual content, the poetry set to music by the great composers is on a level as far above that of today's popular music as the heavens above the earth, or the earth above the underworld. When you listen to Victoria setting Jeremiah, Haydn setting Milton, Schubert setting Goethe, or Vaughan Williams setting Herbert, you know what great poetry united to great music sounds like.

I have compared today's pop music to junk food. It seems to me that we could relate styles of music to four types of food:

+   Genuine sacred music = heavenly food, such as the angels feast upon

+   Beautiful secular music = royal food, fit for a king's high table
+   Good folk music = whole food, suitable for healthy consumption
+   Modern popular music = fast food/junk food, suitable for no one

Change is difficult. But more difficult still is trying to live a contradiction and suffering the inescapable consequences. It is better to suffer the pain of severance and aspire to the promise of a higher, purer pleasure than to settle for mediocrity (or worse) and to shelter illusions of pseudo-open-mindedness. "The most ominous of modern perversions," says Nicolás Gómez Dávila, "is the shame of appearing naïve if we do not flirt with evil."

A young man once wrote a letter to me explaining that his attraction to traditional Catholicism had also begun to have an effect on the music he was listening to. He began to feel that he should avoid certain kinds of music and gravitate toward other kinds—he was getting into the three most popular Baroque composers, Vivaldi, Handel, and Bach—and asked me if I could help him understand why he was going through this unexpected "conversion" and if I had any advice. (The name has been changed.)

Dear Johnny,

I have to say it's music to my ears to hear of your conversion to the beautiful in general and the Baroque in particular. I taught music for many years to college students, and I would say at least 50 percent of the students perked up when they learned about the agreement of philosophers and Church Fathers—great Western intellectuals like Socrates, Plato, Aristotle, Saint Augustine, Boethius, Saint John Chrysostom, Friedrich Nietzsche, Arthur Schopenhauer, Josef Pieper, Roger Scruton, and Joseph Ratzinger, to name just a few—that music both reflects and influences our moral state to a considerable extent, that it is a character-forming force of immense power and intimate influence, arguably *the* greatest force on the natural level. Many students would reach the conclusion that they ought to commit themselves to listening to better music and over time developed a habit of doing so—always with excellent results, and with gratitude months or years later, of which I have many testimonies in the form of emails, letters, and cards.

I have never met anyone who did not fall in love with the great composers after giving them a fair chance. Their music is superior in its depth
of feeling, its subtlety of expression, its lyricism, harmonic complexity, and
overall compatibility with the intellectual and spiritual life proper to man.

Yet it remains difficult for people to appreciate the objectivity of the beautiful—that *x* is more beautiful *in itself* than non-*x*—and this, for two main
reasons. First, the beautiful is perceived by a subject, an individual man, who
must have an apt disposition for it. A person with a devout, well-ordered
soul, open to God and intent on wisdom, will be drawn towards certain
manifestations of order and beauty in any sensible domain, and repelled by
their contraries. And as with moral habituation in general, one can strive
to live a more beautiful life—a life of virtue, prayer, and study—so as to
correspond more fully with beautiful liturgy and fine art. Put simply, the
beautiful object is recognized and rejoiced in by a soul that is either morally
beautiful or actively working to become so.

Second, beauty, like its sister, truth, requires a long and patient acquaintance, a real willingness to learn. The art of music is extremely deep and
subtle, but kids plugged all day long into the Top Ten on the pop chart will
never be aware of that. Only a foolish ignoramus (or worse, an ideologue)
would say that a rap song is equivalent to a fugue by J. S. Bach or a symphony by Beethoven or a movement from *The Planets* by Gustav Holst.
That is like comparing a comic strip to a novel by Jane Austen or Fyodor
Dostoevsky, or a McDonald's to a Parisian bistro. Since modern Western
people, victims of an educational system vacuous at best and ideological at
worst, tend to be dreadfully uneducated about almost everything, we cannot be surprised that their judgments about truth as well as beauty are not
only skewed but ridiculous. *They don't even know what they're talking about.*

Given the extensive changes in musical styles over the past one thousand
years and the unavoidable role of personal interest and taste (even assuming
the best condition of intellect, will, and appetites), one's certainty of judgment is greater the more general one's consideration, and more debatable
as one descends into details. What I mean is that the question "Which is
better, classical music or rock music?" is easier to answer than "Which is
better, the Baroque or the Romantic period?" and that, in turn, is easier than
"Who is the greater composer, Bach or Handel?" So one will find plenty of

ammunition for arguing on behalf of more general principles, but it gets harder to argue for the superiority of this or that period in music history, and harder still to argue for the superiority of this composer over that one. Yet most people are not hung up on the question of Mozart versus Beethoven, but on classical versus jazz versus pop, or, in the Church realm, chant and polyphony versus "praise and worship" or vernacular hymns.

Sacred music exhibits the essential characteristics of the art of music with a particular luminosity and thereby helps us to understand music's role in life more profoundly. I have come to think that all the music we listen to should be *compatible* or *harmonious* with sacred music. This doesn't mean that we should listen to sacred music all the time (that would be weird: it *is* appropriate sometimes to dance, as long as our dancing is of a suitable nature) but rather that our secular life should not be a sealed-off compartment that has nothing to do with our spiritual and liturgical life, or worse, that would compete with it or dilute it or undermine it. There should be a smooth transition from outside the church to inside the church; from inside the church to the Blessed Sacrament; from the Blessed Sacrament to contemplation and the beatific vision. The Catholic view is that our whole lives are to be offered up as a pleasing sacrifice to God, in union with Christ, and on pilgrimage to heaven (see Rom 12:1; Phil 4:8; Col 3:3). In my view, authentic folk music is still compatible in this way; almost everything on the radio stations today isn't.

Unlike less complex forms of aural stimulation, "art music," as in the fine art of music—broadly, the great Western tradition of music of the past millennium, as distinguished from commercialized lowest-common-denominator mass-marketed popular music of our time—needs, and deserves, to be given multiple hearings, with full attention. One needs to give this rich music a chance to speak to one's soul, to convey its beauties to one's mind, to mold one's heart. It's not supposed to be instant gratification; there's more intellectual substance to it than that. A cartoon, for example, tells you right away what it's about, and you laugh at the joke. In contrast, an artfully written novel or play takes time to enter into and appreciate. Like a good wine, it must "breathe." Indeed, a cultivated person would not rush through a gourmet French dinner but would take plenty of time, savor each course, and enjoy the entire ambience, most especially the conversation with other people at the table.

Just as there are great books, which are known to be great by the common consensus of thoughtful people across the ages,[69] and just as there are great paintings and great sculptures, so too there are great works of music, known and felt to be such by educated musicians and music lovers—works notable for their lofty conception, exquisite artistry, and depth of feeling. Ignorance of these is as bad, for someone who seeks to be educated in Western (and Catholic) culture, as ignorance of Dante and Shakespeare in literature, Plato and Aristotle in philosophy, Augustine and Aquinas in theology. Although one cannot train the ear in a day, a month, or even a year, one must bravely decide to make a beginning in developing the skill of what we might call "attentive listening to beautiful sound that is inherently worth listening to." Even though it takes time to develop an ear and a mind for great music, it is never too late to start. (The same could be said of playing a musical instrument or taking up any other worthwhile hobby.) As you listen more, your taste will catch up, your palate will develop, and you will find delight in the music beyond what you imagined possible. As the old saying goes, *ars longa, vita brevis:* art is immense, life is brief. Our lives are much too short to waste on what is inferior.

Cordially in Christ,
Dr. Kwasniewski

---

[69] See Kwasniewski, "Liberal Arts in Contemporary Education: The American Example."

5

The Journey into Great Music

"Okay, I'm willing to explore the great music, but where do I begin? It's overwhelming. I have no idea which composers are which, or what I'd even stand a chance of liking."

I've been asked many times for practical advice on how one should go about bringing good music into one's soul, and how parents may bring it into their home and the lives of their children. In this chapter, I have no intention of continuing my argument against immersion in popular music, most of which I *do* think is bad for the soul, nor will I try to rank the music of one period over that of another—as, for example, by arguing that Baroque music is better than Romantic (even though I personally think it is). My purpose is more modest: I would like to put forth some strategies for building a library of great music and make some particular recommendations.

A preliminary question must be addressed: namely, the degree to which we should be "consumers" of "canned" music. My position, in a nutshell, is that, while recordings of great music have an important place in the life of a modern culturally literate Christian, they must not be allowed to supplant altogether the art of singing, the learning and playing of instruments, and, in general, live music-making and actual concert-going. John Nieto points out the manner in which music has, for too many, become only a passively-consumed product rather than arising from one's own soul: "Once the city has wholly dominated human life it becomes possible to have many goods but they almost always come from somewhere else. Our clothes come from China; our music and our dances come from Los Angeles or New York. We do not sing. We download songs. A generation has grown up that conceives of music as essentially something bought and sold. We live in a world in which folk music is an historical being, a world in which folk music is the product of a music industry."[70]

---

[70] Nieto, "Nature and Art in the Village," 161.

In a letter written on July 30, 1944, Antoine de Saint-Exupéry lamented how modern man had become "castrated of all his creative power," one "who doesn't even know anymore, from the bottom of his village, how to create a dance or a song. The man who is fed a ready-made culture, a standardized culture as one feeds hay to the oxen. This is the man of today."[71] We should strive to escape this shrinking and withering of the human spirit. It is not so much about originality (that is, inventing new music) as it is about cultivating the *musicality* of our nature: even if we sang or played nothing but the folk music of our people or the music handed down by composers, it would still be music that arises from our souls and through our bodies— *our* music, warm, breathing, with a pulse, immanent and not extrinsic.

Still, there are two sides to musical education: one is making music and the other is becoming familiar with the repertoire of great music, the masterpieces that have been gifted to the human race—the works of towering geniuses whose contributions to fine art are no less worth getting to know than the justly celebrated works of the great poets, playwrights, novelists, philosophers, and theologians. Great Books and Great Art belong together, just as good books and good music do,[72] and in the case of music, there is no way to get to know the masterpieces without either attending live concerts (a superior method but not always as convenient or affordable) or listening to a lot of recordings. Modern technology, which has so many downsides, has unquestionably made it easier to find good music if we are keen to find it. An online streaming service like Spotify will make easy work of the exploration: when a listener starts with a popular piece like Vivaldi's *Four Seasons*, Handel's *Water Music*, Bach's *Brandenburg Concertos*, Beethoven's *Pastoral Symphony*, or Vaughan Williams's *Tallis Variations*, the streaming service's algorithms, based on a huge amount of data from user input, will pull up playlists of similar works. Amazon and other online retailers of music make available audio snippets of CDs or MP3 albums, again

---

[71] Translation mine; for the French original, see www.biblisem.net/etudes/stexlagx.htm.

[72] The notion of "good books" is that of John Senior: he means the many things one should read both because they are good, clean, entertaining stuff *and* because they serve as stepping-stones to the more challenging and rewarding Great Books. Similarly, good music, such as real folk music or orderly dance music, is a good in itself and can serve as a stepping-stone to the appreciation of the great masterpieces of the art of music.

allowing for sampling before purchasing. Although it may be considered old-fashioned by this time, purchasing CDs still has many benefits: there is a finite program of music on a particular disc, and the liner notes are usually highly instructive. My family and I have learned an enormous amount from reading liner notes over the years.

You should be able to find something—it's not for nothing that certain pieces in the "classical" genre have been popular for decades or centuries! Listen to these favorite pieces frequently so that you become accustomed to them. Eventually, your tastes will catch up, your palate will develop, and you will find a satisfaction beyond what you imagined possible.

1. Start with composers typically regarded as great. Don't be shy about immersing yourself in their works. To take some well-known examples: Palestrina, Victoria, Byrd, Purcell, Handel, Bach, Vivaldi, Haydn, Mozart, Schubert, Beethoven, Brahms, Dvořák, Tchaikovsky.[73] Although artistic taste can be fickle and untrustworthy—one need only consult the *New York Times* to see the absurd contortions into which art and music critics can twist themselves—it's a simple fact that composers of the fame of the ones just mentioned are widely considered to be great for substantive and compelling reasons. Their music has stood the test of time. Most of the "greats" have been acknowledged as great for many generations now, and it's not for nothing that certain pieces of theirs have been popular for decades or centuries. People keep on listening to their works with enjoyment, orchestras or soloists keep on playing it to appreciative audiences, record companies keep issuing new recordings of it, and radio stations keep programming it. It's remarkable how catchy and delightful a great piece of music, such as Praetorius's *Terpsichore*, Vivaldi's *Four Seasons*, Beethoven's Seventh Symphony, or Mussorgsky's *Pictures at an Exhibition* can be, especially as you become familiar with it through repeated listenings.

---

[73] Many of the great composers were Catholic—in this list, Palestrina, Victoria, Byrd, Vivaldi, Haydn, Mozart, Dvořák. Others were Protestant, such as Purcell, Handel, and Bach. Tchaikovsky was Russian Orthodox. Still others struggled with religious belief, such as Schubert, Beethoven, and Brahms. Nevertheless, even as Catholics benefit from reading the pagan Plato and the Protestant C. S. Lewis, so too can we benefit from the beautifully composed music of non-Catholics, which often includes biblically-based religious music. As argued earlier, the art of music is not a moral virtue but an intellectual virtue, so art must be judged by its intrinsic qualities.

2. Find out what periods, styles, genres, or composers you like the most. The benefit of sampling the famous composers, whose music is *known* to be well written (just as famous novelists are *known* to be good writers), is that you will find out more quickly what kind of music you find most interesting and enjoyable to listen to. Will it be Medieval, Renaissance, Baroque, Classical, Romantic, or Modern? Solo piano, chamber music, orchestral? Sonatas, symphonies, concertos? Purely instrumental, choral music, or solo songs? In the days when "sampling music" often enough meant buying albums, tapes, or CDs at the shop and bringing them home, exploration meant shelling out the bucks. But with free samples on Amazon, the "streaming" music services, online classical radio stations (such as "Boston Baroque Radio"), and YouTube clips, it's possible to listen for free to almost anything and make musical discoveries that will guide you toward a more permanent collection.

3. Listen to these favorite pieces frequently and well. When it comes to music, nothing beats familiarity, and with a longer or more complex piece, or with a style you've never been exposed to before, repeated listening gives the mind a chance to come to grips with the music, and the heart the chance to "sing" with it. Unlike visual art forms, music unfolds only over time and therefore cannot be apprehended and contemplated all at once, the way a painting can be. Repeated listening unifies one's grasp of a piece, of how it unfolds, somewhat like a story or an argument, from beginning to middle to end. The anticipation of this unfolding and the satisfaction of resting in its fulfillment become part of the pleasure.

Once you find a piece of music you enjoy, or as you grow to enjoy it more, I recommend obtaining a good recording of it in a high-quality audio format and listening to it on a decent set of speakers or headphones (not earbuds). YouTube clips are poor in sound quality, and computers and other small devices typically don't have speakers that can handle the dynamic range and sound colors of great music. People sometimes underestimate the difference it makes to have good sound equipment. This is not a waste of money but a good investment for the growth of your intellectual, aesthetic, and cultural life—and if there are children in the picture, it's all the more important.

4. Focus on genres that already appeal to you. For some, a more direct route to the goal of listening enjoyment and cultural elevation would be to identify a favorite *instrument* or *type* of music. Is English choral music your cup of tea on a Sunday? Looking for Gregorian chant and polyphony? Have you always been fond of the mellow cello; the glittering harp; the pleasant guitar; the melancholy lute; the tickled ivories (piano); the trumpet's bright sound; or the pipe organ, king of instruments? Then start your search from that instrument—e.g., "greatest cello works" or some such phrase—and work from there. Again, the online services make this a painless process.

5. **Find a favorite musician or ensemble and collect recordings.** Alternatively or simultaneously, when you find a musician you "resonate with," look him or her up and start exploring his or her recordings. For example, the early music specialist Jordi Savall, his late wife Montserrat Figueras, and the various ensembles they've worked with, such as Hespèrion XXI, are simply outstanding artists in everything they do. I have never found a recording by them that hasn't pleased me.

6. **Take advantage of videos.** I've met a lot of people over the years who find it difficult to just *listen* to classical music; perhaps they are visual people or somewhat fidgety. In this situation, nothing beats a well-produced DVD that explores a composer, musician, time period, or genre. The Christopher Nupen documentaries are some of my favorites. Nupen cleverly weaves together aspects of a composer's life and philosophy, or the trials and accomplishments of a concert musician, with fine performances of individual works. My favorites in the series are *Jean Sibelius*, *Evgeny Kissin: The Gift of Music*, and *Andrés Segovia*.

Another route, which is both affordable and exciting, is the Digital Concert Hall, a subscription to hundreds of recorded and live concerts of the Berlin Philharmonic Orchestra, widely considered the greatest in the world. I know of families that select a concert each week to listen to. It sure beats most of the movies out there.

Some DVDs I have enjoyed in the past, which one may still be able to find: *The Essential Bach* (five DVDs: *Brandenburg Concertos*, performed in the palace of the prince for whom Bach wrote them; *Mass in B Minor*, performed in the Leipzig church where Bach was cantor; *Well-Tempered Clavier*, Book I; various organ works; German Brass Plays Bach); *Byrd: Playing Elizabeth's Tune* (a BBC documentary about the life and times of William Byrd, the Catholic recusant composer who managed to keep the favor of a queen who had the blood of many Catholics on her hands); *Live in Rome: Celebrating Palestrina's 400th Anniversary* (The Tallis Scholars singing the *Missa Papae Marcelli* and Allegri's *Miserere*, among other works, in the basilica of S. Maria Maggiore, where Palestrina served as a choir boy and later choirmaster); *Cecilia Bartoli Live in Italy* (marvelous singing and selection of pieces). It is best to find what you like or what intrigues you and then take that as a point of departure for your exploration.

7. **Further educate yourself and your family.** There are many informative and entertaining lectures online, for free, that can expand your musical horizons. See, for example, British conductor Benjamin Zander's TED talk on "The Transformative Power of Classical Music." In the bibliography, I have listed a variety of entry-level books as well as some books for the more advanced.

Music ought to play an important part in any homeschooling curriculum. Children and young adults should, as part of their education, study the rudiments of music theory, history, and appreciation, starting with the fundamental ingredients of music—rhythms in simple and compound time signatures, pitch in bass and treble clef, key signatures, the circle of fifths, scales and intervals—and moving up to immersion in the greatest masterpieces of the art, like the *Missa Papae Marcelli* of Palestrina and the *Saint Matthew Passion* of Johann Sebastian Bach. Students will become, over time, not only witnesses to what is true and lovers of what is good but also ambassadors for the beautiful, captivated by the reflection of the face of Eternal Beauty. In this way they will inherit and magnify the legacy of Pope Benedict XVI, whom posterity is likely to remember as the "Pope of Beauty"—the pope, that is, who opened up new fountains of beauty in a pilgrim Church, parched and thirsty, wandering through the desert of modernity.

Particular recommendations

Those who are interested in Gregorian chant should check out *Benedicta* by the Monks of Norcia, *Chant* by the Monks of Heiligenkreuz, *Requiem* and *Sancta Nox* by the Priestly Fraternity of Saint Peter, and any of the recordings by the Choralschola der Wiener Hofburgkapelle.

For especially beautiful polyphony, I recommend the ensemble Gesualdo Six; start with their recording *English Motets*. For examples of true incul-turation, try listening to the lovely music composed by Catholic converts in Mexico under the guidance of European missionaries, as performed by the San Antonio Vocal Arts Ensemble (SAVAE). Saint Hildegard of Bingen is not the proto-feminist that some modern authors make her out to be; however strange and riotous her visions may be, her origi-nal music is some of the most peaceful and prayerful ever composed, as heard in the recordings of Sequentia. For medieval instrumental music, check out the ensemble La Reverdie, and for early music in general, Hes-pèrion XXI.

Within the Renaissance and Baroque periods, the Tallis Scholars, the Huelgas Ensemble, The King's Singers, the Cambridge Singers, the Hil-liard Ensemble, Stile Antico, Tenebrae Choir, Voces8, Profeti della Quinta, L'Achéron, Scherzi Musicali, Les Traversées Baroques, Les Arts Florissants, the New London Consort, the Praetorius Consort, the Gabrieli Consort, the English Concert, Accademia Bizantina, and the Freiburger Barock-orchester are a few of the many excellent ensembles to listen to. Again, selecting these online will lead to others worth knowing about.

Dr. Andrew Childs has prepared a wonderful list of a hundred great clas-sical pieces, with brief commentaries and classifications into three catego-ries: AA = All Ages; TYL = Try It, You'll Like It; HL = Heavy Lifting.[74] Dr. Susan Treacy in her engaging book *The Music of Christendom* provides a list of "100 Essential Masterworks of Classical Music: A Starter List" that she says "every Catholic should endeavor to know."[75]

Dr. Michael Pakaluk, a professor of Ethics at the Catholic University of America, has kindly given me permission to publish here his excellent advice on helping children fall in love with classical music.

> Any child who can sit still and read for half an hour can be taught
> to love classical music. It's your choice as a parent: do you want your
> child to grow up liking classical music or not? You can govern this.

---

[74] This list may be found here: www.angelusonline.org/index.php?section=articles& subsection=print_article&article_id=2807.
[75] See Treacy, *Music of Christendom*, 231–35.

I learned this truth from William F. Buckley's autobiography. I don't remember the story exactly. But he says something like when he was a child he visited some relative in Austria (I think), and, after dinner, everyone had to sit quietly for an hour and listen to classical music. He said that at the end of that month he had changed to loving, appreciating, and having an understanding of classical music. All that was required was that he sit down and be quiet.

For high school and college students, I recommend leaping right in with symphonies. Listen to some symphonies of Haydn (for example, The Philosopher, Surprise, Military, Oxford, Horn-signal, Farewell), then Mozart (Prague, Jupiter, Haffner), then all of Beethoven and Brahms, Tchaikovsky [symphony numbers] 4–6, Dvořák 7–9, Borodin 2, Bruckner 4, 7, 8, 9, Mahler 1, 2, 4, 5, 6, Sibelius 2 and 5, Prokofiev 1 and 5, Shostakovich 1, 5, and 10, Rachmaninoff 2, Hanson 2 (for those who can't get enough Sibelius). I'm sure I left many things out even of my own preferred pieces, but that's a good list that would take a year to go through. The order from older to more recent is important I think for quicker understanding.

For younger children I recommend shorter pieces from suites, ballets, and "programmatic" works (pieces which aim to tell a story). For example, begin by playing only "Morning" from Grieg's *Peer Gynt* Suite No. 1. Play it over and over until the children clamor to hear "Morning" again. Then add other parts of the suite. Other good choices along those lines: Bizet's *Carmen* Suites and *L'Arlésienne* Suites, Dukas's *Sorcerer's Apprentice*, Mussorgsky's *Night on Bald Mountain*, Tchaikovsky's *Nutcracker* (Disney knew what he was doing), Prokofiev's *Peter and the Wolf*, Albéniz's *Iberia*—generally the kinds of pieces they have on albums entitled "100 Classical Favorites."

Surprisingly it does not take long until even young children (7 years old or so) can listen to the last movement of Beethoven's 9th and love that. We played that movement every Saturday morning over pancakes for about four weeks and everyone got hooked on it, especially Mark, age 7.

The principle of repetition is extremely effective. We were going to hear the NSO in concert playing the *Three Sea Interludes from Peter Grimes* by Benjamin Britten. So I played them every day for two weeks. Guess what? These pieces became everyone's most beloved music, especially for (then) 8-year-old Mark. These are highly subtle and sophisticated pieces, I would note.

I really recommend the Digital Concert Hall, which is a subscription for video of the Berlin Philharmonic. Why? Music is meant to be seen as well as heard. Children are fascinated by watching the musicians. The Berlin Phil is far superior in playing to almost everything you'll find for free on YouTube. It costs about $120 for a one-year subscription if you are a teacher or student and is well worth trying for one year. Ask for and get the academic discount if you can.

Lastly, it's crucial to realize that the art of composing fine music is by no means limited to past ages or centuries. The modern period, all the way to the present, is full of new music of the highest quality (although admittedly there is plenty of unappealing modernist claptrap in the mix; one can simply avoid that as one would avoid potholes along the road). What follows are some of my favorite works from the twentieth and twenty-first centuries. While it does seem like a good plan to start with "tried and true" composers like the "killer Bs" (Bach, Beethoven, Brahms),[76] I think it's important to get to know more recent composers who stand in the great Western tradition and whose work is worth listening to.

+ Edward Elgar, *Enigma Variations* (1899). Okay, not twentieth century, but close enough.
+ Gustav Holst, *The Planets* (1916).
+ Benjamin Britten's *Simple Symphony* (1934).
+ Ralph Vaughan Williams, *Tallis Fantasia* (1910); *Fifth Symphony* (1943).
+ Maurice Duruflé's *Requiem* (1948).

---

[76] I borrow the expression "killer Bs" from musicologist Robert Greenberg. For recommendations on where to start with Beethoven, see Kwasniewski, "Ludwig van Beethoven."

+ Arvo Pärt's *Te Deum* (1984) and *Berliner Messe* (1990), Estonian Philharmonic Chamber Choir, conducted by Tōnu Kaljuste, ECM label. (Or try any work of his.) Arvo Pärt, born in Estonia in 1935, began his life as a Soviet avant-garde composer and gave up modernism as he discovered medieval music and Russian Orthodoxy. If you enjoy Pärt, you have a lot to look forward to, as he is the world's most frequently performed living composer and many recordings have been made of his music.

+ Henryk Górecki's *Symphony No. 3, "Sorrowful Songs"* (1976). Many recordings; my favorite is still David Zinman and the London Sinfonietta on Nonesuch. Górecki was a devout Catholic who wrote a special piece for the visit of John Paul II to Poland in 1978, "Totus Tuus."

+ John Tavener, *The Protecting Veil, The Last Sleep of the Virgin*, and other choral music. Tavener can be a bit strange, but he may appeal to some with his Byzantine-sounding harmonies and his meditative minimalism.

+ Gerald Finzi's *Lo, the Full Final Sacrifice* and other choral works. Gorgeous English choral music.

+ Rolf Lislevand, *Nuove Musiche* and *Diminuito*. These two ECM recordings feature world-class musicians improvising on Renaissance musical themes. Sounds odd but works well.

+ Jordi Savall, *Lachrimae Caravaggio*. To my knowledge, this is the only original composition by Savall to have been recorded. It's dark and moody, exquisitely rendered on early music instruments such as viols and cornets.

+ Eleni Karaindrou (b. 1941), *Eternity and a Day*, ECM label. Karaindrou is a modern Greek composer who has written some of the best film scores that our age can boast.

+ Pēteris Vasks, of Latvia (b. 1946), writes lush and lyrical music. His setting of the Lord's Prayer, done right after the fall of Soviet Communism, is among the most poignant choral works of our time. To begin exploring, try: *Cantabile* for String Orchestra; *Cor Anglais Concerto*; *Message*; *Musica dolorosa*; *Lauds*.

- Frank LaRocca (b. 1951) has written choral music of extraordinary beauty and poignancy.
- Norwegian composer Ola Gjeilo (b. 1978).
- Catholic composer Mark Nowakowski (b. 1978), represented in the Naxos catalogue with his String Quartets.
- Elam Rotem (b. 1984) composes magnificent new works in a Baroque style.[77]

I had better stop there, because the topic is really endless.[78] We all stand to benefit from broadening and deepening our listening habits and thus our ongoing "musicalization," the shaping of our souls by sonic beauty. I hope you will take this chapter as a gentle provocation to dive in deeper.

---

[77] See Kwasniewski, "Interview with Early Music Composer Elam Rotem."
[78] For many more recommended modern composers, see Reilly's *Surprised by Beauty*.

PART II

Music Fit for the King of Kings

The Role of Sacred Music in the Church's Life

6

Sacred Music as an Occasion of Grace for Modern Man

SINCE THE CHURCH'S liturgy is the Passover Feast, it has to bring us out of the world, out of Egypt. For this reason, it ought to have a certain "strangeness"; it should be a challenge to the comfortable categories by which we live in the secular world, surrounded by familiar idols. In the liturgy, we are trained to leave behind the mind of the world and put on the mind of Christ. This means that what is "unclean" to worldlings must be embraced by us—for example, silence and religious chant—and that what is "clean" for worldlings must be held by us as unworthy and profane, such as pop music and amplified blather. Sir Richard Terry describes the contrast as follows:

> I think we may say that modern individualistic music, with its realism and emotionalism, may stir human feeling, but it can never create that atmosphere of serene spiritual ecstasy that the old music generates. It is a case of mysticism versus hysteria. Mysticism is a note of the Church: it is healthy and sane. Hysteria is of the world: it is morbid and feverish, and has no place in the Church. Individual emotions and feelings are dangerous guides, and the Church in her wisdom recognises this. Hence in the music which she gives us, the individual has to sink his personality, and become only one of the many who offer their corporate praise.[79]

One example of the hysteria of which Terry speaks is the insistence—which, in the minds of some, has grown to the magnitude of an unshakeable first principle—that the people must always and everywhere understand everything that is being sung or said during the liturgy, and that they

---

[79] Terry, *Catholic Church Music*, 47.

themselves must usually be the ones singing it. True, if people *never* knew what the words meant, they would be at a disadvantage when it came to internalizing the instruction offered by the music. But at the same time, there is something inherently elevating and nourishing in beautiful sacred music itself, sung with piety and skill. The words of Arvo Pärt seem exactly on target: "Music must be given the chance to express itself. . . . In my view, the very existence of music is jeopardized by today's society's obsession with communication."[80] If we are concerned only about communicating, we lose the deeper expression, often a wordless *jubilus* or something ineffable hidden in the words themselves, that is at the heart of divine worship, the encounter with the numinous Other who is yet more intimate to myself than I am.

In the *Summa theologiae*, Saint Thomas Aquinas crafts an incisive objection against praising God with chants: "The praise of the heart is more important than the praise of the lips. But the praise of the heart is hindered by singing, both because the attention of the singers is distracted from the consideration of what they are singing, so long as they give all their attention to the chant, and because others are less able to understand the things that are sung than if they were recited without chant. Therefore chants should not be employed in the divine praises."[81] His refutation of the objection deserves to be carefully pondered:

> The soul is distracted from that which is sung by a chant that is employed for the purpose of giving pleasure [only]. But if the singer chant for the sake of devotion, he pays more attention to what he says, both because he lingers more thereon, and because, as Augustine (*Confess.* x, 33) remarks, "all the varying affections of our spirit have modes proper to them in voice and song, whereby, through some secret affinity, they are stirred." The same applies to the hearers, for even if some of them understand not what is sung, yet they understand why it is sung, namely, for God's glory: and this is enough to arouse their devotion.[82]

---

[80] In the liner notes for *Silencio: Music by Arvo Pärt, Philip Glass, Vladimir Martynov,* Gidon Kremer, Kremerata Baltica, Nonesuch 79582-2.
[81] *ST* II-II, Q. 91, art. 2, obj. 5.
[82] *ST* II-II, Q. 91, art. 2, ad 5; translation corrected.

Is this really true? Do we have any evidence to support the Angelic Doctor's claim?

The wonder and strangeness of sacred music

I used to teach a week-long music course for high school students in which I would share recordings of pieces by Bach or Beethoven, Mozart or Palestrina, to illustrate aspects of what we were reading about and discussing. Although a few of the students had been exposed to such masterpieces before, I was struck (as I always am) by how many had never heard music like this. The Western world has the most extraordinary and superabundant heritage of music of any civilization that has ever existed or will ever exist—a thousand years of musical glory!—and for most of our contemporaries, it is as if the great composers had never even existed or had never written any of their great works. The bright side is that, after only a week together, nearly all of these young people are excited about the music they are hearing. They ask me to write down the composers' names and the titles of the works so that they can look them up. It always makes me happy to do so, as I feel that I am spreading a little "sweetness and light" in an age characterized by darkness and philistinism.

But what is always most poignant is when, after listening to chant and polyphony, the young men and women say, "I have never heard such beautiful music before. If only my parish back home would have music like that!" Or, "I suggested learning some chants to our choir director, and she said chant was forbidden after Vatican II." Or, "It's really hard for me to pray at my parish, because of the guitars and the clapping." Or, "How can people be so stubborn about excluding sacred music when Vatican II says that chant should have pride of place, and after it, polyphony?" A comment like the last one always arises when we read and talk about the chapter on sacred music from *Sacrosanctum Concilium*; section 116 is a big eye-opener.[83]

---

[83] Precisely translated, SC 116 reads: "The Church acknowledges Gregorian chant as characteristically belonging to the Roman liturgy, with the result that, other things being equal, in liturgical actions Gregorian chant should hold the first place. But other kinds of sacred music, especially polyphony, are by no means excluded from liturgical celebrations [by chant's pride of place], so long as they accord with the spirit of the liturgical action."

Within this conversation about sacred music, I played for them Antonio Lotti's *Crucifixus à 8*. This work is a stunning portrayal of the Passion of Christ, enveloped in an atmosphere of resignation and tranquility culminating in the final pianissimo major chord. In cascading layers of skillful dissonance, Lotti evokes the agony of Our Lord; in one effortless cadence after another, he displays the peacefulness of the soul of Christ, resting in the Father's will. It is a cathartic *tour de force*—all through the magic of music. How do the students react? They are rapt; they say it was gorgeous and painful at the same time. It was just what Lotti intended it to be: an experience of the Passion, a sonic icon. In my view as a teacher, it is an occasion of grace.

This is the religious experience, the subjective appropriation of the mysteries of Christ, that the Christian faithful should be able to have as a regular part of their worship. Yet it is a religious experience that most of the faithful have been denied for fifty years or more. I do not suggest that such an experience is *identical* to the act of divine worship, but it is a source or support of it and *ought* to be present with it, in accordance with man's nature as a rational animal, a thinking being with feelings, a sensual creature with a lofty spiritual identity and vocation.

Not every choir can manage an eight-part motet like Lotti's, but sacred music at the same level of excellence can be sung regularly by well-trained ensembles at parishes, if only there is a director with good principles and a pastor with an open mind. Nor can we forget that there is an almost endless repertoire of simpler chant and polyphony to draw upon, as I did for years with amateur choirs. The effect is well described in the words of the story *The Mass of Brother Michel*: "The chant, rising from the altar, flooded the chapel and poured into the empty soul of Michel its serene and austere beauty. He listened, enraptured."[84]

Whenever I listen to or sing a work like Lotti's *Crucifixus* or any masterpiece of sacred music, I cannot help thinking that the Catholic Church today is like a dining room lined with cabinets holding the most stunning plates, silverware, and glasses, wherein we are served our meals on Styrofoam plates with plastic cutlery and paper cups. Perhaps the meal is the same, but what a difference it makes how the meal is served! People recognize far

---

[84] Kent, *The Mass of Brother Michel*, 48–49.

better the specialness of the banquet, the value of the food and drink, when it is served in beautiful vessels and with loving attention to how the service is executed. The faithful by and large do not have a *clue* about the riches that belong to them—the riches that Vatican II said should be "fostered and pre-served with great care" (SC 114). Fortunately, those cabinets are still there, with their precious contents ready to be discovered anew.[85]

Possessors of a rich tradition

The Second Vatican Council states that "steps should be taken so that the faithful may also be able to say or to sing together *in Latin* those parts of the Ordinary of the Mass which pertain to them" (SC 54)—that is, the Gloria, Credo, Sanctus, and Agnus Dei; no doubt the responses are also included.[86] Why? Because they are our *heritage*. They come to us from centuries of faith and prayer and art. Our heritage defines who we are. And frankly, it's not too much to ask people to know the songs, poems, and prayers of their ancestors. How hard is it to learn that "Kyrie eleison" = "Lord, have mercy"? I've told you and now you know it (if you didn't already). Or the Gloria—this is a hymn that has not changed at all in 1,500 years. We say it week in, week out. One doesn't have to be a rocket scientist to learn what the

---

[85] For a compact overview of magisterial teaching on sacred music, including the role of trained choirs, see "It's Time We Stopped the Musical Starvation Diet" in Kwasniewski, *Tradition and Sanity*, 183–205.

[86] The 2011 American edition of the *General Instruction of the Roman Missal* [*GIRM*]—containing the guidelines for the celebration of the Novus Ordo—reiterates this point: "The main place [musically] should be given, all things being equal, to Gregorian chant, as being proper to the Roman Liturgy. Other kinds of sacred music, in particular polyphony, are in no way excluded, provided that they correspond to the spirit of the liturgical action and that they foster the participation of all the faithful. Since the faithful from different countries come together ever more frequently, it is desirable that they know how to sing together at least some parts of the Ordinary of the Mass in Latin, especially the Profession of Faith and the Lord's Prayer, according to the simpler settings." It never ceases to amaze me how the Establishment goes from decade to decade literally ignoring the rules it establishes for itself. One must also note that John Paul II forever refuted the notion that chanting done by a schola, or music sung by a trained choir, fails to foster the active participation of all the faithful. See his *Ad Limina Address to the Bishops of Washington, Oregon, Idaho, Montana, and Alaska* (October 9, 1998), a key portion of which is quoted below on p. 130–31.

Latin words of the Gloria correspond to in English (e.g., "miserere nobis" = "have mercy on us"). So, the idea that we must never use a sacred language for worship because it would prevent "active participation" is ludicrous—a thinly-veiled excuse for not embracing our heritage, as the Council itself and the popes before and after it have asked us to do.

My experience, in many different settings, has been exactly the opposite. When they are finally exposed to it (as the Council demanded), young people are proud to be the possessors of such a rich tradition: it makes them *think* about their faith even more, *react* to it as something obviously different from what the world has to offer, and *embrace* it more fully. In general, when we give Catholics *more* to take pride in and take possession of, we should not be surprised to find that they rise to the challenge and glory in the result.

Making things "accessible" by simplification and modernization has been tried and found wanting, again and again. One wonders, with not a little vexation at human myopia, how many more decades will have to pass in which trite tunes and superficial verbiage will be shoved down the throats of Catholics around the world, while the crisis of the mainstream Church continues, escalates, radicalizes, and implodes. I see in my mind's eye the pathetic spectacle of a Mass, ca. 2035, in which an ancient priest preaches to an empty church while, just off to his left, three or four elderly women croak out Haugen-Haas tunes to the accompaniment of a broken-down piano.

In some dioceses, the retranslation of the Roman Missal, launched in 2011, occasioned the choice and imposition of musical settings of the Mass that were even worse, in their discontinuity from tradition and their egregious lack of good taste, than the tripe that had been served up before. Is *this* what the new translation was supposed to get us? One wonders if the operative motto might be: "Boldly Leading the Way into the 1970s." Quite as if *Sacrosanctum Concilium* 116, John Paul II's *Ecclesia de Eucharistia*, Pope Benedict XVI's *Sacramentum Caritatis*, and a host of other documents had never even been written. The strategy of the dying liberals is to ignore, ignore, ignore the tradition in the hopes that it will just go away.

Yet it refuses to go away. On the contrary, in keeping with the motto of the Benedictine abbey of Montecassino, *succisa virescit* ("hewn down, it grows again"), the chapels of traditional Catholicism will continue to expand, bursting with children in homeschooling networks, altar boys in

cassock and surplice, choirs and scholas, sodalities, and so many of the trim-
mings and trappings of a genuine Catholic culture—or, I should say, counterculture. The grim watchmen of the liberal Church either pretend not to
notice this demographic shift or sharply dismiss it as reactionary nostalgia
and postmodern escapism. We can be patient and put up with the whining
and hand-wringing of our foes, for they will live only a few short years more
on this earth, but the Tradition of the Church, already two thousand years
old, will effortlessly outlast them—indeed, will never die, and will live on
in the hearts of all who love the beautiful and the eternal. Daily winning to
herself converts and champions, the traditional Church in her perpetual
youth is the real answer to the crisis of our wayward age.

More than ever, we must educate a new generation of Catholics in the art
of noble music and, in particular, the treasury of sacred music that belongs
to us. We need to make more people aware of our Catholic composers by
talking and writing about them, and above all, by learning and singing their
music at Mass. Beauty in the fine arts has already largely disappeared from
popular culture; let us, then, become *missionaries for the beautiful!* The work
of renewal and restoration has just begun, and we must all play, to the best
of our ability, whatever part Divine Providence has assigned to us.

Why Catholic worship demands the greatest art

Was it really necessary, then—as so many church leaders were saying
decades ago and as they continue to repeat, like scratched vinyl records—
for the Church to change her forms of worship to suit "modern man"? Was
it necessary to jettison our glorious musical heritage and replace it with
newly fabricated utility music that mimicked the styles of the secular world?
This, after all, was the argument used to justify abolishing Latin, chant, and
Renaissance polyphony: all of these are products of other time periods,
other cultural contexts; they are "antiquated" and don't "speak" to us where
we are right now.

But this is evidently false. Many people not only *can* respond to this
music and art but already love it or find it intriguing and convincing, *authentic*, when exposed to it. They love the sound of Latin and chant, the look
of Gothic cathedrals, stained glass windows, noble statuary. Witness the

ongoing popularity of recordings of medieval and Renaissance music, or the steady appearance of art books filled with photographs of the great churches, altarpieces, and tapestries of yore. Such things are perennially appealing to everyone, from the illiterate to the highly educated. All you have to do is watch the looks of amazement and wonder on the faces of visitors to cathedrals in Europe. Majestic beauty still speaks powerfully of the divine, the eternal, the immortal, the spiritual. It is sensuous catechesis, experiential mystagogy. We human beings need it.

It is the purpose of good liturgy and music to *train* the senses, to habituate people to beauty, to lead them to a higher way of living, thinking, and feeling. We are born as simpletons who can learn to find contentment in far less than our human dignity deserves and is capable of. The old masterpieces are God's gifts to Christian civilization and should therefore serve as the norm used to measure all other contributions. "For the gifts and the call of God are irrevocable" (Rom 11:29). Indeed, it would be utterly backwards to let the tastes of popular culture in its deviation into mass-marketed pseudo-art dictate what Catholics ought to esteem and rely upon.

We call certain works of art "great" because their value transcends time, even as the Latin language is timeless, a common possession of all nations and the property of no one.[87] To what nation does the *Missa Papae Marcelli* of Palestrina belong? To what period is the *Requiem* of Mozart confined? To which social class are the Magnificat fugues of Pachelbel restricted? To what special occasion are the Gregorian Propers limited? Foolish questions! Great sacred music and all great pieces of fine art belong to everyone. They are the inheritance and blessing of all members of the Mystical Body of Christ, the joy of all souls wherever the Catholic Church builds her churches and consecrates her altars. Or who would say that the works of Johann Sebastian Bach—such as the *Mass in B Minor*—are "antiquated" and can no longer move people's hearts? Bach's music moves the heart as profoundly as it can be moved.

Pope Benedict XVI's words about Saint Romanus the Melodist are apropos:

---

[87] See Kwasniewski, "Why Latin Is the Right Language for Roman Catholic Worship," and "Latin, the Ideal Liturgical Language of the West" in Kwasniewski, *Resurgent in the Midst of Crisis*, 158–65.

Palpitating humanity, arduous faith, and profound humility pervade the songs of Romanus the Melodist. This great poet and composer reminds us of the entire treasure of Christian culture, born of faith, born of the heart that has found Christ, the Son of God. From this contact of the heart with the truth that is love, culture is born, the entire great Christian culture. And if the faith continues to live, this cultural inheritance will not die, but rather it will continue to live and be current. Icons continue to speak to the hearts of believers to this day, they are not things of the past. The cathedrals are not medieval monuments; rather they are houses of life, where we feel "at home," where we find God and each other. Neither is great music—Gregorian chant, Bach or Mozart—something of the past, rather it lives in the vitality of the liturgy and our faith. If faith is alive, Christian culture will never be "outdated," but rather will remain alive and current.[88]

Those who keep close tabs on the fine arts know that there have always been and continue to be excellent modern pieces of art in all artistic media. In the area of sacred music alone, the repertoire for organists and for choirs is always expanding with worthy new additions. Such works can be effortlessly integrated into the larger panorama of tradition since they naturally emerge from it and enrich it symbiotically, embodying the same ideals and serving the same purposes. There was never any need for a violent derailment of the past and a slap-dash effort to replace it with products of inferior quality. While great music is immortally youthful, mediocre music embarrassingly shows its age.

All the ancient religions of the world maintain centuries-old (or even millennia-old) customs of worship, ritual language, artifacts, and music. This is a sobering observation since it indicates that Catholics alone—or certainly greatly in excess of others—have abandoned their vast artistic and liturgical heritage in favor of a narrow contemporary agenda. Catholicism appears as the religion willing to change most radically its most solemn observances, thus showing that it takes its own traditions *least* seriously;

---

[88] General Audience, May 21, 2008, in the translation made by *Zenit* and published at *Whispers in the Loggia* of the same date. For an alternative translation, see www.vatic an.va/content/benedict-xvi/en/audiences/2008/documents/hf_ben-xvi_aud_20080 521.html.

and it is an easy step to conclude from this that it does not really believe anymore what it has professed for most of its history.

If I were not already a Catholic but were searching for the true religion, this massive disconnect between what the Church *says* it is and how it has acted in the past half-century might have put me off the trail. I would have reasoned: "Orthodox Jews, Eastern Orthodox Christians, High Church Anglicans, Moslems—all of them have clung faithfully and steadfastly to their age-old traditions, have cultivated them and treasured them, and would never give them up. Surely there is abundant wisdom in their attitude if they believe they have the truth. But after Vatican II, Catholics threw out what had been considered most sacred and solemn, most beautiful and worthy. Even the leaders are confused, full of self-doubt, timid and submissive to the modern world. I conclude that the Catholic Church hardly knows what it is doing. Folly on such a scale is convincing proof that the spirit of religion, of fidelity and continuity, is not there."

If this conclusion is unacceptable and false, then so must be the shortsighted, ungrateful behavior towards tradition that supports the inference. The only solution? Cling faithfully and steadfastly to age-old traditions. "Thus saith the Lord: Stand ye on the ways, and see and ask for the old paths which is the good way, and walk ye in it: and you shall find refreshment for your souls" (Jer. 6:16).

The eternal, not the contemporary

I have never made any attempt to hide my passionate devotion to the works of composer Arvo Pärt (b. 1935), already mentioned more than once in this book. Not only do I love his music, but I also love his wise words about music and musicians. Even though he is famously reticent to speak, it's also true that once he gets going, we can always expect profound insights.[89] In an interview, he had this to say about why the music of some composers will always be relevant, always fresh and contemporary to us:

> It is said that many works of art from earlier times appear to be more contemporary than works of today. This combination of "art"

---

[89] On his life-changing and career-galvanizing discovery of ancient sacred music, see Kwasniewski, "Arvo Pärt on Gregorian Chant."

and "contemporary" is in itself absurd. However, what are we to make of this? Certainly not that a musical genius has a prophetic eye for future centuries. I think that the so-called contemporary nature of Bach's music will not disappear in the next 200 years, since, from an absolute point of view, it is simply of an integrally higher quality. The secret of this "contemporary" character lies not so much in how greatly the author embraces his time, but more in the way he perceives all of existence, with its joy, its suffering, and its experiences. . . . Art should concern itself with the eternal, not the contemporary.[90]

That final statement enunciates a salutary corrective against the idolatry of the present—the mentality that our times demand something specific to them that is somehow different from what is simply demanded by human nature, its quandaries, exigencies, and aspirations, or from what is called forth by the encounter with the mystery of the living God. The reason Bach's music can never grow stale or irrelevant or inaccessible is that he is speaking the cosmic language of the human heart, not the local vernacular of a momentary human society.

We can apply these insights to sacred music, especially to the Gregorian chant and Renaissance polyphony repeatedly singled out by the papal magisterium. Their very rhythms and melodies, textures and syntax, speak to us of the spiritual, the eternal, the numinous, the consecrated cosmos in which Jesus Christ is the Eternal High Priest and we are the living members of His Mystical Body. It sounds like a cliché to talk about timeless music, and yet, as the coming chapters will show, there are identifying features of chant and polyphony that *guarantee* their timelessness, their perennial suitability for the act of divine worship.

To speak thus is to speak at the level of musical style, of pure music. But we must not forget the *texts*, which are the directive principle, the underlying motive, the burden of the communication; it is these texts that summon the chant and the polyphony to announce them worthily, to be their

---

[90] Pärt spoke these words in an interview on Estonian Radio in 1968; cited in Saale Kareda, "Back to the Source," in Restagno, *Arvo Pärt in Conversation*, 167–68; for commentary, see Hillier, *Arvo Pärt*, 64–66.

servants in the work of beautiful proclamation. In this connection I was struck by Arvo Pärt's remarks about why, when writing a choral work, he always chooses sacred texts, even though his commission may leave him free to choose any text.

> I have always allowed myself to be guided by texts that mean a lot to me and that for me are of existential significance. It is a root that reaches very deep and that lifts me upwards. It is basically the same fruit that has nourished the world for centuries. If we view a period of two thousand years we recognise that people have changed very little. That is why I believe the sacred texts are still "contemporary." Seen in this light there are not significant differences between yesterday, today, and tomorrow because there are truths that maintain their validity. Mankind feels much the same today as he did then and has the same need to free himself from his faults. The texts exist independently of us and are waiting for us: each of us has a time when he will find a way to them.[91]

Now, re-read this passage while thinking about the Propers and the Ordinary of the Mass—the Introit, Gradual, Alleluia, Offertory, and Communion antiphons, the Kyrie, Gloria, Credo, Sanctus, Benedictus, Agnus Dei—that have given shape and meaning to the Eucharistic sacrifice for a millennium and a half. Are these sacred texts not permanently, intrinsically contemporary, proclaiming truths that always maintain their validity? And is that not one of the many reasons we moderns, already prone to excessive change and pluralism, need the unifying, stabilizing, and consolidating effect of the sacred chants and sacred texts handed down to us?

In the sixties and seventies it was often said that the Church had to reconfigure herself from top to bottom because "Modern Man" needs something different from his forebears. But modern man is not essentially different from the man of any age; his spiritual needs are fundamentally the same as they have always been. What people today need is not something new, changing, ephemeral, fashionable, but something timeless and perennial, connecting them across the ages with their forebears and uniting them to the Lord in

---

[91] Restagno, *Arvo Pärt in Conversation*, 55.

adoration. The life of prayer and worship that sustained centuries of faith—the glorious army of confessors, virgins, martyrs, holy laity—will sustain us too, better than any modern innovations. Thanks to the profound teaching and compelling example of Pope Benedict XVI, which remain alive and fruitful in spite of successive assaults against them, we have entered a new era of rediscovering a lost heritage and rejoicing in its wondrous beauty. The Church of the future will have a growing number of people who ask for, and deserve to receive, all that the Church herself, and she alone, can offer them.

I was born years after the Council had closed, and just after the promulgation of the Novus Ordo. In my own life, I distinctly remember the excitement, the wonder, of discovering amazing riches in the tradition of the Church, a treasure that had been seemingly deliberately buried and hidden: the chaste beauty of plainchant, the dignified and resonant sound of Latin, the shimmering beauty of old vestments, the sprinkling rite (*Asperges*), even something as simple as the use of incense at the elevation of the consecrated gifts. But my new discoveries went far beyond this feast of symbolism and banquet of beauty, which answered to a burning need for reverence; they included the full social teaching of the Church, her ascetical and mystical theology, her scholastic wisdom, her saints and their colorful stories.[92]

This experience of joyful, exuberant rediscovery—accompanied, it is true, by a heart-sickening sense of betrayal that so many and such great gifts had been thrown overboard or stuffed into a closet—is something that *many* people from my generation (and younger generations) are feeling. Catholics who are most serious about their faith, who want to know it intimately, live it fully, and pass it on to their children, are more and more traditional in their beliefs and aspirations. It seems that a large number of older clergy are nervous about, or even openly hostile toward, the change that is brewing in the Church—that is, the determined return to tradition and the rejection of the revolutionary overturning of it that characterized the decades following the Council. This change, nonetheless, is happening and it will not stop, regardless of papal ukases or episcopal crackdowns.

---

[92] See "A Threefold Amnesia: Sacred Liturgy, Social Teaching, and Saint Thomas" in Kwasniewski, *Resurgent in the Midst of Crisis*, 182–97. See also the interviews contained in *Tradition and Sanity*.

7

"Breathing the Air of the Sacred": Music and the Liturgy

The Church, acknowledging that man is not merely an intellectual being who can subsist on thoughts alone but a creature who approaches reality through his senses, has always emphasized the importance of incorporating sense-perceptible signs into her acts of worship. Even if we assent to supernatural truth *sola fide* ("by faith alone"), we do not engage with it *solo intellectu* ("by intellect alone").

As Saint Thomas Aquinas explains in his treatise on the sacraments, Christ provided His Church with sensible signs of His abiding presence, conduits of grace through which the Holy Spirit works in the hearts of the faithful. Used in the proper way, these sacred signs—water, bread, wine, oil, words of absolution—not only represent the action of Christ, they *effect* His work because He works through them, they are the means by which He visits and sanctifies the believer. Because man is not a disembodied mind but an integral whole composed of body and soul, it is most fitting that God should bestow His gifts upon the faithful by elevating humble things of common experience into efficacious means of sanctification.[93]

This sacramental transfiguration[94] extends far beyond its own immediate sphere, as we can see in the rich heritage of the fine arts. What began as the glories of the pagan world—architecture, sculpture, painting, music, poetry—became, in the Church's hands, the servants of divine mysteries, ministers of the unseen world, reflections of the beauty of God. The sacredness of the liturgy is adorned and elevated by the use of beautiful things: icons that seem to capture the timeless essence of sanctity, statues that

---

[93] See *ST* III, QQ. 60–62.
[94] See Digges, *Transfigured World*.

remind us of the communion of saints and the purpose of our lives, stained-glass that depicts episodes from the Gospel and the history of the Church with an eloquence unrivaled by words. Contemplative plainchant, soaring polyphony, the majestic sound of the pipe organ—these, too, are no small part of the Church's evangelization of the senses and imagination of man.

Abusus non tollit usum

The fine arts have enjoyed a long but not always peaceful relationship with the worship of God. When fine art serves to enhance worship by focusing our minds on Him and His saints and angels, it deserves the greatest praise, but when it offers distractions and fascinations that detract from the central act of sacrifice and thanksgiving, it risks setting up itself as the reason for attending Mass. That this has often happened in the history of the Church should come as no surprise. To admire excessively the works of human hands is a perennial temptation, as the commandment against the worship of graven images bears witness.

As happens with all errors, the extreme of paying too much attention to artistic and cultural forms of expression can lead, by way of reaction, to the extreme of rejecting them entirely, under a false notion that men can worship God "more purely" if sensible signs—statuary, organ music, polyphony, stained glass, sacerdotal vestments, and the like—are removed from churches, whittled down to a minimum, or uglified by aesthetic modernism.

The proposed remedy is far worse than the disease. To suppress the traditional liturgical arts, to strip bare the sanctuary in order to "purify" or "simplify" it, as the Calvinists did in the sixteenth century or as modernists did in the twentieth, is not at all to improve worship but rather to make it no longer fit for the creatures of flesh and blood, sight and hearing, that we are—the creatures whom the Word became flesh to save and for whom He shed His Blood, the creatures whose blindness and deafness He wishes to heal by physical contact.

The wave of banality and populism that has stormed Catholic churches for some half-a-century now is scarcely any better, one must admit, than getting rid of artwork altogether. To suppress the fine arts or to replace them with something flimsy and trite is to dishonor the precious gifts that

God has given to mankind through centuries of vibrant Catholic devotion and genius.

Neglected truths about sacred music

Experiences with many liturgies, some blessed and some regrettable, have afforded me much opportunity to think about these things. For the better part of thirty years, I directed polyphonic choirs and chant scholas. The music we performed was predominantly from the Renaissance, that glorious flowering of Catholic artistic culture. Whenever we sang plainsong, we were drawing even more deeply from the historical and devotional fountains of the Faith: a large number of the chants for the Roman rite date back to the first millennium, when flourishing monasteries set the tone for European society at large.

My work with liturgical music brought home to me certain vital but nowadays neglected truths.

The first truth is that one does not "make music for the liturgy" or "fill in the empty spaces when the priest is busy," like someone doodling to pass the time. One learns to *let the liturgy itself*, with its own spirit, its age-old prayers and profound gestures, *shape and govern one's choice of music*; indeed, in the traditional worship of East and West, the music is more or less dictated by the rite.

The second truth I learned is more paradoxical: as its final end, liturgical music should have its own dying in mind. Of course I don't mean the death of the music itself—far too much good music has been allowed to die out, to the inestimable disadvantage of the faithful. Rather, I have in mind the lesson Christ taught us: we must lose ourselves, forget ourselves, that we may be all the more attentive to Him, all the more willing to *listen*. In performing or in hearing music, many people experience a lifting of the soul to heavenly heights where the beauty and peace of God eternally reign. This self-transcendence in the presence of God is one of the aims of the sacred liturgy, and music is meant to aid us in raising our souls to Him—or better, in allowing Him to raise us up. The lesson we learn is one of self-forgetfulness or self-effacement, the humility of those who assist at the Holy Sacrifice: *non nobis, Domine, non nobis, sed nomini tuo da gloriam:*

not to us, O Lord, not to us, but to Thy name give glory (Ps. 113:9). If the people are lifted up to meditation on divine things through our music, we musicians should thank God that they are no longer thinking of the melodies and the singers. "He must increase but I must decrease" (Jn 3:30), said John the Baptist, forgetting himself, guiding his followers to Jesus Christ. In *that* sense, music should die to itself.

In order to serve its purpose, music for the liturgy must breathe the air of the sacred. But what does that mean in practice? It should not be raucous or assertive; it should not advertise its own cleverness or tunefulness. It should not be *noisy*—there is far too much noise in the world already, from airplanes to radio stations. At one extreme, some liturgical music is too operatic, as are many pieces written in the late Romantic period; at the other extreme, pieces fashioned in a "folk" or "popular" idiom are too cutesy and sing-songy.

The best qualities of sacred music have also been the most enduring in the Church's history: pure melodies, tranquility, modesty, prayerfulness. Are "music ministers" there to put on a show and to keep the people pleasantly occupied—or do they sing in order to elevate the devout soul to the worship of the Almighty? It belongs to the essence of true music ministry that it *efface* itself, leaving the limelight and receding into the walls, dissolving like incense. Only when the music is so apt for the liturgy that a congregation ceases to think about it as one would think of any secular art form or entertainment can the musicians assume their rightful place: servants to the common good of the parish, singing on behalf of the Church and by the authority of Christ.[95]

Chant: reasons for its neglect

The Church's official documents have always insisted that her beautiful ancient melodies known as Gregorian chant be given foremost place in the liturgy—a place not to be compromised by other styles or types of music, even when they are worthy.[96]

---

[95] See Kwasniewski, "The Catholic Choir and Choirmaster: Handmaid of the Liturgy and Guide of the Faithful."

[96] The following chapters will quote many of these documents and comment on them. This wise commendation of chant lost much of its force when Paul VI appeared to repudiate it: see Kwasniewski, *Once and Future Roman Rite*, 108–43.

There seem to be at least three reasons for this neglect of chant.

The first reason is a widespread loss of silence, sacrality, prayerfulness, in the celebration of the liturgy itself. Such a dramatic loss could only have taken place where people were already inured to the noisiness and profanity of our world, and no longer realized how great is our need for meditation and recollection if we are to pay honor to God and make strides in living out the Christian life. In such a situation, chant is a non-starter.

The second reason is more subtle and more perilous. In many respects, the way Catholics conceive of the Holy Mass has been gradually tainted by humanism. The focus shifted from the atoning sacrifice of Christ on Calvary to the "community gathered together to celebrate." These two elements need not be in conflict,[97] but given the modern tendency to emphasize the social side of Christian worship, there is a danger that the transcendent mysteries we re-enact may become peripheral, downplayed, even forgotten. The moment a liturgy ceases to be focused upon the Cross of Christ—the unbloody renewal of His Sacrifice on Calvary in the light of His resurrection and ascension—it also ceases to minister to the true spiritual needs of Christians: adoration, thanksgiving, penitence, and supplication.

A humanistic notion of the goal or focus of worship brings about a false sense of what congregational participation means. According to the view (seldom stated but often accepted) that *man is the center of all things*, the purpose of liturgy would be primarily to glorify and praise man, or to make him feel good about himself. Perhaps God would be invoked as an afterthought, but there is little room for God when men think so highly of themselves.

The believing Catholic stands at the pole opposite to the humanist: in humility, he knows that unless he communes with Christ, he shall have no life in him. As for community, he knows that whatever conduces to good prayer—prayer focused entirely on the divine Majesty and His angels and saints—brings about the fullest union of one Christian with another in their common purpose of knowing, loving, and serving God. Anything less is a sham.

The third reason stems from the foregoing reasons: many parish music directors are unaware of the rich heritage they neglect, or they even take

---

[97] See Kwasniewski, "We, Too, Are the Sacrifice We Offer."

advantage of their position to create liturgical "experiences" wholly out of keeping with the faith of the Church. Whether out of dislike for an unfamiliar kind of music or out of more dubious aims of "modernizing" parish life, such directors often fail to cultivate the talent and interest needed for preparing and executing chant, hymnody, or polyphony in a worthy manner.

"I didn't notice the music"

Countless times over the years, I've heard comments like this after Mass, from people young and old: "The music was so beautiful—it really helped me to pray." "That song brought tears to my eyes." Or, from a visitor: "If only my parish back home would have music like the stuff you did today!" People who go to Mass to worship God are deeply grateful when the music focuses their hearts on Him and helps to prepare their souls for the sacred mysteries we celebrate.

But the best comments are those that, measured by the world's standards, a performer would least want to hear: "I didn't really notice the music, because I was so caught up in the beauty of the Mass." "I was praying really intensely, and I think the chants and the rest of it sort of floated me along."

If church musicians do their job well, their work will contribute to the good of the faithful gathered together for worship; the musicians will humbly disappear before God's glory. If all of the elements that constitute our public worship were blended together properly, the music would assume its indispensable role—not as a center-stage attraction, much less a sonic hairshirt, but as one crucial piece of a complex ensemble of symbols: the vestments worn by the priest, the sweet smell of incense rising to God, luminous stained-glass windows depicting the life of Christ or the saints, statuary to remind us of our older brothers and sisters in the Faith.

Each of these traditional elements carries with it both history and instruction, a link with the past and a strong reminder of who we are as Catholics, pilgrims of changeless faith in a world of constant change. The components of the Roman liturgy bear witness, in a tangible, accessible way, to the sublime truths we profess in our innermost souls.

8

Gregorian Chant: Perfect Music for Christian Worship

ONE MIGHT THINK that something called "plainchant" or "plainsong" would afford scant matter for conversation; after all, its very name says it's plain and it's chant.

In reality, Gregorian chant is anything *but* plain, except in the sense that its beautiful melodies are meant to be sung unaccompanied and unharmonized, as befits the ancient monastic culture out of which they sprang. What we call "Gregorian chant" is one of the richest and most subtle art forms in Western music—indeed, in the music of any culture. This chapter will first give a rapid sketch of chant's history, then address why we *sing* our liturgy rather than merely speak it, and finally delve into the characteristics that make Gregorian chant uniquely suited to the Catholic liturgy.

The ancient origins of chant

To understand the origins of chant, we must go back to the Church's Hebrew roots. The tradition of chanting Scripture, a practice known as *cantillation*, began at least one thousand years before Christ's birth. Various Old Testament books, especially the Psalms and the Chronicles, testify to the central function of music in temple worship. Some Gregorian melodies still in use are remarkably close to Hebrew synagogue melodies, most notably the "Tonus Peregrinus" used for Psalm 113, *In exitu Israel de Aegypto*; the ancient Gospel tone; and the Preface tone.

The Israelite knew two basic forms of liturgical worship: the bloody sacrifice involving the death and destruction of an animal, which took place in the temple in Jerusalem, and the chanting of the psalms and other readings done in synagogues wherever the Jews lived. The once-for-all sacrifice of the unblemished Lamb of God on the Cross fulfilled even as it terminated the animal sacrifices of the temple. The Psalter of David, for its part, was seen as the messianic book *par excellence*, and thus, we find Saint Peter, Saint Paul, and the Apostolic Fathers citing it heavily in their preaching and letters. So far from letting it go as they did the animal sacrifices, the first Christians retained the Psalter as their beloved "prayer book," because now it could be prayed in and through Christ, who hallowed its words on His sacred lips.

The Psalter is the "verbal incense" of our prayers and praises, the homage of our intellects, while the animal sacrifice signifies the total surrender of our being to God. In the Mass, these two are wondrously combined into the rational sacrifice consisting of the perfect offering of Jesus Christ upon the altar, who unites our prayers and praises to His and makes them worthy of the Ever-Blessed Trinity. The Eucharist makes present the reality and fruits of this supreme sacrifice in an unbloody manner suitable for those who have been redeemed. Thus, Christian liturgy sprang from the integration and sublimation of Psalter and Sacrifice. Furthermore, the traditional Roman rite of Mass, which is primarily a sacrificial offering, is permeated throughout with verses from the Psalms; and that other great public prayer of the Church, the Divine Office, is primarily composed of Psalms, yet with incense burned at the altar during the Gospel canticles—an acknowledgment of the one supreme sacrifice that unites heaven and earth.

The early Christians continued to chant psalms and other prayers in the Hebrew manner familiar to them from the Temple worship in Jerusalem and from the synagogues spread throughout the Roman world. But Christians also absorbed influences from surrounding Greek and Roman music, particularly in the development of the system of eight "modes." This system—like so much else—developed separately in the Latin and Byzantine realms, roughly corresponding to the Western and Eastern halves of the ancient Roman Empire. To this day, most chants of the Latin and Byzantine traditions fall into eight modes, but the only thing these modes have in common is that there are eight of them.

Chant developed prodigiously in the first Christian millennium. By the time we reach Pope Saint Gregory the Great, who reigned from 590 to 604, a body of chant already existed for the Sacrifice of the Mass and the daily round of prayer (Divine Office). Even as he gave final form to the Roman Canon, which is the defining trait of the Latin rite,[98] Saint Gregory organized this musical repertoire; as a result, the chant has ever afterwards been called "Gregorian" in his honor. Over time, not just the psalms and their antiphons were cantillated, but also the Scripture readings, orations, intercessions, litanies, instructions (e.g., *Flectamus genua*, Let us bend the knees), and, in general, anything meant to be proclaimed out loud. The core of the Gregorian chant repertoire dates to before the year 800; the bulk of it was completed by the year 1200.

The chant of the Roman church was not the only chant being used in the Latin-speaking sphere of the Catholic Church. Ambrosian chant could be heard in Milan, Mozarabic chant in Spain, and Gallican chant in Gaul. As different as their melodies and particular texts were, these regional types of chant shared the exclusive use of the Latin language and the system of eight modes. Due to Charlemagne's centralizing ambitions and his allegiance to the papacy, the Roman rite was brought into the Frankish empire. During its transalpine sojourn, many Gallican elements were incorporated into the Roman rite. Later on, these migrated back to Rome. The medieval Roman liturgy was, therefore, an amalgamation of ancient Roman and Gallican sources.[99]

Since chant was *the* music, custom-made, that had grown up with the Church's liturgy, wherever the latter traveled, the former traveled with it. No one dreamed of separating the texts of the liturgy from their music; they were like a body-soul composite, or a happily married couple. Or one could compare the chant to the vestments worn by a liturgical minister. Once this ceremonial apparel had developed, no one in his right mind would get rid of the chasuble, stole, alb, amice, and maniple. These are the garments that the ministers of the king are privileged to wear! So too, the chants are the garments worn by the liturgical texts. We might even dare, with medieval freedom, to apply the words of Psalm 103 to the chant in relation to the liturgy: "Thou hast put on praise and beauty: and art clothed with light as with a garment." In the transfiguration of Christ, there were two elements: the mortal body of our Savior and the radiance of glory He allowed to shine through His body from a soul already enraptured in the beatific vision. The chanted text is a transfigured text, radiant with an otherworldly glory that reminds us of our true home.

---

[98] See "The Roman Canon: Pillar and Ground of the Roman Rite" in Kwasniewski, *Once and Future Roman Rite*, 216–60.

[99] On this history and on the role of chant within it, see Fiedrowicz, *The Traditional Latin Mass*, 3–35; 178–89.

Why do we sing liturgical texts?

Before proceeding, we should tackle a more basic question: Why do we *sing* our liturgical texts? Why not just *speak* them?

In all world religions, we find the chanting of religious texts. Such a note-worthy likeness, even in cultures and civilizations separated by centuries and vast distances with little or no interaction, suggests that we are looking at a *natural* connection between the worship of the divine and the singing of texts involved in the rites—that is, a connection based on the nature of man, of word, and of music.

This universal practice derives from an intuitive sense that holy things and the holy sentiments that go along with them should not be talked about as ordinary everyday things are but elevated to a higher level through melo-dious modulation—or submerged into silence. Authentic rituals, therefore, tend to alternate between silences (either for meditation or while a liturgical action is being carried out) and chanting (which may or may not be accom-panied by some other action).

Acts of public worship are rendered more solemn, and their content more appealing and memorable, by the singing of clergy, cantors, choir, and congregation. Moreover, the contrast between singing (human expression at its highest) and silence (a deliberate "apophatic" withholding of discourse) is more striking than the contrast between speaking and not speaking. The former contrast is like the rise and fall of ocean waves, while the latter con-trast seems more like switching a lightbulb on and off.

Speech is primarily discursive and instructional, aimed "at" an audience, while song, which more easily and naturally unites many singers and listen-ers into one body, is capable of being in addition the bearer of feelings and of meanings that go beyond what words can convey, greatly augmenting the penetrating power of the words themselves. We find this additional dimen-sion especially in the melismata of chant, the lengthy melodic elaborations on a single syllable that give voice to inner emotions and aspirations that words cannot fully express. "The word that surfaces on our lips frees itself from its limitations and expands into song," as Giacomo Baroffio puts it;[100] chant "is music that infuses deep spiritual recesses with words and breaks the limits of

---

[100] Baroffio, *Re-Tractations*, 23.

lexical meaning by expressing with sound the ineffable vibrations that otherwise would not be able to free themselves from the human heart."[101]

Here's a wonderful example of a melisma-filled chant from the Paschal season: the Offertory chant for Easter Thursday, which takes a verse from the Old Testament, from Exodus chapter 13, and applies it to the newborn Christians: "In the day of your solemnity, saith the Lord, I will bring you into a land flowing with milk and honey, alleluia."

The words "day," "Lord," "I will bring," "land," "flowing," and "milk" are all treated melismatically, with melodies more elaborate than a simple statement of the word would require. The "alleluia" is given the fullest such treatment, in keeping with its role as a word of pure praise of the Lord.[102] The effect is one

---

[101] Baroffio, 37.

[102] The term *"jubilus"* was applied by Amalarius of Metz in the ninth century to melismatic chant phrases. According to Saint Thomas in his commentary on Psalm 32:2–3: "Such a jubilant melody is an ineffable gladness that words cannot express, but by the voice is given to be understood an immense breadth of joys. Now what cannot be expressed are the good things of glory: 'No eye has seen, nor ear heard...' (1 Cor 2:9). And therefore the Psalmist says 'sing well unto him' with jubilation because they cannot be expressed with [ordinary] song." Modern scholars apply the term *jubilus* particularly to

of highlighting or lighting up those words, or, in a more homely metaphor, sucking from each of them the nectar of the flower or the juice of the fruit.

No one has commented more insightfully than the philosopher of music Victor Zuckerkandl on the almost mystical power of song to unite singers with each other, and the subject with the object. He writes:

> Music is appropriate, is helpful, where self-abandon is intended or required—where the self goes beyond itself, where subject and object come together. Tones seem to provide the bridge that makes it possible, or at least makes it easier, to cross the boundary separating the two.[103]

> The spoken word presupposes "the other," the person or persons to whom it is addressed; the one speaking and the one spoken to are turned toward each other; the word goes out from one to the other, creating a situation in which the two are facing each other as distinct, separate individuals. Wherever there is talk, there is a "he-not-I" on the one hand and his counterpart, an "I-not-he," on the other. This is why the word is *not* the natural expression of the group.... [S]inging is the natural and appropriate expression of the group, of the togetherness of individuals within the group. If this is the case, we may assume that tones—singing—essentially express not the individual but the group; more accurately, the individual in so far as he is a member of the group; still more accurately, the individual in so far as his relation to the others is not one of "facing them" but one of togetherness.[104]

> Whereas words turn people toward each other, as it were, make them look at each other, tones turn them all in the same direction: everyone follows the tones on their way out and on their way back. The moment tones resound, the situation where one party faces another is transmuted into a situation of togetherness, the many distinct individuals into the one group.[105]

---

the long melisma on the final syllable of "alleluia" in the Proper of that name.
[103] Zuckerkandl, *Man the Musician*, 24–25.
[104] Zuckerkandl, 27–28.
[105] Zuckerkandl, 28–29.

And finally:

> If his words are not merely spoken but sung, they build a living
> bridge that links him with the things referred to by the words, that
> transmutes distinction and separation into togetherness. By means
> of the tones, the speaker goes out to the things, brings the things
> from outside within himself, so that they are no longer "the other,"
> something alien that he is not, but the other and his own in one.
> ... The singer remains what he is, but his self is enlarged, his vital
> range is extended: being what he is he can now, without losing his
> identity, be with what he is not; and the other, being what it is, can,
> without losing its identity, be with him.[106]

Ultimately, it comes down to this: *we sing when we are at one, or wish to be
at one, with our activity or the object of our activity.* This is true when we are
in love with another person. It is most of all true when we are in love with
God. That is the origin of the incomparably great music of the Catholic
tradition. Saint Augustine says, "Only the lover sings." We sing ... and we
whisper ... and we fall silent.

In the course of his discussion, Zuckerkandl makes a point that reminds
me painfully of growing up in the Novus Ordo with congregations *reciting*
together the Gloria or the "Holy, Holy, Holy": "Can one imagine that people come together to *speak* songs? One can, but only as a logical possibility; in real life this would be absurd. It would turn something natural into
something utterly unnatural."[107] The recitation of normatively sung texts
at a Low Mass "works" only because the priest *alone* is saying the texts, and
doing so at the altar, *ad orientem*.[108] He is not addressing the words of the

---

[106] Zuckerkandl, 29–30.
[107] Zuckerkandl, 25.
[108] My principal objection to the "dialogue Mass" (that is, a traditional Latin Low Mass
where the congregation makes the responses with the servers and recites parts of the
Ordinary of the Mass with the priest) is that, on the one hand, it cancels the meditative
priestly utterance of the words, which endows them with a certain objective rituality,
yet on the other hand, this common speaking lacks the specific benefits of singing the
texts as at High Mass. It spoils the recollected encounter with the words of the liturgy
that is the Low Mass's key strength, even if the latter is lacking in the splendor of the
High Mass.

song to anyone except God. They thereby acquire a ritual status comparable to that of the recited Canon. The speaking of sung texts is not liturgically ideal; really this form of Mass developed for the personal devotion of the priest when celebrating at a side altar with a clerk. To have a large church packed with people and then to *say* the songs rather than singing them should strike everyone as odd.[109]

There are also practical reasons for singing. As experience proves, texts that are sung or chanted with correct elocution are heard with greater clarity and forcefulness in a large assembly of people and in large buildings than texts that are read aloud or even shouted. The music carries the words and penetrates the listeners' ears and souls. In ancient times, epic and lyric poetry, and even parts of political speeches, were chanted for this very reason.

Electrical amplification was unnecessary when architects knew how to design spaces that resonated properly and when liturgical ministers learned how to sing out. A well-built church with well-trained singers has no need of artificial amplification. Moreover, contrary to one of the key assumptions behind the wreckovation of our rites, not everything in the liturgy has to be heard by everyone.

It is hard to imagine a modern-day airport without speakers for announcements. It is, in contrast, a tragedy when the same technical, pragmatic, impersonal, and unfocused type of sound-production invades churches. In a church, the microphone kills the intimacy, humility, locality, and directionality of the human voice. The voice now becomes that of a placeless giant, a Big Brother larger than life, coming from everywhere and nowhere, dominating and subduing the listener. Putting mics and speakers in a church does not enhance a natural process; it subverts it. There is no continuum between the unaided voice and the artificially amplified voice: they are two separate phenomena, with altogether different phenomenologies.

When ritual texts are adorned with fitting music, their message "carries," both physically and spiritually. As we will see, Gregorian chant is nothing other than the ideal musical presentation of the Latin liturgical texts.

---

[109] See "The Peace of Low Mass and the Glory of High Mass" in Kwasniewski, *Noble Beauty, Transcendent Holiness*, 235–55.

The rise and fall . . . and rise and fall of chant

Gregorian chant flourished in the period ca. 600 to the mid-sixteenth century. The Council of Trent (1545–63) reaffirmed the place of chant in the liturgy and discouraged the use of excessively complex polyphonic music, especially when it was based on secular tunes or obscured the intelligibility of the liturgical texts.

Nevertheless, a decline occurred in the use and quality of chant, caused in part by the increasing splendor, variety, and quantity of polyphonic music. Monteverdi's *Vespers of the Blessed Virgin Mary* and Handel's *Carmelite Vespers* are two fine examples of the kind of musical works that supplanted simpler forms—at least where patrons could afford it. The accent on *splendor* was particularly emphasized by the Counter-Reformation, which coincided with the Baroque phase of the fine arts. This meant that, to some tastes, chant was just a little too . . . *plain* for the perceived needs of the moment.

Chant continued to be used, of course (it was literally inconceivable to have a solemn liturgy without chant until after Vatican II), but it was sidelined. Old melodies became abbreviated or corrupted, neumes were forced to conform to a regular beat like the metered music of the day, and new chants were written that lacked the inspiration and savor of the originals. One who picked up a *Graduale* in Germany in the nineteenth century would find melodies stripped of their melismata or melodic embellishments so that they could be chanted as quickly as possible, and the choir could "get on with" the "real" music in parts or with instruments. This utilitarianism took away the chief beauty of the chants and spoiled the internal balance of the parts of the liturgy.

Restoration of such an immense treasure of the Church—and such an integral part of her solemn liturgy!—was bound to come sooner or later. It came through the combined efforts of a monk and a pope. Dom Prosper Guéranger (1805–75) founded Solesmes Abbey in 1833 and built it up into a powerhouse of monastic observance, including the fully chanted Divine Office and Mass. The monks of Solesmes pored over hundreds of ancient and medieval manuscripts in their work to restore the chant's distinctive melodies and rhythms. Soon after his accession in 1903, Pope Saint Pius X met in Rome with monks of Solesmes and placed on their shoulders the monumental task of publishing the liturgical books of chant, with corrected melodies and rhythms. The monks complied, and Pius X gave their work his stamp of approval. From this papal directive was born a long string of influential publications from (or licensed by) Solesmes, most of which are still in use today—most notably the *Liber Usualis*, the *Graduale Romanum*, and the *Antiphonale Monasticum*.

A straight and logical line connects Solesmes and Pius X to the sixth chapter of *Sacrosanctum Concilium*, the Second Vatican Council's Constitution on the Sacred Liturgy.[110] Here is what Vatican II had to say on the subject:

> The musical tradition of the universal Church is a treasure of inestimable value, greater even than that of any other art. The main reason for this pre-eminence is that, as sacred song united to the words, it forms a necessary or integral part of the solemn liturgy. . . .
>
> Accordingly, the sacred Council, keeping to the norms and precepts of ecclesiastical tradition and discipline, and having regard to the purpose of sacred music, which is the glory of God and the sanctification of the faithful, decrees as follows.
>
> Liturgical worship is given a more noble form when the divine offices are celebrated solemnly in song. . . .
>
> The treasure of sacred music is to be preserved and fostered with great care. Choirs must be diligently promoted. . . .
>
> The Church acknowledges Gregorian chant as specially suited to the Roman liturgy, with the result that, other things being equal, it ought to be given the foremost place [*principem locum*] in liturgical services.
>
> But other kinds of sacred music, especially polyphony, are by no means excluded from liturgical celebrations, so long as they accord with the spirit of the liturgical action. (*SC* 112–14, 116)

I have to say that the first time I read these words many years ago, I was dumbfounded. They corresponded to nothing whatsoever that I had ever experienced as a Catholic growing up in America in the 1970s and 1980s, attending a church with purple carpets, Star Trek lighting, and heavily amplified

---

[110] I am aware that this constitution has received, and deserves, criticism (see my article "*Sacrosanctum Concilium*: The Ultimate Trojan Horse"), but the document's sixth chapter is thoroughly traditional. That, indeed, is why it was almost completely ignored by the progressives after the Council: there was nothing for them to cherry-pick from it.

singers emotively rendering "On Eagle's Wings" or "Yahweh, I Know You Are Near." The original Liturgical Movement out of which *Sacrosanctum Concilium's* stirring words took their origin was devoted to restoring and recovering the richest and most beautiful traditions of Catholic prayer.[111] Unfortunately, an explosive combination of false antiquarianism and novelty-mongering modernism threw a gigantic wrench into the works, leaving a war zone of competing visions in which we are still entrenched—and in which chant has suffered near extinction. The good news is that the tide is beginning to turn, here and there, as chant returns to monasteries, cathedrals, parishes, chaplaincies. Chant will never die because it is *perfect* liturgical music.

Now, the Council Fathers offer no explanation of *why* Gregorian chant is the music proper to the Roman rite—or why, more broadly speaking, ancient chant is proper to the celebration of the liturgy. Were they simply taking it for granted? That might have been naïve of them. It goes without saying that it cannot be taken for granted today, at least in the West. I therefore wish to provide a rationale for the consistent and predominant use of Gregorian chant in the Roman rite. If we can identify chant's special qualities, it will be easier to see why it naturally grew up together with the liturgy and why the Church has recommended it so highly over the centuries, down to our own times. Eight qualities make chant distinctive among musical forms: primacy of the word; free rhythm; unison singing; unaccompanied vocalization; modality; anonymity; emotional moderation; unambiguous sacrality.

Primacy of the word

Chant is, above all, music *in service of God's revealed word*, to which it grants primacy. It is *sung prayer*, a form of that *logikē latreia*, or "rational worship," that Saint Paul in the Epistle to the Romans (12:1) says we are to offer up to God. The chant exists to proclaim and interpret divine words or human poetry inspired by those divine words. In this respect, it is unlike much later music, where the text serves almost as an "excuse" for the music, a necessary scaffolding for human voices, or where texts of human authorship can be of inferior quality or theologically problematic.

---

[111] On the Liturgical Movement, see Kwasniewski, *Reclaiming Our Roman Catholic Birthright*, 48–53, and *Noble Beauty*, 89–133.

Most Gregorian chants deliver to us God's own words in Scripture, sung in musical phrases that draw out the words' depth of meaning. "It is not a question of adding music to the words, nor even of setting words to music," says Father Hameline. "Instead it is a question of making the words bring forth the music they already contain."[112] Chant is an *exegesis* of the text: the melody and rhythm are not casually or incidentally related to the text, but unpack and savor its truth, emphasizing this or that aspect of it, lingering over this phrase, probing that one.[113] Chant may thus be called "musical *lectio divina*." It illuminates the words much as medieval scribes illuminated capitals and decorated the margins of their books.[114]

To show how chant is musical *lectio divina*, let's have a look at the Communion chant from the Second Sunday after Epiphany.[115] Connected with the Gospel of the day—Saint John's account of Our Lord's first "sign," the miracle at the wedding feast at Cana—listen to how the chant brings out the drama in the text: "The Lord says: Fill up the water jars with water and carry them to the chief steward. When the chief steward had tasted the water-made-wine, he says to the bridegroom: You have kept the best wine until now. This first sign Jesus did in the presence of His disciples." Notice, first of all, that the text of the Evangelist has been modified in subtle ways: the composer (or whoever it was who first chose the proper text) has

---

[112] Quoted by Hourlier, *Reflections on the Spirituality of Gregorian Chant*, 27.

[113] For detailed illustrations, see Johner, *Chants of the Vatican Gradual*, and Murrett, *The Message of the Mass Melodies*.

[114] See Rampi, "Gregorian Chant, the Song of the Liturgy." Like chant, polyphony at its best—especially after the Council of Trent—also prioritizes the divine word and seeks to convey feelingly some aspect of its inmost meaning so that it may penetrate the soul. John Saward writes of William Byrd: "Like Victoria, and again in the spirit of the Tridentine reform, Byrd strives to make the text as clear as possible: the music is for the Word, not the Word for the music. In the preface to the first part of the *Gradualia*, he explains how close study of the text of the Roman liturgy moved him to find the right notes for the setting. In other words, the music is the fruit of meditation, of *lectio divina* of the Scripture and the liturgical books. In the four-part Mass, for example, he gives solemn stress to the words *unam, sanctam, catholicam et apostolicam ecclesiam* in the Creed, and in the supplication at the end of the *Ave Verum Corpus*, he begs for mercy from Jesus in the Host." Saward, *The Beauty of Holiness and the Holiness of Beauty*, 172–73.

[115] This is its traditional location in the liturgical year of the Roman rite. See Kwasniewski, "Basking in the glow of Epiphany."

approached the narrative with a librettist's artistic freedom and a sense of what to bring to the fore, without of course falsifying anything.

I-cit Dó- mi-   nus : * Im plé-te hýdri-   as a- qua   et ferte archi-tri-clí- no. Cum gu- stás- set archi-tri- clí- nus aquam vi-num fa- ctam, di-   cit spon-so : Servá- sti vi- num bo- num us-que adhuc. Hoc signum fe-cit Je-sus primum co-ram discí- pu- lis su- is.

This wonderful chant presents to us an exegesis of the Gospel text, an interpretation. There's even some word-painting (of a sort) going on. When the servants are filling up the water jars, the chant gives us a repeated figure of minor thirds, suggestive of the action of scooping with jars. Then this water-made-wine is brought to the chief steward and the melody climbs, like a procession that arrives at his mouth. At the moment he tastes the wine, the melody does a curious little turn, as if in surprise at the unexpected flavor. And when he exclaims "You have kept the best wine for last!" the melody just soars, as if he's in ecstasy: he knows he'll never taste the like of this vintage again. The final period ("Hoc signum . . .") is far simpler, as if, having come down from that height, we need to focus our minds with "sober inebriation" on what just happened: the first act of omnipotence that came from the hand of Jesus, a sign of who He is and of what He has come to do—and which He was careful to do in the company of His disciples, for their sake, to prepare them for the wedding feast in due time, the "hour" when He Himself will be the Bridegroom, and when it will not be water that is turned into wine, but wine into blood.

Free rhythm

Precisely because of the primacy it allows to the text, Gregorian chant is "ametrical" or "non-metrical"—the only music of its kind in the Western tradition. Its musical phrases follow the natural rhythm of Scripture, which is not written in meter. Unlike the pagan poets of Greece and Rome, the Hebrews did not have *metered* poetry. The Greek and Latin translations of the Psalms, faithful to the character of the original, are not metrical either. Moreover, the Church Fathers were opposed to the use of strongly rhythmical music in the liturgy—"music with a beat"—as it smacked too much of pagan cults. Because chant is not confined to a predetermined grid of beats, such as duple or triple time (think: march or waltz) but conforms to the syllables of the words, its phrases seem to float, flow along, meander, and soar. It breathes rather than marches ahead; it moves with a wave-like undulation, or like birds circling in the sky. A large part of the special "aura" of chant is caused by its unconstrained fluidity and freedom of motion, which seems to break out of the hegemony of earthly time and the constraints of the flesh represented by the beat.

In the Solesmes method made famous by Dom Mocquereau and Dom Gajard, one can illustrate the non-metricality of chant by counting groups of twos and threes (binary and ternary groupings).[116] As criticized as this approach has been—written off as an imposition of modern structure upon medieval materials—no alternative method has proved capable of equaling the old Solesmes method in lyricism, tranquility of spirit, ensemble unanimity, and liturgical fittingness, let alone pedagogical clarity and ease. Since these qualities are important for worshipers and music-makers, my vote still goes with the old Solesmes method in general, although I do not mind incorporating ideas from the more recent Solesmes research, such as the repercussion of notes in a distropha or tristropha, the omission of the so-called vertical episema, the extension of a one-note horizontal episema

---

[116] For good overviews, see Gajard, *The Solesmes Method*; Anonymous, *Laus in Ecclesia*.

over its neighboring note, and greater attentiveness to changes in tempo. Still, it is always my advice that new or large scholas should sing together with the old method, while only the cantors or a small schola of picked singers should try to bring in any of the newer insights, and only to the extent that it produces results edifying for all.

Unison singing

Because Gregorian chant focuses on the *word of God* as it gathers us into the one Body of Christ, it is eminently fitting that it be sung *in unison*—that is, everyone singing the same melody at the same time. As a 1974 document from the Vatican puts it (another document that was, incidentally, ignored by nearly everyone): "Gregorian chant will continue to be a bond that forms the members of many nations into a single people, gathered together in Christ's name with one heart, one mind, and one voice. This living unity, symbolized by the union of voices that [otherwise] speak in different languages, accents, and inflections, is a striking manifestation of the diversified harmony of the one Church."[117]

The subtle rhythm of chant and the much-admired inventiveness and intricacy of its melodies are possible only because of this insistence, at once practical and symbolic, on unison singing. Few things witness more impressively to the unity, antiquity, and universality of the Church than a large congregation chanting the *Credo* together at Mass, demonstrating *in action* that the Church is one, holy, catholic, and apostolic.

Harmonized music adds splendor to ceremonies, but it involves a certain sacrifice in melodic purity and complexity. While I am passionately fond of polyphonic Mass Ordinaries and have composed a few myself, I nevertheless believe that there are irreducibly distinct and great qualities in the plainchant Masses that make them singularly appropriate to the spirit and letter of their liturgical texts.

We can make a few generalizations about the Gregorian chants of the Ordinary. The *Kyrie*, with its melismatic melodies, has the character of intensely pleading for divine mercy. Its traditional ninefold structure gives

---

[117] Introduction to *Jubilate Deo*. For more on this ill-starred project, see Benofy, "*Jubilate Deo* Latin Chants."

it a doubly underlined Trinitarian character.[118] As befits a longer text, the *Gloria* chants are syllabic or neumatic (that is, each syllable of the text is set to one musical note or, at most, a few notes) and full of solemn joy, in keeping with a hymn intoned by angels in honor of the Redemption. The *Credo* melodies are simple and stately, graceful and balanced, perfectly paced for the prayerful confession of the dogmas of faith.[119] Like the Gloria, they tend to avoid melismata, except for the Amen. The chant settings of the *Sanctus*, hymn of the angels *par excellence*, are particularly solemn, owing to the proximity of this prayer to the offering of the Holy Victim. The Sanctus often features broad, lofty, noble, soaring, ecstatic melodies. The *Agnus Dei*, a miniature litany that complements the penitential Kyrie, features a tripartite structure. The melodies are focused, imploring, and reserved, since they are being chanted in the very presence of the King, now gracing the altar of sacrifice.

A brief note about drones: the modes of chant lend themselves well to the addition of a well-chosen "drone" or, to use its Greek term, "ison"[120]— that is, a pitch, usually lower, sustained by some part of the schola, humming or singing on an open sound. The use of drones can be very effective aesthetically; since the drone is not itself moving, it does not conflict with the purity of the melody but rather tends to enhance its profile. The harmonies that naturally emerge from the moving line against the unmoving line are an additional beauty added to the melody. All the same, one must be careful that both the drone and the melody remain stable in pitch, otherwise unpleasant results may ensue; and one must also be careful not to overdo a good thing. If every chant in the liturgy has a drone, then what

---

[118] I say "doubly underlined" because the nine invocations are arranged as three groups of three (3x3 or 3+3+3).

[119] Albert Schweitzer says that the Credo is an awkward and difficult text to set to music, as it was written without any clue that it would later be sung: "The *Symbolum Nicaenum* is a hard nut for a composer to crack. If ever there was a text put together without any idea of its being set to music it is this, in which the Greek theologians have laid down their correct and dry formulas for the conception of the godhead of Christ." Schweitzer, *J.S. Bach*, 2:317. He also speaks of "the woefully unmusical Nicene Creed" (1:54). It seems hard to escape the conclusion that Schweitzer was unfamiliar with the Gregorian settings of the Credo, which are so elegant in form and so singable.

[120] See Ahmad, "Droning at Mass," and "Singing Upon the Book"; Clayton, "Using Drones as Harmony."

was once felt as a special touch can become a tedious convention. As with polyphony, so with drones: they work best in a larger context where unison chant is plentiful.

As William Mahrt frequently says, "polyphony makes chant sound so pure; chant makes polyphony sound so luxurious." There is a liturgical and aesthetic complementarity between one-voice and multi-voice music that brings out the strengths of each. Polyphony emerged from the chant and benefits from having it as a reference point and a balancing force, while the unison singing, fixed on the delivery of the Word, is the primordial and archetypal response of the musical and religious soul.[121]

Unaccompanied vocalization

Chant is traditionally sung "a cappella," or without instrumental accompaniment.

To this day, Eastern Christian tradition does not allow instrumental music in the liturgy: it has clung to the ancient rule that in the temple of God, only the human voice should be heard—the God-given, inborn instrument of the rational creature made (and remade) in the image of the incarnate *Logos*, Christ, the "New Song," as Saint Clement of Alexandria calls Him.[122] While the Western Catholic tradition starting in the Middle Ages was friendlier to the development of both accompanied and instrumental music—and with magnificent results!—it cannot be denied that Roman Catholics have often faced the difficulty of keeping their church music *sacred*, or to put it negatively, keeping the profane *out* of the temple. As Joseph Ratzinger points out, there have been three major periods of encroaching secularism: the century before the Council of Trent, the century before Pius X's motu proprio *Tra le Sollecitudini*, and the half-century after Vatican II, down to the present day.

Although this fourth characteristic is perhaps the least startling (especially since there are other types of vocal music frequently sung unaccompanied,

---

[121] For this reason, there is nothing "lacking" in a Mass that is only chanted, whereas a Mass that substitutes polyphony for *all* of the Proper and Ordinary chants should be either a rare occurrence or avoided.

[122] From the *Exhortation to the Greeks*, in Strunk, *Source Readings in Music History*, 61–63.

such as Renaissance polyphony), it remains true that the sound of the naked human voice raised up to God in prayer is singularly *real*, sincere, humble, focused—and less vulnerable to the kind of distractions that come with the use of instruments, especially when played virtuosically, rambunctiously, or just plain loudly.

Sometimes chant is quietly accompanied by a modest organ accompaniment, but this is not optimal. People learn over time to sing better, more confidently, and with more satisfaction when they are not "leaning" on an organ for support. The use of organ accompaniment on special feast days as a way of augmenting the splendor of the ceremonies is, however, a distinct and defensible custom.

Modality

A *mode* may be defined as a particular sequence of whole steps and half steps, among which there is a *dominant* (or reciting) tone and a *final* tone on which the music comes to rest. Exploiting the possibilities afforded by the eight-pitch Western scale, chant coalesced into what may be classified as eight modes: four "authentic" modes (1, 3, 5, and 7), called Dorian, Phrygian, Lydian, and Mixolydian, and four "plagal" modes (2, 4, 6, and 8), called Hypodorian, Hypophrygian, Hypolydian, and Hypomixolydian. A plagal mode has the same final but starts a fourth below it and ends a fifth above it.

All pre-Baroque Western music (and some post-Baroque music too) was written using these modes. "Scarborough Fair," for example, is in the Dorian mode, as are many other English folksongs. Due to the prodigious development of harmony in the Renaissance and of harmonic theory in the Baroque era, music after 1600 crystallized around what came to be called *major and minor keys*, which correspond (more or less) to only two of the original eight modes. While the major/minor system of tonality allowed for sophisticated chord sequences and dramatic modulations, it forced melodies into tighter confines, and the subtle variations in feel or mood made possible by the modes were lost—except in chant. And how wonderfully various are these modal moods! Medieval musicologists assigned a special descriptive epithet to each mode: the first was called *modus gravis*; the second, *modus tristis*; the third, *modus mysticus*; the fourth, *modus harmonicus*; the fifth, *modus laetus*; the sixth, *modus devotus*; the seventh, *modus angelicus*; and the eighth, *modus perfectus*.[123]

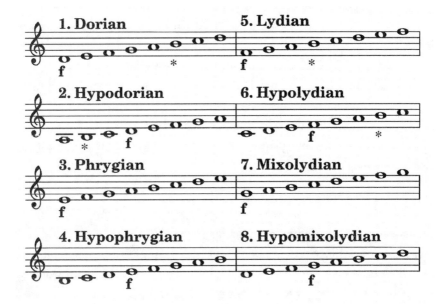

* Under certain conditions, the B is flatted in modes 1, 2, 5, and 6.

Because our ears are so habituated to the major/minor key system (and have been for centuries), Gregorian chants, which employ eight modes that seldom conform to our modern musical expectations, strike us as otherworldly, introspective, haunting, incomplete; to use a term that has been applied to Byzantine Lenten spirituality, it is music of a "bright sadness."[124] We should rejoice in this fact, which illustrates a general rule: an ancient art form is *more*, not less, likely to be associated by a modern believer with the holiness and unchanging truth of God, His strangeness or otherness, His transcendent mystery, the special homage He deserves, and the need for our conversion from the flesh to the spirit—that is, from a worldly mentality to a godly one: "Be not conformed to this world; but be reformed in the

---

[123] The serious or somber mode, the sorrowful or sad mode, the mystical mode, the harmonious mode, the joyous mode, the devout mode, the angelic mode, the perfect mode.
[124] On this pivotal concept (*charmolypê*) in Eastern Christianity, see Bouteneff, *Arvo Pärt*, 139–95.

newness of your mind" (Rom. 12:2). The art form's very *differentness*, which the passing of ages has accentuated, itself acquires theological and religious significance. We see the same thing with the use of ancient liturgical languages, silver or gold chalices, ornamented priestly vestments, the wearing of veils by women, and Romanesque or Gothic architecture. In ancient times, Latin was a widely spoken language; ordinary people wore simple chasubles; precious metals were used at aristocratic banquets; women never went anywhere without covering their heads; and, in the Middle Ages, even merchants and fishmongers worked beneath Gothic arcades. Today, none of these things endures *except* in the Catholic Church; all of them have acquired *expressive and impressive power* due to their longstanding exclusive association with divine worship. In other words, I want to say that we have advantages, in a sense, that ancient and medieval people didn't have.[125]

Non-metricality and modality are the two characteristics that most obviously distinguish chant from all other music. One could argue that in our interactions with chant, we moderns actually *benefit*, incidentally, from our jaded hearing, because our habituation to major and minor keys and the constant beat of metrical music opens us to an experience of strangeness in listening to the ametrical, modal melodies of chant. They strike our ears as mysterious or elusive, floating, at times meandering, incomplete in their cadences.[126] This has exact symbolic parallels with the liturgy as the finite opening on to the infinite and with human nature as itself incomplete, requiring God's action and grace. As the sacraments hover between the already and the not yet—looking back to Israel whose types are fulfilled in Christ, looking forward to heaven of which the Eucharistic liturgy is an image and foretaste—so the chant mingles authoritative utterance with tentative pleading, the finality of Christian revelation with eager longing for the coming of the Savior and His definitive reign.

---

[125] Then again, they had advantages we don't have: a profound cultural unity; a harmony of different domains (such that it made sense for churches, palaces, government buildings, merchant warehouses, schools, and so forth to have similar architecture); an integrity of feeling and belief that sought the best and most beautiful aesthetic forms for all things, humble and lofty alike.

[126] Hence, although drones or isons can add a beautiful touch to the chant, one should not forget that unaccompanied and unharmonized Gregorian chant is particularly well suited to a culture such as ours that is sonically saturated.

Anonymity

Anonymous monks, cantors, and canons composed the vast majority of Latin chants. What a healthy corrective to the egotism that often comes with artistic creativity and performance! Chant quenches distinctive personality—both in that we usually do not know its author and in that we cannot "shine" or stand out in a rock-star way when singing chant in a schola or congregation (if it's being sung correctly!). It works against the desire for show, encourages a submersion of one's individuality in Christ, and makes us act and feel as members of the Mystical Body. Like other traditional liturgical practices, chant strips us of the old Adam and clothes us with Christ. This process of conversion needs to be *gentle* and *continual* if it is to be ultimately successful. It cannot be the result of fits of enthusiasm, emotional highs, or psychological violence.[127]

Emotional moderation

It would be a mistake to say chant is without emotion. The melodies are deeply satisfying to sing and to listen to (when well executed). They plumb the depths of joy and exultation, bitterness and sorrow, yearning and trustful surrender. They express many fine shades of feeling. They can even induce tears in one who is spiritually sensitive. However, the emotions in chant are moderate, gentle, noble, and refined.[128] They induce and conduce to meditation—to the flight of the spirit into God, who is Spirit (cf. Jn 4:24). In this way, chant is well suited to the ascent of prayer, which begins

---

[127] See Kwasniewski, "Why Charismatic Catholics Should Love the Traditional Latin Mass" and "Confusion about Graces."

[128] As Joseph Shaw writes, "In the chant and in the texts and ceremonies of the [traditional] Mass, the liturgy has a great emotional range, from penance and grief, to expectation and joy, but this is expressed with a great economy of means, and without emotional manipulation." Shaw, *How to Attend the Extraordinary Form*, 18. Thomas Merton had made a similar observation: "The cold stones of the Abbey church ring with a chant that glows with living flame, with a clean, profound desire. It is an austere warmth, the warmth of Gregorian chant. It is deep beyond ordinary emotion, and that is one reason why you never get tired of it. It never wears you out by making a lot of cheap demands on your sensibilities. Instead of drawing you out into the open field of feelings where your enemies, the devil and your own imagination and the inherent vulgarity of your own corrupted nature can get at you with their blades and cut you to pieces, it draws you within, where you are lulled in peace and recollection and where you find God." Merton, *The Seven Storey Mountain*, Pt. 3, ch. 4, p. 417.

with a symbol or text that we encounter, on which we ruminate, from which desire is kindled, and which, when God favors us, rests in His embrace, as we gaze on Him.[129] As Father Delalande says:

> All the sentiments with which it [the chant] may be charged lose their passionate, independent, and anarchical character in it and come forth composed and overpowered by divine peace. Roman chant can express love, hate, and desire; hope, confidence, boldness, or sadness, weariness, and terror. Yet conformity to the will of God and security in the arms of His merciful love envelop and penetrate them all. . . . The work of detachment thus begun is increased by the incomparable purity of Gregorian chant; it causes the soul to enter into a world of divine peace by snatching it away from the myriad cares which stand in the way of free exchanges with its Creator. . . . We cannot frequent works of such spirituality and detachment without feeling called upon to purify, detach, and spiritualize ourselves. In the long run we shall be repelled by whatever is vulgar, insipid, sentimental, or affected.[130]

The "temperance" of chant takes on a special importance in our times, when so many people live a fast-paced (if not frantic) life, wearied from excessive stimulation—the constant input of music, movies, videos, the internet. Although chant has positively affected mankind for centuries as a summons to greater interiority, an aid for achieving restful silence, and a guardian of right spiritual hierarchy, for us moderns it carries additional value as a medicinal remedy, a health-giving purgative. As Giacomo Baroffio says, "Liturgical prayer teaches us to put ourselves on a wavelength independent of worldly chaos. . . . Gregorian chant has the power to sing, to divert the heart from preoccupations, because it orients itself to God in adoration

---

[129] I am referring here to the four stages of *lectio divina*, which Guigo the Carthusian identifies as *lectio, meditatio, oratio*, and *contemplatio*.

[130] Delalande, "Gregorian Chant," in *Introduction to Theology*, 238–39. He goes on to say, "What hinders us from finding God is not that God is absent from us but that we are absent from that self in which God dwells. The atmosphere created by the sung prayer of the Church has a marvellous capacity for turning us in upon ourselves and upon our inner guest" (239).

and silence."[131] Pope Leo XIII says something similar in a letter from 1901: "In truth, the Gregorian melodies were composed with much prudence and wisdom, in order to elucidate the meaning of the words. There resides within them a great strength and a wonderful sweetness mixed with gravity, all of which readily stirs up religious feelings in the soul, and nourishes beneficial thoughts just when they are needed."[132]

Unambiguous sacrality

Gregorian chant arose *exclusively* for divine worship, and lends itself to no other (profane) use. The full significance of this fact is seldom appreciated: it means that chant is something inherently sacred—that is, set apart for God alone. It is the musical equivalent of incense and liturgical vestments, which are not used except for divine worship. Such things are the privileged "honor guard" and "attendants" of Christ, powerfully evoking His presence and effortlessly guiding us into that presence.

Chant, says Joseph Swain, is "the musical icon of Roman Catholicism."[133] As such, it contrasts with secular styles of music that, when brought into the church, have an ambiguous signification: are we dealing with Our Lord or with the world (or even worldliness)? Are we lowering God to our own level or asking Him to lift us up to share in His divinity? It's often been remarked that the potent connection between chant and Catholicism is well exploited by Hollywood movie directors, who, whenever they want to evoke a "Catholic atmosphere," make sure there is some chant wafting in the background. Perhaps, in *this* case, our clergy would be right to take their bearings from the secular world's business sense!

---

[131] Baroffio, *Re-Tractations*, 25; 33. In the last letter he ever sent, dated July 30, 1944, Antoine de Saint-Exupéry wrote, "Ah, General, there is only one problem, only one problem in the world. One alone. To restore to men a spiritual meaning, spiritual preoccupations. To shower down on them something like a Gregorian chant. If I had faith, it is quite certain that, after this time of a 'necessary and thankless job' [referring to World War II], I would put up with nothing but Solesmes." French original: http://www.biblisem.net/etudes/stexlagx.htm; translation mine.

[132] Quoted by Hourlier, *Reflections*, 27.

[133] Swain, *Sacred Treasure*, 95. Swain's discussion of chant (pp. 95–117) is among the best I have ever seen and repays close study.

Recapitulation

Taken together, the eight characteristics just examined—primacy of the word, free rhythm, unison singing, unaccompanied vocalization, modality, anonymity, emotional moderation, unambiguous sacrality—show that Gregorian chant is not just a little bit different from other types of music but profoundly different. It is liturgical music through and through, existing solely for divine worship, perfectly suited to its verbal, sacred nature and well suited to aid the faithful who associate it with that worship and who find it both beautiful and strange, as God Himself is.

Human beings are created to contemplate God. Gregorian chant prepares us for this contemplation and inaugurates it. Chant evokes and draws us towards the beatific vision. In particular, the melismata express "the ineffable sighs and groanings" of the Spirit (cf. Rom 8:26). Gregorian chant—and, in a different but complementary way, the quiet low Mass—brings something of the revitalizing spirit of the cloister, the tranquility of the monastic "search for God," into every church. If monasticism is simply the Christian baptismal vocation lived out as radically and integrally as possible, then our liturgy, too, should have this monastic core identity, purity, and efficacy. Without it, we are already on a downward course into superficiality, distraction, and worldliness.[134]

We can see better now why chant is a necessary or integral part of the solemn liturgy, why it gives a nobler form to the celebration, and why it is specially suited to the Roman rite and deserves the foremost place within it— all of which was asserted without ambiguity in *Sacrosanctum Concilium*, as we have seen. When performed in an edifying manner, chant *in and of itself* "accords with the spirit of the liturgical action," which cannot be *assumed* for any other style of music.[135] In other words, chant furnishes the very definition of what it means to "accord with the spirit of the liturgical action," and other musical works must line up to be evaluated, as it were, by this supreme

---

[134] As Baroffio puts it rather bluntly, "The marginalization and expulsion of Gregorian chant from the liturgy have encouraged the spreading of cackles and mawkishness that, beyond their artistic inconsistency, are not able to direct hearts to God." Baroffio, *Re-Tractations*, 42.

[135] Renaissance polyphony, having emerged directly from the chant and sharing some of its properties, very nearly lends itself to the same assumption—which is why it is the only other style expressly mentioned by Vatican II.

criterion. As Saint Pius X says in his motu proprio *Tra le Sollecitudini*: "It is fully legitimate to lay down the following rule: the more closely a composition for church approaches in its movement, inspiration, and savor the Gregorian form, the more sacred and liturgical it becomes; and the more out of harmony it is with that supreme model, the less worthy it is of the temple."

Appreciating the impetus of Pius X

Few documents have had so lasting an impact on the cultivation of sacred music as did Pius X's instruction *Tra le Sollecitudini*, promulgated on November 22, 1903, the feast of Saint Cecilia, patroness of musicians. The pope's purpose in writing this motu proprio was to set in motion a general reform of sacred music in the life of the Church. His notion of reform was never (and could never be) to jettison the past and usher in novelties; rather, he urged all to return resolutely to the wellsprings of Tradition and to let the rushing flow of that clean water clear away the debris that had gathered in decadent periods.

By decadent, Pius X did *not* have in mind the Middle Ages, the glorious era of Christendom, which postwar liturgists generally regarded as a falling-away from the homely simplicity of early Christians. As Pius XII was to state forty-four years later in *Mediator Dei*, the Holy Spirit stirs up liturgical developments in each age as further ways to sanctify the people of God. These developments stand in a continuous line so that what comes about in a later century builds upon and elaborates what is already present earlier on in a more rudimentary form. For example, the transition from Christians in antiquity receiving Communion in the hand while standing (but *not* in the manner in which it is practiced today) to Communion on the tongue while kneeling was an organic development that flowed out of the reverence and adoration toward the Holy Eucharist that was never absent yet continued to grow under the influence of the Holy Spirit until it found an outward form best suited to the truth professed.[136]

Corruptions are also possible when a new feature or practice contradicts the letter or spirit of what is already in place. Thus, to take up the same example,

---

[136] On these points, see Kwasniewski, *Holy Bread of Eternal Life*, 89–145; *Once and Future Roman Rite*, 196–215.

the *reintroduction* of Communion in the hand was a clear corruption, not a development or a restoration. More to the point, the introduction of ornately operatic styles of music into the Mass during the Classical and Romantic periods was a corruption because it turned the liturgy into a concert and detracted from its otherworldly orientation. It was none other than Saint Pius X who expressed this view: though doubtless an admirer of the music of Haydn, Mozart, and Italian composers *on their own terms*, he judged their style poorly suited to the temple of God and the holy mysteries enacted therein. As *Tra le Sollecitudini* explains, God had already generously provided an intensely contemplative music for the liturgy of the Roman rite—namely, Gregorian chant—a music that grew organically with this rite, has always adorned it, and sets the tone for all sacred music fit for use in the temple of God.

Pius X's teaching decisively shaped the subsequent magisterium, from his successors Pius XI and Pius XII through Vatican II's *Sacrosanctum Concilium* down to Benedict XVI's *Sacramentum Caritatis*. In all of these documents, we find an unqualified recognition of the primacy of Gregorian chant for the Roman rite, even though there is also a welcoming of musical compositions in other styles, as long as they harmonize with the liturgical action—which, unfortunately, cannot be said to be true for most of what passes for "church music" nowadays, as we will discuss in later chapters.

The noble vision of Pius X is not unrealistic or unachievable. Throughout the first half of the twentieth century and well into the 1960s, schools all over the world were teaching children to sing chant; priests chanted the High Mass (even if Low Mass was more popular) and religious communities chanted their Divine Office. Chant was such a prominent marker of Catholicism that Hollywood could instantly create "Catholic atmosphere" with a few seconds of chant. It may come as a surprise to know that Thomas Merton, who became so controversial later for his political involvement and interreligious activities, was staunchly opposed to the abandonment of Latin and chant. As he wrote in 1964 to the abbot general of the Cistercians of the Strict Observance:

> This is what I think about the Latin and the chant: they are masterpieces, which offer us an irreplaceable monastic and Christian experience. They have a force, an energy, a depth without equal. All

the proposed English offices are very much impoverished in comparison—besides, it is not at all impossible to make such things [Latin and chant] understood and appreciated. Generally I succeed quite well in this, in the novitiate, with some exceptions, naturally, who did not understand well. But I must add something more serious. As you know, I have many friends in the world who are artists, poets, authors, editors, etc. Now they are well able to appreciate our chant and even our Latin. But they are all, without exception, scandalized and grieved when I tell them that probably this Office, this Mass will no longer be here in ten years. And that is the worst. The monks cannot understand this treasure they possess, and they throw it out to look for something else, when seculars, who for the most part are not even Christians, are able to love this incomparable art.[137]

The difficulty, rather, came from a false notion of "updating" or modernization—the view, which grew slowly in influence and finally dominated the liturgical reform and its implementation, that older prayer forms and modes of art are foreign to modern people, alienating, excessively demanding, a temptation to elitism and escapism. But such a negative judgment does not appear to have been common among Catholics around the time of the Council, who did not *ask* for their cultural heritage to be taken away from them; nor is it the view of Catholics today who, rediscovering these things, appreciate their beauty and appropriateness, like the thoughtful "seculars" Merton talks about.

Life reminds us again and again of the truth of Chesterton's quip: "The Christian ideal has not been tried and found wanting. It has been found difficult; and left untried." If the great man will permit me to adapt his statement: The Gregorian ideal for liturgical music has not been tried and found wanting. It has been found difficult; and left aside. Yet even here, one may question just how difficult it is. Yes, the Propers (the cycle of chants specific to Sundays and feasts) can be quite challenging and require a trained schola.[138] But the

---

[137] Thomas Merton, letter of September 11, 1964 to Dom Ignace Gillet, in *The School of Charity*, 236.
[138] Even the Propers become familiar and easier over time thanks to their annual repetition; this holds even more for the Commons of various categories of saints. It doesn't take long before the oft-repeated Communion antiphon *Fidelis servus et prudens* is committed to memory!

Ordinary of the Mass—the Kyrie, Gloria, Credo, Sanctus, Agnus Dei—and the common responses can be and often are sung with gusto by everyone, including little children who unselfconsciously deliver what they have received by ear. In working as a choir director with youth for thirty years, and as one who has taught chant or worked with those who have taught chant to every category of people, I know the reality: whenever chant is *wanted*, it flourishes to the benefit of all. It has been *unwanted* by some, and therefore left untried.

Gregorian chant has never been more available for those who seek it. All the old liturgical chant books have been republished; all the Solesmes books for the rite of Paul VI are still in print; new resources like *The Parish Book of Chant* are plentiful; most chants can be listened to online or printed off at a few clicks; free tutorials can guide self-study, and well-attended workshops happen year in, year out. This great treasure of liturgical music will not go away; it will rise again from the ashes, as the Church recovers the sacredness of her worship.

Although there are hopeful signs that Catholic liturgical music, after decades of lucrative secularization and horizontal banality, is beginning to experience a *true* renewal in continuity with the Church's tradition, we are still far from seeing Pius X's sound principles universally implemented in parishes. The primary characteristic of modernity, according to many scholars, is its "deep pluralism," and that mentality seems to obtain among Catholics in their liturgical worship: "All we like sheep have gone astray, every one to his own way" (Is. 53:6). May the combined prayers of Saint Cecilia, Saint Gregory, and Saint Pius X move us once again to take up, with veneration, "the musical icon of Roman Catholicism" (Swain), for the glory of God and the sanctification of souls.

9

Understanding the Place of
Gregorian Chant in the Mass

In his First Epistle to Saint Timothy, Saint Paul says that he is not sure
when he can come to visit Timothy, but meanwhile he is giving him instructions "so that . . . you may know how one ought to behave in the household
of God, which is the Church of the living God, the pillar and bulwark of the
truth" (1 Tm 3:14–15).

This statement raises a question for us too: How ought *we* to behave—
or, as other translations have it, "conduct ourselves"—in the Church? More
particularly, since the liturgy is the expression and summation of the
Church's life, how ought we to behave when we enter a church and step
into the sacred domain of the liturgy that takes place within its walls? The
liturgy, with all its complex dimensions—vertical and horizontal, transcendent and immanent, literal and symbolic, visible and invisible, heavenly and
earthly—is a microcosm of the whole of Catholic life. The way Holy Mass
is celebrated, the way we worship in and through it, not only expresses
everything we believe but also, and for that very reason, shapes our faith
and transmits it. If the celebration misses the mark, the result over time will
be a malformed and eventually falsified faith.

Pope Benedict XVI once spoke of the need to "intensify the celebration of the faith in the liturgy, especially in the Eucharist."[139] Sometimes
Catholics feel that simply showing up for Mass is participation enough;
why should we, or how could we, *intensify* that participation? I have often
been surprised at how frequently even men and women of orthodox faith
and irreproachable morals are unaware of the profound centrality, the all-
encompassing role, the Church's liturgy should have in their own personal

---

[139] Apostolic letter *Porta Fidei* (October 11, 2011), no. 9.

and family lives. We may detect the influence of a Protestant, individualist mentality that has to be gently but firmly put aside, not just in our thoughts but in the structuring of our daily life. Catholics should take time to read Pius XII's encyclical *Mediator Dei* (1947), the single finest magisterial treatment of the subject of the liturgy.[140]

The High or Solemn Mass and the Low Mass

Ancient Hebrew worship involved both singing and speaking; so did early Christian worship. By the time of the Middle Ages, the custom of the private "Low Mass" (called low because it was merely recited, and therefore not of the same elevated character as a chanted Mass) had developed in order to favor the daily celebration of the Eucharistic sacrifice by each and every priest, particularly ordained monks in monasteries.[141] The main Mass of the day, however, was always sung in full—a practice that remains alive to this day in observant monasteries. The Catholic ideal of public worship, especially for Sundays and solemnities, is the sung High Mass, the *Missa solemnis* (with the full complement of major ministers—i.e., priest, deacon, and subdeacon) or at least the *Missa cantata* (priest alone). At its best, the Liturgical Movement, a revival in liturgical spirituality in the nineteenth and twentieth centuries, promoted the ideal of the solemn sung Mass, as do the magisterial and papal documents of the past one hundred years.

Not only should the singing of chant be frequent in our churches, but the faithful, when assisting at that High Mass, should sing the chants that pertain to them—namely, the responses (e.g., "Et cum spiritu tuo," "Amen")

---

[140] *Sacrosanctum Concilium* was patterned heavily after *Mediator Dei*, a fact to which earlier drafts of it bore witness in the form of a multitude of citations. The citations were suddenly removed at the last moment before the final vote on the document, when the Council Fathers felt under pressure to approve it and could not send it back for revision. See Benofy, "Footnotes for a Hermeneutic of Continuity." Unquestionably, the general theology of the liturgy is dealt with at greater length and with superior penetration in Pius XII's encyclical than in the conciliar decree. Moreover, the encyclical deftly refutes or tempers certain tendencies of the Liturgical Movement that were later given free rein. For several examples, see Ureta, "A Brief Study of Certain Theological Deviations in *Desiderio Desideravi*." I take a closer look at *Mediator Dei* in chapter 13.
[141] See "The Loss of Graces: Private Masses and Concelebration" in Kwasniewski, *Resurgent in the Midst of Crisis*, 139–48, and Kwasniewski, "Celebration vs. Concelebration."

and the Ordinary of the Mass, usually sung in an alternating fashion with the choir or schola. This chanting together is a significant *external* aspect of "active participation" rightly understood; it is one of the most precious exterior signs of our unity as members of Christ's Body. There is an *internal* aspect too—namely, that we be attentive to the meaning of what we say and do, and really mean it and internalize it through meditation. These internal operations are enhanced over time by the external actions; vocal prayer goes more deeply into the memory and imagination of the one who sings it, and from there it can exercise a more beneficent influence on our interior life. There is no opposition or contradiction between external and internal except where the internal participation, which is more fundamental, is attacked or undermined in the name of an exaggerated external *activism*, where people are "kept busy" talking or being talked at or serving in various "ministries," and leave the church without ever having once genuinely prayed.[142]

I wish to emphasize, lest there be any misunderstanding, that the Low Mass developed in the bosom of the Church under the guidance of Divine Providence and the influence of the Holy Ghost for the immense benefit of the clergy and the faithful. It nourishes a profound priestly spirituality, teaches (and rewards) the art of meditating on the liturgy in a manner comparable to *lectio divina*, and, practically speaking, allows for the daily celebration of Mass in such a way that clergy can offer the Holy Sacrifice with regularity and the laity can assist on workdays. My lavish praises of the sung Mass do not cancel out the devotional role of the Low Mass. Rather, I seek to balance a healthy love of this simpler form of celebration with the place of honor rightfully occupied by the magnificent fullness of our public worship when executed with all the ritual and music that traditionally belong to it, which carry specific theological, spiritual, aesthetic, and psychological benefits of their own.

What are some of the advantages to the Sung or High Mass? For one thing, since this form of the Mass has a fuller ceremonial, with more roles and more

---

[142] For discussions of the true and false meanings of *participatio actuosa* (actual or fully realized participation), see the following chapters in my books: "How the *Usus Antiquior* Elicits Superior Participation" in *Noble Beauty*, 191–213; "A New (Old) Perspective on Active Participation" in *Reclaiming Our Roman Catholic Birthright*, 55–75; "How *Not* to Understand Active Participation" and "When Piety Is Mistaken for Passivity, and Passivity for Piety" in Kwasniewski, *Ministers of Christ*, 131–51.

music, it permits a fuller participation of all the people—celebrant, assisting ministers, choir or schola, and congregation alike. Famously, the Second Vatican Council promoted "active participation," but we shall see that the council had in view several lofty aims, many cuts above the low aims and aimlessness of today's parochial mediocrity. "Mother Church earnestly desires that all the faithful should be led to that full, conscious, and actual participation [*participatio actuosa*] in liturgical celebrations which is demanded by the very nature of the liturgy. Such participation by the Christian people as 'a chosen race, a royal priesthood, a holy nation, a redeemed people' (1 Pet. 2:9; cf. 2:4–5), is their right and duty by reason of their baptism."[143]

How will this right and duty be exercised? Among other things, the Council declares that "steps should be taken so that the faithful may . . . be able to say or to sing together *in Latin* those parts of the Ordinary of the Mass which pertain to them" (*SC* 54), and that—to give a more accurate translation of the passage—"The Church acknowledges Gregorian chant as characteristically belonging [or specially suited] to the Roman liturgy, with the result that, other things being equal, in liturgical actions Gregorian chant should hold/obtain the first place" (*SC* 116).[144] The phrase "other things being equal" (*ceteris paribus*) means that *even if* we assume there is other music of equal artistic value and liturgical appropriateness, such as Renaissance polyphony, the chant *still* takes possession of the first place— and why? Because it is the ancient musical form in which the liturgical texts are clothed; it is thoroughly sacred in character; and it is our native inheritance, binding us to God and to one another with the ties of tradition. It is clear from the inclusion of all of these statements in *Sacrosanctum Concilium*

---

[143] *SC* 14. On the meaning of the phrase *participatio actuosa*, see the preceding note.

[144] "Ecclesia cantum gregorianum agnoscit ut liturgiae romanae proprium: qui ideo in actionibus liturgicis, ceteris paribus, principem locum obtineat." As Fr. John Zuhlsdorf comments on this paragraph: "If you aren't praying with Gregorian chant, 50 years after the Council, then you are 50 years out of step with what the Council mandated in the strongest terms. The Council Fathers in *Sacrosanctum Concilium* go on to talk about the use of other kinds of music and they provide a welcome flexibility. But none of those other provisions eliminates or supersedes or mitigates what *SC* 116 says. In other words, we shouldn't justify the use of Gregorian chant. The Church has done that for us. We have to justify the use of something *other* than Gregorian chant." Zuhlsdorf, "What does *Sacrosanctum Concilium* 116 really say?"

that there can be no inherent contradiction between, on the one hand, the primatial status and use of Gregorian chant and, on the other, the actual participation of the faithful.

Unfortunately, most Catholics have never attended a Mass according to the rite of Paul VI that respected and implemented these clear words from Vatican II. Indeed, Paul VI himself did not respect and implement them.[145] In a supreme irony, complete fidelity to *Sacrosanctum Concilium* on this and many other points will be found today only in the chapels, parishes, and schools where the ("unreformed") traditional Latin Mass is being celebrated. There we are likely to find, as a common practice, the congregation singing the Ordinary of the Mass in Latin (or, for the Kyrie, Greek) as well as the responses like "Et cum spiritu tuo," "Amen," "Deo gratias," and "Sed libera nos a malo." These prayers that everyone may sing together or may sing alternating with the choir—the Kyrie, Gloria, Credo, Sanctus, Agnus Dei—are structurally central to the Mass. In chanting them we are fulfilling the Council's request. In such communities, one will also find the regular chanting of the Mass Propers, the most beautiful melodies ever composed in human history.

The same council said, "The use of the Latin language is to be preserved in the Latin rites" (SC 36.1). The prerogatives of Latin were enunciated more than once by the Council Fathers, whose speeches and liturgies were conducted almost entirely in Latin.[146] Here is not the place to refute the gratuitous claim that the liturgical reform that took place primarily in the decade 1964–1974 fulfilled the stipulations and desiderata of *Sacrosanctum Concilium*, when it most certainly did not.[147] What is germane to our purpose is to grasp that—and why—we should chant the liturgy as given to us by tradition.

---

[145] See "Revisiting Paul VI's *Apologia* for the New Mass" in Kwasniewski, *Once and Future Roman Rite*, 108–43.

[146] See Kwasniewski, "Why Latin Is the Right Language for Roman Catholic Worship," and the following articles of mine: "The Council Fathers in Support of Latin: Correcting a Narrative Bias"; "What They Requested, What They Expected, and What Happened"; "Daringly Balanced on One Point."

[147] The literature on the question of how the liturgical reform deviates from *Sacrosanctum Concilium* is vast. For several examples, see Stickler, "Recollections of a Vatican II Peritus"; Reid, "*Sacrosanctum concilium* and the Reform of the *Ordo Missae*"; Reid, "The Liturgy, Fifty Years after *Sacrosanctum Concilium*"; Reid, "Does *Traditionis Custodes* Pass Liturgical History 101?" in Kwasniewski, *From Benedict's Peace to Francis's War*, 252–59; Shaw, "Vatican II on Liturgical Preservation"; Shaw, "What Sort of Mass

Why should the communal Mass be sung?

The normal practice for the first thousand years of undivided Christianity was to sing the Mass. This practice remained and still remains the norm for Eastern Christians, both Catholic and Orthodox, who are *required* to sing the Divine Liturgy. The development of a recited or Low Mass in the West as a devotional exercise for individual priests had a trickle-down effect into many parishes. By the era of Pope Pius X, a recited Mass with little or no music was the type of liturgy most familiar and available to Catholics. Pius X launched a movement to recover not only Gregorian chant and polyphony in general but the High Mass in particular. To this pope is attributed the advice: "Don't pray *at* Holy Mass, pray the Holy Mass."[148] In 1969, the Vatican journal *Notitiae*, not always a repository of sound advice, nevertheless formulated a happy variation:

> That rule [permitting vernacular hymns] has been superseded. What must be sung is the Mass, its ordinary and proper, not "something," no matter how consistent, that is imposed on the Mass. Because the liturgical service is one, it has only one countenance, one motif, one voice, the voice of the Church. To continue to replace the texts of the Mass being celebrated with musical pieces that are reverent and devout, yet out of keeping with the Mass of the day, amounts to continuing an unacceptable ambiguity: it is to cheat the people. Liturgical song involves not mere melody, but words, text, thought, and the sentiments that the poetry and music contain. Thus the texts must be those of the Mass, not other texts, and singing means singing the Mass, not just singing during Mass.[149]

Did "Vatican II' Want?"; Anonymous, "The Old Liturgy and the New Despisers of the Council"; Shaffern, "The Mass According to Vatican II." This question is also taken up in chapter 11.

[148] This saying is not meant as an activist agenda for abandoning personal prayer and devotional exercises in favor of a regimented communal task but rather a call to enter into the rich prayers, antiphons, and readings of the liturgy itself as a basis for the lifting of the mind and heart to God.

[149] *Notitiae* 5 (1969): 406, quoted in Anonymous, "Can Hymns Licitly Replace Propers?," which goes on to note: "Even more remarkably, the document was cited in 1993 by the US Bishops' Committee on the Liturgy: *BCL Newsletter*, Volume XXIX, August-September 1993."

In line with the teaching of Pius X, the Second Vatican Council taught: "Liturgical worship is given a more noble form when the divine offices are celebrated solemnly in song, with the assistance of sacred ministers and the active participation of the people" (SC 113). The implication is that Catholics should *aspire* to give worship a more noble form by celebrating it in song—in other words, that the sung Mass should once more attain prominence. This implication was drawn out by the Sacred Congregation of Rites in the Instruction *Musicam Sacram* of March 5, 1967:

> Liturgical worship is given a more noble form when it is celebrated in song, with the ministers of each degree fulfilling their ministry and the people participating in it. Indeed, through this form, prayer is expressed in a more attractive way, the mystery of the liturgy, with its hierarchical and community nature, is more openly shown, the unity of hearts is more profoundly achieved by the union of voices, minds are more easily raised to heavenly things by the beauty of the sacred rites, and the whole celebration more clearly prefigures that heavenly liturgy which is enacted in the holy city of Jerusalem. Pastors of souls will therefore do all they can to achieve this form of celebration. (no. 5)

In other words, the chanted celebration of Mass should be a familiar experience, not a rare exception. The same document states, "For the celebration of the Eucharist with the people, especially on Sundays and feast days, a form of sung Mass (*Missa in cantu*) is to be preferred as much as possible, even several times on the same day" (no. 27).[150] The rationale for

---

[150] As if to underline that singing is not an add-on but part of the inherent structure of the Mass, the instruction goes on to establish three degrees of musical participation for Mass (see nn. 28–31): one begins by singing what pertains to the first degree, then adds that which pertains to the second, and finally moves on to the third, according to the capabilities of the congregation and choir. The first degree includes the entrance rite (with the Collect), the Gospel acclamation, the *oratio super oblata*, the preface dialogue and preface, the Sanctus, the doxology of the Canon, the Lord's Prayer with its introduction and embolism, the Pax, the Post-Communion, and the dismissal. The second degree adds the Kyrie, Gloria, Creed, Agnus Dei, and the Prayer of the Faithful. The third degree adds the Introit, Offertory, and Communion antiphons, the Gradual, Alleluia, or Tract (if chanted in full), and the Epistle and Gospel. The first degree depends on the priest's chanting of his own parts as given in the *Missal*. In the Church's

singing the Mass flows from the very nature of liturgy, as we saw in the last chapter. Indeed, the Church's tradition provides chants for *every day* of the year and for every occasion. There is no such thing as a Mass that cannot be chanted, down to its most particular elements. In the words of Father Delalande:

> It is too obvious to be denied that a celebration sung in the Gregorian manner is more solemn than a celebration which is merely recited; but this statement is especially true in the modern perspective of a celebration which is habitually recited. The ancients had provided melodies for the most modest celebrations of the liturgical year, and these melodies were no less carefully worked out than those of the great feasts. For them the chant was, before all else, a means of giving to liturgical prayer a fullness of religious and contemplative value, whatever might be the solemnity of the day. Such should also be our sole preoccupation in singing. As long as people look upon the Gregorian chant solely as a means of *solemnising* the celebration, there will be the danger of making it deviate from its true path, which is more interior.[151]

---

tradition, the priest's chants have always been simple, involving only a few notes of melody; they may even be sung *recto tono* in a case of necessity. The second degree enriches the beauty and solemnity of the rite by bringing out the richness of the prayers of the Ordinary of the Mass. The third degree completes the musical elevation of the liturgy by ensuring that its meditative texts (antiphons and lessons) are sung. Admittedly, this piecemeal approach can be and has been criticized; for one thing, it does not give enough weight to the sung Propers, which are the gems of the Gregorian repertoire, nor does it appreciate the liturgical function of the chants as the natural accompaniment to certain actions (such as the entrance procession or the communion procession). Wisely, the rubrics of the traditional Latin Mass demand that *every* prayer that is meant to be sung *must* be sung. Still, one may say on its behalf that *Musicam Sacram* is an attempt at finding practical ways to move toward the ideal of the sung liturgy. Since the *GIRM* (for the rite of Paul VI) expressly cites *Musicam Sacram*, there can be no doubt that the latter, although it appeared in 1967, is still to be considered pertinent.

[151] As cited and translated by Dom Marc-Daniel Kirby, "Sung Theology," in Caldecott, *Beyond the Prosaic*, 148, n. 62. For an alternative translation, see Delalande, "Gregorian Chant," 249, n. 17. Taken together, the essays by Kirby and Delalande, the chapter by Swain, and the book by Mahrt (*Musical Shape of the Liturgy*) offer the most comprehensive and profound analysis of the liturgical fittingness and spiritual benefits of chant.

Dr. Jennifer Donelson begins her classes on liturgical chant with "Top Ten Reasons to Sing the Mass":

1. Intensifies the sense of sacrality
2. Encourages active participation
3. Respects the dignity of the text of the liturgy and Scripture
4. Centers singing on the Mass itself, not on paraliturgical songs
5. You disappear; Christ appears
6. Singing is often an aid for understanding (diction, audibility)
7. Gives a better sense of the grammar of prayers
8. Gives a better sense of the structure of the Mass
9. Strengthens the sense of community rather than isolation
10. *Sensus ecclesiae, not sensus individualis*[152]

Chanting the Mass is more in accord with Catholic tradition. It is in harmony with what anthropology, sociology, and psychology tell us about how ritual activity is best done if it is to be satisfying, renewing, and connecting. It is more in keeping with the consistent teaching and counsel of the magisterium. Lastly, it is crucial for the evangelization of modern (or postmodern) man through "the way of beauty."[153] Therefore, chanting the Mass is vital to moving beyond the doldrums of excessive verbosity to the heights of prayerful engagement with the sacred mysteries.

Confirmation from three Piuses

Saint Pius X wrote in his 1903 motu proprio *Tra le Sollecitudini*, "These qualities [of holiness, good artistic form, and universality] are to be found in the highest degree in Gregorian chant, which is consequently the chant proper to the Roman Church. . . . The ancient traditional Gregorian chant must, therefore, in a large measure be restored to the functions of public

---

[152] The chanted liturgy gives the participants a "sense of the [whole] Church" at prayer rather than an "individual sense" of what this or that person or group may wish to do.

[153] For a thoughtful reflection along these lines, see the concluding document of the 2006 Plenary Assembly of the Pontifical Council for Culture: *The «Via Pulchritudinis», Privileged Pathway for Evangelization and Dialogue*, www.vatican.va/roman_curia /pontifical_councils/cultr/documents/rc_pc_cultr_doc_20060327_plenary-assemb ly_final-document_en.html. See also the mighty synthesis by James Matthew Wilson, *The Vision of the Soul*.

worship.... Special efforts are to be made to restore the use of the Gregorian chant by the people, so that the faithful may again take a more active part in the ecclesiastical offices, as was the case in ancient times" (no. 3). Pope Pius XI had this to say in his 1928 apostolic constitution *Divini Cultus*:

> Voices, in preference to instruments, ought to be heard in the church: the voices of the clergy, the choir, and the congregation. Nor should it be deemed that the Church, in preferring the human voice to any musical instrument, is obstructing the progress of music; for no instrument, however perfect, however excellent, can surpass the human voice in expressing human thought, especially when it is used by the mind to offer up prayer and praise to Almighty God.... In order that the faithful may more actively participate in divine worship, let them be made once more to sing the Gregorian Chant, so far as it belongs to them to take part in it. It is most important that when the faithful assist at the sacred ceremonies ... they should not be merely detached and silent spectators, but, filled with a deep sense of the beauty of the Liturgy, they should sing alternately with the clergy or the choir, as it is prescribed. If this is done, then it will no longer happen that the people either make no answer at all to the public prayers ... or at best utter the responses in a low and subdued manner. (no. VII)

When Pius XI says "sing alternately with the clergy," he means, for example, when the priest chants "Dominus vobiscum," everyone responds: "Et cum spiritu tuo"; or, in the *usus antiquior*, at the end of the Lord's Prayer, everyone chants together: "Sed libera nos a malo." The point about alternating with the choir is seen in the Kyrie: the choir chants the first petition, then everyone chants the second petition, then back to the choir for the third, and so forth.

Pope Pius XII writes very beautifully in his 1947 encyclical *Mediator Dei*:

> A congregation that is devoutly present at that sacrifice in which our Savior, together with His children redeemed by His sacred blood, sings the nuptial hymn of His immense love, cannot keep silent, for "song befits the lover" (Saint Augustine, *Sermon* 336), and, as the ancient saying has it, "he who sings well prays twice." Thus the

Church militant, faithful as well as clergy, joins in the hymns of the
Church triumphant and with the choirs of angels, and all together
sing a wondrous and eternal hymn of praise to the most Holy Trinity in keeping with the words of the Preface: "we entreat that Thou
wouldst bid our voices too be heard with [the angels'], crying out
with suppliant praise." (no. 192)

In his 1955 encyclical *Musicae Sacrae*, Pius XII added, "It is the duty of
all those to whom Christ the Lord has entrusted the task of guarding and
dispensing the Church's riches to preserve this precious treasure of Gregorian chant diligently and to impart it generously to the Christian people. . . .
In the performance of the sacred liturgical rites this same Gregorian chant
should be most widely used and great care should be taken that it be performed properly, worthily, and reverently" (no. 44).

The conclusion we can take away from these papal documents—and
there are more in the same vein that came after 1955[154]—is that *we the people* are repeatedly and directly asked by Holy Mother Church to SING THE
MASS. It is our right; it is our duty; it is actually instrumental in our sanctification as liturgical beings. As Catholics who follow the authentic magisterium, we should all be singing the chants of the Ordinary. Of course,
exceptions can be made for special occasions, when a polyphonic Mass sung
by the choir augments the people's festive joy and gives a new impetus to
their meditation on the mysteries.

Now, you may ask, what's all this praise of Gregorian chant? To borrow a
saying from the world of the pipe organ, the popes certainly pull out all the
stops when speaking about chant. But so does the Second Vatican Council,
whose unambiguous witness on this point is all the more striking given the
almost total ignorance or repudiation of it in practice:

The musical tradition of the universal Church is a treasure of inestimable value, *greater even than that of any other art.* The main reason
for this pre-eminence is that, as sacred song united to the words,

[154] See, e.g., Kwasniewski, "John Paul II on Sacred Music"; Rutherford, *Benedict XVI
and Beauty in Sacred Music.* Ratzinger/Benedict XVI is well known for his many writings on sacred music and authentic liturgical participation, whereas the preconciliar
magisterium's teachings on the subject are often neglected nowadays—including at
times by traditionalists!

it forms a necessary or integral part of the solemn liturgy. Holy
Scripture, indeed, has bestowed praise upon sacred song, and the
same may be said of the Fathers of the Church and of the Roman
pontiffs who in recent times, led by Saint Pius X, have explained
more precisely the ministerial function supplied by sacred music in
the service of the Lord. Therefore sacred music is to be considered
the more holy in proportion as it is more closely connected with
the liturgical action, whether it adds delight to prayer, fosters unity
of minds, or confers greater solemnity upon the sacred rites. . . .
Accordingly, the sacred Council, keeping to the norms and precepts
of ecclesiastical tradition and discipline, and having regard to the
purpose of sacred music, which is the glory of God and the sanctification of the faithful, decrees as follows. (SC 112)

And, from what has already been quoted on previous pages, we know
what it decreed. Notably, Vatican II was the first ecumenical council in the
two-thousand-year history of the Church to expressly name Gregorian chant
as the music proper to the Roman rite and to establish officially its normative
status and primacy of place. Why did the twenty earlier ecumenical coun-
cils not mention this? Certainly not because it had been a matter of indifference or uncertainty, but rather, because it had simply been taken for granted
back then, whereas in the middle of the last century there was debate about
whether it was finally time to substitute a different kind of music for the traditional chant. Perhaps "modern man" needed something else? And Vatican II's
answer was crystal clear: *there can be no substitute.* What modern man most
needs is to drink deeply of timeless tradition, not to let himself be trapped in
the limits of his own age and its superficial tastes and assumptions.

Why, then, have so many people ignored what Vatican II asked for? Of the
many reasons that can be given, surely the most salient is that militant liturgical progressives not only ignored, rejected, or twisted the words of chapter
6 of *Sacrosanctum Concilium* but also, even before and during the Council,
already laid plans to overthrow the traditional Roman liturgy *tout court*—not
just in its music but in its texts, rubrics, and ceremonies, its theological content
and spiritual orientation.[155] Joseph Ratzinger/Pope Benedict XVI frequently

---

[155] How this came about is a story that has been told elsewhere. See, *inter alia*, Sire,
Phoenix from the Ashes; Davies, *Pope John's Council*; Davies, *Pope Paul's New Mass*;

spoke of the need to recover continuity with the Church's liturgical tradition against the partisans of rupture, an effort he launched on two fronts: a "reform of the reform," largely by way of papal example, that would restore to Paul VI's rite some of the content it had unjustifiably lost; and a removal of impediments to the renewed use of the Tridentine liturgy or *usus antiquior*. Ratzinger's vision was largely pragmatic, pastoral, and patient, an opening of space for "mutual enrichment" and "liturgical peace," and did not directly address some of the deeper wounds caused by the revolution of the 1960s.[156]

Diverse musical roles in the liturgy

Let us dig deeper into *why* we sing *what* we sing at Mass, and what are the roles of the various people present. The Mass is a manifestation of the essence of the Church as the Mystical Body of Christ; therefore, it reveals hierarchical communion. That is why there are chants that only the ministers sing; chants that only a cantor or schola sings; and chants that everyone sings.

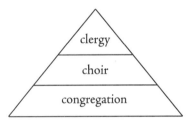

The parts sung by bishop, priest, or deacon (and, in the *usus antiquior*, by subdeacon or lector) are theirs by virtue of their distinctive sacramental identification with Christ, the Head of the Church, and therefore can never be sung by one who is not ordained.[157] This shows us unambiguously that the ordained minister is not a mere delegate of the community, as in a

Chiron, *Paul VI*; Chiron, *Annibale Bugnini*; cf. Kwasniewski, *Once and Future Roman Rite.*

[156] Tragically, his successor in the papacy canceled out this vision of liturgical peace and reopened the wounds that had only just begun to heal. For a multifaceted discussion, see the pieces collected in Kwasniewski (ed.), *From Benedict's Peace to Francis's War.* In any event, the magisterium has never been other than consistent in its praise and promotion of chant—before, during, and after the Second Vatican Council—and that is sufficient for the case being made in this book.

[157] I am referring to the traditional understanding of holy orders and minor orders, a full account of which is given in Kwasniewski, *Ministers of Christ.*

modern democratic government or a Protestant assembly, but a true head and ruler of it, appointed by God.

Then there are the "Propers" of the Mass, entrusted to the schola—that is, the choir of trained singers. There are five such Proper chants: the Introit, the Gradual, the Alleluia, the Offertory, and the Communion (in Lent, the Alleluia is replaced with a Tract; in Paschaltide, the Gradual is replaced with an additional Alleluia). An integral part of the Mass since deep within the first millennium,[158] the Propers structure liturgical time and space in important ways; they nourish our devotion as they accompany the different actions of the Mass; they instruct the faithful by placing the Word of God in their ears and in their hearts. In more recent times, the Propers have tended to be strangely forgotten, especially in the desert decades after Vatican II. Nowadays a great effort is being made to recover them so that the celebration of Mass might be more faithful to our tradition.[159]

Finally, as we have already discussed, there are the chants in which the congregation may join: the responses and the Ordinary. The responses enjoy the dignity of entering into the transtemporal dialogue between Christ and the Church as represented by the priest in the sanctuary and the people in the nave: this is the exchange between the Bridegroom and His Bride! The Ordinary chants, for their part, are like tall, massive pillars of the rite: the penitential Kyrie, the joyous Gloria, the stately Credo, the angelic

---

[158] Already by the eighth century we possess complete "graduals" containing the texts and music of the Propers. The music in these early manuscripts takes the form of neumes, since the use of multiple lines with positioned square notes developed only later on.

[159] The GIRM specifies (for the Novus Ordo!) the Gregorian antiphons from the Graduale Romanum as the preferred songs for the Entrance, the Offertory, and the Communion. In parishes where hymns have become an adamantine custom, the Propers may be introduced alongside the hymns. For example, a cantor or choir could sing the Introit immediately before the bell rings for the procession, and then the Entrance hymn might follow; or, alternatively, after the Entrance hymn, when the priest reaches the altar and begins incensing it, the Introit may be sung. The same practice can be followed at the Offertory and at Communion time. This, all by itself, can have a remarkable effect on the way the liturgy is perceived and experienced by the congregation. It begins to be perceived more as the work of God than as the work of man, as a formal offering permeated with the Word of God. On the Communion antiphon in particular, see Kwasniewski, "Breaking News: The Communion Hymn is an Optional Add-On."

Sanctus, and the pleading Agnus Dei. These punctuate the Mass at signifi-cant moments: the preparatory confession of sin, the exuberant rejoicing in God's revelation of His glory to us, the response of faith to that revelation, the humble adoration of the Lord of hosts, the surrender of ourselves to the Lamb who takes away our sins: the circle is complete.[160] If someone were to say, "All that I get to sing at Mass are the Mass parts—the choir does the rest," he would betray an inadequate, reductive understanding of those "parts." Private study of good commentaries on the Mass is a valuable way to deepen one's appreciation for each element of the liturgy.[161] Priests should also preach more regularly on the riches of the Mass texts, both the Ordinary and the Propers;[162] a sermon series on the Kyrie, Gloria, Credo, Sanctus, and Agnus Dei would be a way of greatly expanding the liturgical knowledge of the faithful.

Sometimes one will encounter Catholics who feel offended when a choir sings chant or polyphony and they cannot join in but must simply listen. They object that they are supposed to be "actively participating"—and how can they possibly do this in such a situation? Pope John Paul II responded to this objection in a paragraph that should be engraved on a plaque and displayed in the vestibule of every parish:

> The liturgy, like the Church, is intended to be hierarchical and polyphonic, respecting the different roles assigned by Christ and

---

[160] The character of the text and the liturgical function of the Sanctus and the Agnus Dei make the old custom of kneeling for both of them entirely fitting. The most ba-sic problem with "contemporary"-style settings of the Ordinary is that the tunes and rhythms are at cross-purposes with the exalted words being sung and their role in the unfolding liturgical action. Chant settings bring out the words as prayers rising up to God like clouds of incense, expressions of sacred mysteries we are unworthy to utter with our lips, glimpses into the heavenly Jerusalem. That is what the chant style of singing accomplishes, in its simple, humble, modest, and yet exultant way.

[161] See, e.g., Dom Prosper Guéranger's *The Traditional Latin Mass Explained* and Fiedrowicz's *The Traditional Mass*.

[162] Even the *GIRM* (no. 65) points in this direction: "The homily . . . should be an ex-position of some aspect of the readings from Sacred Scripture *or of another text from the Ordinary or from the Proper of the Mass of the day* and should take into account both the mystery being celebrated and the particular needs of the listeners" (emphasis added). And yet it is exceedingly rare to hear anything other than the readings preached on, which has created a vacuous monotony in postconciliar homiletics.

allowing all the different voices to blend in one great hymn of praise. Active participation certainly means that, in gesture, word, song, and service, all the members of the community take part in an act of worship, which is anything but inert or passive. Yet active participation does not preclude the active passivity of silence, stillness, and listening: indeed, it *demands* it. Worshippers are not passive, for instance, when listening to the readings or the homily, or following the prayers of the celebrant and the chants and music of the liturgy. These are experiences of silence and stillness, but they are in their own way profoundly active. In a culture which neither favors nor fosters meditative quiet, the art of interior listening is learned only with difficulty. Here we see how the liturgy, though it must always be properly inculturated, must also be countercultural.[163]

How we should sing—and why people don't sing

Persistent and persevering effort are required to habituate a congregation to singing chant reasonably well. It can certainly be done; I've seen it happen with average communities. What is required is a *lot* of repetition, preferably one Mass setting per liturgical season to allow for maximum familiarization.[164]

How should the chant be sung? First and foremost, chant should be lively, moving forward with momentum. Chant is never to be sung too slowly or lethargically. It is not a funeral dirge. When it comes to the pacing of chant, there is always a danger, given the law of entropy, of slowing down over time. When I used to direct music for a college chaplaincy, I noticed that people sang more slowly at certain times of the year and needed to be gently prodded to pick up the pace. We have to make a conscious effort not to be

---

[163] *Ad Limina Address to the Bishops of Washington, Oregon, Idaho, Montana, and Alaska*, §3.

[164] For an inspiring account of the tremendous success obtained by Msgr. Martin B. Hellriegel (1890–1981), see his 1956 article "'Active Participation' in Chant," reprinted by *Adoremus* on January 1, 1994 and available at https://adoremus.org/1994/01/active-participation-in-chant. One must, needless to say, overlook a few of his Liturgical Movement prejudices. Notable is the success he had with teaching chant to children, as Justine Ward did, and as Ward Method teachers still do.

heavy like syrup but light like birds on the wing. Remember, the monks who gave us the chant had to sing many hours a day, so they couldn't afford to wallow in it—they wrote music that is meant to be vibrant and energetic, while still being meditative and peaceful. These characteristics are by no means contradictory. The pace may be governed in two practical ways. The first is to have a discreet organ accompaniment for the chanting. The second is to make sure the choir or schola is singing in such a way as to be heard easily by the people—not, of course, with a boisterous operatic style, but still with a strong unison presence that others may rely upon. Amplification, however, should be avoided at all costs. Nothing is more distracting and more harmful to the anonymous and chaste spirit of the chant than having to hear a cantor booming it through speakers.

Chant's rhythm is an organic one, like the beating of the heart or the ebb and flow of the tide. It should be sung in a legato style, smoothly; not every note is equal or should be equally emphasized, as in a badly played military march. One will hear the ebb and flow of the melody as the phrases rise and fall. Corporate breaths for the choir should not be too frequent; phrasing should match thoughts as much as possible. All of this is the province of the music director, who needs to take steps not only to train the members of the choir or schola but also to help the people sing better. If the parish has a school attached to it, the children should be learning and singing chant on a regular basis. As the Ward Method shows, children pick up chant faster and better than adults do. It is easy for them to imitate and to memorize, and they have no fear of Latin. Chant workshops may be offered for the choir and for interested parishioners. Cantors, organists, and choir directors should certainly attend something like the Sacred Music Colloquium of the Church Music Association of America, or another of its chant programs. Clear Creek Abbey also offers courses, while the Gregorian Chant Academy offers online possibilities.

The more you sing and hear the chants of the Church, the more connatural they become to your soul; they rise up within you as spontaneous prayers. They shape your memory and imagination, and thus your prayer life becomes more and more suffused with the Church's own memory and imagination. It's like the way children speak in the manner of their mothers or fathers and use their gestures because of so many years of living together under the same roof. When we come before Our Lord at the end of our lives, it will be a great consolation to us if He sees written into our souls the face and voice and gestures of His beloved Bride, the Church, of whom His own Virgin Mother is at once the most perfect member and the supreme exemplar.

Excuses people make for not singing

In my lifetime, here are the main excuses I have heard as to why people don't sing, or at least don't sing much in the household of God.

"I can't sing." Really? Not even quietly? Do you *want* to sing better? There's only one way to get there: by trying. Few people are genuinely "tone deaf"; nearly everyone can make it to the point of singing the responses and simpler chants of the Ordinary of the Mass, though it takes intentionality and a bit of effort, like all worthwhile things in life. Although I seldom have occasion to quote Protestants favorably, John Wesley had it exactly right when he said, "If singing is a cross to you, take it up, and you will find it a blessing." The more we sing, the more it makes sense to sing and the more joy we find in good songs. There is much truth in the ancient saying *qui bene cantat bis orat*, "he who sings well, prays twice." The first meaning of "well" here is not that one must always hit the right note but rather that one sing with love and understanding. *That* is what it means for the people to sing well at Mass. No one needs to sing loudly in order to participate in a simple song, like the Salve Regina or other Marian antiphons. Even a quiet voice—*sotto voce*, as the Italians say—is better than no voice at all. In the end, no one can replace or substitute for *your* voice. Your singing voice is the instrument God gave you in your mother's womb, the only instrument you always carry, and the one that God most desires to hear, because it bears *your* personality.

"I don't feel like it." This, gentle reader, is sheer laziness. If someone plans to do in life only what he or she *feels* like doing, I strongly recommend avoiding marriage, priesthood, or religious life. This "I'll sit back and listen" attitude seems to be linked up with a longstanding problem: many Catholics seem to lack all inclination to *sing* at Mass.[165] Part of the reason is the embarrassingly

---

[165] A phenomenon well and humorously analyzed by Thomas Day in *Why Catholics Can't Sing: Revised and Updated with New Grand Conclusions and Good Advice.*

poor artistic quality of postconciliar music, awkward in range and rhythm, but surely the problem stems also from an unfortunate history of thinking about the Mass as something "the clergy do" rather than something *every* Christian genuinely participates in, with distinctive roles for each member of the Mystical Body. The Mass is my offering and yours as much as it is the priest's, albeit in wholly different modes: he is metaphysically empowered by his priestly ordination to offer the unbloody Sacrifice on behalf of all, making the Lord sacramentally present in our midst, while we are metaphysically empowered by our baptism to unite ourselves in faith and love to this Holy Sacrifice and to receive Our Lord into our body and soul.[166]

"I don't know how to read music." How will you get better at it if you don't even try? The four-line square note system of notation used for Gregorian chant might look intimidating if you're not a musician or if you've been trained only with modern musical notation, but it is a remarkably *intuitive* approach and easy enough to get used to if you keep your eyes on it while you're first listening to chant and making your tentative forays. Back in high school, when I first came across a copy of the *Graduale Romanum* and had no teacher who could explain it to me (in the '80s, chant was never sung in my parish or in any church I had ever been to), I bought a chant CD and listened to it over and over while attempting to follow along in the *Graduale's* pages. After some time, the relationship between the sound on the recording and the symbols on the page grew clearer to me, and it was not long before I was chanting for love. Not everyone will be as determined as I was to master the notation, but looking at the chant while singing it at Mass or hearing it sung will certainly bring you over time to a sense of how it works.

"Music is for the choir, for specialists, not for plain folks like me." That's false: music is for everyone. My own children, by the time they were five or six, were belting out the Salve Regina and other chants before they could read the alphabet, let alone any musical notation. Every human being was created with a natural musical instrument that the Creator intended each of us to use regularly. If a child can do it, we, striving to be child-like, can do it too.

---

[166] See Pius XII, *Mediator Dei*, nos. 76–111; cf. Kwasniewski, "Is the Laity's Offering of the Mass a Post-Conciliar Re-Discovery?" and "Refuting the Commonplace that 'Liturgy' Means 'Work of the People.'"

"Singing disturbs my personal prayer." This is a Quaker mentality. Liturgy is public worship. Public prayer and private prayer are like the systole and diastole of the heart, or the inhalation and exhalation of breath. Breathe in with mental prayer, breathe out with communal vocal prayer. Naturally, the liturgy has silence within it; there is not an *opposition* between collective and personal—we ought to have the precious leisure of communing intimately with Our Lord after receiving Him in Holy Communion, and there is no reason to see a choir's singing of the Propers or of devotional motets as detracting in any way from one's own participation. Nonetheless, the Mass is fundamentally and essentially a public and vocal prayer offered by the Church to God, and therefore a prayer that is public and vocal for each one who participates in it, always in keeping with one's proper role and respecting a relative freedom of personal prayer within communal prayer.

10

Don't Change the Sign, Change Yourself

In spite of its ritual complexity, a solemn Mass in the *usus antiquior* comes across as a seamless and flowing single action that carries the worshiper along from start to finish, without awkward caesuras or transitions. At the same time, some of the most impressively beautiful traditional liturgies I have assisted at moved along with a surprising fleetness by the hand of the clock, yet without the slightest appearance of haste or hurry. Both of these aspects—the sense of a natural ebb and flow and the "Roman efficiency," which complements "noble simplicity" rightly understood—are the result of centuries of gradual perfection in prayers and chant, ceremonial and rubrics, like the slow smoothing of pieces of glass as they are tumbled in the ocean. Everything "clicks" the way it's supposed to, each step leading into the next, distinct yet overlapping, and one is caught up in the wonderful momentum of it all. Regardless of how much time it takes, it helps one *forget* about time by its power to pass beyond time.

A major cause of this sense of "passing beyond time" is the Roman rite's ancient chant, sung in modes that surpass our restricted melodic conventions and with a free-floating rhythm that baffles our expectation of beat (and therefore "keeping time"). Anthropologists of religion tell us that every ancient religion has a sacred chant all its own because of a deep human instinct for distinguishing what is sacred from what is profane, setting apart certain signs, be they linguistic, musical, or ceremonial, from all others that belong to the workaday human world. The Jews and the Moslems have ancient tones to which they chant their holy writings, the Buddhists and the Hindus likewise. Alice von Hildebrand observed, "Not only is the quality of sacredness a mark of all religions, but it is so essential to religion that the very moment sacredness disappears religion vanishes with it."[167] This innate human awareness, woven into our soul by God the Creator, was brought to completion by the same God when He revealed to us how best to worship Him, as he did first for the chosen people of Israel, and, in the fullness of time, as Our Lord Jesus Christ did for the Church, the new Israel, when He gave her the sacrifice of His own Body and Blood.

The Latin Church's sacred chant was born out of a confluence of Jewish cantillation and Greco-Roman song, the same diverse cultural milieu that shaped our liturgy and our theological language. As a result, there developed in the first millennium a music *proper* to the Roman rite, a music that grew up with it from the beginning and was never left aside. No matter how many subsequent musical developments there were, no matter how elaborate became the Masses of Palestrina or Mozart, Gregorian chant always remained a vital component of the liturgy; it was never discarded as a primitive historical form destined to be supplanted by the progress of fine art. Indeed, later polyphonic and homophonic music makes continual reference to this immense treasury of chant, so much was it the common language of all church musicians—even for Protestant composers such as Johann Sebastian Bach, who used a chant melody as a *cantus firmus* in the Credo of the *Mass in B Minor*. One does not simply leave behind tradition, for it preserves the origin and makes it ever present. Tradition is the gift that each generation must give intact to the next.

The most fundamental problem, then, with the postconciliar "popular" church music is that it is quite simply fabricated, altogether new. It has no organic connection with the tradition of the Church and with the music that has never ceased to grace her worship in every generation, even if not every congregation was privileged to hear it in its fullness. The new church music is religious music *ex nihilo*; in no way a development of the tradition, it is rather a rejection of it, a break, a totally new direction. Its direction is from the world and to the world, not from the Church and to the Church. It is meant to be "relevant," to "appeal," to "speak to people where they are." This has never been the purpose of sacred music or even of the liturgy itself, nor can poor-quality art stay relevant or appealing for long (if it ever was to

---

[167] Von Hildebrand, *Introduction to a Philosophy of Religion*, 32.

begin with). The purpose of divine worship is to worship the divine, not to entertain or even to catechize people. When we adore God in the manner handed down to us by tradition, *we* are the ones who are made relevant to the divine (so to speak), *we* are the ones re-formed. We are taken to a place where we were not before, but where we should be and must go.

When watching Philip Gröning's documentary on the Carthusians, *Into Great Silence,* I was struck by a scene near the beginning. A number of monks are having a conversation outdoors. One of them asks if they should get rid of the ceremony of the washing of hands before meals, as he claims another monastery has done. An older monk replies, "Our entire life, the whole liturgy, and everything ceremonial are symbols. If you abolish the symbols, then you tear down the walls of your own house. When we abolish the signs, we lose our orientation. Instead, we should search for their meaning . . . one should unfold the core of the symbols. . . . The signs are not to be questioned, *we are.*"

This, then, could be our battle cry: "Don't change the sign, change yourself." An artist who sets about producing a work of art for the Catholic Church should conform himself to the prevenient sign, the historic symbol, the given sacrament, rather than distorting or even abandoning it in order to pursue his own tastes and agendas.

Pride of place in the Roman rite

In his great motu proprio on sacred music, Pope Pius X wrote:

> These qualities [holiness, goodness of artistic form, universality] are to be found, in the highest degree, in Gregorian chant, which is, consequently, the chant proper to the Roman Church, the only chant she has inherited from the ancient fathers, which she has jealously guarded for centuries in her liturgical codices, which she directly proposes to the faithful as her own, which she prescribes exclusively for some parts of the liturgy. . . .
>
> On these grounds Gregorian chant has always been regarded as the supreme model for sacred music, so that it is fully legitimate to lay down the following rule: the more closely a composition for church approaches in its movement, inspiration, and savor the

Gregorian form, the more sacred and liturgical it becomes; and the more out of harmony it is with that supreme model, the less worthy it is of the temple.

The ancient traditional Gregorian chant must, therefore, in a large measure be restored to the functions of public worship, and the fact must be accepted by all that an ecclesiastical function loses none of its solemnity when accompanied by this music alone.

Special efforts are to be made to restore the use of the Gregorian chant by the people, so that the faithful may again take a more active part in the ecclesiastical offices, as was the case in ancient times.[168]

We already know what the Second Vatican Council taught in chapter 6 of *Sacrosanctum Concilium*. Here is one of many commentaries on that document by Pope John Paul II: "Sacred music is an integral part of the liturgy. Gregorian chant, recognized by the Church as being 'specially suited to the Roman liturgy' (SC 116), is a unique and universal spiritual heritage which has been handed down to us as the clearest musical expression of sacred music at the service of God's word."[169] Neither did Pope Benedict XVI mince his words:

Certainly as far as the liturgy is concerned, we cannot say that one song is as good as another. Generic improvisation or the introduction of musical genres which fail to respect the meaning of the liturgy should be avoided. . . . [W]hile respecting various styles and various sufficiently laudable traditions, we desire, as was requested by the Synod Fathers, that Gregorian chant be suitably esteemed and employed as the chant proper to the Roman liturgy. . . .

. . . Speaking more generally, I ask that future priests, from their time in the seminary, receive the preparation needed to understand and to celebrate Mass in Latin, and also to use Latin texts and

[168] Instruction *Tra le Sollecitudini*, no. 3, https://adoremus.org/1903/11/tra-le-solleci tudini. Curiously the Vatican website has this pivotal twentieth-century document in only four languages: Latin, Italian, Spanish, and Portuguese. The English translation may be found at dozens of other places on the web.
[169] *Address to the Participants in the International Congress of Sacred Music*, no. 3.

execute Gregorian chant; nor should we forget that the faithful can be taught to recite the more common prayers in Latin, and also to sing parts of the liturgy to Gregorian chant.[170]

There is no lack of statements such as the ones cited above; whole books have been filled with them. We have clear teaching about the nature of the sacred liturgy and, *based upon this*, equally clear teaching about the nature of sacred music. Yet the vast majority of Catholic clergy and faithful, in the period after the Council and right into our own day, act and think as if they are ignorant of both—that is, what the liturgy (especially the Mass) truly is, and what music is proper to it because of what it is.

Do we trust the wisdom of Catholic tradition?

What, then, are we to make of clergy and laity who *do* know what the Church teaches, who *have* read the relevant documents—and who nevertheless follow their own (different) way, picking and choosing, mostly choosing not to implement what the documents call for, all based on a certain personal vision of what the Church *ought* to be doing or not doing, or based on "my experiences with x, y, and z" or "this is what the people need/expect" or "this is our local culture"?

A parallel exists between people who know what the Church teaches about sacred music and reject it and those who know what the Church teaches about contraception and reject it, or pay lip service to it as an "ideal" so that it may be safely ignored. One might hear the argument: "Well, if everyone were perfectly generous or self-controlled, they could either have large families or use NFP (or a combination of both), but most married people are just not *capable* of that kind of virtue. It's not realistic to ask them to live that way. It could even be bad for their spiritual lives."[171]

---

[170] Post-synodal apostolic exhortation *Sacramentum Caritatis*, nos. 42, 62; translation corrected in light of the original Latin text at www.vatican.va/content/benedict-xvi/la /apost_exhortations/documents/hf_ben-xvi_exh_20070222_sacramentum-caritatis .html. For some caveats, see Kwasniewski, "The 'Latin Novus Ordo' Is Not the Solution."

[171] See John Paul II, encyclical letter *Veritatis Splendor*, nos. 102–3; cf. Kwasniewski, *Treasuring the Goods of Marriage*, ch. 18.

Who is unaware that priests arguing this way, or justifying their silence by a sense of defeatism, have more or less undermined among the faithful the reception of the Church's teaching on the intrinsic evil of contraception and the social plagues it unleashes? The causes of this massive dissent on the part of the clergy are complex, but at the root stands a tragic fact: they do not trust that the Holy Spirit leads the Church into the fullness of truth by the solemn teaching of her shepherds who repeat and apply her millennium-spanning tradition; they do not believe that this tradition is a rock-solid foundation for pastoral ministry, preaching, catechesis, or spiritual direction.

We find a parallel in the realm of sacred music. "Well, if everyone were already musically educated and capable of contemplative prayer, Gregorian chant (and polyphony, for that matter) would undoubtedly work very well for them—but let's be realistic: the people in the pews listen only to popular music, they can't relate to something unless it's emotionally satisfying to them, and if we threw chant at them, they'd feel completely put off and probably leave."

To which one might make a response like this: "Father (or Choir Director or Youth Minister, etc.), we don't need to introduce a lot of chant all at once, but what we must do without delay is humbly put our trust in the Church's tradition and her pastoral wisdom. This will involve two steps: first, learning about the goal to be worked toward and wholeheartedly embracing it (that is the invisible step that calls for a leap of faith); second, moving the liturgies gradually but decisively in the right direction, at the same time educating the faithful through homilies and handouts, classes and workshops." So far from being impossible, this approach has been patiently implemented in many parishes with surprisingly positive results. Or should we be surprised?

Whether the subject is the evil of artificial contraception and the good of respecting the divinely-bestowed procreative and unitive meanings of the nuptial act, or the evil of inappropriate music at Mass and the good of authentic sacred music, what is demanded of each and every Catholic is to put on the mind of Christ, which we put on by firmly adhering to the tradition of the Church. What is demanded of us is nothing less than a surrender to the providence of God, with a lively trust that He will bless this surrender. "Trust in the Lord, and do good" (Ps. 36:3).

So good is the heritage we have received that nothing, *nothing* needs to be added to it in order to have the fullest and most fitting solemnity of divine worship. Certainly, an abundance of beauty has been added century by century to the musical treasury of the Church. Who would question for a moment the artistic splendor and liturgical suitability of the polyphonic masterpieces of the Renaissance, not to mention countless other compositions down to our own times? Still, Pius X reminds us of a truth supported both by his admirable principles and by personal experience: a Mass sung exclusively in chant is not deficient or defective in any way, for it is clothed with the resplendent vesture of the King—the musical raiment with which Tradition, inspired by the Holy Spirit, has covered the Western liturgy, a glory of pure melody like nothing else in the history of the world.

Given these royal robes—handmade, custom-fitted, bequeathed to each generation, held out to the People of God by one vicar of Christ after another—can we seriously look elsewhere for the music of the liturgy? Can we ever be forgiven if we persistently ignore, demote, or denigrate this patrimony? The magisterium of the Church has been clear and consistent about the primacy of Gregorian chant in the liturgy; limiting ourselves to the past century and a quarter alone, we can see an unbroken chain from Pius X to Pius XI to Pius XII to Vatican II to John Paul II to Benedict XVI.[172]

The postconciliar fabricated secularized church music must be repudiated, in the name of tradition, in the name of sound spirituality, and in the name of a council that solemnly taught: "There must be no innovations unless the good of the Church genuinely and certainly requires them; and care must be taken that any new forms adopted should in some way grow organically from forms already existing" (SC 23). Let there be an end to excuses and a beginning, at last, to the renewal of chant called for by the *pars sanior* of the Liturgical Movement and voted for by the Council Fathers.

---

[172] The consensus, needless to say, is far broader than the last century and a quarter. See Hayburn, *Papal Legislation on Sacred Music*.

"Don't let the best be the enemy of the good"

How often have we heard this saying? When it conveys the value of patience in implementing change and the value of incrementalism as a prudent method, it expresses human wisdom. When used to justify stasis or stagnation, as it too often is, it functions rather as an excuse.

A case in point would be the reaction of many to those who advocate a serious return to the plainchant tradition, whether in its original Gregorian form or in vernacular adaptations that mirror the modes and rhythms of their model. "Are you serious?" they say. "You don't know what it's like on the ground; your head must be in the clouds. The Catholic faithful have no idea what chant is, they've never heard it, they can't sing it, and the music ministers don't know how to navigate it either. And besides, it's hopelessly out of date. Sure, you can point to popes who recommend it, but that was then, and this is now. We have a new style of music that suits the contemporary Church, and who are you to say that it's bad or harmful? Maybe, just maybe, chant's artistically superior, but you're in danger of judging by art alone, not by pastoral needs. And besides—don't let the best be the enemy of the good."

You see, all of this is an elaborate dodge or feint. It skirts around the real questions by taking refuge in that infinitely malleable concept "pastoral."[173] The *real* questions are, however, as follows.

Is there a type of music that the Church teaches should have pride of place in the Roman rite? Yes, of course; we have seen what Vatican II and subsequent popes have said. Chant, the optimal sacred music for the liturgy, is put forward as a baseline to start from and an ideal to work towards.

Given that this is so, is there a Roman rite liturgy on the face of the earth where it would not be most fitting to use chant? Leaving to one side the necessity or desirability of a quiet "low Mass," where there is no intention of having any music at all, the answer is a resounding No: there could not be any liturgy in which some other type of music would be *more* fitting to use than chant, although there are occasions when other worthy music may *join* the chant as a compatible partner.

---

[173] See Rodheudt, "Pastoral Liturgy and the Church's Mission in Parishes," in Reid, *The Sacred Liturgy*, 273–89.

Can everyone learn to sing chant, or is it very difficult to do? In many ways, this is the strangest question of all, and deserves a fuller response. Over the span of a thousand years, thousands of chants were passed down by oral tradition, long before musical notation was invented. That shows the "sticking" power of this marvelously melodious, infectiously singable, and truly popular music. As a music teacher, I have taught high school students with no prior musical background to read, sing, and enjoy chant in the course of a few days. Its simpler pieces are vastly easier to sing than most Western art music or the contemporary schlock employed at many a Mass today. As a college professor, I saw students who came in as blank slates graduate four years later with dozens of chants memorized and a ready familiarity with where to find things in a chant book, not because they made a special study of them but simply because they regularly attended Mass in our chapel, where we sang a lot. As a parent, I heard my children, well before they could read or write, singing with gusto the Kyrie of Mass XI, the Gloria of Mass VIII, Credo III, the seasonal Marian antiphons (*Salve Regina, Alma Redemptoris Mater, Ave Regina caelorum, Regina caeli*), *Ave verum corpus*, and still other chants, which they learned by hearing them sung at Mass or at Compline.

"Okay," someone might rejoinder, "but *you* are a musician yourself!" It may come as a surprise to learn that I was not born equipped with musical knowledge but had to acquire it, often by difficult and circuitous routes. In high school, I stumbled on an old copy of a *Graduale Romanum* in the library (it was a school run by Benedictine monks who, alas, no longer sang the chant) and found it intriguing and wanted to be able to read it. No one could explain it to me, and the internet was hardly functional at that time. My solution was to go to the local record store and buy a CD of monks singing chant, then locate the chants in the book using the index, and then listen over and over until I could see how what they were singing matched the squiggles on the pages. It was a rough and ready approach, but it got me going, and helped me fall in love with these achingly beautiful melodies. As for my children, we did not make a point of having a special music curriculum at home, or drills in chanting. They picked up the chants as children pick up so much else (for good and for ill): by osmosis, from their local environment.

The situation today is vastly better than the one I faced in the late 1980s. We have downloadable chant tutorials, live online classes, specialized workshops for clergy, and in-person chant courses around the country. Bestselling chant recordings linger for weeks on Billboard music charts (so much for the notion that "this old music is obscure and unappealing"!). It has never been easier for everyone involved, from clergy to laity, to get effective and inexpensive training. And did I mention that the music itself is either available for free or, in the case of vernacular chant, not especially pricey? We are living now in a veritable chant renaissance—a moment when it is possible, perhaps for the first time ever, to implement the teaching of Vatican II across the entire globe, from the rising of the sun even to its setting: "The Church acknowledges Gregorian chant as characteristically belonging to the Roman liturgy, with the result that, other things being equal, in liturgical actions it should take possession of the first place" (SC 116).

A former teacher of mine, an admirable philosopher and musician, once contacted me to ask if I was advocating that Latin chant replace all other music being used in the church. He was concerned that I might be endorsing too extreme a position. I replied that it was certainly *not* my position that Latin chant should replace everything else; that I love polyphony, classic English hymnody, and noble instrumental music; and that all of these can and should have their places in the worship of the Church today. Indeed, I even think that a certain limited pluralism is a good thing: some parishes or chapels ought to become known for the quality of their chant, others for their blend of chant and polyphony, others for their addition of hymnody to chant—and still others for their quiet and contemplative Masses. There is abundant room for ancient and modern sacred music that has the requisite qualities of holiness, artistic excellence, and universality; there is room for extensive silence too, always provided that chant, which is part of the very fabric of the Roman rite, is not marginalized or omitted altogether (here I have in mind the Ordinary of the Mass, the orations, dialogues, and Preface, and the responses and acclamations of the people).

More than anything, we must not let the *good* be the enemy of the *best*. The chanted Roman liturgy is our birthright as Roman Catholics; it is a privilege to be able to sing this great music; and it is an injustice and a travesty when the chant is not generously shared with choirs and congregations.

The music that grew up intertwined with the texts and ceremonies of the Roman rite, the music in which this rite is enshrined and through which it is most profoundly expressed, is the music that Holy Mother Church reasonably expects to be the clothing of our public worship, whatever ornamentation or decoration we may borrow from other traditions or other periods.

It simply does not help to run away from this fact of our identity, our inheritance, and our vocation. Like all other historic rites in the Catholic Church, the Roman rite is a well-articulated set of prayers, chants, ceremonies, and implements, structured as a sequence of chanted texts accompanied by symbolic gestures. The sacred liturgy is an organic whole, a body-soul composite, that Our Lord Jesus Christ established in its germinal form and that the Holy Spirit has brought to maturity over the course of centuries in diverse ritual traditions.[174] Thus, as Pope Benedict XVI frequently reminded us, the liturgy belongs to the Church precisely as a gift inherited, not as a construct to be manipulated, a container for whatever "relevant content" we may want to inject. So it is, too, with the music of the liturgy, which, as Vatican II reminded us, is intimately connected with the liturgical action: this music must *in itself* clearly and consistently bear that history, that tradition, that gift, and impress it upon the souls of the faithful so that all of us may be shaped and formed by its beauty.

Advocates of the widespread restoration of Gregorian chant—or, for that matter, of any traditional element or aspect of liturgy—are not suggesting that only the best is good enough and that everything lesser must be abandoned. Rather, they are striving to implement the teaching of Holy Mother Church by correcting the bad, enriching the good, and crowning it all with the best, in accord with the given nature of the liturgical rite. And why? Because this is what Catholics do, and this is who Catholics are.

---

[174] See Kwasniewski, *Once and Future Roman Rite*, 32–77, 94–95, 287.

11

A Blueprint for Parish
Musical Restoration

SINCE THE RELEASE of *Traditionis Custodes* on July 16, 2021, we have witnessed the rejuvenation of a decades-old lie or myth—namely, that the Novus Ordo is the fulfillment of the Second Vatican Council's Constitution on the Sacred Liturgy and expresses the will of the Council Fathers. This false narrative has been refuted so many times it is hard to keep track,[175] but error is stubborn and, like a weed, keeps coming up no matter how often one plucks it out.

Sacrosanctum Concilium is a deceptively placid document with a complicated prehistory and subsequent history. It was drafted by a committee of which Annibale Bugnini was the secretary. Documentary research has shown that Bugnini deliberately steered the writing of the draft in a direction that would permit postconciliar manipulation and innovation; this explains why the document is full of loopholes and conflicting statements.[176] There is also plenty within the document that, at face value, looks and sounds quite traditional; indeed, it *had* to be that way in order to gain the desired unanimity of votes (in the event, the document was passed 2,147 to 4). The drafts discussed at the Council were peppered with copious references to Pius XII's *Mediator Dei*.[177] Even Archbishop Marcel Lefebvre put his name on the list of signatories. We must therefore recognize, and many did recognize subsequently, that a high-stakes game was played. The document was written to sound conservative in order to reassure the participants in the Council that they need fear no revolution, but it also

---

[175] See note 147 above.
[176] See Kwasniewski, "*Sacrosanctum Concilium*: The Ultimate Trojan Horse."
[177] In a remarkable act of last-minute sleight-of-hand, these references were removed from the final text just before it was put to the vote. See note 140.

had to include sufficiently open-ended provisions to allow Bugnini and the other liturgical radicals to carry out, with Paul VI's support, their already planned reinvention of the Church's life of worship.[178]

Is your liturgy like what Vatican II describes?

I shall take the principles and recommendations of *Sacrosanctum Concilium* at face value, as nearly all the bishops present at the Council did, in order to envision what our local liturgical scene would look like if we were following the concrete indications of the document *ad litteram*.

1. The Eucharist would be perceived by all as a "divine sacrifice," in which, as in the Church herself, action is subordinated to contemplation (cf. *SC* 2). The Mass would be understood to be, and would be called, a "holy sacrifice" (*SC* 7, 47, et passim) and the liturgy in general "a sacred action surpassing all others," whose purpose is "the sanctification of man and the glorification of God" (*SC* 10; cf. 112). Indeed, the liturgy would seem like a foretaste on earth of the heavenly liturgy of the new Jerusalem (*SC* 8).

2. The faithful would be well catechized and well disposed to receive the sacraments fruitfully (*SC* 11), and would understand the nature of the liturgy and how to participate well in it (*SC* 14), led by the example and instruction of the clergy (*SC* 16–19): "through a good understanding of the rites and prayers they should take part in the sacred action conscious of what they are doing, with devotion and full collaboration" (*SC* 48). In this way, they would be unlike the majority of Catholics today, who, according to many surveys, are unaware that the Mass is the re-presentation of the Holy Sacrifice of Calvary or that the Eucharist is the true Body and Blood of Jesus Christ—and who also don't sing very much, in spite of decades of cajoling.

3. The liturgy would look much as Catholic liturgy has looked for centuries, since "there must be no innovations unless the good of the Church

---

[178] Let us not forget two important facts. First, already in the March 1949 (!) edition of *Ephemerides Liturgicae*, Annibale Bugnini had published an article "Per una riforma liturgica generale" (published in English as "For a General Reform of the Liturgy," *NLM*, November 16, 17, 18, 21, and 22, 2022) in which he proposed an overhaul of the Roman rite in its entirety; and second, that Giovanni Battista Montini, the future Paul VI, always perceived him as the key figure for spearheading this overhaul, as Yves Chiron documents in his biographies of both men.

genuinely and certainly requires them; and care must be taken that any new forms adopted should in some way grow organically from forms already existing" (SC 23).

4. The ordained ministers would be the only ones performing the actions *they* are supposed to do, while the laity would be involved in those ways that pertain to them: "in liturgical celebrations each person, minister or layman, who has an office to perform, should do all of, but *only*, those parts which pertain to his office by the nature of the rite and the principles of liturgy" (SC 28; cf. 118).

5. No one, "even if he be a priest," would ever "add, remove, or change anything in the liturgy on his own authority" (SC 22.3).

6. The use of the venerable Latin language would be a frequent and appreciated occurrence, since "the use of the Latin language is to be preserved in the Latin rites" (SC 36.1). The vernacular will be utilized, of course, but only for certain parts of the liturgy (SC 36.2), and the clergy would remember the Council's request that "steps should be taken so that the faithful may also be able to say or to sing together *in Latin* those parts of the Ordinary of the Mass which pertain to them" (SC 54).

7. Liturgies would frequently be celebrated in their most noble form—namely, "solemnly in song" (SC 113). Most of the singing would be closely connected with the actual texts of the Mass (cf. SC 112, 113) and the music would be such as "adds delight to prayer, fosters unity of minds, or confers greater solemnity upon the sacred rites" (SC 112). There would be an important role for trained choirs or scholas, which preserve and foster the treasure of sacred music—a treasure of inestimable value (SC 112, 114–15). The people, for their part, would sing acclamations, responses, psalmody, antiphons, and songs—and everyone would observe reverent silence at the proper times (SC 30). None of the texts of the songs would be in any way objectionable from a doctrinal point of view, since they would be drawn directly from Scripture or the liturgy itself (SC 121).

8. Notably, Gregorian chant, being "specially suited to the Roman liturgy," would be given "pride of place in liturgical services" (SC 116). Other forms of sacred music would not thereby be excluded—such as, preeminently, polyphony (SC 116). And of course, the pipe organ would be "held in high esteem" as "the traditional musical instrument which adds a wonderful splendor to

the Church's ceremonies and powerfully lifts up man's mind to God and to higher things" (*SC* 120). Other instruments would be used only if they "are suitable or can be made suitable for sacred use, accord with the dignity of the temple, and truly contribute to the edification of the faithful" (*SC* 120). Hence, such instruments as piano, guitar, and drums, which, in the Western world, originated in profane settings and are still associated with genres like secular classical, jazz, folk, and rock, would never be used for sacred music.[179] None of this is surprising, since the Council Fathers announced their purpose of "keeping to the norms and precepts of ecclesiastical tradition and discipline, and having regard to the purpose of sacred music, which is the glory of God and the sanctification of the faithful" (*SC* 112).

9. Communion under both kinds would be rare—for example, to newly professed religious in the Mass of their religious consecration or to the newly baptized in the Mass that follows their baptism (*SC* 55). Similarly, concelebration would be relatively rare (*SC* 57).

10. Sunday Vespers would be a much-loved weekly occurrence, to which large numbers of faithful flock: "Pastors of souls should see to it that the chief hours, especially Vespers, are celebrated in common in church on Sundays and the more solemn feasts. And the laity, too, are encouraged to recite the divine office, either with the priests, or among themselves, or even individually" (*SC* 100).

11. The liturgical year would be of enormous importance in the life of the community, marked by the observance and promotion of each season's traditions and customs (cf. *SC* 102–10). Images and relics of the saints would be publicly honored (*SC* 111). Sacramentals and popular devotions would abound, such as Eucharistic Processions, Adoration and Benediction of the Blessed Sacrament, the Stations of the Cross, the Rosary, the Brown Scapular, and customs connected with saints' days, because all of these things deepen the spiritual life of the faithful and help dispose them to participate more fully in the sacred liturgy (cf. *SC* 12–13).

12. The church architecture and furnishings would be "truly worthy, becoming, and beautiful signs and symbols of the supernatural world . . . turning men's minds devoutly toward God" (*SC* 122). There would be nothing that could disturb or distract the faithful, since the bishop would have

---

[179] See chapter 18 below.

"carefully remove[d] from the house of God and from other sacred places those works of artists which are repugnant to faith, morals, and Christian piety, and which offend true religious sense either by depraved forms or by lack of artistic worth, mediocrity, and pretense" (124), since what are rightly sought are "works destined to be used in Catholic worship, to edify the faithful, and to foster their piety and their religious formation" (SC 127).

Question: Is this what *you* experience, week in, week out?

What became of the great promise of the original Liturgical Movement? It is hard to escape the impression that *Sacrosanctum Concilium* was largely a dead letter within a year or two of its promulgation. Should we be happy or sad about that? Indifference seems to be far the greater reaction. And surely that is unworthy of Catholics.

If those of a more traditional mind have pointed out ambiguous or problematic passages in the conciliar documents (including *Sacrosanctum Concilium*), they would also be the first to recognize the abundant presence of traditional doctrine—nearly all of which has been systematically ignored or even contradicted in the name of the "spirit of Vatican II." Pope Benedict's Christmas Address of December 22, 2005, where he systematically exposed and refuted the false understanding of Vatican II, is one of the milestones of the postconciliar magisterium and has changed the entire conversation about the Council. There can no longer be a serious discussion of the Council or of the liturgy that does not bring in the expressions the pope introduced on that occasion—the "hermeneutic of rupture and discontinuity" and the "hermeneutic of reform in continuity" (referred to in some later documents simply as the "hermeneutic of continuity").[180] The conversation has been decisively reoriented. What has yet to be reoriented is the way the Mass is celebrated in most places.

Throughout my adult life, I have discovered that these points from Vatican II are *most* being lived, week in and week out, in the chapels of the Priestly Fraternity of Saint Peter, the Institute of Christ the King Sovereign Priest, and similar institutes, religious houses, and diocesan parishes where the traditional Roman rite is celebrated. This is not to say that the *usus antiquior* itself embodies every recommendation made (for better or

---

[180] See *Sacramentum Caritatis*, n. 6; Address to the Italian Episcopal Conference on May 24, 2012.

for worse) by the Council Fathers, but rather that the grand theological vision of *Sacrosanctum Concilium*—the centrality, dignity, and solemnity of the sacred liturgy, with the devout chanting of its prayers by priest, schola, and people—is being implemented in these communities and in very few others. That should give us considerable food for thought. Sadly, churchmen who are in the grip of the lie or myth of which I spoke at the start of this chapter are waging a sleepless campaign against precisely such communities because they refuse to follow the so-called "spirit of Vatican II" that consigns the bimillennial tradition of the Church to oblivion in the name of a supposed new ecclesiology and an already stale and failed project of *aggiornamento*.

While proponents of the New Liturgical Movement have reservations about many of the formulations in *Sacrosanctum Concilium*, it is nevertheless obvious that both those who adhere to the *usus antiquior* and those who promote a "reform of the reform" model are far more faithful to the explicit teaching of the Council than any of the progressives have been or wish to be.

A model pastoral letter on sacred music

If an enterprising bishop decided one fine day, "Enough is enough! We must do something about the deplorable condition of music in this diocese," what concrete steps might he take? Could he write a letter *ad clerum* (to the clergy), laying out a comprehensive program of reform based on the traditional principles found in *Sacrosanctum Concilium*? What follows is the sort of letter a bishop or other superior might send to his clergy to promote the liturgical renewal so eloquently called for and expounded in Benedict XVI's writings. This letter succinctly addresses the desperate need for elevating the style and quality of music in parishes. May it be helpful in some way to all pastors who are striving to purge what is unworthy of the temple of God and reestablish excellence in sacred music.

Dear Sons in Christ,

"Let nothing be preferred to the Work of God," as Saint Benedict memorably says in his *Holy Rule*. The Father of Western Monasticism left us a clear reminder that, whether we are monks or not, the service of Our Lord in the divine liturgy—what Benedict called the *opus Dei*—is our principal task while on earth, our greatest responsibility before the Creator of heaven and earth, the most profound source of our sanctification, and a work of love handed down from ages past into which it is our joy to initiate each new generation of believers.

Unfortunately, in the decades following the Council, it seemed as if many in the Church became confused. They ran away from this primary task and got preoccupied with what may have been important but was certainly secondary. Their commitment to the sovereign work of the Lord grew weak, and soon they treated the most sacred mysteries in a casual and irreverent way. Many of the treasures of our faith were forgotten or repudiated in the mistaken view that they had nothing to say anymore to modern people. Pope John Paul II and Pope Benedict XVI worked against secularization and the forgetfulness of God that affected the realms of doctrine, morals, and worship. As pastors, it is our duty to avoid anything that may contribute to ecclesiastical self-destruction and to promote, in a clear-sighted and principled way, the sanctification and salvation of the faithful entrusted to our care.

To do so, we must first of all consistently adhere to Catholic tradition and the magisterium of the Church. Any Catholic church should be, and *look* and *sound* like, a microcosm of the one Catholic Church; the same is true of the liturgy that takes place within. That is why the Instruction *Redemptionis Sacramentum* can say: "It is the *right* of the community of Christ's faithful that especially in the Sunday celebration there should customarily be true and suitable sacred music" (no. 57). In accordance with the teaching of the Second Vatican Council—"steps should be taken so that the faithful may also be able to say or to sing together *in Latin* those parts of the Ordinary of the Mass which pertain to them" (*SC* 54); "the musical tradition of the universal Church is a treasure of inestimable value, greater even than that of any other art" (*SC* 112); "the treasure of sacred music is to be preserved and fostered with great care" (*SC* 114); "the Church acknowledges Gregorian chant as specially suited to the Roman liturgy: therefore, other things being equal, it should be given pride of place in liturgical services" (*SC* 116)—as well as the constant teaching of the sovereign pontiffs from Pius X down through Benedict XVI, I shall be requiring pastors and music ministers to expand the use of, or to reintroduce if they have fallen into disuse, chanted proper antiphons and the chanted Ordinary of the Mass.[181]

The "Propers" of the Mass—in the Mass of Paul VI, we may point at least to the Introit or Entrance antiphon, Offertory antiphon, and Communion antiphon—are an integral part of the Roman rite of Mass and ought to have preeminence, as is suggested by their primacy in the *GIRM* (see nos. 48, 74, 87). The scriptural and theological riches of the Proper texts given in the official liturgical books and the wonderful congruency of chanted antiphons with the liturgical action for which they are intended recommends them above all other texts and types of music. While it is possible and at times desirable to use exclusively the proper antiphons for accompanying the liturgical action (extended, as needed, by psalm verses and the repetition of the antiphon), it is certainly permissible to chant the antiphon and then proceed to a suitable motet or congregational hymn; I leave the particulars to your own judgment, which must consider the abilities of the singers and the sensibilities of the faithful. What I am requiring is that these three antiphons *always* be sung at the principal Masses of Sundays and holy days, whatever else may be sung.

The "Ordinary" of the Mass—the Kyrie, the Gloria, the Creed, the Sanctus, the Agnus Dei, the Lord's Prayer, and the dialogues between priest and people—is likewise to be sung on Sundays and holy days, in English or in Latin (Greek for the Kyrie). When the Ordinary is sung in English, preference should be given to modal melodies that have the characteristics of plainchant. Naturally, it will take time to learn a number of chants, so it may be best to start with a certain core, such as the Kyrie, Sanctus, and Agnus Dei, and add to it as time goes on.

Gregorian chant is not simply one style of church music among many; it is the music of the Roman rite *par excellence*, and therefore deserves chief

---

[181] This, too, is consistent with the advice of the USCCB in *Sing to the Lord: Music in Divine Worship* (see, inter alia, nos. 30, 61, 72–80, 117), even if this document has no magisterial weight.

place in our services. Pope Benedict XVI asked us to rediscover our tradition and, at long last, to implement what Vatican II taught (cf. *Sacramentum Caritatis*, no. 42). It would therefore be fully appropriate and desirable that chant be used at every Mass at which music is planned. Every Mass should be reverent and sacred, as worthy as we can make it of the unfathomable gift and mystery of the Lord's Body and Blood.

In some missalettes and in nearly all hymnals there is at least one Gregorian chant Mass, and often several, that can be employed. Resources for expanding the parish use of plainchant in Latin as well as in the vernacular (English and Spanish) are available from such publishers as the Church Music Association of America, Corpus Christi Watershed, CanticaNOVA, Ignatius Press, Illuminare Publications, and St. Boniface Roman Catholic Church (for the *St. Michael Hymnal*).

As chief liturgist of the diocese, responsible for good order and decorum in the house of God, I ask that you instruct music ministers to stand no longer in or near the sanctuary at the front of the church, but to sing from the choir loft, or, if there is no choir loft, from the back of the church. Decades of confusion and poor instructions have caused many to believe that the ideal location for musicians is at the front, visible to everyone, but this positioning contravenes in every respect the true nature and role of the musician at Mass. Musicians are not supposed to be in the foreground but in the background; their essential contribution is to help the Christian people to meditate on the sacred mysteries, which is best accomplished by music that is itself more contemplative, not too loud, strident, or dominating. When placed front and center, singers and instrumentalists cannot avoid being seen as performers and drawing attention to themselves, no matter how humble their intentions may be.[182]

In this connection, it is also important to recall, as the popes have done into our own times, that the preferred instrument for musical accompaniment in the Roman rite is the pipe organ (cf. SC 120; Pius XII, *Musicae Sacrae*, no. 58; Instruction *Musicam Sacram*, no. 63). Churches that do not have a pipe organ should be fitted with one at the nearest opportunity. If

---

[182] An exception could be made for a church equipped with an antiphonal choir in the chancel or transept, from which a schola of men vested in cassock and surplice may sing.

it does not seem possible to raise the requisite funds, a high-quality digital organ may be installed. The piano and the guitar shall be phased out, inasmuch as the Church has repeatedly taught that instruments associated with worldly music are not suitable for liturgical use. It is true that these instruments have been around for a long time now, but their abiding cultural associations, the manner in which they tend to be played, and the style of music written for them combine to show that we are dealing not so much with the sacralization of once-secular instruments as with the secularization of once-sacred music. Accordingly, as of Christmas next year, the only instruments that may be played during the liturgy will be the pipe organ (or its digital equivalent as verified by the diocese) and traditional string and wind instruments. Of course, voices by themselves are more than sufficient for the singing of the Church's music, and the organ by itself, the "king of instruments," suffices for accompaniment or solo playing.

In pursuit of these important goals, which require professional training and continuing education, diocesan funds will be made available annually to assist in sending parish music directors, choir directors, cantors, and organists to the Sacred Music Colloquium, the Chant Intensives, and other events sponsored by the Church Music Association of America and related organizations. We are also making plans to bring teachers into the diocese for workshops. Each pastor will be asked to select a certain number of musicians from his parish to attend educational events, in proportion to the size of the parish and the scope of its music program. In the next two months, the Office of Divine Worship will send you more information on these educational events, together with several suggested chant settings for the Ordinary of the Mass, a list of permitted hymnals and recommended music resources, and more details on the installation of pipe organs and digital organs.

The requirement to reintroduce the chanted Propers and Ordinary and to alter (if necessary) the location of musicians goes into full effect as of the upcoming First Sunday of Advent, any customs to the contrary notwithstanding. By Christmas, all three aforementioned Propers are to be sung on Sundays and Holy Days, either in simple tones or in fuller melodies; by the feast of Candlemas, February 2, all parts of the Ordinary as well. The requirement to shift to the pipe organ will go into effect as of Easter Sunday; the long-standing tradition of utilizing no musical instruments during Lent will be of assistance in this regard.

In number 35 of the final list of propositions of the Fathers of the thirteenth General Assembly of the Synod of Bishops in October 2012, we read these stirring words: "The worthy celebration of the Sacred Liturgy, God's most treasured gift to us, is the source of the highest expression of our life in Christ (cf. SC 10). It is, therefore, the primary and most powerful expression of the new evangelization. God desires to manifest the incomparable beauty of his immeasurable and unceasing love for us through the Sacred Liturgy, and we, for our part, desire to employ what is most beautiful in our worship of God in response to his gift. In the marvelous exchange of the Sacred Liturgy, by which heaven descends to earth, salvation is at hand, calling forth repentance and conversion of heart (cf. Mt 4:17; Mk 1:15). Evangelization in the Church calls for a liturgy that lifts the hearts of men and women to God. The liturgy is not just a human action but an encounter with God which leads to contemplation and deepening friendship with God. In this sense, the liturgy of the Church is the best school of the faith."

That is the noble vision we must take for our own and put into practice. The source and summit of the new evangelization will be the sacred liturgy worthily, reverently, and beautifully celebrated, drawing upon all that is best and noblest in our Catholic tradition. This, dear priests and deacons, is the demanding and rewarding path we shall follow as we strive to adore the Father in spirit and in truth and to lead our people ever more deeply into the unfathomable mysteries of His love.

Cordially yours in Christ,
✠ Most Rev. Harmon E. Ristohrer

Indeed, a bishop *could* do something like that; and a certain enterprising and courageous American prelate named Alexander K. Sample took a step in the right direction during his tenure as bishop of Marquette when he issued the pastoral letter *Rejoice in the Lord Always* in January of 2013.[183] In promulgating

---

[183] The full text may be found at the website of the Diocese of Marquette: www.diocese ofmarquette.org/UserFiles/Bishop/PastoralLetter-RejoiceInTheLordAlways.pdf.   In a fortunate spirit of continuity, the bishop's successor in the see of Marquette, Bishop John Doerfler, endorsed the letter as well; it remains on the diocesan website under the Sacred Music heading.

this document, with its clear explanations and actual legislation for parishes, His Excellency combined the two ways mentioned above: he put the mind of the Church into writing and, using his episcopal authority, introduced diocesan laws that would establish sacred music at the parish level so that the Catholics of his diocese could, in accord with Vatican II, at last experience the primacy of chant and of other music from the Church's priceless patrimony. This successful step nevertheless prompts a painful question: Where are the roughly 150 other pastoral letters of the same nature that should be emanating from episcopal thrones around the United States?

As it is in our own day, so it was at the turn of the twentieth century: the situation of church music was extremely wretched, impoverished, and desperate. When Giuseppe Sarto (the future Pius X) was preparing to assume the office of Patriarch of Venice and requested Gregorian chant for his inaugural Mass, his choirmaster Lorenzo Perosi wrote in dismay that he could hardly find any chant books in Saint Mark's Basilica and hastily ordered thirty copies of the *Kyriale* from Solesmes. About six months after his inauguration, he released a pastoral letter (May 1, 1895) implementing a "minimum" program for musical reform, with diocese-wide requirements that might well be taken up as a model today by truly forward-thinking bishops: "The Cardinal ordered that, at least once a month, in all the churches [of Venice], the Kyrie, Gloria, Credo, Sanctus, and Agnus Dei should be sung in Gregorian chant, as well as the Introit, the Gradual, the Offertory, the Communion chant, and the office of Vespers. He forbade the piano and bands in churches, and ordered that every parish should set up a school of Gregorian chant. He also created a [diocesan] Sacred Music Commission, with the task of promoting the study and performance of sacred music and chant, and of making sure that the prescribed norms were observed."[184] Cardinal Sarto was elected pope only eight years later, and this time he waited only three months before issuing the momentous motu proprio *Tra le Sollecitudini*. Thus we can see how a true reformer, a good shepherd, acts quickly to remedy the evils that oppress his flock.

---

[184] Chiron, *Saint Pius X*, 104; see 101–4 on the situation in Venice, and 139–40 on the motu proprio.

12

Music of High Artistic Value

When reading papal documents about sacred music, we often find popes speaking about the need for music that possesses a certain sacrality, conduces to meditation, and exhibits high artistic quality. The popes are assuming that there is (or can be) general agreement—at least among pastors, liturgists, and musicians—about the kind of music that deserves these accolades as well as the kind that does not. In other words, the papal documents assume that the criteria are universally accessible.

I do not mean to say that a given musician will *agree* that solemn music is the most appropriate for the liturgy; in fact, there are many church musicians who would say "Palestrina's solemn, for sure, but it's much too serious and somber for modern-day church-goers. We prefer something lighter and happier-sounding, something you can sing along with and feel good about," et cetera. This is significant, is it not? People *know* what is meant by "solemn music," regardless of whether it helps them pray or bores them to tears. Many contemporary church hymns are intended to be, and are recognized as, precisely not solemn. A decision has been made, then, to reject one of the criteria of sacred music—namely, that it should respect and venerate the transcendent awesomeness of the divine mysteries.

Similarly, when it comes to artistic quality, few people in positions of pastoral authority are so poisoned by relativism that they would not be able to perceive the objective excellence that belongs to many older works of musical art and to judge them superior simply as exhibits of skilled craftsmanship or products of genius. Still, having made this judgment, many would then argue that such works are no longer culturally relevant; they are too difficult to perform, they do not "actively involve the people," and so on. Once again, a certain quality is shown to be capable of being *recognized*, even if it is not considered a relevant criterion—even if, indeed, it is repudiated.

The papal teaching addresses precisely the question of criteria; it does not attempt to teach people how to listen to music or how to discriminate between different qualities of music. If such discriminatory abilities are lacking, the papal teaching can have no meaning for us. If it ever comes to pass that we can no longer distinguish finely-crafted art from trite toss-offs, a solemn atmosphere from a sentimental or familiar one, or sacral intentions from profane idioms, then the magisterium on sacred music would be totally irrelevant in practice because its very words would carry no weight, no meaning, no force.

What do I conclude from this? That the most important long-term solution for the current crisis in sacred music is *education, education,* and *more education.* If faithful Catholics (clergy and laity alike) are not continually educated in the amazing and glorious heritage of sacred music that is ours by God's gift, we can expect even the clear requirements of the Church to carry less and less *meaning.*

Oliver Bennett observes, "In a 'dumbed-down' culture, the idea of an art which might be 'ennobling and spiritualizing' was destined to be mocked."[185] Try this experiment. Tell someone who doesn't care for polyphony, Gregorian chant, or the classic pipe organ repertoire that the reason you prefer these types or genres of music for the church is that they ennoble and spiritualize the listener. It can be guaranteed that your claim will be written off as either patronizing or incomprehensible and irrelevant. Bennett goes on to say:

> Why should this rise in relativism be seen as a manifestation of decline? Surely the collapse of old forms of cultural authority should be celebrated as a liberation from repressive forms of cultural domination? . . . The idea of "cultivation," with its connotation of self-improvement, had been one of the chief casualties. It was replaced by an anthropological notion of "the cultural," in which distinctions of value were dissolved and everyday activities, however banal, [were] elevated to the status of "culture." With the same logic, what had once been perceived as the greatest achievements of art turned out to be just another manifestation of "the cultural." This, of course, played straight into the hands of the advertising

---

[185] Bennett, *Cultural Pessimism,* 129.

industry, whose ceaseless hyperbole attempted, in the interest of sales, to bestow the status of "culture" on even the most banal and mediocre of products.[186]

This is the kind of relativism and even nihilism that church musicians, liturgists, and lovers of tradition face—a relativism that can undermine the comprehension of the vocabulary that papal documents have confidently used, relying on the native intelligence and judgment of educated people. If we want to usher in a day when the consistent criteria of Pius X, Pius XII, John Paul II, and Benedict XVI are actually followed, we must work today to ensure that their aesthetic and theological language can be well and duly understood, especially among young Catholics.

Church music versus utility music

One place to begin this education is with the sharp contrast between traditional sacred music and "utility music" (*Gebrauchsmusik*). By their own admission, the architects of the liturgical reform tended to favor the latter over the former because their sole criterion was creating a new body of vernacular music that was catchy and easy to sing (though, ironically, it is often not so easy to sing!). Here is how Joseph Ratzinger describes it: "Many liturgists have thrust this treasure [of the traditional music of the Catholic West] aside, calling it 'esoteric' and treating it slightingly in the name of 'an intelligibility for all and at every moment, which ought to characterize the post-conciliar liturgy.' Thus instead of 'church music'—which is banished to cathedrals for special occasions—we only have 'utility music,' songs, easy melodies, catchy tunes."[187]

But there are at least two major problems with this shift from the lofty ideals of traditional sacred music to the simplistic repertoire of the postconciliar era, whose populist agenda has triumphed except in fortunate pockets of survival or restoration. The first problem is what one writer aptly calls "a truncated range of emotional experience":

> One of the failings of mainstream parish music today (and I mean the style more than the text) is that it appeals to and expresses a

---

[186] Bennett, 134.
[187] Ratzinger, *The Ratzinger Report*, 127–28.

truncated range of emotional experience. Mostly it suggests a sense
of contentment and satisfaction, often to the point of superficiality.
There seems to be little about struggle, disappointment, pain, suffering, and finding peace even within great difficulty. If "happy" is all
that our parishes offer, what happens when tragedy strikes? Sometimes it seems that our missalettes are training us to live in denial,
so that when we have to deal with terrible illness, war, depression,
we are asked to buck up and get with the happy program or go
somewhere else.[188]

Again, Ratzinger pointedly agrees with this diagnosis: "Every phase of
life has to discover its own specific maturity, for otherwise we fall back
into the corresponding immaturity."[189] Superficial, frivolous elation is far
removed from the solemn joy or "sober drunkenness," *sobria ebrietas*, of the
mystics. As Arvo Pärt once remarked, "Music, like other arts, is a result of a
certain way of thinking. What do you think about life?"[190]

Ratzinger is famous for his exposure of the Dionysian, diabolic spirit
behind rock music. Apart from some aberrations that occurred more in
the seventies than today, the devil knew he could not get unfiltered rock
music into the churches. So he got his cloven hoof into the Mass by a softer,
subtler device: insipid, uninspiring, artistically banal, relentlessly horizontal music that derives from rock and pseudo-folk music but has at times
something of an *appearance* of reverence without the substance. In this way,
it was possible to retard an entire generation's transformation in Christ by
institutionalizing the sensual shallowness of profane existence.

The second problem is the very loss of artistic greatness itself, manifested
in a diminished range of aesthetic response to the majesty and holiness of
God. The utility music in contemporary liturgy suffers not only from emotional impoverishment but also from intellectual vacuity. It does not challenge, elevate, expand, and refine the senses of man so that he may become
a more fit vessel for divine action and for the suffering of divine mysteries.

---

[188] This passage was copied from an article by Jeffrey Tucker that has subsequently
disappeared from the internet.
[189] Ratzinger, *Christianity and the Crisis of Cultures*, 111.
[190] Interview in November 1978, published in *Teater, Muusika, Kino* no. 7 (1988), retrieved from https://sheetmusiclibrary.website/2022/02/27/arvo-part-sheet-music/.

In an interview, the philosopher Roger Scruton speaks of the critical role played by fine art and the treasury of artistic works:

> I agree with you that the high [European] culture in which I have always put my trust has been effectively destroyed by its own appointed guardians, and that without the religious core it persists only as a fragile shell. . . . But this [renewal] means, as you say, rejecting the premise of modern life, that God is dead, and starting all over again, seeking for the living God, and hoping to be visited by his grace. If people are prepared to live the religious life, then their example will once again make this course available to the mass of mankind, and there will be hope. At the same time, we must constantly fight those who are trying to destroy the memory of the spiritual way of life, and assailing all those things in which that memory is contained. In particular we should exercise our aesthetic choices in art devoted to the ideals of beauty and order, and refrain from the kind of desecration that has become the norm in modern art schools.[191]

For Scruton, art represents or contains the *memory* of a spiritual way of life: it is the embodiment or echo of some experience, some way of seeing or hearing, that has happened deep within the artist's mind and heart, and, as a result, it can become the activating occasion for such an experience in the mind and heart of another. The great work of art gives the viewer new eyes, the listener new ears. It is as if every work of art is a mnemonic device that demands of us the recollection of some truth or mystery we have transiently encountered in life—and art will evoke or assist this recollection more or less depending on its inherent "goodness of form" (to use a phrase from *Tra le Sollecitudini*).

Saint Thomas Aquinas lends support to Scruton's insights with these words: "In the emergence of artworks from art, a twofold coming forth may be considered: first, that of the very art from the artist, which he discovers in his own heart; and secondly, the emergence of the works of art from the art thus discovered."[192] So, art has a twofold birth: the first is an interior

---

[191] Torretta, "The Person in Battle," 65.

[192] *In I Sent.*, Dist. 32, art. 3, ad 2: "In egressu artificiatorum ab arte est considerare

origination of the work, which, being from the artist's heart, is akin to his nature, his character, his soul; the second is the outward emergence of that work into the world where it can be seen or touched or heard by others, and can gently but powerfully mold them. The work of art is born *in the heart*, and is shaped according to the heart's total formation—psychological, cultural, spiritual.

Without denying the crucial role of trained skill and an unpredictable factor of genius, Scruton and Aquinas suggest that art is an unfailing barometer of a person's worldview and of an age's aspirations and ideals. This is no less true of music than of any other art; indeed, it may be most of all true of music, which has a more intimate connection with the human heart, and more immediately moves and molds its listeners and performers. Hence, what we need most of all today is a renaissance of music that will challenge, elevate, expand, and refine our powers of spiritual perception and bolster our ability to live a godly life in the midst of the world's corruption—a corruption of which the most subtle form is a self-satisfied mediocrity that aspires to nothing great or difficult, an utter lack of magnanimity and magnificence. In the provocative words of Joseph Ratzinger:

> A Church which only makes use of "utility" music has fallen for what is, in fact, useless. She too becomes ineffectual. For her mission is a far higher one. As the Old Testament speaks of the Temple, the Church is to be the place of "glory," and as such, too, the place where mankind's cry of distress is brought to the ear of God. The Church must not settle down with what is merely comfortable and serviceable at the parish level; she must arouse the voice of the cosmos and, by glorifying the creator, elicit the glory of the cosmos itself, making it also glorious, beautiful, habitable and beloved. Next to the saints, the art which the Church has produced is the only real "apologia" for her history. It is this glory which witnesses to the Lord, not theology's clever explanations for all the terrible things which, lamentably, fill the pages of her history. The Church is to transform, improve, "humanize" the world—but how can she

---

duplicem processum; scilicet ipsius artis ab artifice, quam de corde suo adinvenit; et secundo processum artificiatorum ab ipsa arte inventa."

do that if at the same time she turns her back on beauty, which is so closely allied to love? For together, beauty and love form the true consolation in this world, bringing it as near as possible to the world of the resurrection. The Church must maintain high standards; she must be a place where beauty can be at home; she must lead the struggle for that "spiritualization" without which the world becomes the "first circle of hell." Thus to ask what is "suitable" must always be the same as asking what is "worthy"; it must constantly challenge us to seek what is "worthy" of the Church's worship.[193]

Pope Benedict XVI sought to revive in the Church a vivid faith in, and wonderment at, the *glory* of Christ Jesus—and, consequently, faith in and wonderment at His magnificent gift of Himself in the Holy Eucharist, deserving of our adoration, our total dedication of all powers of body and soul, the very best that we can give. Like John the Baptist, he was a voice crying out in the wilderness of the modern Church, preparing the way of the Lord. It is time for us to heed the call to repentance and artistic conversion as we prepare to receive Christ in our hearts, in our churches, in our liturgies.

Musical harmony softens hard hearts

When Pope Benedict XVI approved the centuries-old *cultus* of Hildegard of Bingen, and even more when he named her a Doctor of the Church, I had been thinking that I ought to get to know her better. Up till now, she has seemed to be the province (or the victim) of herbalists, tree-huggers, ex-clerical modernists, and suspiciously languid early music groups that dress up in faux medieval costumes to chant Hildegard's lyrics. I wanted to know more about the *real* saint, the mighty Benedictine abbess who received mystical visions, wrote copious treatises and poems, and corresponded with some of the great minds of her age.

I chanced upon a reliable collection of her mystical writings at a used bookstore and snatched it up. Reading it was an eye-opening experience as I learned of Saint Hildegard's profound (and thoroughly orthodox) theological genius, her marvelous fluency with metaphors and imagery, and her blazingly intense intellectual concentration on the mystery of God, with

---

[193] Ratzinger, *The Feast of Faith*, 124–25.

whom she is passionately in love. As an example, consider the following passage on music from Saint Hildegard's work *Scivias*:

> Musical harmony softens hard hearts, inducing in them the moisture of contrition and summoning the Holy Spirit. So it is that those voices that you hear are like the voice of the multitude when they lift up their voices on high. For the faithful carry their jubilant praises in the singleness of unanimity and revealed love, towards that unity of mind where there is no discord, when they make those on earth sigh with hearts and mouths for their heavenly reward. And the sound of those voices passes through you in such a way that you understand them without being hindered by dullness. For wherever divine grace has been at work, it removes all shadow of obscurity, making those things pure and full of light that had been concealed by the carnal senses in the weakness of the flesh.[194]

If musical harmony is meant to soften hard hearts, induce contrition, and summon the Holy Spirit, is our music really doing this for the people in the pews? Moreover, are the faithful really engaged in "jubilant praises [of God] in the singleness of unanimity and revealed love"—is our music focused on the *divine Majesty*, in an idiom that fosters the unanimity rooted in revelation and leading to unity of mind, *sighing for their heavenly reward?* This sounds like a perfect description of Gregorian chant, which is surely the model Saint Hildegard had in mind. I do not know of a single piece of "contemporary church music" that embodies and expresses *sighing for our heavenly reward*, whereas the simplest Gregorian antiphon translates this transcendent longing into music.

Have the shepherds and ministers of the Church done everything they could to help the faithful understand and enter into the Church's worship, or have they made a truce with the carnal senses and the weakness of the flesh (think "praise and worship" music), surrounding the sacred mysteries with shadows of obscurity and causing the spiritual progress of the faithful to be hindered by dullness? If Saint Hildegard were here today, what would she say of our music, our intentions, our standards, our aspirations?

One might, in fact, develop a musical examination of conscience . . .

---

[194] Bowie, *Hildegard of Bingen*, 83.

Good stewards of God's gifts

These days, we are often told that we need to examine our consciences about our relationship to the natural world. Are we being good stewards of creation? Are we polluting or contaminating the soil or the water? Are we practicing responsible agriculture and husbandry? Are we reusing and recycling? Are we tempted to keep the air conditioning on too high?

Whatever we make of environmental hot button issues in detail, all of us should be able to agree with Pope Benedict XVI's call to work towards a proper "human ecology"—that is, an optimal environment for *man's* flourishing, which means proper intellectual and cultural nourishment, enveloped by the justice, courtesy, and charity proper to our human and Christian dignity. The most important thing, by far, is that we be *good stewards of our souls and one another's lives.* The entire non-rational material world is not worth as much as one human child, just as a single act of supernatural love or charity is worth more than all acts of natural virtue, and one mortal sin is worse than all physical catastrophes that could ever hit the earth.

Taking our cue then from Benedict XVI, could we not say something analogous about "musical ecology"?

We must be good stewards of the wealth of our tradition, which the Lord has graciously summoned forth from centuries of faithful Christians, including the greatest artistic geniuses the human race has ever known, and innumerable musicians who have translated their scores into sounds that elevate the soul and pay homage to the "one God and Father of all, who is above all, and through all, and in us all" (Eph. 4:6).

As good servants of human ecology, ordered by nature to the beautiful and lifted by grace to the pursuit of the face-to-face vision of Beauty Himself, we must not pollute the air with banality or noise; we must not contaminate the souls of worshipers with trite songs lacking in beauty and worthy lyrics. We must avidly "recycle" by continually drawing on the resources already present, even as we strive to augment those resources with well-made contributions of our own.

Modern music outside of the Church is often a toxic swamp of unbridled sensuality and angry rebellion, when it is not a mind-numbing pudding of New Age vibes or soft jazz or background Muzak. The Church must be a refuge from this toxicity, a place where the complex ecosystem of

Catholicism is protected and fostered, a spiritual garden where we catch an echo of the distant but thrilling music of the heavenly hosts.

Here, then, is an examination of conscience for church musicians—at least those who are working in genres other than Gregorian chant, which is perfect Church music and harbors no evils to be dispelled.

1. Are the lyrics we are singing purely and unambiguously Catholic, focused on Our Lord or on the saints, and expressive of the Church's established doctrine? (Put negatively: Are the lyrics mingled with political correctness; fashionable causes such as feminism, socialism, egalitarianism, or environmentalism; worldly attitudes or horizontal reductionism?)

2. Does the music have a beautiful melody that follows the laws of good melodic form—namely, a natural and singable arc in each period and intelligent reference to modal or tonal centers?

3. Is the rhythm natural and orderly, emphasizing the strong beat and de-emphasizing the weak beat, and avoiding frequent syncopation?

4. Is the harmony of sufficient interest, diversity, and nobility, without being avant-garde or sentimental?

5. Would someone with a serious training in church music be able honestly to describe the music we are using as having the qualities of holiness, good artistic form, and universality, such that it would savor of nothing worldly, would stand comparison with repertoire of acknowledged excellence, and would have the ability to cross cultures because of its inspiration from the liturgy and suitedness for the liturgy?

6. Given that Pius X said that Gregorian chant is the supreme measure of good church music, and that the further music is from chant, the worse it is for the liturgy, would the music I am performing sound "right and just" alongside a Gregorian chant, or would the two dramatically clash in style and effect?

7. Is this music worthy of my rational dignity and supernatural calling in Christ? Is it an invitation to meditate and contemplate the *Logos*, the eternal wisdom of God?

8. Would Our Lord Jesus Christ, the Blessed Virgin Mary, Saint Paul, Saint Thomas Aquinas, Saint Catherine of Siena, Saint John Vianney, Saint Padre Pio, or any other saints you admire listen to this church music with enjoyment or at least benevolent toleration? (I admit, this is not an

easy question to answer, given that probably any Christian prior to 1800 would have fallen off his chair with apoplexy listening to a Mass by Bruckner or a motet by Duruflé. A saint's personal tastes are never the final measure of art, but in general I think we can say that the saints—because they were serious in their life of prayer and penance and took the divine liturgy seriously—would, and did, instinctively react against anything that seemed really "off." In any case, it is better in such matters to err on the side of caution. When one is approaching the Burning Bush, one should not be wearing gasoline-saturated rags.)

As regards the music we write, perform, or listen to *outside of* the temple of God, the foregoing questions could still serve as points for reflection, inasmuch as good music in general should favor our Christian maturity, as discussed in part I. But we could add a few further questions:

9. Would I want to *look* like or *live* like this or that performer I am enjoying? Would I want to be friends with that performer or his or her tagalongs? Would I pick a friend or a spouse for one of my own children from their milieu?

10. Are the lyrics in accord with Catholic faith and morals, or are they promoting hedonism, sensualism, materialism, cynicism, a worldly mentality, et cetera?

This musical examination of conscience is one that the Church ought to be promoting a great deal more than eco-consciousness. I do not imply that we should be flippant about the natural environment, but I am certain that we need to be much more concerned about *human* ecology—the habitats of our churches, the optimal conditions for prayer and praise, the duty of integrating our lives around the mysteries of Christ—so that we may give due honor and glory to the most Holy Trinity. The ecological mess men have made (and let's not deny that it really exists, even if it *isn't* the world's worst problem) is bound up with a gradual departure from Christian wisdom and an embrace of moral depravity, whereby the unrestrained desires of the ego are given free rein. To solve any large-scale problem will require, first and always, returning to that wisdom, restraining and retraining those desires, and seeking what is truly worthy of the image of God. That's as true for music as it is for any other area of human endeavor.

13

Ecclesial and Ethical Consequences of Poor Church Music

MUCH HAS BEEN written about the manner in which Church music has, in the postconciliar period, deviated from its properly liturgical purpose and sacral characteristics.[195] I will limit myself here to observing that there has been a tendency for the lyrics of Catholic hymns or songs to be emotionally saturated, narcissistic, pantheistic, horizontal, this-worldly, and, at times, effeminate.[196] They focus not on objective (usually divinely revealed) truths and man's appropriate response to them—sober jubilation, humble adoration, devout thanksgiving, sincere contrition—but on subjective states, how we should feel, how we are together as one family, how we will overcome prejudices, judgmentalism, differences, and such "social evils."

The musical language follows suit, with "lounge chords," syncopations, meandering melodies, and awkward leaps replacing the more orderly rhythms, dignified melodies, and stylized harmonic progressions of classic hymnody, or better yet, the peaceful and flowing lines of Gregorian chant, illuminating ancient texts in angelic arcs.

A musical repertoire that is people-oriented rather than God-oriented, turning us towards each other rather than to the Blessed Trinity and

---

[195] See, inter alia, Day, *Why Catholics Can't Sing*; Swain, *Sacred Treasure*; Jeffrey Tucker, *Sing Like a Catholic*.

[196] Lucy E. Carroll has exposed these aspects of modern Catholic lyrics: "Singing for the Supper or the Sacrifice?"; Carroll, "A Choir Director's Lament on Lyrics for Liturgy." Anthony Esolen has frequently addressed the double problem of "bad poetry, bad theology" in vernacular church music; an online search will turn up dozens of articles. He also makes the case for the "good poetry, good theology" of classic hymnody in his book *Real Music: A Guide to the Timeless Hymns of the Church*. See Kwasniewski, "What a Catholic Hymn Should Be"; "What Vernacular Hymns Can Be"; "Happy 200th Birthday, 'Silent Night.'"

the mysteries of salvation, inculcates the false impression that worship is something we do *from* and *for ourselves*, a communal self-help ritual that vaguely gestures at the divine but in a way that validates our own assumptions. (It was, after all, in a similar though artistically superior way that Protestants in the sixteenth century used music to express, transmit, and validate their doctrines and supplant Catholic dogma. It remains a scandal that the best music to be met with in Catholic churches today is often the Protestant hymnody of the last several centuries rather than our own distinctively Catholic musical repertoire in monophony and polyphony.)

In expressing themes of togetherness, equality, and non-judging attitudes, the message of popular liturgical songs is too easily assimilated to or confused with secular ideas of equality between all humans and especially between men and women (on every level),[197] thwarting necessary judgments about states of objective human disorder or discordance from natural law and divine law. One might put it this way: if contemporary church music tells me that Mass is all about forming a warm, affective community of people who are "there for each other," and I buy into that message, then of course I can't deny someone the "symbol" of belonging in that community: the full participation in the Communion rite. I'd risk hurting that affective community by making a person feel offended and excluded.

This is exactly the mentality we are up against in a world run by Amorites.[198] It will eventually undermine every aspect of Catholicism if it is not vigorously combated because it is an acid that breaks down intellectual assent to propositional truths and spiritual commitment to inflexible principles—that is, it negates revealed religion as such.

The direction of popular liturgical music after the Council therefore furnishes the archetypal instance of the ecclesial surrender to the seemingly invincible forces of secularization. The music reflects and strengthens a worldview or mentality that is at odds with traditional Christian doctrine, morality, and devotion, thus playing into the hands of those who would see

---

[197] See "Doctrinal Foundations of All-Male Sanctuary Service" in Kwasniewski, *Ministers of Christ*, 31–40, et passim.
[198] A way of referring to proponents of the pastoral accommodationism of *Amoris Laetitia* as codified in the Buenos Aires guidelines.

Church doctrine altered, morals recast in a flexible postmodern form, and devotions reconceived as delivery systems for political agendas.

Put simply, if the great Catholic liturgy and its centuries-old music can be changed overnight, written off as irrelevant and virtually abandoned at the whim of the Church's shepherds, why cannot women become deacons, or some types of contraception be approved, or remarried divorcees be admitted to Communion? While such reasoning would be simplistic and misleading, it cannot be denied that there are powerful forces at work in the Catholic Church that would suggest and support this very inference, and pastors have done far too little to counteract those forces.

These difficulties concerning music surface also in matters of architecture, furnishings, sacred vessels, and liturgical vestments—indeed, any area in which the categories of fittingness and beauty *must* be dominant concerns. There is an intimate relationship between beauty and evangelization, as Bishop James Conley explains:

> We speak of beauty as something "transcendent." Every instance of real beauty points beyond itself, toward the infinite perfection of God. . . . We can think of beauty as a kind of language, through which God speaks to our hearts and souls. . . . The first point—and the most essential—is that we must present the truths of faith in a beautiful way. Our liturgical worship, in particular, must reflect God's own beauty and holiness. Worship, after all, is the basis of Christian culture. The beauty of the sacred liturgy is meant to radiate outward into the world. Liturgical beauty shapes the common life of believers, and it can also help to attract those who are outside the Church. A leading liturgical scholar, Monsignor Nicola Bux, has said that: "a mystical liturgy celebrated with dignity can be a great help for people searching to find God." . . . Monsignor Bux is right. To renew Catholic culture, and evangelize our contemporaries, we must restore beauty to the sacred liturgy. If we cannot restore beauty and holiness to our sanctuaries, we will not be able to restore it anywhere else.[199]

---

[199] Conley, "Ever Ancient, Ever New."

The recovery of the beautiful in worship—the specifically and unmistakably *sacral* beautiful, one might say—is an urgent priority for the Church in an era of obsessive utilitarianism, "scientific" material reductionism, technological excess, and saturation with banality and superficial messages. The works of the fine arts of the Catholic tradition have a spiritual power, deriving from their inherent qualities and consecrated status, that is capable of awakening modern man to an awareness of an entirely different realm of being and manner of action.[200] In particular, liturgical beauty plays a part in ordering the communion of persons in marriage to God, its source, strength, and shield, restraining the downward tendency of fallen human beings to turn in on themselves and their own fleshly desires, and making it easier to keep one's mind on the things *of the spirit* and to live according to the desires of the spirit (cf. Rom 8:5; Gal 5:16–17).

If the lyrics and style of church music do not continually elevate the soul to God in such a way that a habit of meditation and even rudimentary contemplation can be formed, it is not clear that they will not have the *contrary* effect in the long term, producing habits of distraction or emotional self-absorption.[201] This will not assist the individual in his pursuit of holiness, nor will it assist married couples in their striving for a shared life of prayer, purity, and fidelity.[202]

As Bishop Conley's observations imply, the paucity of vibrantly and transcendently beautiful works of art in Christian worship is a tragedy of the first order. In such a cultural vacuum, man's longing for the transcendent God and His supernal beauty—a longing that draws man out of himself towards his divine exemplar and relativizes earthly desires by placing them in a greater context—finds no oxygen, no flame, no kindling. God's

---

[200] See Pontifical Council for Culture, «*Via Pulchritudinis*».

[201] Later chapters will return to the dangers of emotionalism in church music.

[202] Here is the bare-bones argument: Those things that communicate or constrain Catholic beauty have an effect for good or for ill on the spiritual life of married couples; we have lost the things that communicate Catholic beauty and added things that constrain it; therefore, there has been an evil effect on the spiritual life of married couples. The liturgical reform is a contributing cause to the breakdown of marriage and family in the last half-century; it must therefore be resisted and supplanted as part of the strategy of renewal. For detailed arguments, see Kwasniewski, *Ministers of Christ* and other works.

providential plan of a mutually reinforcing escalation in which our ability to recognize and resonate with the beautiful in nature and in human persons is awakened and energized by our being steeped in the beautiful in divine worship and vice versa can take effect only if there is the requisite beauty to be immersed in. The spread of body piercing, prolific tattoos, and other forms of mutilation and defacement seem to show that, as a culture, we are blind to the simple beauty of the human body and deaf to the reality of the human spirit. How can this defective consciousness not affect the most natural of all relationships, that of man and woman, in which the body and the spirit are uniquely interwoven? One is reminded of the words of *Gaudium et Spes* in one of its less woolly moments: *Creatura enim sine Creatore evanescit. . . . Per oblivionem Dei ipsa creatura obscuratur.* "For without the Creator, the creature disappears. . . . When God is forgotten, the creature itself is darkened" (no. 36).

Music for the Eucharistic Sacrifice

The most common argument I've heard over the years for why we should allow Christian "pop" music in Church is the consequentialist or utilitarian argument: "Look how well it works. It gets people to Mass and keeps the youth involved." Interestingly, I've never heard a Catholic try to defend the folksy or pop-style music on purely artistic or liturgical grounds, and only rarely have I seen Protestants try to do that. The baseline for the entire discussion seems to be a rough-and-ready pragmatism.

The problem with this argument is twofold. First, even on a practical level, it's not really true, or very unevenly so. The number of Catholics attending Mass is in steady decline and has been for decades, *especially* in the category of young people. The music we have cobbled together after the Council just doesn't seem to be *so* appealing, broadly speaking, that it can staunch the bleeding or turn the tide. It seems to put off at least as many people as the number it may appeal to.

Second, and more importantly, a popular style of music, complete with guitars and pianos and that unmistakable rock-ballad or easy listening feel, is not at all compatible with the Church's understanding of the Mass as a true and proper sacrifice offered to God. Let's admit (for the sake of argument) that we could pack a building full of people by using that kind of music. Would this music be able to *convey* to the worshipers what the Mass actually *is*, how they should be disposed to it, and how they should think of what they are doing? Or would it subtly or openly inculcate a different doctrine that would eventually result in heterodoxy?

It must be recalled that the issues we are dealing with today are by no means peculiar to our time but arise in one form or another during any period of history in which secular music exercises an undue influence on the music of the Church. Pope Pius XII's encyclical on the sacred liturgy *Mediator Dei*—a major source for *Sacrosanctum Concilium*—offers us luminous insights on the topic at hand. In the pages that follow we will comment on a number of germane passages.

> 47. The entire liturgy, therefore, has the Catholic faith for its content, inasmuch as it bears public witness to the faith of the Church.

Note well: the *entire* liturgy has *the Catholic faith* for its content. This entirety, then, includes the music of the liturgy, in both its words and its strictly musical attributes. Pius XII is saying that the texts, melodies, rhythms, *all* of these should bear public witness to the Church's faith. It comes as no surprise that Pius X, Pius XI, Pius XII, Vatican II, John Paul II, and Benedict XVI pointed to Gregorian chant and polyphony as pinnacles of this public witness, and underlined the need for new compositions to imitate the spirit of these exemplars.

> 68. The august sacrifice of the altar, then, is no mere empty commemoration of the passion and death of Jesus Christ, but a true and proper act of sacrifice, whereby the High Priest by an unbloody immolation offers Himself a most acceptable victim to the Eternal Father, as He did upon the cross. "It is one and the same victim; the same person now offers it by the ministry of His priests, who then offered Himself on the cross, the manner of offering alone being different" (Council of Trent).

The Mass is not a social gathering with a humanitarian aim, it is not even a symbolic drama in which we play-act the death of Jesus. It is a true and proper sacrifice, the unbloody re-presentation of the sacrifice of Calvary.

Our Lord Jesus Christ's once-for-all immolation on the Cross is made present and active for us sinners, who would otherwise be lost forever. He comes to be present in this awe-filled, world-changing, life-shaking, heaven-rending sacrifice. For our part, do we appreciate what is happening on the altar? Do our actions, attitudes, responses, artistic expressions, accurately convey our interior awareness of this great mystery, before which we should fall in self-abnegation, profound humility, trembling adoration? Or does the music (for example) lead us to feel, think, and act as if this mystery and miracle were not taking place?

> 152. While the sacred liturgy calls to mind the mysteries of Jesus Christ, it strives to make all believers take their part in them so that the divine Head of the mystical Body may live in all the members with the fullness of His holiness. Let the souls of Christians be like altars on each one of which a different phase of the sacrifice, offered by the High Priest, comes to life again, as it were: pains and tears which wipe away and expiate sin; supplication to God which pierces heaven; dedication and even immolation of oneself made promptly, generously, and earnestly; and, finally, that intimate union by which we commit ourselves and all we have to God, in whom we find our rest. "The perfection of religion is to imitate whom you adore" (St. Augustine).

Does our music convey that we are falling down in worship before the all-holy Lord, the God of heaven and earth—the serving of whom leads to eternal life, the offending of whom leads to eternal death? And is this God a fearful mystery for us, present in our midst, or has He been domesticated into a kind of friendly ambiance within which our self-referential ceremonies take place? Are the souls of the people like altars of immolation? Is the unspeakably pure and demanding holiness of God the dominant note of what we are doing and singing?

> 188. Three characteristics of which Our predecessor Pius X spoke should adorn all liturgical services: sacredness, which abhors any profane influence; nobility, which true and genuine arts should

serve and foster; and universality, which, while safeguarding local and legitimate custom, reveals the catholic unity of the Church.

We must admit it: when reading these words of Pius XII, it is as if we are looking at another *world*, not just another decade or era. When is the last time you have met someone who is concerned to "abhor any profane influence"? Catholics today readily compromise their faith, morals, and worship by embracing the latest fashions rather than rejecting worldly poison. Far from abhorring the profane, they court it, welcome it, and submit to it, making what ought to be a badge of shame into the boast of a new identity and mission. Indeed, a popular (though at least partially exaggerated) interpretation of Vatican II presents it as the moment when the Church finally welcomed the world into her bosom and discarded, once and for all, the ascetical divide between sacred and secular: there was to be no such thing as *sacred* liturgy, because all the world is our new liturgy, all of it is blessed by God, and the Church has only to listen, learn, and adapt herself to man in order to bring forth Christ in him. Man is always already in Christ, and he needs only to be made aware of that dignity. Such is the cartoon-version *nouvelle théologie* that made the rounds.[203]

When is the last time you have heard "nobility" put forward as the general description of the aim of human arts and skills, when these are brought into the service of God? Nobility—the pursuit of the utmost excellence, tasteful beauty, integrated virtue—should be the single word that captures the essence of the Catholic attitude and mentality, the single word that should sum up the tone of seminary education in catechetics, homiletics, dogmatics, morals, and, above all, liturgy. It is, unfortunately, hard to resist the impression that the cult of the ugly, the compromise of the ignoble, and the toleration of the casual and the slipshod are instead the prevailing traits.

Last but not least, is there universality still left when the ever-malleable and evolving popular inculturated liturgy, burdened by compulsory "optionitis,"[204] makes every community one visits a new sociological experiment as to the meaning of "Catholic" in this or that town, diocese, or country?

---

[203] See Kwasniewski, "Karl Rahner and the Unspoken Framework of (Much of) Modern Theology."
[204] See Kwasniewski, "Indeterminacy and Optionitis."

As a friend pointed out to me, many Catholics have no assurance of either universality or stability: even if their parish has done the liturgy nobly and beautifully for many years, the whole thing can be undone overnight by the next cleric in charge—and, regrettably, almost all of the unwanted changes, deformations, reductions, cancellations, modifications, and novelties can be justified in the name of some permission or other. Let us be clear about this: outside the tranquil world of the *usus antiquior* and those few communities fortunate enough to enjoy its exclusive use, there is simply no universality, and but little stability, for Catholics of the Latin rite.

> 80. It is, therefore, desirable, Venerable Brethren, that all the faithful should be aware that to participate in the Eucharistic Sacrifice is their chief duty and supreme dignity, and that not in an inert and negligent fashion, giving way to distractions and day-dreaming, but with such earnestness and concentration that they may be united as closely as possible with the High Priest, according to the Apostle, "Let this mind be in you which was also in Christ Jesus" (Phil 2:5). And together with Him and through Him let them make their oblation, and in union with Him let them offer up themselves.

Magnificent words! The "chief duty and supreme dignity" of the Christian is "to participate in the Eucharistic Sacrifice." Our chief duty and supreme dignity is not social work; it is not evangelization or catechesis or education; it is not political activism; it is not breaking down barriers of prejudice; it is not the defense of human rights. Our dignity consists above all in worshiping the true God at His holy altar—and making of ourselves an oblation that is pleasing to Him by attaching ourselves devoutly to the supreme offering of Jesus Christ the High Priest. If this is not what we are thinking and intending to do during Mass, we have *missed the entire point* of the liturgy. We are doing violence to it, abusing it, making it serve our own ends rather than serving its inherent end.

When it comes to music, in particular, we see how often the Mass is sorely abused, inasmuch as a worldly style of music not only permits but encourages "distractions and day-dreaming" that take us far away from the "earnestness and concentration" with which we should be joining ourselves to the High Priest and saving Victim. Just pondering these words of Pope

Pius XII will make us realize how many times the Mass is violently derailed from its very purpose and made to serve a human agenda that is ultimately inert and negligible.

No wonder—as many fine priests and bishops have begun openly to admit—no wonder the New Evangelization has looked so flaccid and been so fruitless. We spend much time talking among ourselves about how to make Christianity appealing, attractive, relevant, meaningful, but we neglect the single most important thing that we are called to do as Christians: worshiping the Lord in the beauty of holiness and receiving from Him, through our Catholic Tradition, the sacred, noble, universal, and stable forms by which we are to order ourselves and the whole of creation back to their primal font and glorious end. Whenever and wherever Catholics have committed themselves wholeheartedly to this program—and for its own sake, because God is worthy of it!—the propagation of the Gospel has taken place quietly, irresistibly, with a joy that is not of this world.

We have seen how the truths expounded by Pius XII in *Mediator Dei* necessitate that everything we do and make for the liturgy, especially music, be in full accord with its inherent nature and qualities, if we expect God to be pleased with what we offer and our own sanctification to result. What about the *interior* attitude of the worshiping Christian?

> 81. It is quite true that Christ is a priest; but He is a priest not for Himself but for us, when in the name of the whole human race He offers our prayers and religious homage to the eternal Father; He is also a victim for us, since He substitutes Himself for sinful man. Now the exhortation of the Apostle, "Let this mind be in you which was also in Christ Jesus," requires that all Christians should possess, as far as is humanly possible, the same dispositions as those which the divine Redeemer had when He offered Himself in sacrifice: that is to say, they should, in a humble attitude of mind, pay adoration, honor, praise, and thanksgiving to the supreme majesty of God. Moreover, it means that they must assume to some extent the character of a victim, that they deny themselves as the Gospel commands, that freely and of their own accord they do penance and that each detests and satisfies for his sins. It means, in a word, that

we must all undergo with Christ a mystical death on the cross so that we can apply to ourselves the words of St. Paul, "With Christ I am nailed to the cross" (Gal 2:19).

Emphasis on Christ as Priest and Victim is rarely met with today, and yet, there is no way to understand how Our Lord saved mankind except by reference to the sanguinary redemption by which He purchased for us forgiveness of every sin, eternal life, and the outpouring of the Holy Spirit, which brings with it all the means necessary to be holy in this world.

In short, we owe *everything we are* and *everything we do* as Christians to Christ's perfect oblation on the Cross. The Mass was given to us precisely to place us in mind of, in the presence of, *and in real contact with* this saving mystery of love. Our mystical participation in it is the wellspring of our life and the pattern to which we are conformed.

If our experience of the Mass and its "externals" seems to say to us little or nothing of the "religious homage" offered to the eternal Father by Jesus Christ, the high priest of our confession and victim for our sins; if it does not cultivate in us *explicit* acts of "adoration, honor, praise, and thanksgiving to the supreme majesty of God" (including the very consciousness of His majesty!); if it does not lead us ever deeper into the sacrificial death of Christ so that we understand ourselves to be, *and desire ourselves to be*, victims with him in a "mystical death on the cross," then one might well wonder whether it is serving its supernatural purpose at all. For sure, the mystery is still present if the consecration is valid, but are *we* present to the mystery? Has the liturgy, have the texts, ceremonies, music, and other elements, made us present to the Lord, Priest and Victim, as they are meant to do?

> 100. . . . While we stand before the altar, then, it is our duty so to transform our hearts, that every trace of sin may be completely blotted out, while whatever promotes supernatural life through Christ may be zealously fostered and strengthened even to the extent that, in union with the immaculate Victim, we become a victim acceptable to the eternal Father.

The liturgy is supposed to develop our "supernatural life through Christ," which has its root in our *interior life*. The "interior man," the "new Adam" in us, needs to be *cultivated*—his existence is caused by baptism, certainly, and he receives new powers at confirmation, but his growth and maturation cannot be taken for granted and will not happen automatically. The old Adam will take over again and reign supreme if we do not take seriously "the duty to transform our hearts" until we become "a victim acceptable to the eternal Father." The liturgy itself ought to be such as will cultivate our interiority, our inner life, our genuine awareness and desire for spiritual goods, for the heavenly fatherland. I am reminded of a passage in *Veritatis Splendor* where, speaking of the search for the meaning of life, John Paul II observes, "This is in fact the aspiration at the heart of every human decision and action, the quiet searching and interior prompting which sets freedom in motion" (no. 7).

A richly filled and ordered space for "quiet searching and interior prompting": this is what the traditional Roman liturgy provided and still provides with a special abundance. The music of our worship, too, should promote this intimate searching for God, the fundamental motivation of the inner man, in a way that is perhaps initially disquieting as it displaces us from our worldly assumptions and expectations.

> 101. In fact, the prescriptions of the sacred liturgy aim, by every means at their disposal, at helping the Church to bring about this most holy purpose in the most suitable manner possible. This is the object not only of readings, homilies and other sermons given by priests, as also the whole cycle of mysteries which are proposed for our commemoration in the course of the year, but it is also the purpose of vestments, of sacred rites and their external splendor. All these things aim at "enhancing the majesty of this great sacrifice, and raising the minds of the faithful by means of these visible signs of religion and piety to the contemplation of the sublime truths contained in this sacrifice" (Council of Trent, Sess. 22, c. 5).

A failure to "raise the minds of the faithful . . . to the contemplation of the sublime truths contained in this sacrifice" is not just an incidental problem or marginal mistake; it is something close to a total liturgical disaster, a failure to prepare the faithful to take part worthily in the Lord's sacrifice and to approach Communion with the proper dispositions. It is therefore a failure to build up the Body of Christ in such a way that the Mass will actually *benefit* the particular members of the Church *ex opere operantis*, by their very acts of "adoration, honor, praise, and thanksgiving to the supreme majesty of God." In short, it saps the strength, disturbs the order, and hinders the mission of the Church Militant.

The attitude, the dispositions, the state of mind and heart of the Christian worshiper as described by Pope Pius XII imply a significant responsibility on the part of clergy and church musicians to offer the liturgy in such a way that these goods can be genuinely fostered in the Church. May we do our part, be it big or little, as cleric, religious, or layman, to put into practice the vocation of adoring love to which Our Lord has summoned us. We must evaluate liturgical music and all other aspects of our public worship in light of the truth that "the entire liturgy . . . has the Catholic faith for its content" and that this content includes, as one of its most precious components, the mystery of the awesome sacrifice of Calvary made present in the Most Holy Eucharist. The teaching of *Mediator Dei* helps us to discern the kinds of music most suitable for the humbling and exalted honor of assisting at and sharing in this divine offering, this "work of God."

14

Driving the Musical Merchants
Out of the House of Prayer

WHY ARE TRADITIONAL Catholics opposed to the use of guitars for church music? Why, in general, do we think that a popular, contemporary musical style is incompatible with the spirit of the liturgy? I take as my point of departure the following words of Saint Paul: "Do not model your behaviour on the contemporary world, but let the renewing of your minds transform you, so that you may discern for yourselves what is the will of God—what is good and acceptable and mature" (Rom 12:2).[205]

My basic objection to the popular idiom of guitar music in church, whether the tunes are sentimental or snappy, is that it is nothing other than a conforming of our minds to a secular age, to the artistic, psychological, and spiritual standards of our times.[206] It resembles the sound of Bob Dylan and Billy Joel—though such "folksy" singers seem straight-laced in comparison with the noise pollution, the grinding violence and abject sensuality, of the music many now listen to recreationally.

It is as if the mass-marketed "rock anthem" is implicitly recognized as a new standard of excellence, to which even music for the worship of God must be conformed. God, too, must be wooed by a streetlamp lover; he has to be cajoled and whined at about sin and grace, much as a popular singer cajoles and whines about whatever cause is in the air—the Vietnam

---

[205] As rendered in the NJB, capturing well the air of challenge. The RSV renders it: "Do not be conformed to this world but be transformed by the renewal of your mind, that you may prove what is the will of God, what is good and acceptable and perfect."
[206] This assessment is made frequently by Joseph Ratzinger: see, e.g., *Feast of Faith*, 97–126; *New Song for the Lord*, 111–27; *Spirit of the Liturgy*, Pt. 3, ch. 2, "Music and Liturgy." A fine summary of his principal arguments is given in Michael J. Miller's "Cardinal Ratzinger on Liturgical Music."

war, Third World poverty, the AIDS epidemic. The sound has to gesture towards the misty-eyed ballad or the happy-cat hop. However one may describe the music, its origin and likeness to secular forms is unmistakable.

This is not the first time we have faced this problem in the history of the Church's liturgical music. The last great epidemic of musical secularism was the age of opera, lasting through the eighteenth and nineteenth centuries, when nearly all church music was dashed off in strict operatic style, a hardly-disguised relative of the moralizing epics and predictable romances played out on the stage night after night when the audience assembled mainly to hear the gorgeous voices of the lead tenor or soprano.

When Pope Pius X sought the reform of church music, he had in mind principally its *resacralization*, its recovery from the worldliness of opera. He wanted to restore a music that was crafted *for the church* and *for her liturgy*, a tranquil and soul-searching music that channels attention not to performers but to divine mysteries, fostering an atmosphere of contemplative prayer—a music of many moods and modes, gently and subtly playing upon the emotions, yet always at the service of something greater than itself, something *essentially non-emotional*: the "rational worship" (*logikē latreia*) of which Saint Paul speaks in the letter to the Romans (12:1). For Paul, the "true circumcision" belongs to those who "worship God in spirit, and glory in Christ Jesus, and put no confidence in the flesh" (Phil 3:3).

The point is this: although our baptized bodies are the temple of the Holy Spirit (cf. 1 Cor 6:19; 2 Cor 6:16) and we are to worship the Lord with heart *and* voice (cf. Ps 83:3), our worship is not at the level of body, it is not a sensual moving and being-moved but a spiritual sacrifice and adoration supported by a well-disciplined body whose passions are chastened, whose emotions are purified.

Truly Catholic sacred music has the power to move us, in accord with the dignified "dance" of the liturgy, to an ever-higher love of the Lord with our heart, mind, soul, and strength. It is thus a humble instrument of man's divinization, his becoming God-like in grace and charity. Music should help, or at least not hinder, the progressive maturation of the soul in her journey through the Teresian mansions, in her arduous ascent of Mount Carmel, up to the summit, the transforming union, the mystical marriage.[207]

---

[207] See, for a lucid account of the stages of prayer, Thomas Dubay's *Fire Within*.

Music that remains stylistically at the level of sensuality, thereby stimulating and feeding "everyday" emotions within the souls of its listeners, is not music fit for divine worship, because it does not help the soul to mature in spiritual dignity, it does not purify the passions and elevate the mind to a more heavenly plane of existence. Indeed, a casual, talkative style of celebrating Mass coupled with a popular musical idiom will give rise to a stunted psyche, an artificially prolonged adolescence of the emotions, out of keeping with the spiritual perfection the Lord intends to impart through the sacred rites and mystic sacraments of the Church.[208] It does not provide the optimal environment for that quieting of the heart, that subsiding of the hyperactive will, which Saint Teresa of Avila sees as an indispensable preparation for the trials and blessings God has in store for souls who persevere through the first three mansions. The soul, she says, has to grow more and more *receptive*, not getting caught up in a sort of mental activism that makes it nearly impossible for the God who speaks with a "still, small voice" (cf. 1 Kgs 19:12) to act sovereignly, on His own initiative.

The Christian has to develop a heightened capacity for waiting and listening, for welcoming and receiving, and finally, please God, for surrendering to His delicate invasion into the soul, to bask in the warmth of His light. Gregorian chant and Byzantine chant, the polyphony and homophony they inspired, and modern sacred music wrought in the same tradition have the necessary qualities of sacredness, artistic excellence, and universality that the Church's authentic liturgy itself possesses and demands. Nothing secular, banal, superficial, or noisy is worthy of the "divine, holy, pure, immortal, heavenly, life-creating and awesome mysteries of Christ."[209]

Another way of seeing the same point is to recognize, as the Western tradition has done for more than two thousand years, that music is a kind of language *in and of itself.* Words *added* to music give it an additional character or communicative scope, but music as such is already a language that speaks to the human soul. As Josef Pieper reminds us, "music does not

---

[208] On the irreducible *sacredness* of the rite of Mass and what this implies for liturgical praxis (particularly in contrast to the ever-growing trend of "secularization" observable after the Council), see Pazat de Lys, "Towards a New Liturgical Movement."

[209] From the Divine Liturgy of Saint John Chrysostom.

speak of things but tells of weal and woe."[210] It speaks a certain message, or better, creates an atmosphere; it conveys an implicit worldview, stirs up feelings, evokes chains of ideas. By itself it cannot convey a *particular* message with the finely-chiseled precision of words, but neither is it amorphous and without power to communicate deeply what is in the bones and blood of its maker—or, at any rate, what he has the ability to plant within it by an act of imaginative sympathy.[211]

But it is not only the immediate composer of the music that matters. What is far more decisive is the style he inherits from his teachers, his models, his contemporaries, his era. Just as one cannot change meanings of words at random if one expects to speak to others, so one cannot just invent an altogether new musical language from scratch.[212] The basic language and its many distinctive dialects are already there, to be unconsciously internalized or consciously exploited. A piece of music carries with it and conveys not only what its maker may be thinking and feeling but the thoughts and feelings of the culture out of which the musical style or its elements emerged.

So, if one takes a folksy Bob Dylan tune, with guitar accompaniment, and substitutes Christian lyrics for the anti-war screed that might equally well have suited the music, is one really producing a work of *Christian* art—or is it rather a hybrid of a thoroughly secularized musical language with a textual veneer of Christian sentiments? The *underlying language*, the one that most

---

[210] Citing (with approval, in this case) Schopenhauer; see Pieper, "Thoughts about Music," 42. Herbert McCabe has an arresting comment along these lines: "Poetry is language trying to be bodily experience, as music is bodily experience trying to be language." *God Matters*, 131.

[211] I say this because one finds a great composer like Gabriel Fauré, who was agnostic, writing one of the most beautiful modern settings of the Requiem Mass. This he could do because his training and his talent enabled him to enter into a religious framework and follow its conventions. The result is a work that has power to activate a deeply religious response. For reasons given at the end of chapter 1, it actually matters more *how an artist is trained* than it does whether he has good motives, a pious attitude. A devout Christian trained as a musician nowadays runs a much greater risk of producing mediocre or even spiritually debilitating products than an agnostic from one hundred years ago. This is because the intellectual virtue of art is one that is acquired by dint of really hard work based on "cultural capital." If you take away the capital, the power to invest falls away; the results are of little substance.

[212] Arnold Schoenberg attempted it; the results are known to all. For a fuller account, see Kwasniewski, "Anton Bruckner, Sacred Tonality, and Parsifal's Redemption."

shapes the soul, is the *musical* language. In the familiar sayings:"talk is cheap" and words "go in one ear and out the other." Music is rich, its influence powerful, its resonance in the body long-lasting, almost "hard-wired." The living body reacts more spontaneously to the *music* than to the *words*.

I have seen firsthand young Christian students of charismatic persuasion playing "secular" music in their rooms and then singing "religious" music in church, yet the two types of music to a large extent *overlap* as far as the musical language is concerned—that is to say, both are secular *music*, though the lyrics of the latter are religious. In other words, the atmosphere of church and liturgy and prayer suffers pollution or infection from the antinomian atmosphere of Woodstock, the sing-alongs of a carefree beach party, the cool chords of a smoky bar. And it hardly needs to be added that the *manner* in which the "music ministers" in question sing and play their instruments—a manner untrained, rough-edged, sliding and slurring from note to note, without sensitivity, subtlety, or purity of tone—perfectly fits the musical language, which, as music history shows, originated in a worldly revolt against a religiously animated high culture.

We would not want (I hope) the aesthetic of billboards or the architecture of a supermarket for our churches, yet many welcome and even celebrate their equivalents in music. The only reason this can happen at all is that music affects our judgment more than any other art; we do not become blind to visual beauty as quickly as we become deaf to audible beauty. Music goes more deeply into the soul, into its passions and emotions; it affects us at the intersection of spirit and flesh, it gets "under the skin," it goes into the very sense-appetites and shapes them by motion, by repetition. Just as the habits of virtue or vice are formed in the sense-appetites by repeated action, so too are certain habits formed in the same appetites by repeated sensual stimulation. What we listen to does not remain "outside" of us but enters *into* us and changes our way of feeling, reacting, perceiving. That means we cannot help being affected morally by long-term exposure to any kind of music.[213] The music will make our passions—and through the passions, our souls and our selves—*like unto itself*. Conversely, people gravitate toward music that most reflects or voices their conscious and unconscious

---

[213] See Cole, *Music and Morals*.

preoccupations or expectations. Those who are longing for transcendence and for eternal beauty will seek a music that somehow gives expression to this longing, this transcendence.

We are also confronted by a problem peculiar to our age: it is easier to grow up today without experiences of beautiful music—be it chant or Palestrina, Bach or Beethoven, Debussy or Pärt—than it is to grow up without experiences of visual beauty. Objects of sight are readily available, the beauties of nature and of culture are abundantly distributed. As a teacher, I have seen, to my great dismay, that many young adults have never tasted even once the glories of well-composed secular *or* sacred music; it is a realm that practically does not exist for them. Listening to Handel or Brahms for the first time at the age of twenty is as difficult as learning a foreign language from scratch; it would have been far better for the children to have been immersed in the music of such great composers from the time of their infancy. Nevertheless, I have also seen, as a teacher of music appreciation, that anyone can acquire education and good taste in music. It is never too late.

Traditional church music is derived from and indebted to sacred precedents: Christian plainchant was born out of Hebrew chanting of the psalms, Renaissance polyphony grew out of plainchant (when singing a motet by Palestrina you can *feel* the Gregorian influence upon every line), Baroque styles emerged from Renaissance ones; and it is clear how the energetic nineteenth-century revival of chant and polyphony—a movement encouraged by popes and bishops—restored to the liturgy a dignity and serenity lacking in the period dominated by a florid operatic style, with its bombast and superficiality.

Although not always successful in preventing their influence, the Church has always been suspicious of styles that evolved *outside of* the temple, in secular entertainments. In fact, the word "profane" means "outside the threshold of the temple." This category includes useful but essentially non-sacred genres like drinking songs for the tavern, marching songs for the battlefield, and romantic songs for wooers and wooed.

Particular specimens of these types of music had a more or less direct influence on Church music from time to time, but efforts were made either to prevent this from happening or to purge the borrowings of any distracting reminders of "vulgar" life. The reason is simple. As the faithful sing in

the Divine Liturgy of Saint John Chrysostom: "Let us who mystically represent the Cherubim and sing the thrice-holy hymn to the life-creating Trinity now set aside all earthly cares." Or, as Saint Thomas observes, apropos of
the Roman rite of Mass:

> In this sacrament [of the Eucharist] both a *greater* devotion is
> required than in the other sacraments, owing to the fact that the
> whole Christ is contained in it, and also a *more extensive* devo-
> tion, because in this sacrament the devotion of the whole people
> is required, for whom the sacrifice is offered, and not only the
> devotion of those receiving the sacrament, as in the other sacra-
> ments. And for this reason, as Cyprian says (*On the Lord's Prayer,*
> ch. 31), "The priest, saying the preface, prepares the minds of the
> brethren, by saying: 'Lift up your hearts,' in order that, when the
> people respond: 'We have lifted them up to the Lord,' they may be
> reminded that they should think on nothing other than God."[214]

The liturgy of the Mass ought to stir up so deep and wide a devotion in
the people, as befits so great a sacrifice, that we may think on nothing other
than God! In this life we cannot emulate the cherubim perfectly, so as to be
perpetually caught up in the heavenly liturgy; *some* earthly thoughts and
emotions will cling to us. But the Church has always voiced her protest
whenever composers and musicians allow those earthly thoughts and emotions to set up camp inside the temple and dominate the scene.

Inspired by Jesus's teaching, nourished by His life-giving Body and
Blood, our calling as Christians is to bring holiness *from* the altar *into* the
world and, as much as we can, to transform the world, renew it, sanctify it
by the power of the sacred mysteries. Christians have never seen it as their
duty to bring elements of the fallen world *from* the outside *into* the temple,
remaking liturgy, preaching, and art forms into reflections of *that* world.
For even if they are "toned-down" reflections, still they have their origin not
from God but from the world, and they carry worldliness with them. Might
there not be a connection between, on the one hand, postconciliar attempts
to replace the hierarchical nature of the Church with a democratic model

---

[214] *ST* III, Q. 83, art. 4, ad 5.

borrowed from Enlightenment humanism and, on the other hand, the decline in the quality of sacred and religious music, which now celebrates man instead of God, and only really succeeds in showing the banality and poverty of man without God?[215]

If we want to know how the Psalms or other texts from Scripture should be sung, we should listen to the successors of the Israelites chanting the Hebrew "songs of Sion"—namely, the faithful monks and nuns who have committed their lives to "singing wisely" (cf. Ps 46:8). An attentive ear can hear the musical parallels between Jewish cantillation and Christian psalmody, whether Latin or Byzantine.[216] If you listen to a recording of the monks of Le Barroux, Fontgombault, Norcia, or Heiligenkreuz, you will hear the sound of *sung prayer*—reverent, adoring, and contemplative, savoring the sacred words like honey (cf. Ps 118:103), with passions at peace and the mind lifted up to heaven and to the Most Holy Trinity.

Eaten up with zeal (see Jn 2:17), Jesus drove the money changers out of the temple precincts, even though what they were doing was a good bit *less* objectionable than much of what goes on in the very sanctuary of Catholic churches today. Why did Our Lord, gentle as He was with sinners, act that way? It is because Christ, more than any worshiper who has ever lived or ever will live, knows the importance of purity of worship, the need to keep a separation between the worldly and the sacred. He alone felt and knew to the depths of His uncreated being how unworthy of the living God were the motives, manners, and merchandise offered by those businessmen.

When a person enters the temple, he puts behind him the business and pleasures of the world and strives to worship God with his whole heart, his whole mind, his whole soul. And this wholeness of dedication and

---

[215] See Ratzinger, "Image of the World and of Human Beings."

[216] A friend pointed out to me that "Vietnamese Catholics sing hymns with resemblances to Vietnamese Buddhists' chanting of the Pali scriptures" and suggested that perhaps Christian forms can and do arise from non-Christian ones—or sacred from secular. In response, I noted that one could similarly point out that the *L'homme armé* Masses (of which there are over a hundred, written by some of the greatest Renaissance composers) were set to the tune of a soldiers' pub song. It *is* possible to take something from the surrounding world and sacralize it. The key is *how* to do this. It seems that the Renaissance composers worked a sort of magic spell on the song to make it suitable as a *cantus firmus*. If you listen to Du Fay's setting, you cannot hear anything reminiscent of a pub anymore. A process of absorption and purification has taken place.

devotion is supposed to spill over from the temple into the world so that the more a person worships, the more he is conformed to the mysteries he celebrates, bringing the aura, echo, and fragrance of their beauty into his secular pursuits. The goal is not to secularize the sacred and make it more "accessible" to the mentality of the age (this would border on sacrilege) but rather to sanctify the secular by ordering *it* to God.[217] A consecrated church building is the domain of the sacred, not the home for an adapted, accommodated worldliness. The Church is supposed to win our minds and hearts for the sacred so that this victory may permeate the rest of our lives in the world. "Christian rock," or even the mild folksy style of the St. Louis Jesuits, is nothing less than a victory of worldliness, a byproduct of unresisted cultural imperialism, a contamination of the silence and plainsong that should reign in the house of God, where the spirit breathes freely and the emotions are gently stilled.

Many books and articles have been written on ecclesiastical guidelines for music intended for worship and on the noble ideal of *singing the Mass*, not merely singing *at* Mass—doing so, moreover, in continuity with the glorious heritage of sacred music that the Spirit of the Lord has breathed into His Church down through the centuries. Here, I wish only to suggest a good starting point for an "examination of musical conscience" that may lead to a change of heart, to new resolutions and concrete initiatives. Session 22 of the Council of Trent challenges us to do all that we can to make our offering of the liturgy worthy of its inner nature:

> What great care is to be taken that the holy sacrifice of the Mass be celebrated with all religious devotion and reverence, each one may easily conceive who considers that in the sacred writings he is called accursed who does the work of God negligently (Jer 48:10). And since we must confess that no other work can be performed by the faithful that is so holy and divine as this awe-inspiring mystery, wherein that life-giving victim by which we are reconciled to the Father is daily immolated on the altar by priests, it is also sufficiently clear that all effort and attention must be directed to the end

---

[217] See Kwasniewski, *Ministers of Christ*, 65–102.

that it be performed with the greatest possible interior cleanness and purity of heart and exterior evidence of devotion and piety.[218]

In particular, bishops are asked to "banish from the churches all such music which, whether by the organ or in the singing, contains things that are lascivious or impure."[219] Those who know about *Renaissance organ music*, even of a purely secular character, will readily understand that what the Fathers of Trent were up against was as nothing compared to the invasion of musical profanity that has descended on most Western parishes today.

Such words call us to rethink and deepen our conceptions of musical and liturgical fittingness. When all is said and done, we still hear Saint Paul calling out to us across the ages, with the Fathers of the Church, with the Council of Trent, with Saint Pius X, with Benedict XVI: "Do not model your behaviour on the contemporary world, but let the renewing of your minds transform you, so that you may discern for yourselves what is the will of God—what is good and acceptable and mature" (Rom 12:2, NJB). We must drive the musical merchants of modernity out of the Father's house of prayer—not only in the temple of God, without a doubt, but also in the temple of our lives, in our souls and bodies redeemed by the Blood of Christ and dwelt in by His Spirit.[220]

---

[218] *The Canons and Decrees of the Council of Trent*, 150.
[219] *Canons and Decrees*, 151.
[220] See Mt 21:12–13, Mk 11:15–18, Lk 19:45–46, 1 Pt 1:19, 1 Cor 3:16.

15

Traditional Sacred Music versus "Contemporary Worship Music"

WHENEVER THE POPES speak about sacred (i.e., liturgical) music, the first quality they put forward is holiness or sanctity, which they describe as worthiness of or suitability for the celebration of the sacred mysteries of Christ, and freedom from worldliness or even that which is suggestive of the secular domain. The Fathers of the Council of Trent frowned upon the use of secular melodies even when transformed into the style of sacred music, and Pius X fought valiantly against the influence of Italian opera. It was not that such music was not good as far as the rules of composition were concerned; it was that the music carried strong associations with celebrating the goods of this life and not the heavenly goods of the life to come. If the musical style is borrowed from the outside world and brought into the temple, it profanes the liturgy and harms the spiritual progress of the faithful.

Liturgical music should not only *be* but also *seem* to be exclusively connected with and consecrated to the liturgy of the Church. It is not enough for a type of music to have been written for the sake of performance in a church; it is crucial that it be felt or experienced as associated with divine worship.[221] To some extent, this will be a matter of cultural conditioning: some people will know more about liturgy and its panoply of fine arts than others. But as followers of Jesus Christ, the incarnate Word who extends His real presence throughout space and time, we acknowledge as a principle of faith that there are hallowed traditions of prayer, ceremonial, and music, slowly matured over many centuries, that practically "cry out" Catholicism—signs that identify us and bind us to each other and to Our Lord. Over the course of more than

---

[221] To use the language of the moral theologians, a good intention is not enough; the act must also be right in kind as well as in its circumstances.

three decades of experience singing in a variety of churches and settings, I have been astonished by the way in which Catholics, even relatively unchurched or uncatechized ones, immediately recognize Gregorian chant as distinctively Catholic and, more often than not, appreciate some presence of it in the liturgy.

The reason Gregorian chant is held up as the supreme model of sacred music and the normative music of the Roman rite is not far to seek. It is music that grew up together with the liturgy, fraternal twins from the cradle. It is the musical vesture of the words of divine worship, the servant of its actions. Its exclusive function is to clothe in music God's holy words to us, and our words to Him and about Him; it has no other realm or purpose.[222] When we hear chant, there is no ambiguity or ambivalence about what it is or what it is for; it breathes the spirit of the liturgy and cannot be mistaken for secular music in any way. Something similar is true about the pipe organ, which, after one thousand years of nearly exclusive use in churches, is so completely bound up with the ecclesiastical sphere that its sound equates with "churchliness" in the ears of most people.[223] The long line of popes who have commented on sacred music maintain that these strong and deep associations are good and important.

It follows that music with a "double identity," music that involves teleological and tropological ambiguity, is problematic. Many contemporary church songs are nothing other than religiously-themed pop songs, as one can see by examining the chord sequences, the shape of the melody, the particular use of syncopation, the style of the singing with which it is marketed, and the ease with which percussion could be added or has been added.[224] We can develop this critique if we look at the three criteria enunciated by Pope Pius X and expounded by Pope Pius XII: holiness or sanctity, goodness of form or artistic soundness, and universality (which one might also think of as catholicity).[225]

---

[222] See chapter 8.

[223] At least in the West and in those parts of the world touched by western Christian influence—which, after the Age of Exploration, includes nearly the entire face of the earth.

[224] One might search online for the following examples: Toby Mac, "Me Without You"; Robin Mark, "Days of Elijah"; Darrell Evans, "Trading My Sorrows"; Michael Card, "My Shepherd"; Matt Maher, "Lord, I Need You" and "Kyrie"; Hillsong, "Oceans."

[225] Pius X's *Tra le Sollecitudini* (1903) and Pius XII's *Musicae Sacrae* (1955) take up

Holiness

Sacred music is not to have any reminiscences of secular music, either in itself or in the manner in which it is performed. Consider this thought experiment: play a random sampling of contemporary American church music for someone who does not speak English, and ask (in his own language, of course) what he thinks the songs are all about. He might reasonably assume that they were secular love songs. A different way of running the same experiment: take the same piece of music, substitute lyrics about falling in love or world peace, and see if the words are incongruous with the musical style. In contrast, think of the absurdity of singing such lyrics to the music of a Gregorian chant, Palestrina's "Sicut cervus," a Bach chorale, or Duruflé's "Ubi caritas."[226]

Moreover, the instrumentation and technique all by itself, with the use of strummed guitars and/or piano, strongly conveys the atmosphere of secular music, since these instruments originated in, and are still associated with, a variety of styles that have in common their *extra-ecclesiastical nature*: the Romantic concert-hall repertoire, jazz, early rock, country, and contemporary folk. The style of popular Christian singing is one of its biggest problems. The voice slides from pitch to pitch, with the scooping and warbling that derive from jazz and pop styles. In its origins, this manner of singing was intended to be a more passionate, "realistic" style, as opposed to the highly trained and therefore "artificial" voices of operatic singers. But it is no less opposed to the pure tone and lucid harmony aimed at in polyphonic ensembles and the tranquil unanimity aimed at in unison chanting, both of which symbolize the unity and catholicity of the Church.

---

these points most explicitly, but there are numerous parallels in Pius XI, Paul VI, John Paul II, and Benedict XVI.

[226] I am aware that great composers such as Josquin des Pres and Orlando di Lasso composed secular motets in a style that would strike many listeners today as reminiscent of church music. But this, I think, points to the benign and purifying influence of Christianity at its cultural height, when all of the fine arts were affected and elevated by the noble standards set in the sacred domain. Since daily life was more of a unity, sacred and secular music were able to share a greater kinship. Bach's secular music is as well-crafted as, and with a similar aesthetic to, his sacred music. Something analogous could be said of Monteverdi, Vivaldi, Handel, or Bruckner.

Goodness of form

Generally speaking, songs in the "praise and worship" genre feature simple (at times simplistic) melodies and harmonies, and express a narrow emotional range. They are lacking or weak in the qualities that are objectively most appropriate to the liturgy and therefore also to sacred music: grandeur, majesty, dignity, loftiness, transcendence. Whatever function they may have, they do not *express or evoke* their divine subject or the human person's spiritual nature with appropriate musical means. The regular metrical beat and the predictable, sentimental melodies suggest a confinement to earthliness and the comfort of familiarity, as opposed to the free-floating word-based rhythms and the soaring, at times capricious, modal melodies of traditional chanting, which so well evoke the eternity, infinity, and "strangeness" of the divine.

If someone were to object that the Holy Eucharist is a humble sacrament, given under the signs of simple bread and wine, and that humble music, décor, and ceremonial is more appropriate than something elaborate and rich, the response would be that this is *never* the way the Church has acted, whenever she has been free to express her innermost nature. Her liturgy in the first centuries had, of necessity, to be relatively simple, since Christians were a bitterly persecuted minority who had to meet in secrecy, without shrines or temples of their own. After the legalization of Christianity by Emperor Constantine, the liturgy moved out of the homes and catacombs into great basilicas, and all of its latent doxological energies were released. The basis of the Christian cult, the Word made flesh—the splendor of the eternal Father irrupting into our world of sight, sound, taste, touch, and smell—furnished the best (indeed irresistible and illimitable) reason for incarnational worship, for outward and upward expansion in regard to its publicity, formality, solemnity, and glory. Thus, the Council of Trent declares: "Since we must confess that no other work can be performed by the faithful that is so holy and divine as this awe-inspiring mystery, wherein that life-giving Victim by which we are reconciled to the Father is daily immolated on the altar by priests, it is also sufficiently clear that all effort and attention must be directed to the end that it be performed with the greatest possible interior cleanness and purity of heart and exterior evidence of devotion and piety."[227]

John Paul II makes explicit what Trent implies: "Like the woman who anointed Jesus in Bethany, *the Church has feared no 'extravagance,'* devoting the best of her resources to expressing her wonder and adoration before the *unsurpassable gift of the Eucharist.* ... With this heightened sense of mystery, we understand how the faith of the Church in the mystery of the Eucharist has found historical expression not only in the demand for an interior disposition of devotion, but also *in outward forms* meant to evoke and emphasize the grandeur of the event being celebrated."[228]

Universality

If Pius X is correct, music that has the first two features (holiness and artistic soundness) will have a third quality, universality—it will in some way be accessible to all believers and recognizable as appropriate for the liturgy. This is the trickiest quality of the three, because some cultures are so primitive or uneducated that initially they may not have "ears" to appreciate the sanctity and beauty of a certain type of music that other Catholics already take for granted as sacred. On the other hand, Benedict XVI posits that the great music of the Western tradition has a universal power to move souls;[229] he is therefore also of the opinion that the greatest sacred music has an inherent power to speak to God-thirsting souls and to convert them to Christ. Certainly we can see in the historical record that Gregorian chant and polyphony were welcomed and taken up by peoples to whom European missionaries preached, leading to amazing examples of inculturated

---

[227] Council of Trent, Session 22, in *Canons and Decrees*, 150.

[228] John Paul II, encyclical letter *Ecclesia de Eucharistia*, nos. 48–49. See Kwasniewski, *Holy Bread of Eternal Life*, and the catena of classic texts in Bishop Athanasius Schneider's 2015 lecture at the Angelicum, "The Treasure of the Altar." One might also meditate on Raphael's famous painting, the *Disputa*, as an "icon" of how we should think about the glory and holiness of the Most Blessed Sacrament.

[229] As evidence, consider the immense enthusiasm generated around the globe by the music of composers like Bach and Mozart, some of whose best modern interpreters are Japanese, Korean, and Chinese musicians for whom Western music is a foreign import. Surely this is one of the best demonstrations of the universality of the uniquely rich heritage of music born from the fusion of Greco-Roman art with Christian culture.

but recognizably Catholic music, a blend of the European aesthetic with native colors and accents.[230]

A test for whether a style of music proposed for church is truly universal is to ask whether imposing it on a foreign country or people would be a kind of imperialism. With Gregorian chant, the answer is in the negative, because, like Latin, chant belongs to no single nation, people, period, or movement: it developed slowly from ancient times to more recent centuries, across the entire map where Christianity was planted; its composers are predominantly anonymous; it is the native musical clothing of the Latin-rite family of liturgies (something that cannot be said of polyphony, as praise-worthy as it is). In short, wherever the Latin liturgy traveled throughout the world, there too Gregorian chant traveled, and it has never been perceived as anything other than "the voice of the Church at prayer."[231]

In contrast, the *style* of Praise & Worship songs is obviously contempo-rary, American, and secular. If missionaries were to impose these songs on some indigenous tribe elsewhere in the world, it would be comparable to asking them to dress, eat, and talk like Americans. It is, in that sense, com-parable to jeans, Coca-Cola, and iPhones.

But what about emotions?

A student once objected to me that Saint Augustine considers affection of the heart so essential a component of prayer that if one's heart is not stirred, one is not truly praying—even if one has the right thoughts and the right intention. Out of this patristic axiom, my interlocutor extrapolated the conclusion that emotionally rousing music, such as one finds in Praise & Worship, is helpful for animating prayer, perhaps even necessary for some people or in some circumstances.

Let us admit, in keeping with the reverence we owe to the Church Fathers and Doctors, that Augustine is right on this point, even if we are

---

[230] The San Antonio Vocal Arts Ensemble (SAVAE) has done a great service in record-ing many programs of Catholic music from Central America that display this marvel-ous confluence; Chanticleer has done the same with some of the music of the Spanish in California. There is, in fact, a great wealth of properly inculturated sacred music that is nevertheless strongly characterized by the qualities on which the popes insist.

[231] See Friel, "Between Universality and Inculturation."

also aware that these great saints are not automatically right about every-thing.[232] Nevertheless, we cannot assume that *our* conception of "affection of the heart" is what *he* meant by it. Nor can we assume that Augustine would have approved of contemporary Christian music, given that he famously objected to what he considered to be the "sensuality" of Ambrosian liturgi-cal chant, which would doubtless not seem especially emotional by today's standards! In the *Confessions* we see him struggling with whether or not music should have *any* role in liturgy, because of the danger that it may draw too much attention to itself or to its performer. He finally concludes that it can and should have a role, but only if it is restrained. A beautiful singing of a psalm might lead to tears, but these are the tears of the spiri-tually sensitive.[233] Augustine's "affection of the heart" is a gentle movement of the heart towards the divine and away from reliance on the senses and the appetites of the flesh. The words of a modern Byzantine commentator about icons apply just as well to music for church, which ought to have an iconic function: "Icons lift our soul from the material to the spiritual realm, from a lower level of being, thought, and feeling, to a higher level."[234]

We have to be extremely careful how we understand the role of emotions in worship. Unless we are sleeping or totally distracted, our emotions will inevitably be engaged in some way, at some level. It is not really a ques-tion of emotionlessness versus emotionalism but a question of whether the emotional state we are in is (1) a state of self-contained boredom, (2) an excitation and agitation of feeling, or (3) the quiet intensity of looking and listening for the truth above and beyond oneself. The first and the second differ in the degree of activity, but they do not differ in regard to whether there has been a genuine transcendence of oneself and one's worldly frame of reference.

---

[232] After all, some opinions in Saint Augustine's works, abstracted from mitigating factors, became the germs of Lutheran, Calvinist, and Jansenist heresies. Even the Church's Common Doctor, Saint Thomas Aquinas, was in material error regarding the Immaculate Conception.

[233] See *Confessions* X.33; cf. the discussion of Augustine in chapter 17 below.

[234] See Cavarnos, *Guide to Byzantine Iconography*, 241–45. Delalande, Hourlier, Kirby, Swain, and Mahrt all explain the elevating power of Gregorian chant, its "iconic" or even "theophanic" function.

The need for sobriety

A culture predisposed to think everyone should be "on a high" as often as possible via athletics, drugs, sex, or rock concerts will likewise incline people to think that prayer and the worship of God ought to be the same way. One should feel "on a high." Sacred music, however, has never aimed at such an emotional high. In fact, it has conscientiously avoided it, to guard against the danger of fallen man becoming submerged in (and so, limited by) his feelings. As Dom Gregory Hügle observes, "Divine Providence has arranged that liturgical music should be austere and unyielding to personal whims; the sentiments of profound reverence mingled with fear and love break the snares which Satan has laid for the church singer."[235]

Sacred music gently moves man's emotions in order to foster the intellectual activities of meditation and contemplation. This approach corresponds to the timeless advice of the spiritual masters, who, while recognizing that emotion (feeling, passion) has a legitimate value, are cautious about deliberately stoking it or tapping into it for religious purposes. Emotion is more likely to have a clouding or distracting effect than a clarifying or concentrating one; instead of facilitating the ascent of the mind to God, it can lead to an illusion of self-transcendence that is evanescent and disappointing. For example, the much-loved spiritual author Brother Lawrence of the Resurrection opines: "Outside feelings of surprise, a person should not allow himself to be carried away with his feelings, because God should remain the Master and center of our attention."[236] Brother Lawrence warns: "Those who conduct themselves in the spiritual life only by following their particular dispositions and feelings, who believe that they have nothing more important to do than to examine whether they are full of devotion or not— this sort of person could not possibly be stable or certain in his conduct, because these things change continually, whether by our own negligence, or by the order of God, who varies His gifts and His conduct towards us according to our needs.[237]

An expert on Carmelite mysticism, Father Thomas Dubay, writes in his *magnum opus*: "Holiness does not consist in delights at prayer. . . . When

---

[235] *The Caecilia*, vol. 61, no. 1 (January 1934), 36.
[236] Lawrence, *The Practice of the Presence of God*, 64–65.
[237] Lawrence, 151.

God does not give the feelings of devotion even to generous people, they should not be in the least upset but should rather merely conclude that this emotional dimension is not presently necessary."[238]

Flannery O'Connor—an author who surely knew how to incite and harness emotions in her fiction—nevertheless considered sentimentality "an excess, a distortion of sentiment, usually in the direction of an overemphasis on innocence."[239] By presenting a "shortcut to lost innocence," sentimentality obscures the difficult path of asceticism that is the universal Christian way. In O'Connor's words, "We lost our innocence in the fall of our first parents, and our return to it is through the redemption which was brought about by Christ's death and by our slow participation in it. Sentimentality is a skipping of this process in its concrete reality and an early arrival at a mock state of innocence, which strongly suggests its opposite." On this quotation Father Uwe Michael Lang comments: "A timely antidote against the spiritual sentimentality of much present musical practice can be found in the earlier Christian tradition with its insistence on sobriety in liturgical music."[240]

The basic problem with Praise & Worship

To summarize our critique: Praise & Worship music is not suitable for liturgical use. Its style reinforces a false conception of the Church's liturgy (Mass, Divine Office, other sacramental rites) as communal gatherings in which subjective feelings, informality, and spontaneity play a large role. In reality, as Guardini and Ratzinger show, the liturgy is characterized by objectivity, formality, and unspontaneity—and only thus is it capable of being for us the fixed principle of our thoughts and actions, the rock on which we can build our interior life, the infinitely pleasing worship that is offered not so much by us as by our High Priest, and by us in union with Him.[241]

---

[238] Dubay, *Fire Within*, 221.
[239] Quoted in Lang, *Signs of the Holy One*, 144.
[240] Lang, 144.
[241] On the theological, liturgical, and psychological assumptions and consequences of contemporary worship music, see Fr. Christopher Smith's article "Why Praise & Worship Music Is Praise, But Not Worship," and the follow-up article "Let's Revisit 'Praise and Worship Music is Praise But Not Worship.'"

The Mass, in particular, must not be so weighed down with sentimental-ity and subjectivity that its essence is clouded by its accidents and we lose sight of what it actually is: the mystical re-presentation of Christ's supreme sacrifice on Calvary. We know this truth *only* by faith-informed intellects, and never by a psychosomatic faculty, whether it be the external senses, the imagination, or the emotions. We participate in this objective, public, solemn offering primarily by uniting our mind and will to the prayers of the priest and to the realities they point to. At the same time, the "exter-nals" of the liturgy should lead our minds and hearts in the direction of the faith-perceived mystery so that what we sense and what we believe do not seem to be at odds but rather converge in harmony. The sensible elements of the liturgy are meant to evoke and gesture towards the imperceptible mystery, inviting us to make acts of faith, hope, and charity in the presence of Our Lord's redeeming sacrifice and to participate in it most intimately by receiving Holy Communion. All of this is something that totally transcends the emotional realm as such, and while it is true that the Lord sometimes grants strong emotions to individuals as an encouragement or prompting or consolation, we relate to the essence of what is taking place through our intellect and will properly cleared, focused, and directed.

Moreover, there cannot be a place for contemporary pop-inspired or pop-influenced music in the liturgy because it violates several of the prin-ciples repeatedly given in authoritative Church documents. The fact that many priests and bishops do not enforce these rules and do not seem to care is beside the point, just as the fact that most Catholics dissent from *Humanae Vitae* (including many members of the clergy) does not justify contraception. Many Catholics are in a state of colossal ignorance, habit-ual carelessness, and sometimes outright disobedience, and we must plainly admit that the current crisis of identity, doctrine, and discipline in the Church is an unsurprising result.

I would go further and say we need to be moving away from the fashion or fad of using music derived from contemporary popular styles for *any* liturgical or devotional activity. We would do well in Eucharistic Adoration, for example, to allow silence to predominate and, at judicious moments, to make use of simpler chants. Silent prayer, combined with chant, allows peo-ple of very different temperaments, personalities, ages, and situations they may be going through to be united in prayer in a way that can be adapted to the needs of each. A more "stirring" form of music, while it may have a place in Christian recreational settings, does not facilitate group prayer (*a fortiori*, liturgical prayer) in the way that silence and chant do.[242]

Just a matter of taste?

At this point, an attempt at deflection is usually made: "Well, that's your opinion, but I guess we'll just have to agree to disagree. *De gustibus non disputandum*—there's no arguing about tastes."

This, too, is a false position that cannot stand up to serious scrutiny. As we learn from Plato and Aristotle, there are qualifications on the basis of which some people can and will make better judgments than others in matters of virtue, science, and aesthetics.[243] Aristotle saw that the closer a man lives to the golden mean, the better he can judge what is deficient or excessive. For his part, Plato saw that those who have the wisdom of age are, *ceteris paribus*, better judges of what is good for youth than youths are. Those who have more knowledge, training, and experience in the realm of sacred music, liturgy, and theology (for all three are necessary) will have better and more trustworthy opinions and judgments. Such people—Pope Benedict XVI is a shining example—have developed a sensitive ear and a reliable taste for what is better and worse, more or less suitable, according to the principles of art, liturgy, tradition, and the magisterium.

Consequently, we should take their opinions and judgments most seriously, and not fall prey to a form of voluntarism whereby, because we

---

[242] Romano Guardini makes a similar point about liturgical prayer in general: "Prayer is, without a doubt, 'a raising of the heart to God.' But the heart must be guided, supported, and purified by the mind. . . . If prayer in common, therefore, is to prove beneficial to the majority, it must be primarily directed by thought, and not by feeling. It is only when prayer is sustained by and steeped in clear and fruitful religious thought that it can be of service to a corporate body, composed of distinct elements, all actuated by varying emotions. . . . Dogmatic thought brings release from the thralldom of individual caprice, and from the uncertainty and sluggishness which follow in the wake of emotion." From chapter 1 of Guardini, *The Spirit of the Liturgy*; in the commemorative edition of Ratzinger's work of the same name, 280–82.
[243] We can also add spirituality to the list. All this is hard to swallow in our egalitarian era.

like something, or are *accustomed* to it, we will bend over backwards to try to find arguments in favor of it, or fall prey to a form of nominalism whereby we end up wanting to deny principles or essences in favor of what we think are self-evident facts. Nominalism and voluntarism, major intellectual elements of the Protestant Reformation, are unquestionably responsible for the downfall of Western realist philosophy, which is the necessary substrate for Christian theology. When you add voluntarism and nominalism together, you end up with relativism. We should be on our guard against importing this trio of -isms into our life of prayer and worship; we should not even dally with them.

It is beyond dispute, too, that as a culture our general musical level has declined, and this has negatively affected the artistic quality of music in every genre, from radio songs to movie scores to Broadway shows to church compositions. Hence, we should favor masterpieces from the past in order to educate and elevate our taste and know what is the "gold standard" to look to when evaluating new pieces or when attempting ourselves to add to the treasury of sacred music. What is needed, in short, is a lifelong discipleship to great sacred music. We must apprentice ourselves to the masters if we wish to enter into the discipline, assimilate it, and eventually produce fruits worthy of the Divine Majesty and of the Christian soul, which is *capax Dei*—capacious enough to receive God Himself.

Is the Church's traditional music too hard?

When my son, who was no prodigy, was five years old, he could sing the four major Marian antiphons (*Salve Regina* and so on); by the time he was six, he could sing the *Missa Orbis factor*, the *Missa De angelis*, and other chants familiar in our church, without being able to read the music. My daughter was the same way. Other boys and girls in the community were no different. Since children are gifted learners by ear and many chants have captivating melodies, children quickly pick up these chants if they live in communities that prize them.

That, indeed, is how tradition was and is always passed down: naturally, painlessly, orally, through a common treasuring of traditional things and a common use of them. In the heyday of the Gregorian chant revival before Vatican II, Justine Ward had developed an incremental method by which schools across the world were successfully teaching chant to thousands of children.[244] There were public liturgies at which crowds of boys and girls would beautifully chant the Ordinary of the Mass. At the principal Mass of the Eucharistic Congress in Chicago in 1926, a choir of 62,000 children drawn from hundreds of parochial schools came together to chant the Mass.[245] Such endeavors could easily have kept growing and continued well into our day, propelled by Vatican II's encomium of chant, but the 1960s and 1970s were not a propitious time for the preservation of tradition. Those in charge of institutions gambled on the supposed evangelistic benefits of modernization and let go of precious cultural treasures, even when sociologists of religion were predicting a renewal of interest in tradition among those searching for meaning in an increasingly chaotic post-Christian West and were expressing doubts about the staying power of shallow contemporary substitutes for perennial things.

If we look East to the Byzantine sphere, we can still find congregations accustomed to singing liturgical texts in three or four harmonized parts. This is common throughout the Eastern Christian world. Western Christians quickly pick it up, as I experienced firsthand in Byzantine liturgies at the International Theological Institute in Austria and at Wyoming Catholic College. At Taizé in France, an ecumenical monastery of sorts, large congregations of worshipers, Catholic and Protestant, sing repetitious Latin and vernacular chants, harmonizing in four parts. Visitors pick up these songs quickly and never forget them. While I do not consider most Taizé music to be artistically excellent, one may count in its favor that it generally avoids trite emotionalism and seems capable of fostering prayer.

Truly, the capacity of the human soul for great music is limitless. We should not underestimate either the capacity or the need for excellence in this domain. No one should ever assume that young people today cannot become cultured or acquire a wide intellectual purview, as if being primitive or illiterate is an unavoidable condition of modern youth. It is a social and cultural *choice* we have made in creating the artificial post-World War II category of

---

[244] See Hellriegel, "'Active Participation' in Chant."
[245] See Kwasniewski, "A Blast from the Past."

"the teenager."[246] In reality, as Guardini asserts, "A fairly high degree of genuine learning and culture is necessary in the long run in order to keep spiritual life healthy. By means of these two things, spiritual life retains its energy, clearness, and catholicity. Culture preserves spiritual life from the unhealthy, eccentric, and one-sided elements with which it tends to get involved only too easily. . . . [The Church] desires, as a rule, that spiritual life should be impregnated with the wholesome salt of genuine and lofty culture."[247]

The Church has an obligation to immerse her children into her own heritage, from birth onwards. As Jean Piaget demonstrated, the early years of a child are the "cultural womb" that completes the process of gestation. All Catholic children should be singing the *Salve Regina* and the *Gloria* by the age of five or six. A failure to give this heritage of beauty and spiritual strength to the little ones so prized by Our Lord is a kind of high treason against the supernatural polity of the People of God.

To priests, especially, I say: Do not underestimate the capacity of the young, and of the laity in general, to enjoy, appreciate, participate in, and grow spiritually from the traditions of the Catholic Church. A true spiritual hunger exists in the world. It is not only growing, but also unfortunately assuming deviant forms because it does not find satisfaction in much of what is being offered in the name of "relevance" and "inculturation." Offer rich fare, explaining how one should dine upon it, and the people will, at last, be able to be satisfied.

All great things are demanding

Father Samuel Weber makes a crucial point: there is need for hard work and discipline any time something great is at stake. We regularly expect such commitment from business people and sports teams; why should we not expect it of music ministry? Is that arena really so much less demanding and worthy of our attention, care, and effort? "Speaking from experience," says Father Weber,

> I would agree that Gregorian chant may require a greater discipline, more attention and sacrifice of time and energy in order to "make

---

[246] See Platt, "Myth of the Teenager."

[247] Guardini, *Spirit of the Liturgy*, chapter 1; in the Ignatius Press commemorative ed. of Ratzinger's *Spirit of the Liturgy*, 294.

it happen" in our parishes. But difficulty is not a real impediment. In our American society we greatly value sports. I'm a Green Bay Packers fan myself, rabid, actually. I'm really grateful to the Packers for all the hours they spend in practice and preparation for their games. All the sacrifices they make. It's worth it. The payoff is really something awesome. We, the fans, would settle for no less. Doesn't this same expectation apply to the things of God? It really isn't that hard to understand, is it?

St. Augustine taught the people of Hippo: *Cantare amantis est.* Singing is characteristic of a lover. If the supreme love is, as we believe, between Christ, the Bridegroom, and the Church, his Bride—can any effort be spared to express this love in true beauty? Is any sacrifice too much? We don't have to guess at the song. This tremendous Lover of ours tells us the song that he wants to hear from our lips and our hearts. This is our Catholic faith. What more need be said? Let us begin![248]

But why is it that, in Father Weber's words, "we don't have to guess at the song"? Because Our Lord Jesus Christ, through the Church's tradition and her magisterium, "tells us the song that He wants to hear from our lips and our hearts." The problem of poor church music will be overcome when, and exactly to the degree that, ecclesiastical tradition and magisterial teaching are embraced with respect, humility, and gratitude. The single greatest problem of the Church of our time is the loss of *any* conception or idea of tradition, much less the kind of knowledge and appreciation of it that a healthy condition of Catholicism presupposes.[249]

The worst thing would be for a society to have no laws whatsoever. But the second worst thing is to have good laws and not to follow them or even to know that they exist. The latter, alas, is the current condition of the Catholic Church in regard to far too many aspects of her life. The consistent legislation on sacred music affords a notable example of laws unknown,

---

[248] Weber, "Sacred Music that Serves the Word of God."
[249] See "Tradition as Ultimate Norm" in Kwasniewski, *Once and Future Roman Rite*, 1–30.

ignored, or held in contempt. A society whose members routinely violate its laws is in a perilous condition and certainly cannot be said to be flourishing. Things tend to be quite different, happily, among Catholics who treasure the traditional Roman rite and its immense musical heritage.[250] Henri Adam de Villiers, director of the Schola Sainte Cécile in Paris, notes that the nobility of the liturgy itself calls forth and rewards the efforts of his amateur singers:

> Now this liturgy is demanding: one cannot just do whatever, and personal subjectivity must take a back seat, because one must above all follow the path of a centuries-old tradition of sacred music. The traditional liturgy is demanding, but this also means that it is a true school in excellence that draws us upwards and makes us give the best of ourselves. That is why this liturgy has begotten so many artistic wonders throughout history, not only in the realm of music, but also in the other arts, notably architecture. I believe that our choristers—who are only simple parishioners—are very sensitive to that aspect: their generous personal investment is an enthusiastic response that aims to measure up to the traditional liturgy's inherent beauty. God is the Sovereign Good and the Sovereign Beautiful—and the liturgy is a foretaste of His glory, an epiphany, Heaven on earth! So mediocrity can't be allowed![251]

Let us begin, if we have not yet started; let us continue, if we have already begun; let us bring to perfection all that concerns the divine, holy, pure, immortal, heavenly, life-creating, and awesome mysteries of Christ, for the glory of God and the sanctification of the people. Perfection is an elusive goal, never entirely reached in this life; but just as we must strive for the fullness of charity, so too must we strive for the fullness of divine worship, in which that charity is powerfully nurtured and beautifully confessed.

---

[250] Even in this realm, however, certain difficulties arise that require prudent correction. See my article "The Catholic Choir and Choirmaster."

[251] DiPippo, "We Sing of God Alone and for God Alone, Through the Traditional Liturgy."

16

True and False Musical Inculturation

In *A New Song for the Lord*, Joseph Ratzinger devotes a particularly luminous chapter to the subject "The Image of the World and of Human Beings in the Liturgy and Its Expression in Church Music."[252] Ratzinger masterfully shows how the music we employ in church always embodies and communicates an ecclesiology, a Christology, and an anthropology—it is *that* significant! There is no escaping it: every piece of music we perform in church expresses and inculcates in its listeners a certain perception of both natural and supernatural realities. This is why church musicians will have much glory or great shame on judgment day.

Whenever I assigned this chapter to students, a certain question always came up in class discussions. Didn't the missionaries who went to the New World assimilate elements of the culture of peoples they encountered, including aspects of their music? Vatican II tells us that we should do the same thing wherever the Gospel is preached. Can we not take up elements of today's popular culture around us, such as rock or pop styles of music, and turn them into vehicles for evangelizing our contemporaries?

My answer—at least as far as the realm of the *liturgy* is concerned—is a resounding no, for the following reasons.

Inculturation, correctly understood, is the process of carefully discerning and integrating harmonious elements of an indigenous culture into the teaching and practice of the Faith so as to make the Faith at home in a culture. In this way, the people to whom it is being introduced experience it not as something completely foreign to them but as something that completes and elevates the good already present in their midst. The Church does indeed promote inculturation so understood:

---

[252] In Ratzinger, *A New Song for the Lord*, 111–27; also in *Collected Works* 11:443–60.

Since the Kingdom of Christ is not of this world (cf. Jn 18:36), however, the Church or People of God in establishing that King-dom takes nothing away from the temporal welfare of any people, but on the contrary, it fosters and takes to itself the abilities, riches, and customs of each people, insofar as they are good, and by taking them up, purifies, strengthens, and ennobles them. The Church in this is mindful that she must bring together the nations for that king to whom they were given as an inheritance (cf. Ps 2:8), and to whose city they bring gifts and offerings (Ps 71[72]:10; Is 60:4–7; Rev 21:24). This characteristic of universality, which adorns the People of God, is a gift from the Lord Himself, by reason of which the Catholic Church effectively and continually strives to bring all humanity with all its good things back to their source in Christ, under His Headship, in the unity of His Spirit.[253]

With prudent sensitivity, the great missionaries adopted and adapted some of the customs and art forms they found in order to evangelize the pagans more effectively and to enrich the Church's treasury with the gold of Sheba. We can see examples of such inculturation in vestments, architec-ture, and music. The *Liturgical Arts Journal* and *New Liturgical Movement* websites have run many articles about how Asian missions intelligently pro-moted this approach.[254] Marvelous examples of inculturation can be found in the fusion of European chant and polyphony with Native American instruments and texts.[255]

There are, however, crucial differences between the foregoing examples from the age of missions and the model proposed today for "reaching our contemporaries" in the secular world.

---

[253] Dogmatic Constitution on the Church *Lumen Gentium* (November 21, 1964), no. 13.
[254] See, e.g., Shawn Tribe's articles at *Liturgical Arts Journal*: "The Oriental Chasuble of Dom Pierre-Célestin Lou Tseng-Tsiang, OSB"; "Inculturation: Japanese and Chi-nese Madonnas"; "The Tradition of the Japanese Madonna"; others may be found by searching. The artwork of Daniel Mitsui today draws upon oriental designs with great effectiveness; see, for instance, the "Second Dream of St. Joseph."
[255] As mentioned earlier, the San Antonio Vocal Arts Ensemble (SAVAE) has done admirable renditions of Catholic missionary music from central America.

First of all, there is the overwhelming and undeniable fact that when Catholic missionaries came to native peoples in the Age of Exploration, they brought with them a fully "realized" religion, founded on fixed dogmas, issuing in definitive moral teachings, crowned and nourished by a stable sacred liturgy, all intertwined with a rich culture of art and thought. The missionaries fully intended to plant *this* religion and its culture on foreign soil and to win over the pagans to its truth and superiority.[256] The Catholic Faith, in all its specificity and plenitude, was the non-negotiable controlling paradigm by which indigenous elements had to be judged and into which they had to be fitted. It played the dominant role; like form in the philosophy of Aristotle, it was to be imparted to the receptive matter. In this way, the missionaries never baulked at "the scandal of the particular": they were preaching Jesus of Nazareth and establishing the Church of Rome.

This precedence of a universal *and traditional* Catholic orthodoxy and orthopraxy—the doctrine of the Council of Trent, let us say, and the organically developed sacramental rites of the Roman Church, replete with Gregorian chant—is *not* what proponents of a modernizing inculturation assume; in fact, they are more likely to ignore, marginalize, or exclude such things, failing to see how they could ever be relevant to our contemporaries. In this way, they run the risk of no longer inculturating the *Catholic* Faith. They might even end up fashioning new micro-religions, somewhat like the proliferation of local craft beers (no offense to craft brewers!).

Second, when the missionaries came to the pagans, the latter had no Christian heritage at all. They were a blank slate in this regard, although they were disposed, better or worse, to hear the Gospel due to their pre-existing religious beliefs, sentiments, and rituals. True pagans are not "scientific" atheists, elegant agnostics, smug liberals, or materialistic consumers; they believe in one god or many gods, they fear and placate them, and are ripe for conversion to a more divine and more humane religion. Coming to such religious non-Christians, the missionaries could make a discernment about which elements to take up from a genuinely pagan milieu, all the while remembering that the message they brought was authoritative and controlling.

---

[256] For further thoughts on inculturation, see "A Theological Review of the Amazon Synod" in Kwasniewski, *The Road from Hyperpapalism to Catholicism*, 186–210, at 196–202.

Today's Westerners, in contrast, are post-Christian aliens, estranged from their own history and the great cultural synthesis that could and should be theirs. The history of modern music, whether atonal or jazz or rock or pop, is a history of deliberate rebellion and revolt against the great tradition of Western music, against its high art forms, its slowly developed musical language, and its explicitly or implicitly Christian message. In its origins and its inner meaning, much of modern Western music is a rejection of the Catholic (and European) tradition. As a result, it is not morally, intellectually, or culturally "neutral"; it is already laden with anti-institutional, anti-sacral, anti-traditional significance. This music is not naïve raw material waiting to be Christianized, but anti-Christian propaganda. It rejects the ideals of lofty beauty and grandeur, spiritual seriousness, evocation of the divine, openness to the transcendent, and artistic discipline in favor of vapidity, frivolity, profanity, sensuality, and banality. As David Clayton aptly observes, "The dominant contemporary culture of the West today is the secular culture of anti-culture. It defines itself not by what it is, but by what it isn't. It is founded on a reaction against Christianity. Therefore, it is a distortion of it and as such is parasitical upon it."[257]

Given the specific requirements and expectations that go along with the *cultus Dei*, to admit such music into the temple is to profane the temple, to violate its sacredness. We are looking not at an outgoing *in*culturation but at an invasive "*de*culturation," in which what is proper to a unified historical religion is diluted or obliterated by its opposite.

Third, the pagans had a genuine folk culture—a culture that was, so to speak, of the people, by the people, and for the people. It was vital, personal, immediate. When the missionaries worked on and with this culture, they were working with something organic, spontaneous, and, in a sense, disinterested. In stark contrast, today's pagans are largely passive consumers of mass-produced, low-quality sonic junk food that earns huge profits for capitalist corporations who know how to manipulate the feelings of poorly educated, emotionally volatile audiences.[258]

What the pagans could offer to Christ, then, were local traditions of truly human dimensions, expressive of their identity and creativity as a people,

---

[257] Clayton, *Way of Beauty*, 48.
[258] See Storck, "Mass Culture or Popular Culture?"

not today's monotonous, artistically shallow epiphenomena of cancer-phase capitalism. In those fortunate pagan cultures that were not in thrall to demon worship and ritual violence, the missionaries were confronted with anthropologically rich soil for planting the seed of the Gospel, which they proceeded to do with confident zeal. What they found there permitted actual *enrichments* of devotion and worship. Today's popular culture, on the other hand, to the extent that it has grown up in revolt against the unifying principles, certainties, and demands of Christianity, is a melting pot of conflicting fashionable ideologies, a mishmash of tribalism, globalism, and techno-barbarism. Its underlying anthropology is suited not for saints and heroes but for narcissists and manipulators.

Consequently, the prevailing Western popular culture is impervious to and, at times, *subversive* of, the process of Christian inculturation. What I mean by subversive is this: it is not the secularism that ends up Christianized by the attempt at a merger but the Christianity that ends up secularized. It is not the vast empire of mediocrity that will be molded and transformed but the Catholic Faith. The only hope lies in calm resistance, pursuing a course so obviously opposed to that of the world that we will not cease to be a light shining in the darkness, which cannot overcome us as long as we remain truly light. This is why Pope John Paul II said in *Veritatis Splendor*, "It is urgent that Christians should rediscover the newness of the faith and its power to judge a prevalent and all-intrusive culture."[259] He was speaking about our contemporary culture of liberalism, relativism, and hedonism.

Clayton has vividly outlined the problem:

> So much pop or rock music is of a form that has developed specifically to reflect the culture of hedonism. . . . [T]o ignore this aspect of the style of the music altogether and just change the words to those of Christian hymns runs the grave risk of communicating something very bad regardless of how pious or holy the words of the song may be. Because worship of God is the activity in which we bare our souls the most, it is where we are most vulnerable to adverse influence. I suggest that we should be more conservative

---

[259] *Veritatis Splendor*, no. 88.

and less inclined to take risks in the choice of music in the liturgy than in the local dance hall. The music of our worship should be rooted in the Christian tradition so that it naturally becomes the standard to which all else points. If we make the secular forms the standard by which the liturgical [forms] are measured, the hierarchy has been inverted and the result is disaster for both cultures— the culture of faith and contemporary culture.[260]

In sum: due to its origins in a repudiation of the Christian cultural inheritance, its continual appeal to the appetites of the flesh, its negation of the dimension of mystery, and its consequent poverty of artistic expression, contemporary popular music *cannot* be suitable matter for the process of inculturation; rather, it is a formidable *obstacle* to the conversion of souls and the creation of a true Christian culture.

A Bible passage that has always struck me very forcefully is Romans 12:1–2: "I appeal to you therefore, brethren, by the mercies of God, to present your bodies as a living sacrifice, holy and acceptable to God, which is your spiritual worship. Do not be conformed to this world but be transformed by the renewal of your mind, that you may prove what is the will of God, what is good and acceptable and perfect."

Saint Paul is *appealing* to us by the mercies of God, so this must be serious stuff indeed. And what is he asking us to do? To present our *bodies* as living sacrifices: to make every fiber of our being a pleasing sacrifice to the Lord. And he says that if we do this, it counts as our *spiritual* worship. He could not be clearer in affirming the fundamental unity of man as a creature of body and soul, who worships the Lord *as one being*, not as a mind doing its own thing and a body left behind to do its own thing. Then, as if to explain further what he means, he says that we must not take on the form of this world but rather be transformed through those good, acceptable, and perfect things that express *God's* will. And this will amount to a re-creation of us, a making new of what has become old, stale, and wretched in our fallen nature: "Behold, I make all things new," as Jesus says in the book of Revelation (21:5).

As Catholicism is being reduced in its glory and transformative power by decades of facile conformism to the secular anti-culture and its fads, Saint

---

[260] Clayton, *Way of Beauty*, 41.

Paul's teaching is even more urgent today. Nowhere can this be seen more evidently than in the realm of music for the liturgy. Saint Paul's solemn appeal to give ourselves body and soul to the spiritual worship of God, resolutely turning our backs on this world's depraved, tawdry, or imperfect offerings, was ignored, even denied, as churches were filled with insipid or heretical lyrics, worldly rhythms, and secular styles more redolent of Broadway and Woodstock than of Jerusalem and Rome.

Thanks be to God, a reversal is beginning to be seen, and a growing number of musicians are taking a different path—one that is genuinely *new*, with the freshness of the Spirit that hovers over the Church in all ages, not the oldness of the flesh celebrated in the carnal cult of contemporary society. Centuries of magnificent musical treasures inspired by the Holy Spirit are being newly discovered and sung, in accord with the manifest mind of the Church. And new music worthy of the temple of God is being written— music that strives to be good, acceptable, and perfect, by the high standards of the Sacrifice of Praise. In every age, the challenge is the same: Christianity should *inform* culture and *transform* the world rather than be informed by the prevailing secular culture and itself transformed into a second-rate image of the world. We must always be on guard against letting the world mold *our* minds after *its* image rather than letting ourselves be renewed in our minds after Christ's image.

All too often, many incorrectly assume that the only way to communicate the Faith to our youth is to dilute the gospel with the language of their world, the soundtrack of their music. While this approach has had its ephemeral successes, the once-promised mass conversion or reversion of young people to the Lord of the Dance has never materialized, with studies showing an accelerating exodus of youths from all organized religion, including Catholicism, no matter how emotional and relevant we think we are making it.

There is, however, a quiet counter-witness rising up among the same young people to whom things like Life Teen and the charismatic renewal are supposed to appeal, even though they often do not. Now I am not saying that these youths are the norm (if only!), but only that they represent a greater thoughtfulness and spiritual hunger than our society—and all too often, I'm afraid, our Church—believes to be possible in men and women their age.

In the final examination for my music course at Wyoming Catholic College, students were asked to write essays in which they tried to express why certain modern styles of music are not appropriate for the liturgy. While most of what they said was a rehashing of Pius X and Benedict XVI (not a bad thing—would that we had more such recollection in a world of forgetfulness), there were certain statements that struck me as well said and full of wisdom. Here are a number of passages I transcribed from their handwritten finals.

> Man should be struck dumb with wonder at the immortal freshness of Christ's unimaginable sacrifice and wish only to sing what is most like the choir of angels. Bringing in "rock Masses" or Praise and Worship not only fails to grasp the solemnity of the event, but turns it toward the people, who at that moment should be emptying themselves to God. . . . Far beyond accenting the participation of the individual, sacred music must aid men in decentering and forgetting themselves, so that they can melt like wax into the fire of the divine romance.

Another student made a similar point about the incurving trajectory (*incurvatus in se*, as Saint Albert the Great says of self-love) of what is fashionable to our own generation and reflective of our preoccupations:

> Instead of coming to worship God and conform oneself to His rationality, popular styles are necessarily the expression of a particular community. This quality encourages worship to cease movement towards God and reflect back to the congregation: it is *their* music, *their* choice, *their* expression of *their* emotions toward *their* God. Such action is not worship, but self-indulgence.

One has to admit that this student has put a finger on a problem that is now endemic to the Latin rite, with its option-ridden and pluralistic Novus Ordo and the availability of the Tridentine Mass as well as the Anglican Ordinariate—namely, that how we worship as Roman Catholics becomes a matter of choice rather than something inherited, accepted as a given. But discussion of this point belongs to a different context than the present.[261] Another student:

---

[261] See Kwasniewski, *Noble Beauty*, 169–72; *Resurgent in the Midst of Crisis*, 57–70; *Once and Future Roman Rite*, 82–85.

The mysterious nature of the liturgy keeps us from comprehending it, but also draws us closer because of the beauty and depth. If we destroy this sanctity through a desire for acceptance by contemporary culture, then we have abandoned the great mystery.

And another:

Arvo Pärt's music now contributes to the manifestation and diffusion of God's holiness, artistry, and universality.

Could this not be said of all worthy sacred music? Its three qualities, as Pius X defined them in *Tra le Sollecitudini*, end up being a means by which God's own perfect possession of those qualities is made known in the world: for He alone is holy in Himself (*Tu solus sanctus*); He is the great Artist of the universe whose wisdom fashioned all things; He is the one and only Lord of the universe, near to all who call upon Him in truth (see Ps 144:18). Yet another:

"Relevant" music should not bow to the influences of the century, but rather the truly relevant music of the liturgy ought to influence the people of the century to refocus and worship the presence of the Lord within the Mass.

I like how this student redefined relevant as that which is inherently so, and therefore informs and impresses itself on people, to make *them* relevant, in a way, to *it*, and to the Lord it announces. We are the ones who are clay in the potter's hands, and we need to be reshaped until we are relevant to God, rather than the other way around. A different student had written in similar fashion:

Far from seeking a temporary, debatable, and always shifting "relevance," church music must retain within itself elements that will keep it relevant to tradition.

That's a striking thought: our practices, summoned to the court of truth, must defend their own relevance to the tradition we have inherited. If they are foreign to it, in tension with it, at oblique angles to it, they lose and tradition wins.

Another student, drawing on insights of Ratzinger:

> Liturgical music must reflect the knowledge that liturgical action
> is a historical, cosmic, and mysterious reality. Pop music rejects the
> notion that sacred music takes part in a rich history which draws
> from its past as it develops. It also ignores the notion that worship is
> larger than any one person, any one group, or any one time; it drives
> all sense down into the particular alone. Finally, pop music treats
> worship as something to *do,* not as something to *receive.* In other
> words, the use of popular styles directly undermines the approach
> to God in the most insidious way possible; it preys on the congre-
> gation's own enthusiasm and emotion towards their God and shuf-
> fles it back into themselves. The sacred, far from needing help from
> modern styles, remains relevant: it is a conduit to universal truths.
> With its ground in transcendent reality, true sacred music needs to
> shake off modernizing influences like dust from its feet.

I find in the foregoing words an incisive critique of popular musical
styles in the liturgy. They are bad, spiritually bad, because they are divorced
from history, particularized, and activist, and thus anti-incarnational, anti-
ecclesial, and anti-receptive. Such qualities are in tension with Catholicism.
Again:

> Pop music is not timeless. The music of the Church ought to be
> like her—transcending age, taste, mood, etc. However, pop music
> is specific to our modern time. We have decided to make shallow
> music for shallow men. We must remember that the music of the
> liturgy should reflect the reality it describes. Since the Mass con-
> tains mysteries ineffable and transcendent, should not our music
> reflect this?

Should it not, indeed? That is the "million-dollar question," and it is only our
Catholic tradition, in its lofty ideals and clear priorities amidst artistic variety,
that furnishes an answer not doomed to premature obsolescence. Instead of
the "deculturation" approach, which involves stripping away our distinctive
heritage, we should be harnessing the uncanny "shock value" of tradition.[262]

---

[262] See Kwasniewski, *Once and Future Roman Rite,* 1–30; *Noble Beauty,* 3–31.

I once received a wonderful letter about tradition and youth ministry, which occasioned a fruitful exchange. Because so many of us face week in, week out the issues he and I discussed, I asked and received permission to include some of the correspondence in this chapter.

Dear Dr. Kwasniewski,

I just read *Tra le Sollecitudini* and have a couple of questions. They mainly circle around the weight of the document, and how it interacts with other documents of the Church—questions of authority.

It seems as though any attempt to use the document authoritatively runs the risk of the claim that it's been superseded by Vatican II. For example, when it says sacred music "must be holy, and must exclude all profanity," that is of course not merely a disciplinary matter (one subject to change), but a normative one (it is true in the order of being). One the other hand, because some of the disciplinary matters have in fact been superseded, it seems that it might also allow the rejoinder: "Yes, the music must be holy and must exclude profanity, but just as it's wrong about the use of Latin, and wrong about women singing in the choir, so, too, is it about what *counts* as holy and profane." Another way it might be put: you once critiqued that sad, sad line in *Sacrosanctum Concilium* about "useless repetitions" (SC 34).[263] You classified it as *disciplinary* and therefore prudential and changeable. Might not someone say the same about using profane music? It could be prudent to use it, if it draws someone in.

That claim essentially challenges Benedict XVI's claim that what was sacred for our fathers is sacred for us. I think he's right, but it isn't obvious that he's right. He may be right in the order of being (it's sacred for us whether we realize it or not), and he may be right for people who still believe that the preconciliar church of their fathers is their own church. It isn't clear, however, that the average Catholic in America holds that Latin, Gregorian chant, Communion on the tongue, saints' days, fasting, penances, facing the Lord to pray, beautiful vesture and architecture, etc., which we've received from our fathers, *is* sacred. In fact, at least a small number actually hold those things in contempt.

And I think one of the challenges is to face up to the fact that to some degree, what we find holy *does* change! Think of the human body. It was held

---

[263] See Kwasniewski, "Poets, Lovers, Children, Madmen—and Worshipers."

in contempt by the ancient pagan world, and after having been sanctified by the Lord's Incarnation, it is again held in contempt in this neo-pagan culture. These are things I'm dealing with in my position as youth minister of a huge Catholic parish, where the unspoken expectation is that I'll encourage "youth Masses" and "praise and worship." To me, Pope Pius X offers clear, understandable principles that are obviously expressive of a once common and universal understanding of the liturgy. But you wrote on one occasion that the encyclical *Mystici Corporis* reads today as if it had been written in another universe, and I feel somewhat the same way about *Tra le Sollecitudini*. Indeed, the very idea that there's a tradition to refer to as an authority seems a universe away.

Can you tell me how you wade through these matters?

Yours in Christ,

Duc in Altum

Dear Duc,

Thank you for your honest and heartfelt letter. I understand the problems you're talking about. It's by no means easy to navigate what we are supposed to do when there is so much dissent, contradiction, amnesia, and just plain ignorance. And yet I believe that if one studies what the Church has taught over the centuries and especially during the past one hundred years, one can find a deep continuity there, in spite of the surface squalls.[264]

Moreover, I take it as a given that if a Church document is promulgated with the force of law, as *Tra le Sollecitudini* obviously was, and as *Summorum Pontificum* is in our own day, it remains in force except in those provisions that have been expressly abrogated.[265] So while the prohibition of women in choirs was, in fact, lifted later on, the ban on pianos and bands in church was never lifted, and for good reasons.[266]

---

[264] See chapter 10.

[265] On Pope Francis's attempt to cancel out *Summorum Pontificum*, see my article "Does Traditionis Custodes Lack Juridical Standing?," in *From Benedict's Peace to Francis's War*, 74–78, and other pieces in the same anthology. For those who believe it to have some standing, Fr. Gerald Murray's damage-control analysis merits attention: "Guarding the Flock." For a thorough critique by a canonist, see Fr. Réginald-Marie Rivoire, FSVF, *Does "Traditionis Custodes" Pass the Juridical Rationality Test?* (Lincoln, NE: Os Justi Press, 2022).

[266] See Kwasniewski, "Are Women Permitted to Sing the Propers of the Mass?" and chapter 18 on instruments.

Another thing I think is important is distinguishing between prudential, contingent judgments—for example, "the sanctoral cycle needs to be simplified" or "some vernacular may be allowed in the sacramental rites of the Latin Church"—and matters of principle, such as "the Church offers to God the sacrifice of praise in the Mass and the Divine Office." The latter is something the Church must always do. When one examines the documents on sacred music, one finds a remarkable consistency of principles, albeit different degrees of tolerance or flexibility regarding what corresponds to (or at least does not conflict with) those principles. Here, too, is where a certain amount of philosophical and theological training is simply indispensable—training, regrettably, very few people have. One who has studied Plato, Augustine, Aquinas, Ratzinger, thinkers of that stature, will *understand* where the principles are coming from, and that they are rooted in the nature of man, the nature of music, the mystery of the Incarnation, the stages of the spiritual life (purgative, illuminative, unitive). Then it's a matter not simply of swallowing a magisterial statement but of seeing that the magisterium is enunciating, for our benefit, something that *must be so*. It's like Saint Thomas saying that God reveals His existence to us, even though we can demonstrate it by the use of our natural reason, because most people won't, in fact, reach it that way. But they *could*.

In the area of youth ministry, Catholics have made a serious wrong turn in assuming that what young people want is a second-rate version of what the secular world gives them. The Church cannot compete with the entertainment industry. She is in the business of winning souls for Christ with the proclamation of a beauty they will never encounter in the meat market. This demands a certain otherworldliness, a countercultural challenge, an exposure to our own rich heritage. It is a dead end to pander to the lowest common denominator. In years of working with college students, I have seen that those who are serious about their faith will get more and more serious if they are fed nourishing spiritual food, which includes a more traditional style of liturgy and music. Conversely, they will stay superficial and a bit bored if they are given the usual "fast food."[267]

You'd think the American bishops would try to find a serious answer to the question: Why do we lose a vast swath of young people after confirmation?

---

[267] See Kwasniewski, "Healthy Food for Grown-Ups."

It clearly can't be the lack of youth ministry programs, which exist in their thousands. It is because of an outdated and ineffective paradigm.

If I may add a word about one difficulty you raised—namely, that Pope Benedict XVI might be too sanguine when he says, "What earlier generations held as sacred, remains sacred and great for us too"—I think he is saying not that our current generation already holds it to be sacred and great, but that it remains such *in itself* for anyone who discovers it with an open mind and heart. Hence, he says almost immediately afterward: "It *behooves* all of us to *preserve* the riches which have developed in the Church's faith and prayer, and to *give* them their proper place." This is as if to say: the sacrality and greatness of Catholic tradition places certain demands on us here and now. We are obliged to hold on to these things, to rediscover them if they are in abeyance, and to pass them on to the next generation.

So I see Pope Benedict making a judgment based on the principle of conservation of tradition and of the guidance of the Church by the Holy Spirit, which cannot be contradicted by any later developments. It's one thing to expand on what you've got; it's another thing to reject it.

God Bless,

Dr. Kwasniewski

Dear Professor,

Thank you for taking the time to write a thorough reply. Cardinal Newman saw it coming—the rise of private judgment. One of the mantras of my superiors is, "Let's do what the kids want," to which I reply, "It isn't clear their desires are well formed or should at all be determinative." The exchange presupposes the difference between private judgment and conscience. The Great Tradition *does*, or *should*, serve as a sounding board for our judgments. If the notes of our judgment are discordant with the Tradition, we, not the Tradition, must become better tuned.

But *why* are so many consciences discordant with Tradition and its beauty? What has caused priests and people to belittle Latin or *ad orientem* or chant? These attitudes and others like them should be warning signs that something has gone very wrong. Cardinal Ratzinger puts it concisely: "The guilt lies then in a different place, much deeper—not in the present act, not in the present judgment of conscience but in the neglect of my being which made me deaf to the internal promptings of truth."[268]

Our problems, it seems, lie within the inmost reaches of our being. Back to Cardinal Newman, and to a famous passage:

> The heart is commonly reached, not through the reason, but through the imagination, by means of direct impressions, by the testimony of facts and events, by history, by description. Persons influence us, voices melt us, looks subdue us, deeds inflame us. Many a man will live and die upon a dogma: no man will be a martyr for a conclusion. A conclusion is but an opinion; it is not a thing which is, but which we are "certain about;" and it has often been observed, that we never say we are certain without implying that we doubt. To say that a thing must be, is to admit that it may not be. No one, I say, will die for his own calculations; he dies for realities. This is why a literary religion is so little to be depended upon; it looks well in fair weather, but its doctrines are opinions, and, when called to suffer for them, it slips them between its folios, or burns them at its hearth. . . .
>
> Logic makes but a sorry rhetoric with the multitude; first shoot round corners, and you may not despair of converting by a syllogism. Tell men to gain notions of a Creator from His works, and, if they were to set about it (which nobody does), they would be jaded and wearied by the labyrinth they were tracing. Their minds would be gorged and surfeited by the logical operation. Logicians are more set upon concluding rightly, than on right conclusions. They cannot see the end for the process. Few men have that power of mind which may hold fast and firmly a variety of thoughts. We ridicule "men of one idea;" but a great many of us are born to be such, and we should be happier if we knew it. To most men argument makes the point in hand only more doubtful, and considerably less impressive. After all, man is not a reasoning animal; he is a seeing, feeling, contemplating, acting animal. He is influenced by what is direct and precise. It is

---

[268] Ratzinger, "Conscience and Truth."

very well to freshen our impressions and convictions from physics, but to create them we must go elsewhere.[269]

The vast majority of the faithful should be able to hear the music of the Church, have it resonate deeply in their souls, know that it's true, *and never need to give an account of why.* This is where the problem lies. The vast majority can't give any account of the whys or the wherefores. Confusion has sedated them.

Cardinal Sarah points this out in incisive remarks in his interviews about silence. Catholics are losing the poor. So Newman again:

> Obedience is the test of Faith. Thus the whole duty and work of a Christian is made up of these two parts, Faith and Obedience; "looking unto Jesus," the Divine Object as well as Author of our faith, and acting according to His will. Not as if a certain frame of mind, certain notions, affections, feelings, and tempers, were not a necessary condition of a saving state; but, so it is, the Apostle does not insist upon it, as if it were sure to follow, if our hearts do but grow into these two chief objects, the view of God in Christ and the diligent aim to obey Him in our conduct. I conceive that we are in danger, in this day, of insisting on neither of these as we ought; regarding all true and careful consideration of the Object of faith, as barren orthodoxy, technical subtlety, and the like, and all due earnestness about good works as a mere cold and formal morality; and, instead, making religion, or rather (for this is the point) making the test of our being religious, to consist in our having what is called a spiritual state of heart.[270]

His fear would be even better founded today, for the danger is now almost entirely realized. People in fact don't know *what* to be obedient to.

So how did we get here? The other way to ask the question: What has made the Church so deaf to the internal promptings of truth? This is a pressing question for me. It's one that's at least, but not only, historical in

---

[269] Newman, *The Tamworth Reading Room*, Discourse 6, in *Discussions and Arguments*, 293–94.
[270] Newman, "Saving Knowledge," Sermon 14 in *Parochial and Plain Sermons*, vol. 2, 153–54.

nature. I do think Catholics in America found false friends in the Founders. Enlightenment rights language corrupts Catholic rights language. But surely there has to be more to it.

This long missive ends by connecting what I said with your reflections on youth ministry in particular. We think we can offer degraded versions of the secular entertainment industry, and somehow (by magic?) their hearts will be converted. I have been pressured to do a great variety of things that could be done whether or not Jesus Christ was raised from the dead, and almost nothing contingent upon that reality.

We're working under a false premise: "We will do anything to get the youth to see how much God loves them." Nearly everything I've encountered in contemporary youth ministry is based on this premise. If it takes playing crappy music, fine. If it means having dull, short sermons, fine. If it means making everything as easy and as convenient as McDonald's, fine. So long as they realize "God loves them." But it's faulty because we've lost the resonance with the internal sound of truth. We want to allow the children's private judgments to rule—but not really. *We let the adults' assessment of children's private judgments rule.* Thus, God, Truth in Person, is evacuated, making it impossible for the sentence "God loves you" to resonate. The term "God" is empty.

It doesn't matter if you know that God loves you if you don't know who God is. And if you don't know who God is, then you can't possibly know what love is. So we build an entire edifice (at great cost!), desperate to convey to the children that, *"[Empty term] [empty action]s you."* Little wonder the children lose interest! And a large wonder some stick it out.

May all the saints keep us in prayer.

Yours in Christ,
Duc in Altum

Dear Duc,

The issues you are struggling with are the same ones Cardinal Newman was facing, except that in his day, everything was cinctured about with a sort of Victorian respectability. Still, he saw the revolt against Christianity in his time, and he predicted that it would accelerate and degenerate. Your *reductio ad absurdum* of the "[empty term] [empty action]s you" captures the vacuity of a faith without roots, without heritage, without clear compass points of dogma and anchors of precept. We are floating adrift, and desperately clutching at the flotsam and jetsam of popular culture to see if anything will hold us up and keep us from drowning.

On a more hopeful note, I think the emptiness of the self-referentially modern approach is becoming more and more evident, at least to those who were not brainwashed in it back in the '70s and '80s. A shift in mentalities takes a long time, but consider the fact that healthy families and a large number of priestly and religious vocations are arising in those parts of the Church that have *resisted* mindless modernization (one thinks of traditional monasteries and convents, or parishes affiliated with the Latin Mass). God's victory unfolds over centuries, not over decades, and it always happens in surprising ways.

What made the Church so deaf to the internal promptings of truth? This is a most difficult and painful question to ask. It's hard to set a point in time, but one wonders if there was not a form of rationalism and worldliness that crept in during the Enlightenment period (with obvious exceptions—God raises up saints in every age) and reached its peak in the middle of the twentieth century, when it seemed at last as if man had entered a new age, the age of love, peace, unity, human rights for all. It was the most seductive trap that could ever have been set up: a secular Gospel dressed up with the ideals of Christianity yet without the cross, without Christ. The rupture with tradition happened at this point in a dramatic way: all that old medieval stuff, asceticism, the sacrifice of the Mass, the Latin breviary, scholastic theology—it all had to go; it wasn't optimistic, open-armed, fraternal, metamorphic, futuristic.

It is not going to be easy to rebuild, as the monks in Norcia are experiencing. The earthquake tore down all the churches, and there are piles of rubble everywhere. But there are still people of faith who are determined to rebuild Norcia, to revitalize its economy, and to make it as beautiful as it was before. This seems to be a perfect parable for the Church in general. When you rebuild, it's not a case of nostalgia, because no one can recreate the past, not even God; but one can create the future to be in continuity with the past, to be its new likeness. That is not nostalgia but wisdom, humility, and trust in Providence. That is how I understand my vocation as a tradition-loving Catholic.

Thanks again for your probing questions.

In Domino,
Dr. Kwasniewski

17

Objective Form and Subjective Experience: Life Teen under Scrutiny

IN MY BOOK *Noble Beauty, Transcendent Holiness*, I devoted a chapter (pp. 115–33) to the vigorous debate between certain Benedictines and Jesuits of the early twentieth century over the centrality of the liturgy in the Christian life and, more particularly, in the life of prayer. As I wrote there:

> Faithful to their age-old emphasis on the *opus Dei*, the sons of St. Benedict promoted the line of St. Pius X that the sacred liturgy is the "fount and apex" of the Christian life, the point of departure for all of the Church's pastoral activity and the goal in which her entire mission culminates. The communal liturgy of the Church, ripened over centuries of faith, is the highest expression of the love and wisdom of the Holy Spirit shared between Jesus Christ and His immaculate spouse. One might say that the "Spirit of truth" is at home in the liturgy, which is the most visible and most authoritative manifestation of His invisible presence among us. . . . In contrast, the sons of St. Ignatius, heirs of far-flung missions often undertaken by solitary priests, presented the liturgy as one among many tools useful for personal spiritual growth, with private meditation having a certain pride of place. One seeks and finds the Holy Spirit in the individual practice of the discernment of spirits— done, of course, within the framework of Catholic doctrine and under the guidance of the hierarchy, but still, concentrating on the pursuit of one's own vocation in the world, to which formal public prayer is a useful adjunct, more or less dispensable depending on circumstances.[271]

---

[271] Kwasniewski, *Noble Beauty*, 115–16. Foremost on the Benedictine side were Dom

The ironic outcome was that both sides won and both sides lost in the period of volatile reform after Vatican II. For, on the one hand, liturgy rose to prominence and often became the *only* kind of prayer Catholics talked about or participated in; yet on the other hand what "triumphed was a 'creative,' devotional, sentimental, largely subjective notion of liturgy, a utilitarian and custom-designed approach that is utterly contrary to the Benedictine vision of liturgy as objective, formal, stable, and received, an external standard to which we are subject and to which private devotions and personal preferences are to be subordinated."[272]

Having read this chapter, a parish youth minister wrote to me as follows, sharing his thoughts on the Life Teen phenomenon.

Dear Dr. Kwasniewski,

I have been subjected to two "Life Teen" conferences this summer, and I must say *they* are the true challenge to the return of Tradition. For they don't attempt to be heterodox, just the opposite in fact. Those folks who wish the Church could just "get with the times" are dying off, and their children, if they had any, have apostatized. But the Life Teen business is so painfully anti-intellectual that you can barely argue with it, and so it's tough to defeat. You know things by their fruits, and the fact is that these people are able to exercise a decent attraction for a time. It's the longer view that comes into question, and it requires more subtle arguments about form and the nature of the spiritual life.

Your book touches on the Benedictine–Jesuit divide in terms of liturgy, but I think that it can be pushed even further. On my view the Benedictine life is the practical working out of the Augustinian theological/spiritual synthesis. At the heart of that synthesis is the conflict between pride and humility. Pride is self-indulgence to the point of contempt of God. Humility is God-indulgence to the point of contempt of self. At the heart of this is Augustine's profound self-effacement. He knows how complicated,

---

Lambert Beauduin and Dom Maurice Festugière; foremost on the Jesuit side, Jean-Jacques Navatel and Louis Peeters.
[272] Kwasniewski, 117.

tangled, and inverted things can become. As he says in the *Confessions*: "I have become an enigma to myself."

The Augustinian (and therefore the broadly Catholic) method for resolving that question is through submission to form that is not self-created or self-perpetuating. This, for two reasons. One, the self is untrustworthy and readily deceived, and two, because there is no coming to faith without mediation. That's why he concludes the opening of the *Confessions*: "I call upon thee, O Lord, in my faith which thou hast given me, which thou hast inspired in me through the humanity of thy Son, and through the ministry of thy preacher." The humanity of the Son, that is the one who takes the mediation of flesh through Mary, and the ministry of the preacher—i.e., Ambrose, and the episcopal office more generally.

Thus, it's not by accident that humility, submission to the rule and to the abbot, are the very foundations of Benedictine life. It is through obedience—both to the rule and to the abbot, which are parallel to Augustine's ministry of the preacher and the humanity of the Son—that one draws near to the Lord. Here there is no room for self-expression or self-presence as we've come to understand those things. On the other hand, that's why Benedict constantly exhorts the abbot to patience and magnanimity, never abusing that great authority.

In a similar way, in Benedictine life the liturgy, the *opus Dei*, is the reception of and adherence to form, down to the last detail. Salvation comes through conforming yourself to the mediated image, just as the mediated image, in the case of the Host, becomes salvation, when a priest conforms himself to the given form (no wonder Augustine so well understood *ex opere operato* in his refutation of the Donatists). In other words, "experience" understood as "conscious seeming" has almost no role to play in Augustinian–Benedictine spirituality.

Contrast that with the Jesuit tradition. Experience is everything. Self-presence, self-knowledge can be read (and indeed in the consciously modern period have been read) throughout the *Spiritual Exercises*. It becomes very easy then to cast such things as fixed liturgical forms, rubrics, traditional chant as evils just to the extent that they put a damper on experience. To an experientialist, if something becomes rote, it doesn't seem like anything. Options, flexibility, creativity, become paramount.

Now, I'm not claiming this is what Ignatius had in mind, but in broad strokes, I think one can see clear differences. These are differences that aren't merely contrasting; they are contradictory. The two schools disagree on the nature of knowledge, on the formation of the soul, indeed, on the very purpose of the liturgy.

I may be way off-base on all that, but I think there's something to it.

Best regards,
Life Teen Skeptic

I sympathize with many things my interlocutor is saying; his singling out of subjectivism as a modern vice is correct, and it is hard to dispute that the Jesuits have played a role in the decentering of the Church from her public liturgy. But I have to take some exceptions to his interpretation of Augustine.

Augustine can be and has been used to support just about any position—just think of the Protestant reformers who continually cited him, or later on, the Jansenists. The reason is simply that he is so rich, so comprehensive, and so subtle that he really did see every angle of a problem. He gives us a lot to work with—and to take out of context. In his mature thought, however, there is a perfect balance of the subjective and the objective, or to put it differently, as a Platonist with a deep spiritual hunger for the reality of God, he was absolutely fixed on the Good above us and beyond us, and intimately in love with this Good as it came to possess his own heart. The usual contrasts between, say, "objective spirituality" (i.e., liturgy, sacraments) and "subjective spirituality" (e.g., personal prayer, emotion, experience) fall apart when it comes to him: his most personal experiences were precisely ones of the reality of God as mediated through the order of creation and the order of redemption. He would look at us with extreme puzzlement if we started to make an opposition between Eucharistic worship and personal friendship with God, or between adoration through stable external signs and inward conviction or conversion. He would say: The Eucharist, the divine liturgy, *is* the locus of that friendship, and that friendship cannot exist unless nourished by God Himself. We have to be drawn out of ourselves into the transcendent mystery of God through sacramental signs in order to know and love ourselves aright and to have His indwelling presence in us.

This brings me to an Aristotelian point, which will supply a key premise. Aristotle argues that pleasure is the accompaniment of a good action, in some sense a concomitant or result of it, and that the best pleasures accompany the best actions. So, if you want the pleasure, you have to seek out the action, and if you want the best pleasure, you need to seek out the best action a human being is capable of. The reason we reproach "pleasure-seekers" is that they are aiming for easier, low-hanging fruit, usually of a sensual or emotional kind. The paradox is that if you seek pleasure in itself, you miss the better pleasures, which require a certain self-denial and self-transcendence. The virtuous man aims at good or great actions, and experiences a deeper, purer pleasure in doing them.[273]

Now let us consider worship as an action, and religious experience as a pleasure. Liturgical action, when pursued for its own sake—that is, in adoration and praise of God—is accompanied by the best religious experience. But if we seek the *experience* as our goal, we will be denied the experience at its best, which comes only from pursuing something nobler than a mere experience. Hence, the person who will be most delighted in worship is the one whose motto is: "I want to find *God*"—not the one whose motto is "I want to have an experience of God."

One may draw a parallel here with marriage. If a partner begins with the attitude: "I want an experience of a deep relationship," the marriage is doomed. If he or she begins with the attitude: "I want to do right by this person, no matter what," the marriage can flourish. What is vitally important is that the aim be not some experience gained by using another but simply the other himself or herself: he or she is the aim.[274] It is the same with having children. For a parent to think "I want to have the experience

---

[273] See *Nicomachean Ethics* I.8; VII.11–14; X.4–7. The reason pleasure-seeking leads to a bad end is that action grounds pleasure rather than pleasure grounding action. If you seek the best action, you have a grounded approach to the best pleasure, but if you seek pleasure, the pleasure itself will not guide you as to the best or right action.
[274] Obviously, not as an ultimate end, but as one ordered to God by charity. See Kwasniewski, *The Ecstasy of Love in the Thought of Thomas Aquinas.*

of being a parent/having a child" is a subtle form of selfishness. The parent who thinks "I want to bring a child into the world for his or her own happiness" is instead focused on the good of the other and willing to sacrifice himself or herself to accomplish it.

The result of this analysis is that we should not set form or objectivity over against experience, as if they are in opposition. Rather, form, or a formal action, will always come with an experience. A higher form will come with a higher experience. A lower form will be accompanied by a lower experience.[275] This, I believe, is exactly what Augustine is saying throughout the *Confessions* and other works.

That a lower form will be accompanied by a lower experience is what we see in a phenomenon like Life Teen. It's easy to get the immediate emotional experience; it requires so little in the way of form or action. But it is correspondingly shallow and unsatisfying for that reason, and must be repeatedly sought, perhaps with attempts made at intensifying the same experience. In this way, it is somewhat like drugs, where people start with small doses and eventually try bigger doses or move to more potent drugs, because they are seeking more of that experience, more of that pleasure.[276]

With traditional worship, it is quite different. At first, the form is lofty and remote, the action difficult for our nature. We may feel dry, at a loss, perplexed, even offended at the lack of consideration for our feelings and (what we think to be) our needs. We are confronted with the otherness, the strangeness of God. But if we stick it out, something calls to us in our remoteness from Him. As we dwell with it more, it slowly seizes hold of us and lifts us up to a higher level, to higher perceptions of the truth of what we are doing and Whom we are dealing with. As this worship becomes more connatural, we experience more delight. The delight does not grow stale or cloying but, in fact, builds upon itself without limit, because it is of a spiritual or intellectual order (although not separated from the physical

---

[275] By "higher" and "lower" here, I mean more in accord with man's rational or spiritual nature as *capax Dei*, a nature open to the knowledge and love of God, which are attained most of all in contemplation.

[276] A similar critique could be offered of tendencies in the Charismatic Movement. See Kwasniewski, "Why Charismatic Catholics Should Love the Traditional Latin Mass" and "Confusion about Graces."

domain). At the limit, beyond this life, we enjoy the beatific vision, where the experience and the objective reality, the form, are utterly at one.

Humility, obedience, submission to rule, reception of form, and adherence to form do not need to be (or to be seen as) opposed to experience, self-presence, self-knowledge, and fulfillment. With Aristotle, Augustine, and Aquinas as our guides, we see that the latter are best accomplished by following the narrow road of the former, and the former are necessarily accompanied by the latter in their purest state. But we cannot pursue the latter for their own sakes if we ever wish to practice the former well; indeed, such a mistaken prioritization leads to a skepticism towards and an eventual abandonment of those "objective" foundations and qualities.

It is for this reason that Life Teen and programs like it are harmful to the spiritual development of adolescents, who are at a particularly vulnerable point in their lives, with anxieties about self-image, a tendency towards emotional instability and excess, and the temptation of pleasure-seeking. They will benefit the most, over time, from the traditional emphasis on formal liturgical action to which worshipers anonymously submit, all facing in the same direction and offering a visible sacrifice such as the nature of man requires, avoiding the psychological inflations and distractions of a contemporary style of worship.

I should like to give the last word to Dom Guéranger, as reported by Abbess Cécile Bruyère: "Let us note well that the science of the Christian life is a determined and definite science. Therefore we must not rest satisfied with repeating conventional phrases or with multiplying sentimental formulas ['Oh, ah, I ah-dore you-ou-ou'—PK]; it is by labour, and not by dreaming and excitement, that we must learn the secrets of a science which has its axioms, its deductions and its certain rules. All must be drawn from divine sources, that this science may be truly that of the spiritual life in the Christian Church."[277]

---

[277] Bruyère, *The Spiritual Life and Prayer according to Holy Scripture and Monastic Tradition*, 121.

18

Fitting and Unfitting Musical Instruments for Sacred Music

THE PIPE ORGAN occupies a unique place among instruments to be employed for, or in conjunction with, sacred music in the liturgy. The Church herself says a great deal in praise of the organ's qualities as an instrument for the temple of God:

> The traditionally appropriate musical instrument of the Church is the organ, which, by reason of its extraordinary grandeur and majesty, has been considered a worthy adjunct to the liturgy, whether for accompanying the chant or, when the choir is silent, for playing harmonious music at the prescribed times. . . . Let our churches resound with organ-music that gives expression to the majesty of the edifice and breathes the sacredness of the religious rites; in this way will the art both of those who build the organs and of those who play them flourish afresh and render effective service to the sacred liturgy.[278]

> Among the musical instruments that have a place in church the organ rightly holds the principal position, since it is especially fitted for the sacred chants and sacred rites. It adds a wonderful splendor and a special magnificence to the ceremonies of the Church. It moves the souls of the faithful by the grandeur and sweetness of its tones. It gives minds an almost heavenly joy and it lifts them up powerfully to God and to higher things.[279]

---

[278] Pius XI, *Divini Cultus* (December 20, 1928), VIII.
[279] Pius XII, *Musicae Sacrae* (December 25, 1955), no. 58.

> In the Latin Church the pipe organ is to be held in high esteem, for it is the traditional musical instrument which adds a wonderful splendor to the Church's ceremonies and powerfully lifts up man's mind to God and to higher things.[280]

And a pair of gems from Pope Benedict XVI:

> We have just listened to the sound of the organ in all its splendor, and I think that the great music born within the Church is an audible and perceptible rendering of the truth of our faith.[281]

> Solemn sacred music, with choir, organ, orchestra and the singing of the people, is not an addition of sorts that frames the liturgy and makes it more pleasing, but an important means of active participation in worship. The organ has always been considered, and rightly so, the king of musical instruments, because it takes up all the sounds of creation and gives resonance to the fullness of human sentiments. By transcending the merely human sphere, as all music of quality does, it evokes the divine. The organ's great range of timbre, from *piano* through to a thundering *fortissimo*, makes it an instrument superior to all others. It is capable of echoing and expressing all the experiences of human life. The manifold possibilities of the organ in some way remind us of the immensity and the magnificence of God.[282]

Texts like these indicate that there is something special about the organ whereby its music, when properly chosen and played, is most of all suitable for the church, raising the minds and hearts of the faithful to the contemplation of God's beauty, grandeur, and mystery. A Mass without music (vocal and instrumental) is a Mass that does not fulfill in every possible way the elevating power of the sacred liturgy. Of course, as Cardinal Sarah has been reminding us, quiet prayer is an important aspect of the liturgy, so it should never be absent.[283] We are once again dealing with a Catholic "both/

---

[280] Vatican II, *Sacrosanctum Concilium* (December 4, 1963), no. 120.
[281] Benedict XVI, Meeting with Clergy of Bolzano-Bressanone (August 6, 2008).
[282] Benedict XVI, Dedication of Organ in Regensburg Basilica (September 13, 2006).
[283] See part III.

and," not a Protestant "either/or": a High Mass generally has both periods of natural and meditative silence and periods of chant and other music, and these are complementary to one another.

In defense of the organ postlude

I will admit that ever since the first time I heard a pipe organ follow up on the recessional hymn with a magnificent postlude, it has seemed to be almost self-evident that this is the right and proper way to end Mass. Whether it was a stirring fantasia on the hymn tune, the majesty of a Bach prelude and fugue, the dazzling harmonies of the French Baroque, or a mighty piece from the Romantic or Modern periods, it filled the temple with a sonic image of angelic choirs, a wordless transcendent proclamation of God's glory. It reminded me once again: *Terribilis est locus iste: hic domus Dei est, et porta coeli: et vocabitur aula Dei.* "Terrible is this place: it is the house of God and the gate of heaven, and it shall be called the court of God."[284]

But there are people who are apparently bothered by postludes and find them a loud distraction that stands in the way of making a thanksgiving after Mass. (I will not deign to talk about those who are bothered by the powerful sound of the organ because it prevents the exchange of greetings and comments on the weather.) So I will take up the challenge of showing the fittingness of this practice, which has been with us for several centuries now, since the great age of organ music that dawned in the late Renaissance and reached its height in the Baroque period.

The postlude after Mass is specifically ordered to proclaiming the attributes of God's greatness and majesty, which have been revealed to us in the Holy Sacrifice of the Mass. A postlude is highly appropriate for a time of thanksgiving because throughout the Mass, we have been preparing ourselves, with contrition, with steps towards the altar, with much earnest prayer and supplication, and when the Lord finally makes Himself present to us and even gives Himself to us in Holy Communion, our hearts should be bursting and ready to cry out "Alleluia!" with all of creation. That is what an organ postlude does better than anything else can do: it makes creation resound with the divine praises as we get ready to step forth into the world

---

[284] Gen 28:17; Introit, Mass of the Dedication of a Church.

again. The voice of the organ gathers up into itself the voices of creation, with the wind blowing through the pipes, the metal, wood, and other components standing in for the material world, and the rhythms, melodies, and harmonies expressing the thoughts and feelings of the human soul, which is a microcosm of the universe.

Such a postlude needs to be appreciated for what it is: a musical expression of the soul's exultation. People don't need to be able to *think* during it, much less run through a set of prayers. The music is pre-rational and super-rational; it is more fundamental than any one of the thousands of human languages spoken on earth, and yet reaches beyond them too, conveying what no words, however poetic, can convey. The most appropriate thing to do is allow ourselves to be carried off for a few minutes by the sound that shakes the building. "The voice of the Lord is upon the waters; the God of majesty hath thundered. . . . The voice of the Lord is in power; the voice of the Lord in magnificence. The voice of the Lord breaketh the cedars: yea, the Lord shall break the cedars of Libanus. . . . The voice of the Lord divideth the flame of fire" (Ps. 28:3–5, 7). It's a healthy "apophatic" experience: we are invited to negate our flood of words and thoughts by surrendering to a non-pictorial, non-verbal reality.

Listening to a postlude cannot substitute for personal thanksgiving, which is best done after the music ends. Perhaps one of the problems is that modern people are so often either in a hurry or in an individualist frame of mind. They can't wait to get out of church or, once *in* church, they'd rather be "left alone to their own prayers." Both utilitarian pragmatism and individualistic piety are inimical to the true spirit of the liturgy, which is a divinely-bestowed communal leisure, elevated by the fine arts and vivified by personal devotion. Once again, I would not be understood to be saying that individual piety is not valuable. Far from it. But it is not the purpose of liturgy to give a person space for his or her private prayers. It is the solemn, public, objective, and formal prayer of the Church, the entire Mystical Body, and we must prepare well for it by times of personal prayer outside of the liturgy, as well as earnest prayer during the liturgy, and a time of quiet thanksgiving afterwards.[285]

---

[285] See "On Worthily Receiving the Lord" in Kwasniewski, *Holy Bread of Eternal Life*, 71–88. Parents of small children face special challenges in this regard, but Holy

The Low Mass has many spiritual benefits for the priest and for the faithful who attend it on weekdays. It is my favorite way to pray early in the morning; some of my best memories of the liturgy are of the 6:00 a.m. private Mass my wife and I attended in Austria, or the 6:40 a.m. Mass at the Basilica in Norcia. Nevertheless, liturgy in its fullness is the *Missa solemnis* or, where this is not possible, the *Missa cantata*, wherein we worship God with all the capacities of our body and soul, with silence, speech, and above all song, drawing upon the immense heritage of our traditional sacred music, about which the Second Vatican Council rightly said: "The musical tradition of the universal Church is a treasure of inestimable value, greater even than that of any other art. The main reason for this pre-eminence is that, as sacred song united to the words, it forms a necessary or integral part of the solemn liturgy" (SC 112). For this reason, one must gently but firmly combat the inroads of a "low Mass mentality" into public worship, because it is a form of minimalism whereby the wings of the soul cannot fully spread themselves and soar on the beauty Our Lord has so lavishly given to His people. Seek out silence in personal prayer times; seek contemplative silence in the daily Low Mass; seek blessed silence at the very heart of the High Mass; but do not silence the exuberant expression of the glory of the Lord and the beauty of His handiwork, as they reach our minds through music.

So, the next time you are at church and the pipe organ's postlude thunders forth as the Mass ends, don't try to keep following that devotional book, don't try to "meditate," don't leave for the chattiness of the coffee hour or the seclusion of your car. Just sit and absorb the plenum of sound, the heavenly harmonies, the wordless jubilation. Take up again the thread of thanksgiving when the music fades away.

Pius X's prohibition of pianos

Just as Gregorian chant has the Church's blanket approval—it is the right vocal music to use for any liturgical service, with no need to justify itself—so too, as we have seen, the pipe organ enjoys the same approval. It has already been pre-screened and pre-approved for all liturgical use, anywhere and everywhere.

Church, being a sympathetic mother, expects them to do only what is realistic in the circumstances.

It is quite a different matter with the most popular of all modern instruments, the piano—or, to give it its full and telling name, pianoforte, a concert hall and jazz festival mainstay, a lounge and bar-room fixture, and a pedagogical mountain countless children are made to climb. This brilliantly versatile instrument was developed exclusively in the world of secular entertainment music by Classical-period musicians like Beethoven who were looking for a penetrating sound that would carry well through a concert hall. The piano is, technically, a *percussion* instrument; the whole point of the "Hammerklavier," the precursor to today's instrument, was to seize the listener and pin him to the music *for its own sake*. We are dealing here with a worldly instrument that announces to its audience: "I'm playing now for your entertainment, so sit back and (—fill in the blank—) [sip your drink; tap your toes; read the newspaper; chat pleasantly with your companion; or, in Liszt's day, swoon before the virtuoso].

We come now to November 1903. Reams have been written about *Tra le Sollecitudini*'s general principles, its advocacy of Gregorian chant and polyphony, the checkered history of its implementation, and the irony of the incorporation of its main points into Vatican II's *Sacrosanctum Concilium* only to be followed immediately afterwards by their almost total neglect or contradiction in practice. Yet seldom does the motu proprio's nineteenth paragraph receive the attention it deserves: "The employment of the piano is forbidden in church, as is also that of noisy or frivolous instruments such as drums, cymbals, bells, and the like."

The rationale for this ban—namely, that the piano (to leave aside for the moment other members of the percussion family) was a secular instrument from the start and has always been associated with secular music—is often repeated in subsequent magisterial documents that urge the faithful to avoid any instrument suggestive of styles of music that originate outside of the temple of God. Pope Pius XII teaches in his encyclical *Musicae Sacrae* of 1955: "Besides the organ, other instruments can be called upon to give great help in attaining the lofty purpose of sacred music, so long as they play nothing profane, nothing clamorous or strident, and nothing at variance with the sacred services or the dignity of the place. Among these the violin and other musical instruments that use the bow are outstanding because, when they are played by themselves or with other stringed instruments or with the organ, they express the joyous and sad sentiments of the soul with an indescribable power" (no. 59).

The 1958 document *De Musica Sacra et Sacra Liturgia* of the Sacred Congregation of Rites dwelt on the point more closely: "The difference between sacred and secular music must be taken into consideration. Some musical instruments, such as the organ, are naturally appropriate for sacred music; others, such as string instruments which are played with a bow, are easily adapted to liturgical use. But there are some instruments which, by common estimation, are so associated with secular music that they are not at all adaptable for sacred use. . . . The principal musical instrument for solemn liturgical ceremonies of the Latin Church has been and remains the classic pipe organ" (nos. 60–61).

Even the Second Vatican Council followed this line. After stating that the pipe organ is to be "held in high esteem" as "the traditional musical instrument," *Sacrosanctum Concilium* continues: "But other instruments also may be admitted for use in divine worship, with the knowledge and consent of the competent territorial authority, as laid down in Art. 22 §2, 37, and 40. This may be done, however, only on condition that the instruments are suitable, or can be made suitable, for sacred use, accord with the dignity of the temple, and truly contribute to the edification of the faithful" (no. 120).

Citing both the preceding text and its 1958 precursor to indicate continuity of judgment, the *post*-conciliar instruction on Sacred Music, *Musicam Sacram* of 1967, also from the Sacred Congregation of Rites, hones this judgment as follows:

> In permitting and using musical instruments, the culture and traditions of particular peoples must be taken into account. At the same time, however, instruments that are generally associated with and used only by secular music are to be absolutely barred from liturgical services and religious devotions.[286] Any musical instrument permitted in divine worship should be used in such a way that it meets

---

[286] The stipulations of *Sacrosanctum Concilium* and *Musicam Sacram* should not be "retroactively" softened in view of the unfortunate normalization of the use in church of secular instruments in subsequent decades.

the needs of the liturgical celebration, and is in the interests both of the beauty of worship and of the edification of the faithful. (no. 63)

At the time this document was written, the piano and the guitar were manifestly associated with secular music—concert halls and lounges for the one, campfire singalongs and the 1960s folkish "counterculture" for the other—and definitely *not* with sacred music in church, which was the hallowed domain of voices, the pipe organ, and, on special occasions, string and wind instruments.

We have spoken more of the piano, but let us recall, too, that the acoustic folk guitar had never been an instrument used in church. In the Baroque period, more refined instruments like the lute, archlute, and theorbo were frequently used as part of the *basso continuo* accompaniment with strings and organ, but the solo guitar, even played in a classical style, was not part of the tradition—much less a guitar played in the strumming and syncopated style of folk-music or pop music.[287] The guitar spoke of one thing and one thing only: secular entertainment music. That is why the strictures of the documents quoted above (to which more quotations could be added) apply so unequivocally to it; and these are strictures that no Church document has ever repudiated or relaxed.

Banish all guitars and pianos from the church

The following year, 1968, less than a year before the infamous Woodstock concerts, Pope Paul VI had this to say on the matter:

> The primary purpose of sacred music is to evoke God's majesty and to honor it. But at the same time music is meant to be a solemn affirmation of the most genuine nobility of the human person, that of prayer. . . . Since that is the essential function for sacred music, what ground is there for allowing anything that is shabby or banal, or anything that caters to the vagaries of aestheticism or is based on the prevailing excesses of technology? . . . Vocal and instrumental

---

[287] In my article "Happy 200th Birthday, 'Silent Night,'" I note that *Stille Nacht* was premiered with an arpeggiated guitar accompaniment—but this was due to the pipe organ being broken down and in need of repair!

music that is not at once marked by the spirit of prayer, dignity, and beauty, is barred from entrance into the world of the sacred and the religious.[288]

It is noteworthy how many magisterial texts insist that instruments, in order to gain admittance to the church, must be such as to "edify the faithful." But what exactly does this mean? I would say it means this: apart from traditional instruments *already* enjoying longstanding approval and therefore safely assumed to be edifying when properly played, any *non*-traditional instrument that is disturbing, distracting, or annoying to members of the congregation is *ipso facto* excluded from use in church. It is no exaggeration to say that a simple survey of nearly any congregation in the world would indicate the presence of Catholics who are gritting their teeth every time the folksy strumming begins or the jazzy lounge-chords pour out from the electric piano. These people are certainly *not* being edified, and therefore the instruments in question are violating a fundamental precondition for their legitimate use.

Given the increasingly obvious failure of much of contemporary church music to embody the spirit of sacredness and the link with tradition that Vatican II and a multitude of other documents demand of all new compositions for the liturgy, it is surprising how prevalent guitars and pianos still remain in Catholic worship. This is all the more surprising given that it has never been difficult to discern the mind of the Church on this matter.

What if I told you that Pius X's official ban on pianos in church has never been lifted? But it is quite true. And how seriously ought we to take this fact? Let's have a look at the strong language he employs at the end of the prologue: "In order that no one for the future may be able to plead in excuse that he did not clearly understand his duty and that all vagueness may be eliminated from the interpretation of matters which have already been commanded . . . we do therefore publish, *motu proprio* and with certain knowledge, Our present Instruction to which, as to a juridical code of sacred music, We will with the fullness of Our Apostolic Authority that the

---

[288] Paul VI, Address to the *Associazione Italiana Santa Cecilia* (September 18, 1968), in *Notitiae* 4 (1968): 269–73.

force of law be given, and We do by Our present handwriting impose its scrupulous observance on all."[289]

I would like to suggest that a history of over fifty years of routine and ubiquitous violation of Pius X's clear provision—"the employment of the piano is forbidden in church, as is also that of noisy or frivolous instruments such as drums, cymbals, bells, and the like"—has placed us in a better, if unenviable, position to see the correct theological intuition, the lively spiritual instinct, the keen aesthetic judgment, and the fine liturgical sense that led to its formulation in the first place. These words of John Paul II have never been more timely: "Christians should rediscover the newness of the faith and its power to judge a prevalent and all-intrusive culture."[290]

It is fitting to return, time and again, to the prologue of Pius X's *Tra le Sollecitudini*. One perceives the intense piety and evangelical zeal that motivated the saintly pontiff to issue this "juridical code of sacred music" that has lost none of its relevance:

> Among the cares of the pastoral office, not only of this Supreme Chair, which We, though unworthy, occupy through the inscrutable dispositions of Providence, but of every local church, a leading one is without question that of maintaining and promoting the decorum of the House of God in which the august mysteries of religion are celebrated, and where the Christian people assemble to receive the grace of the Sacraments, to assist at the Holy Sacrifice of the Altar, to adore the most august Sacrament of the Lord's Body, and to unite in the common prayer of the Church in the public and solemn liturgical offices. Nothing should have place, therefore, in the temple calculated to disturb or even merely to diminish the piety and devotion of the faithful, nothing that may give reasonable cause for disgust or scandal, nothing, above all, which directly offends the decorum and sanctity of the sacred functions and is thus unworthy of the House of Prayer and of the Majesty of God. . . .

---

[289] The same document's prohibition of female singers (no. 13) was later lifted under Pius XII: see Kwasniewski, "Are Women Permitted to Sing the Propers?" This implies, however, that provisions *not* lifted remain in force.

[290] *Veritatis Splendor*, no. 88.

. . . Filled as We are with a most ardent desire to see the true Christian spirit flourish in every respect and be preserved by all the faithful, We deem it necessary to provide before anything else for the sanctity and dignity of the temple, in which the faithful assemble for no other object than that of acquiring this spirit from its foremost and indispensable font, which is the active participation in the most holy mysteries and in the public and solemn prayer of the Church. And it is vain to hope that the blessing of heaven will descend abundantly upon us, when our homage to the Most High, instead of ascending in the odor of sweetness, puts into the hand of the Lord the scourges wherewith of old the Divine Redeemer drove the unworthy profaners from the Temple.

19

Pouring the Argument into the Soul

AT ONE POINT in Plato's *Republic*, Thrasymachus, the nihilistic proponent of might-makes-right, asks his interlocutor Socrates, "Am I to take my argument and pour it into your very own soul?" To which query Socrates replies, "God forbid, don't do that!"[291]

I found myself thinking about this in connection with some truly despicable church music to which I once had been subjected: a Mass setting with lounge-lizard jazz harmonies, Broadway melodies, and not a milligram of sacrality. The vivid description given by Thrasymachus is, in fact, just how liturgy operates—especially its music. Liturgy pours an argument directly into our souls, before we have any chance to evaluate what is being done to us. Our reason is not capable of being a filter when the music comes into our ears, when various images pass before our eyes and become lodged in our memory, to be carried with us ever after until they are brought to perfection in heaven, scoured away in purgatory, or permanently fastened to us in hell. What happens experientially shapes us into an image of itself, before we have a chance to evaluate or accept or protest. This is why whoever attends a service is implicitly saying to it: "Shape me, make me like yourself."

God intended that it be so, and it is a fine thing as long as the liturgy is done properly. We *ought* to be formed like clay in the hands of the potter rather than sitting with arms crossed like theater critics.[292] When the sound of chant or bells floats into our ears, when the scent of incense creeps into our nostrils, when the sight of flashing raiment reminds us of an anointed mediator offering holocausts on the altar, then we are caught up in the

---

[291] Plato, *Republic*, 345b, in *Plato: Complete Works*, 989.
[292] On what I call "Mosebach's Paradox"—namely, that the more we know about liturgy, the more likely we are to turn into theater critics—and how to escape from it, see Kwasniewski, *Noble Beauty*, 169–72.

245

worship of the one true God, plunged into His holy mysteries, and renewed before and beyond all rationality. In this act of self-surrender, we water the roots of our everyday consciousness and, one might say, tie the emerging plant and bend it towards heaven.

However, nowhere is the axiom *corruptio optimi pessima* (the corruption of the best is the worst) more true. Socrates uttered his exclamation "God forbid, don't do that!" because he knew that if Thrasymachus could pour nihilism into his soul, his soul would be scorched or frozen before there would be time to react. It is too late to raise difficulties about arsenic once one has ingested it. In like manner, if the content or manner of the liturgy is flawed, God *will* be dishonored and our souls *will* be injured. There is no "perhaps" or "maybe" about it. We submit to a blurred vision of the Mass, the liturgy, the act of adoration, the life of prayer, and thus we deviate from the Catholic Faith as it has been taught and lived by the great saints who came before us.[293]

So, then, we always stand at a crossroads. Is this liturgy in which I am about to participate going to be a healthy and health-giving "argument" to pour into my soul? Will it be God-glorifying in its essence and in its accidents, and therefore perfective of me as a creature made in God's image? Or will it be harmful to the development of the interior life, missing the mark, displeasing to God, because it is an exhibition of willfulness, indolence, narcissism, tawdry pop culture, or any other corrigible defect?

I have heard church music that is so completely unsuitable for the freight of its words and the seriousness of its purpose within the Holy Sacrifice of the Mass that it constitutes a form of spiritual self-mutilation to allow oneself to be sonically assaulted by it, and a form of cruelty to allow impressionable children to be subjected to it. When I have been confronted by such situations (which were usually surprises), I have left the building or taken my family out until the music ended. Afterwards, I considered carefully how to avoid the same problem in the future.

---

[293] I highly recommend Linda Graber's three-part treatment of "Focus vs. Blur: Multi-Sensory Learning, Motivated Focus, and the Mass," published at *OnePeterFive* on January 15, January 25, and February 26, 2016. See also "Sorting Out Difficulties in Liturgical Allegiance" in Kwasniewski, *Reclaiming Our Roman Catholic Birthright*, 281–88.

We ought to get into the habit of thinking about this crossroads *ahead of time* so that we can make sound decisions for ourselves and our dependents based on what we can reasonably expect and hope for in our circumstances. We will be rewarded for our good efforts to seek public worship that truly merits the name "divine liturgy" (as our Byzantine brethren call it), a Mass that truly reflects its fuller name "Holy Sacrifice of the Mass."

As to how far one should be willing to go to find a liturgy that is worthy of God, of man, and of the God-man Jesus Christ, that depends on how bad the nearer options are. If they are bad enough to disturb your inner equilibrium, interfere with reverent prayer, set your teeth on edge, or make you want to lash out at the musicians, it's surely time to travel further afield, or even to consider pulling up tent pegs and moving. Given the massive crisis of faith, morals, and liturgy in the Church, Catholics should no longer expect to entertain, much less achieve, the old-fashioned ideal of long-term stability in a single place. We are never permitted, on account of work, family, or friends, to make a continual sacrifice of our spiritual health or our access to a God-pleasing liturgy, as this would conflict with the primacy of the love of God and the virtuous self-love that belongs to the theological virtue of charity: "Thou shalt love the Lord thy God with thy whole heart, and with thy whole soul, and with thy whole mind. . . . Thou shalt love thy neighbor *as thyself*" (Matt. 22:37, 39). Sometimes we may be forced to postpone a needed move by circumstances beyond our control, but this is manifestly a bad situation, not one that can be taken as permanent. Divine Providence has permitted the ecclesial crisis so that we may be tested as to whether we are, in fact, living according to the command to "seek first the kingdom of God and His righteousness," with faith that everything else we need will be added unto us (cf. Mt 6:33). Most of us know of families that drive one or two *hours* every week to get to a traditional Latin Mass, or families that go to a Byzantine Divine Liturgy in order to avoid the Western morass of their region. This is the stuff of heroism. It is the dry martyrdom that will populate the heavens.[294]

---

[294] Regarding the influence of the Mass on children in particular and the responsibility of parents to ensure a proper liturgical formation, see Kwasniewski, *Reclaiming Our Roman Catholic Birthright*, 87–93, 235–65.

Let us return to Plato. Socrates claims in the *Republic* that as the participants in the dialogue create a city through their speech, what is justice will
eventually emerge. In a way hardly surprising for those acquainted with his
uncanny proto-Christianity, Socrates managed to hit upon a fundamental
truth of worship. Liturgy is a certain "city in speech," within which God's
justice, His righteousness, emerges—or fails to emerge. When we celebrate
the liturgy, we are necessarily creating the *image* of a *city*. Which city is it? It
will be either the City of God, the heavenly Jerusalem, or the City of Man,
the worldly Babylon. What are the traits of these cities according to Saint
Augustine? A modern scholar, Robert Barr, offers a vivid summary:

> The City [of God] knows and worships one God only, and lives
> by His Law. Its directing virtues are *faith* in Him Who intends to
> save the city and *humility* in His sight. This is the faith which is
> necessary for salvation, and without which there is no return to the
> City—for which therefore the martyrs have borne whatever might
> come; and it is this humility which principally distinguishes the
> citizens of the City of God from their irreconcilable enemies, the
> subjects of the Devil.... The City of God is God's temple and true
> Sacrifice. While physically distinct from the Offering of the Mass,
> it is mystically identical with it.[295]

In its venerable forms handed down through the ages, Christian liturgy
is the foremost representation and guarantee of the orthodox Faith, and
by our Marian receptivity to it, we live most fully the virtue of humility in
the face of divine revelation.[296] When we worship in any traditional liturgy,
Eastern or Western, we know that we are safely drawn into the holy city of
Jerusalem, exercising our rights of citizenship, letting the King Himself rule
over our hearts and minds.

Far different is modern committee-fabricated liturgy, replete with dubious theological modifications and extemporaneous adaptations. It is not
an age-old, universally accepted proclamation of the orthodox Faith, a
measure against which all else must be measured, a trustworthy invitation

---

[295] Barr, "The Two Cities in Saint Augustine," 214–15.
[296] See "The Spirit of the Liturgy in the Words and Actions of Our Lady" in Kwasniewski, *Noble Beauty*, 53–87.

to self-surrender. This novel liturgy evokes the City of Man, promoting the all-too-human agendas of its compilers and impresarios. Describing Augustine's view of the citizens of this *civitas terrena*, "earth-born and earth-bound," Barr writes:

> Their interests are private, yet they lust to dominate the world. As a result their city is torn by passion, plague, and revolt. They only unite, it seems, against a common enemy—the City of God: glorying in their numbers and strength, they persecute that city—to the latter's advantage! . . . Really the most deadly persecution the devil and all his hellish minions can launch is that against the Faith itself, by inspiring heresy. He would, if he could, deprive the elect of God's Revelation, of their unanimous subscription to the teaching of the few writers of Sacred History [i.e., the inspired authors of Scripture], and scatter them among the adherents of the number-less philosophers of the City of Confusion.[297]

The City of Man is aptly expressed by two popular songs, one of them completely secular, the other faux-sacred: "We Built This City on Rock 'n' Roll" and "Let Us Build the City of God." In spite of the latter's title, its *logos*, *ethos*, and *pathos* (message, character, and feeling) is unquestionably by, of, and for the City of Man. It is horizontal, humanistic, constructivist, pragmatic, superficial, and dull. If this is what we listen to or sing, we should not be surprised at the results we get: in our souls, the result of cleaving to this world; in our communities, the result of looking to each other for a salvation that comes only from God. God's justice will fail to emerge.

The City of God, in contrast, is beautifully evoked by two truly sacred songs: the Gregorian chant *Urbs beata Jerusalem*,[298] which expresses the beauty of the heavenly fatherland for which we long, and which we glimpse past the veil of the sacred liturgy when it is true to God—

---

[297] Barr, "The Two Cities in Saint Augustine," 215–16. For more on this contrast, see Kwasniewski, "The Liturgy as a Temple."

[298] Changed to *Coelestis Urbs Jerusalem* under Pope Urban VIII. The translation by John Mason Neale is available at https://en.wikisource.org/wiki/Mediaeval_Hymns_and_Sequences/Urbs_beata_Jerusalem.

Urbs beata Jerusalem,	Blessed city of Jerusalem,
dicta pacis visio,	called "vision of peace,"
Quæ construitur in coelo	Which is built in heaven
vivis ex lapidibus,	out of living stones
Et angelis coronata	Encircled with angels
ut sponsata comite.	As a bride with her maids.

—and William Byrd's motet *Civitas Sancti*, which expresses the deep sorrow of the exile who has lost his earthly home. If these are the songs we sing or listen to, the wings of our soul will sprout and grow strong, and we will find ourselves yearning for the Lord more than watchmen for the break of day (cf. Ps 129:6). *This*, this is the city we must build in our souls, in our churches, on our altars. This is the argument, the *Logos*, that we want to have poured into us and into our children.

20

The Campaign against Musically-Shaped Memory

RESEARCH HAS DEMONSTRATED what everyday experience already knew: music is the most powerful of all memory aids. The reason small children so easily remember twenty-six pieces of otherwise unrelated information—the alphabet—is that they learn a song about it. Years after one has last heard a certain song, all it takes is a snatch of its melody for the whole thing to come flooding back. People in comas have reawakened when their loved ones sang or played familiar music to them. Music embeds itself deep in the psyche; its highly articulate structure secures for it a permanence that is often missing from mere text. It takes ten times longer to memorize a spoken poem than the same poem set to a melody.

We know that before the Council, there were still many places that, in spite of Pius X's best intentions, did not use the full chanted Propers but substituted for them "Rossini Propers" or something similarly minimalist; we know that the majority of Masses were recited, not sung or solemn. Nevertheless, there *were* High Masses and fully chanted Propers; this cannot be denied, for eyewitnesses and historical records confirm it. For many religious communities, a fully chanted Mass was normative. Popular liturgical writers could confidently refer to and comment on the chants of Mass, expecting to be understood. "Ad te levavi," "Puer natus est," "Nos autem," "Resurrexi," "Spiritus Domini," "Cibavit eos," "Requiem aeternam," "Gaudeamus omnes" were texts *and melodies* that enjoyed currency and, more importantly, embedded themselves into the collective ecclesial consciousness. They were the stuff of the Church's long-term memory. Everyone knew what "Gaudete" and "Laetare" referred to—namely, the Introits of the particular Sundays in Advent and Lent when rose-colored vestments could be worn.

In his letter *Sacrificium Laudis* of 1966, Paul VI encouraged monks and nuns to retain chant, but he certainly expected Mass everywhere else to be characterized by a *lack* of chant.[299] In his infamous General Audience of November 26, 1969, right before the *Novus Ordo Missae* was to go into effect, he said:

> It is here that the greatest newness is going to be noticed, the new-ness of language. No longer Latin, but the spoken language will be the principal language of the Mass. The introduction of the ver-nacular will certainly be a great sacrifice for those who know the beauty, the power, and the expressive sacrality of Latin. We are part-ing with the speech of the Christian centuries; we are becoming like profane intruders in the literary preserve of sacred utterance. We will lose a great part of that stupendous and incomparable artistic and spiritual thing, the Gregorian chant. We have reason indeed for regret, reason almost for bewilderment. What can we put in the place of that language of the angels? We are giving up something of priceless worth. But why? What is more precious than these loftiest of our Church's values?

He replies, not too convincingly, "The answer will seem banal, prosaic. Yet it is a good answer, because it is human, because it is apostolic. Understand-ing of prayer is worth more than the silken garments in which it is royally dressed. Participation by the people is worth more—particularly participa-tion by modern people, so fond of plain language which is easily understood and converted into everyday speech." It would be difficult to believe that the supreme pontiff, pope of Rome, actually said these words had they not been carefully recorded and committed to print and were they not readily available.[300]

---

[299] The firm line Paul VI appeared to wish to take by means of that document was torpedoed in 1967 by interventions from the new abbot primate of the Benedictines, Rembert Weakland, as the latter recounts in his *A Pilgrim in a Pilgrim Church: Memoirs of a Catholic Archbishop*, 121–23, 130–31. See Kuhner, "Rembert Weakland, Proud Vandal"; cf. Kwasniewski, *Once and Future Roman Rite*, 114–16.

[300] For a full commentary on this speech, see Kwasniewski, *Once and Future Roman Rite*, 108–43. The publication, with Paul VI's approval, of a tiny collection of Grego-rian chant in 1974, *Jubilate Deo*, was an effete and ineffectual gesture at a time when

Later in his address, the pope cautiously suggests that Latin will not per-
ish, but never says that chant will survive. The fact that he rushed to promulgate a missal in 1969 for which there was no corresponding chant book—a
glaring defect that would be repaired only in 1974 when the monks of
Solesmes finally published the revised *Graduale Romanum*, by which point
not only had the horses bolted from the barn but the barn had been razed
and the ground sown with salt—points to the same conclusion: this pope
had no intention of following one of the teachings of Vatican II that could
not be called ambiguous or ambivalent—namely, the assignment of "first
place in liturgical services" to Gregorian chant, as signed by 2,147 Council
Fathers and promulgated by the same pope only six years earlier (*SC* 116).

The loss of chanted Propers of the Mass was therefore a deliberate
strategy, not an accidental fallout. The appearance of the 1974 *Graduale
Romanum* was a sad afterthought that made no impact on parochial life;
the tradition had already been severed. Stories are rife of monks, nuns, fri-
ars, and laity chanting from the *Liber Usualis* one week, and the following week singing folksy English songs from binders or booklets, never to
take up the chant again.[301] What this means, if we go back to our opening
remarks about music as a repository and vehicle of memory (indeed, of an
ever-deepening memory that lives and grows while it endures), is that the
Church was systematically deprived of her most precious liturgical memories in the form of the cantillated Scripture verses with which her worship
had been adorned for at least a millennium and a half.

The result? A rupture or dissolution of memory that, at least as far as individuals and communities are concerned, would be comparable to severe amnesia or to Alzheimer's, with a superficialization of the meaning and content of
worship. It is not that one treasure was substituted for another, but a treasure

chant had very nearly disappeared from the face of the earth. Like the similarly unen-
forced *Sacrificium Laudis*, it is more a badge of shame than of honor.
[301] We are speaking, again, of the mid-sixties, even before the Novus Ordo was implemented. See the important research of Susan Benofy in her pair of articles concerning November 29, 1964: "The Day the Mass Changed, How It Happened and
Why," originally published in the *Adoremus Bulletin* in February and March 2010 but
available in better format at *Catholic Culture*: www.catholicculture.org/culture/library
/view.cfm?recnum=9377 and www.catholicculture.org/culture/library/view.cfm?rec
num=9378.

was lost, and in its place was put a random collection of vastly inferior items that enjoyed neither diachronic nor synchronic universality. The power of music to retain and transmit the Faith was fragmented, atomized, and fluxified. The replacement of the annual reading cycle with two-year and three-year reading cycles,[302] the abolition of many priestly prayers in the Mass (at the start, at the Offertory, before Communion, before the final blessing),[303] the distension of the integral one-week psalter to an expurgated four-week psalter,[304] the optionitis and opportunities for presidential improvisation—all of these moves run strongly against the formation of memory by continual repetition. Together they guaranteed that almost no Catholics—including, tragically, the clergy—would be able to *internalize* the liturgy to such an extent that it became bone of one's bone, flesh of one's flesh. Or, at any rate, what was internalized would be inadequate compared to the inheritance of the Faith. Instead, due in part to the sheer quantity of text and in part to the assumption of recited liturgy as normative, the clergy would have to remain largely at the level of reading texts out of "official books."[305] This reinforced an unhealthy mentality of legal positivism and cut off Catholics from an ingrained, intuitive sense of what is and is not liturgy, what is and is not in keeping with tradition. If one has the liturgy *within oneself* because of its stability of form, manageable compass, rhythm of language, and most of all its standard assigned music, then one attains much more readily that *experiential knowledge* called by Saint Thomas Aquinas "connatural knowledge"—that is, intimate acquaintance of something's essence not by reasoning but by sympathy. One would therefore be in a position to

---

[302] For an overview, see Kwasniewski, "Mythbusting."

[303] See Kwasniewski, "On Liturgical Memory" and "The Relationship between Priest and People in the Latin Mass."

[304] See Kwasniewski, "The Omission of 'Difficult' Psalms and the Spreading-Thin of the Psalter."

[305] Not to mention the shuffling, shifting, and supplanting of liturgical texts and ceremonies that took place with bewildering rapidity throughout the whole period of "reform": each year of the decade from 1962 to 1972 saw more changes in the way the Mass was celebrated than all of the changes from 1570 to 1955 combined. It is as if an intelligence of supreme malice were deliberately endeavoring to undermine the preconditions of both liturgical life and the interior life.

tell when a note jarred against this harmony, when a word or phrase grated against the ear.

In short: the ancient liturgy is capable of *planting itself within*, while the reformed liturgy is spread out in so many texts and books, and multiplied by options, that it would be well-nigh impossible to "have it" within. This makes its user less offended by deviation and more pliant to officialdom, from which the books are handed down.

Imagine Roman clergy from the Middle Ages who had somehow been transported to our time and had sat through a parish Novus Ordo Mass. Assuming they had not died of cardiac arrest, their first question would be: "Where was the *Ad te levavi?*" or "Where was the *Puer natus?* We didn't hear it anywhere." They knew what the Roman liturgy was, *not* because it had been dictated to them by a pope or any conference of bishops but because they had it in their ears, their mouths, their hearts. This was true, be it noted, well before and well after the missal issued by Saint Pius V in 1570, since the text, music, and ceremonial aspects of the various Latin rites and uses enjoyed considerable analogy with one another and a stability of form akin to the massive stone architecture of their churches: they were recognizably from and for the Catholic Church.[306] From the High Middle Ages on, the Roman rite had changed only by certain minor modifications until 1907 when Pius X laid hands on the Breviary and the 1950s when Pius XII disfigured the Holy Week ceremonies.[307]

The worst part about loss of memory is that, after a certain point, the one suffering from it no longer realizes that he has lost it. Traditionalists in the Church today are like nurses trying to remind a patient of who she is or where she came from or who her relatives are, showing pictures from the past, singing a snatch of song, trying in some way, in any way, to reactivate the memory of a beloved mother.

Thanks be to God, not all hope of recovery is lost. For indeed the Church is not a monolithic entity with merely mortal powers but is composed of many members united in their Head. The eternal Head of this Body has

---

[306] Against the myth that Pius V "gave the Church a new missal," see Shaw, "St Pius V and the Mass."

[307] On the twentieth-century reforms, see Kwasniewski, *Once and Future Roman Rite*, 332–75.

never lost His memory and never will; He sends the Spirit of truth to remind the disciples of all that He has taught, not only in His lifetime but in the lifetime of the Church that He governs from heaven, and on which He has bestowed the treasures of liturgical rites and their traditional music. The memory is present in actuality in Him, and in a mixture of act and potency among us, as in a body with some healthy limbs and some diseased or damaged limbs. The prophet says to us: "Strengthen ye the feeble hands, and confirm the weak knees" (Is. 35:3). The *rigor mortis* of legal positivism is giving way to the warm love of tradition for its own sake.[308]

To change metaphors, rebuilding a bridge that has collapsed is difficult but not impossible, if there is a willingness to reconnect the two sides over the abyss. I have been singing the Proper chants for the *usus antiquior* for thirty years now, and have reached a point where they are totally ingrained in me. Every Sunday, practically every holy day, the chants are right there in my soul, brought up instantly when the singing begins. And the same is true for many of my friends and acquaintances around the world, a growing number that includes new recruits, new reverts and converts, cradle Catholics who have been driven by a longing for more to seek out a worship that has and is more. It is no surprise that conversions (and vocations) are prompted and deepened by encounters with the great music of the Church, for, as David Warren points out, this music is intrinsic to her identity and mission:

> Through the centuries, and even to the present day, the faith of the Church has been communicated by music, as much as by words; the very Word, through the Church, embodied in music. The training of choirs, of organists and harpists, of practitioners in every musical art, has been a constant function. It is an essential function; it was never merely decorative. The Mass in its nature is sung, chanted; and the innumerable musical settings of the Mass are intrinsic to its meaning, to its universality, to the dimensionality: it is not "just words." They are ἔπεα πτερόεντα— "winged words"—and music has borne them aloft. I am convinced that the recovery of the musical traditions, within Holy Church, can do more to evangelize than any

---

[308] See Kwasniewski, *True Obedience in the Church.*

quarrelling with the world. For what we must do is not argue, but proclaim; and music in its nature does not argue. It proclaims.[309]

The memory of the Church that some might have thought irrecoverably lost has, by the grace of God, remained alive in the Mystical Body of Christ on earth. A bridge, even if a narrow and rickety one, has been erected again, joining the past to the future by way of the present. What a privilege to be a part of the rebuilding—part of the reactivating and transmission of beautiful, noble, gracious memories.

---

[309] Warren, "Oh Had I Jubal's Lyre." A slight caveat: we certainly *should* argue, against errors and for the Faith (this is what apologetics does at its best), but we must also, and more fundamentally, proclaim the beauty of Christ and of His Immaculate Bride.

PART III

Giving Way to Silence

21

The Endangered Sonic Species

THE CAMPAIGN AGAINST silence—yes, let us call it such—is one of the great follies of our times. Cardinal Sarah has spoken eloquently, out of a deep faith and spirit of adoration, about the dictatorship of noise in secular life and increasingly in the domain of the sacred—a campaign conducted like warfare that takes no prisoners.[310] It is becoming harder and harder to find *any* quiet place in the world: cafés and restaurants pump in music so loud that one can barely hear the person across the table; shops, stores, offices, gas stations, facilities of every description seem to be acting under a cosmic memorandum to avoid silence at all costs; if the ambient noise is inadequate, ubiquitous earbuds will ensure an uninterrupted flow; even many parks and recreational areas have their sweet peace nibbled away by the sound of constant automobile traffic and airplanes crisscrossing the sky. As if this were not challenge enough to health of mind, one can rarely find a Catholic church building or liturgy that respects the profound human need for silent recollection in the presence of the living God, who speaks tenderly to the receptive heart.

Proponents of the restoration of liturgical sanity speak much about sacred music, and no wonder, given the power of music to transport us heavenward into the mysteries of God—or to stifle our prayer with paltry imitations of secular tunes. But we are no less committed to silence, music's necessary counterpart and prayer's inseparable companion. As Saint Faustina Kowalska says in her autobiography, "In order to hear the voice of God, one has to have silence in one's soul and to keep silence. . . . Silence is so powerful a language that it reaches the throne of the living God. Silence is His language, though secret, yet living and powerful."[311]

---

[310] See Sarah, *The Power of Silence Against the Dictatorship of Noise.*
[311] Kowalska, *Diary: Divine Mercy in My Soul,* §118; §888.

Her statement prompts us to consider the silence we ought to have during Holy Mass. The relative proportions of speech, song, and silence are determined by the rubrics of the traditional Latin Mass, but a wide latitude still remains in the determination of the ratio of silence to music. In the Mass of Paul VI, this latitude becomes nearly open-ended, as there are few fixed standards by which the proportions are dictated. In spite of this amorphousness, many Catholics still have a fairly good sense of when there is too little silence for recollection.

To the action of the liturgy we bring ourselves, our voices, our words and songs—but there comes a time when we must yield to a mystery greater than anything we can think, feel, speak, or sing. In the process of making bread, we actively mix together a number of ingredients, but then we have to let the dough sit for a while and patiently await the work of the yeast. It is not enough to know in a merely conceptual way that all of our efforts are inadequate and that the living God is encountered in the still, small voice. Everyone agrees with that in theory, it seems, but too often in practice, liturgy is conducted as if silence were an optional, incidental affair, something to be pursued in private by individuals who feel so inclined but not a distinguishing feature of Catholic worship.

In the liturgies of the Christian East, wave upon wave of singing mounts to heaven, and silence is rare. The liturgies of the Christian West, in contrast, developed in ways that brought in substantial spans of silence interspersed between chanted or recited texts. Without denigrating the value of Eastern practice, Roman Catholics should regard their own approach as no less *dignum et iustum*.[312] The opportunity for a restful abandonment to God alone—letting our activity, however good and necessary it may be, yield to His action, invisible and inaudible—is for us an inseparable element of liturgical life, and one we neglect at the peril of curtailing its natural momentum and trajectory. Spans of silence in the setting of public worship point to a realm entirely beyond what we ourselves are doing or contributing and prompt an experiential knowledge of it.

Within the Western context, if there is no moment in the liturgy when we are not *doing*, but simply *being*, when we are not acting, but resting

---

[312] See Kwasniewski, *Once and Future Rome Rite*, 304–11.

in God's presence—above all, after the reception of Holy Communion—then we risk importing a subtle Pelagianism into our worship, as if it is primarily something *we* initiate, sustain, and complete. A community living out its dependence on divine grace will be one in which the liturgy is enveloped in silence before Mass and after Mass,[313] and one in which silence during Mass is not a bane to be driven away by any and all means. Here I have to express my chagrin about music directors who feel they must fill up every moment during the liturgy with chant, polyphony, or organ music, lest—God forbid!—there be a few moments of quiet, when each worshiper is left to himself in prayerful recollection. Acting thus is to overdo a good thing, like a person who eats chocolate all the time because it's so delicious and has forgotten about the role of water or, for that matter, of fasting. As this book has shown, I always defend the normativity and preferability of the sung Mass, without denigrating the great value of the Low Mass. Yet even in a sung Mass there can and should be moments of silence in which deep recollection is possible so that the singing and ceremonial will bear the most fruit in souls. John Paul Sonnen reminds us, "Liturgical silence is not empty, it is full of answers. . . . Silence is attractive. It calms the soul and body. . . . As the American Renaissance writer Herman Melville once wrote, 'All profound things and emotions of things are preceded and attended by silence.'"[314]

Silence seems to come naturally with the traditional Roman rite or *usus antiquior* because it contains more (and more elaborate) gestures and much for the priest to do on his own, which leaves pools of quiet here and there in

---

[313] With these words, I refer to the general atmosphere before and after Mass; I do not mean to exclude the playing of a tasteful organ prelude or a thundering organ postlude, since such music is quite fitting for the time right before and right after the Mass (see chapter 18). It would take a separate article to consider the pros and cons—mostly cons, in my opinion—of public recitation of the Rosary before Mass. I say this as one who loves the Rosary and prays it daily but who prefers to be quietly recollected before Mass or to say some portion of the breviary. I have talked to many others who feel the same way, but it seems difficult to get the point across to clerical authorities and lay leaders that a twenty-minute public vocal prayer prior to Mass is something of an imposition.

[314] Sonnen, "On Silence in the Liturgy." There is never a need to play organ during the Canon, or to leave no quiet time after Communion and before the Postcommunion prayer.

which the faithful find precious opportunities to intensify their own prayers as the liturgy progresses. Father Roberto Spataro explains the significance of this trait:

> Humility is more than a virtue. It is the condition for a virtuous life. Watch the bows and genuflections the humble man makes faithfully before God in a spirit of obedience, acknowledging His merciful sovereignty, His love without bounds, His creative wisdom. Reason is not tempted to be puffed up, as happens in the revolutionary process, because in the old rite not everything can or ought to be explained by reason which, for its part, is content to adore God without comprehending Him. It turns to Him through the means of a sacred language differing from ordinary speech, because in the harmonious order of creation that the liturgy represents in its rituals, there is never a monotonous repetition or tedious uniformity, but a symphony of diversity, sacred and profane, without opposition, respecting the alterity of each. Here reason also renounces an excessive use of words that unfortunately exists in the liturgical praxis inaugurated by the *Novus Ordo*, interpreted by many priests as the opportunity for pure garrulousness. In the old rite, on the other hand, reason appeals to other dimensions of communication and, besides words pronounced or sung, also gives silence a place. This silence becomes the atmosphere, impregnated with the Holy Spirit, in which believing thought and prayerful word is born.[315]

Above all, the silence that falls during the Roman Canon cordons off the holiest portion of the liturgy, erecting a sonic iconostasis, powerfully signaling that something awesome, ineffable, divine, and miraculous is taking place, and calling all to utmost attention in response to it. No amount of speech or music could ever do the same with remotely comparable success.[316]

The Mass of Paul VI is also supposed to leave room for silence, as its governing document spells out:

---

[315] Spataro, *In Praise of the Tridentine Mass and of Latin, Language of the Church*, 30.
[316] The silent Canon is the subject of chapter 23.

Sacred silence also, as part of the celebration, is to be observed at the designated times. Its purpose, however, depends on the time it occurs in each part of the celebration. Thus within the Act of Penitence and again after the invitation to pray, all recollect themselves; but at the conclusion of a reading or the homily, all meditate briefly on what they have heard; then after Communion, they praise and pray to God in their hearts. Even before the celebration itself, it is commendable that silence be observed in the church, in the sacristy, in the vesting room, and in adjacent areas, so that all may dispose themselves to carry out the sacred action in a devout and fitting manner.[317]

Silence in the new rite nevertheless tends to be elusive and unsatisfactory. Many observers have pointed out that the moments of silence, because they are "staged" and usually at the discretion of the celebrant, come across as artificial and awkward; usually nothing else is going on, so they seem empty or static moments rather than filled with ritual action or restful contemplation. It is easier to get impatient in these clerically controlled silences and to wonder when the next "module" will get started. The root problem here is with sequential liturgy as a paradigm, instead of the traditional (Catholic) approach of parallel liturgy.[318] In a liturgical rite where the clergy are kept busy with an abundance to do and to pray (much of it inaudible to the congregation), periods of silence open up naturally, organically, in an unfocused and ambient way, freeing up a space for the people to pray interiorly while feeling unobserved—engaged but not put on the spot. As a modern commentator on liturgy has written:

> The silence that the priest maintains here [at the foot of the altar] and in different places in the Sacred Liturgy is not an absence of sound. It has no gaps; it is a single great canticle, and the silence acts as an acoustic veil over the whole liturgy to reveal what the liturgy is. The Gregorian Rite has no artificial introduction of silence into the liturgy by the addition of pauses. When silence is at the beck and call of the celebrant, as opposed to the rite, the silence of

---

[317] *GIRM*, no. 45.
[318] See Kwasniewski, *Once and Future Roman Rite*, 159–62, 291, 294.

the priest becomes the whole congregation waiting for him, wondering what is going to happen next. The silence in the Gregorian Rite is given as an integral part of the Mass, determined by the Church through two thousand years of development. And what often seems like silence in our rite is not quite silence; it is rather the priest praying to God in a low voice.[319]

When the priest is "busy" with the liturgy, the people too can be "busy" with the liturgy.[320]

In the modern sequential liturgy, by contrast, normally only one thing can happen at a time, and the people are frequently called upon to make some outward response. The anthropocentric aura of *versus populum* causes every silence to be focused somehow on the celebrant himself. In a clericocentric rite, silences are generally at the mercy of the president; whenever a silence comes, we are habituated to waiting for the priest to start talking to (or at?) us again. It is a tense silence rather than a peaceful one. Since even the silence is something the priest is "doing for us" or toward us, *we* become the object of it rather than God, and prayer comes with difficulty; there is little or no room or freedom for one's own prayer, one's own action. The difference, albeit hard to put into precise words, is rather obvious in the actual experience of the old and new rites.[321] It is the difference between a quiet symphony of praying and a regimented drill with short breaks.

A properly understood liturgical silence overflows the boundaries of Mass itself and seeps into the space before and after like incense diffusing throughout the sanctuary. To quote Father Edward McNamara: "Silence should be observed after Mass until one is outside the Church building, for respect both toward the Blessed Sacrament and toward those members of the faithful who wish to prolong their thanksgiving after Mass."[322] Would that this simple support of Eucharistic piety, churchly decorum, and respect for others could be patiently explained and encouraged far and wide by the

---

[319] Jackson, *Nothing Superfluous*, 97.
[320] See Kwasniewski, "The Relationship between Priest and People in the Latin Mass."
[321] See Kwasniewski, *Noble Beauty*, 72–74.
[322] McNamara, "Sounds of Silence."

clergy![323] Across the United States, congregations burst into chatter the moment the priest exits the church. For all the problems there may have been in the 1950s, this sort of behavior was not even conceivable.

Similarly, for the priest to take some minutes to recollect himself before Mass, especially by praying the traditional vesting prayers (which used to be required and which are now being rediscovered by a new generation), seems only sensible in view of the mysteries about to be re-enacted and the importance of a reverent and recollected frame of mind if he is to obtain as many and as great graces from the celebration as he can, and lead the people into the same prayerful pastures.

No "new evangelization" can possibly succeed, none can even get off the ground, unless we recover a strong sense of the sacred and refocus on the sublime mystery of the Holy Eucharist present on every altar of sacrifice and in every tabernacle, where God deigns to dwell with men. Otherwise, we will spend our days making and hearing empty talk, missing the silence in which the mystery of God impresses itself on our souls. Pope John Paul II reminded the Church:

> One aspect that we must foster in our communities with greater commitment is *the experience of silence*. We need silence "if we are to accept in our hearts the full resonance of the voice of the Holy Spirit and to unite our personal prayer more closely to the Word of God and the public voice of the Church" (*Institutio Generalis Liturgiae Horarum*). In a society that lives at an increasingly frenetic pace, often deafened by noise and confused by the ephemeral, it is vital to rediscover the value of silence. The spread, also outside Christian worship, of practices of meditation that give priority to recollection is not accidental. Why not start with pedagogical daring *a specific education in silence* within the coordinates of personal Christian experience? Let us keep before our eyes the example of Jesus, who "rose and went out to a lonely place, and there he prayed" (Mk 1:35). The Liturgy, with its different moments and symbols, cannot ignore silence.[324]

---

[323] See Kwasniewski, *Reclaiming Our Roman Catholic Birthright*, 168–71.
[324] Apostolic letter *Spiritus et Sponsa* (December 4, 2003), no. 13.

The poignant lines of T. S. Eliot's *Ash Wednesday* come to mind:

> Where shall the word be found, where will the word
> Resound? Not here, there is not enough silence
> Not on the sea or on the islands, not
> On the mainland, in the desert or the rain land,
> For those who walk in darkness
> Both in the day time and in the night time
> The right time and the right place are not here
> No place of grace for those who avoid the face
> No time to rejoice for those who walk among noise and deny the voice[325]

Three things are packed into that last verse: no time to rejoice—for those who walk among noise—and deny the voice. An essential condition for man to be sane and rational and joyful is that he must, at times, let go of his everyday concerns, the whirling wheels of his calculating and planning, the burdens and cares of this life, and enter into the presence of the eternal and infinite God whom he cannot grasp, cannot dictate to, cannot manipulate, but only adore and love. For Eliot, the four dispositions for encountering the Absolute are humility, detachment, silence, and wonder. Their common denominator could be called receptivity, or else the pursuit of holiness. These dispositions are exactly contrary to our modern (anti-)culture of noise, disillusionment, consumerism, and self-advancement.

It is a paradox: we will not find time for rejoicing unless we sacrifice time to "do nothing," to make a burnt offering of our life and our time before the Lord, in a silence without props, without scripts or safe paths or social support. Only by making a choice for inactivity, as it were, will we habituate ourselves to *stop* walking among noise and *stop* denying the voice. Perhaps this is why the prophet Isaiah says: *Cultus iustitiae silentium*—the worship of justice is silence (Is. 32:17 in the Vulgate), as if to say, we owe everything to God, in whom we live and move and have our being (cf. Acts 17:28), and it is justice to worship Him in the silence of our hearts.

Gabriel Marcel, a perceptive philosopher of the interior life, had this to say about the relationship between recollection and mystery: "Not only am

---

[325] Eliot, *Complete Poems and Plays 1909–1950,* 65.

I in a position to impose silence upon the strident voices which usually fill my consciousness, but also, this silence has a positive quality. Within the silence, I can regain possession of myself. It is in itself a principle of recovery. I should be tempted to say that recollection and mystery are correlatives."[326]

Is this not another way of saying: "he that shall lose his life for my sake, shall find it" (Matt. 16:25)? We lose possession of what is more exterior to us and gain possession of the innermost reality—God closer to me than I am to myself, yet higher than the highest in me.[327] If the conditions for recollection are never present in our lives, if we do not fight to create and guard such conditions, we will lose our awareness of divine mystery, which ought to refresh us like springtime rains; we will wander aimlessly in a wilderness of superficiality.

Now, if a modern-day liturgist were reading along, he would be ready to explode by this time: "The way you describe silence in the liturgy . . . it's opposed to the people's *active participation*! That's what matters above all."

That may have been Vatican II's perspective, but it was not Pius X's, nor that of the Catholic tradition he transmitted.[328] Yet even if, for the sake of argument, we went ahead and assumed our liturgist's viewpoint, it would not undermine the argument of this chapter, for one simple reason: *the fundamental precondition for active participation is interior silence.* As Father McNamara explains, a spirit of recollection

does not impede, and indeed favors, full and active participation . . . for each person is more fully aware of what he or she is doing. Our modern world is starved of silence and Holy Mass should be a privileged moment to escape the hustle and bustle of daily life and, through worship and participation in Christ's eternal sacrifice, become capable of giving an eternal value to these same daily and transitory activities. To help achieve this, we should foment by all available means the spirit of attentive and active silence in our celebrations and refrain from importing the world's clamor and clatter into their midst.[329]

---

[326] Marcel, *Being and Having*, 113.
[327] See Augustine, *Confessions* III.6.11.
[328] See Kwasniewski, *Ministers of Christ*, 131–40.
[329] McNamara, "Sounds of Silence."

Remaining in silence before God is, in fact, a particularly noble form of human *activity*—more active than merely speaking or singing, which can easily be done in a distracted frame of mind. Developing the dispositions of heart and mind necessary to be able to derive spiritual refreshment from silence is a school of virtue in which every Christian should be enrolled as a lifelong pupil.[330]

John Paul II articulates this point authoritatively in his 1998 *Ad Limina* address to the bishops of the northwestern United States: "Active participation does not preclude the active passivity of silence, stillness and listening: indeed, it demands it. Worshippers are not passive, for instance, when listening to the readings or the homily, or following the prayers of the celebrant, and the chants and music of the liturgy. These are experiences of silence and stillness, but they are in their own way profoundly active. In a culture which neither favors nor fosters meditative quiet, the art of interior listening is learned only with difficulty. Here we see how the liturgy, though it must always be properly inculturated, must also be countercultural."[331]

Silence and appropriate sacred music convey to our minds the awareness of a transformative mystery, a mystery that is both frightful and alluring, by which we can come to grips with sin and death and pass beyond them into love and life. The Mass is the supreme sacrifice of Calvary made present; this is the reason why Catholic worship pivots on the crucifix. The life-giving death of God is put before us: reason enough for silent awe. As Joseph Ratzinger said back in 1968: "If the Church were to accommodate herself to the world in any way that would entail a turning away from the Cross, this would not lead to a renewal of the Church, but only to her death."[332]

The Counter-Reformation liturgical aesthetic underlined the essence of the Mass as the sacrifice of the Cross by aligning the chasuble's cross-like pattern, the altar of immolation, the tabernacle shrine, and the crucifix in a visually escalating series that reinforced the centrality of the consecration and elevation—as also do the *ad orientem* stance and the silence in which the Canon is enveloped.[333] All of these elements worked marvelously together

---

[330] See Fiore, "Silence before God in the Life and Writings of Saint Thomas Aquinas."
[331] *Ad Limina Address to the Bishops of Washington, Oregon, Montana, Idaho and Alaska* (October 9, 1998), §3 and §4.
[332] Cited in Ratzinger, *Co-workers of the Truth*, 167.
[333] See Kwasniewski, "The Sacrificial Nature of the Mass in the *Usus Antiquior*," and

to concentrate the worshiper's senses, thoughts, and desires on that which is essential and central. They work no less marvelously today, and will do so for all time.

The papal master of ceremonies under Benedict XVI, Guido Marini, compellingly summarized the latter's views on silence:

> Silence is necessary for the life of man, because man lives in both words and silences. Silence is all the more necessary to the life of the believer who finds there a unique moment of his experience of the mystery of God. The life of the Church and the Church's liturgy cannot be exempt from this need. Here the silence speaks of listening carefully to the Lord, to His presence and His word, and together these express the attitude of adoration. Adoration, a necessary dimension of the liturgical action, expresses the human inability to speak words, being "speechless" before the greatness of God's mystery and the beauty of His love. The celebration of the liturgy is made up of texts, singing, music, gestures and also of silence and silences. If these were lacking or were not sufficiently emphasized, the liturgy would not be complete and would be deprived of an irreplaceable dimension of its nature.[334]

For Ratzinger, music and silence are interdependent correlatives. Authentic sacred music is born out of silence and returns gently into silence. It arises not as an imposition on people or as a provocation of them, but as an awed response to God's beauty—an attempt at interpreting, among us, the heavenly music far above us. Similarly, a truly prayerful silence is one that is, of its very nature, receptive to appropriate sound, whether spoken or sung. The right music is capable of emerging harmoniously from silence and merging peacefully into it; the wrong music does violence to silence, overpowering and stifling it.

If an ecclesial community does not have a regular experience of profound and *meaningful* silence, the souls of the faithful cannot be expected to respond

---

"The Removal of Tabernacles and the Desacrificialization of the Mass."

[334] Interview of Msgr. Guido Marini with Maddalena della Somaglia in *Radici Cristiane* 42 (March 2009), trans. Shawn Tribe and published as "Msgr. Guido Marini Speaks Again on the Liturgy, Its Forms and Its Importance." Cf. Marini, *Liturgical Reflections of a Papal Master of Ceremonies*, 30–32, 85–87.

sympathetically to the "musical tradition of the universal Church," which the Second Vatican Council called "a treasure of inestimable value, greater even than that of any other art," and which the same council instructed us to "preserve and foster with great care" (SC 112, 114). You cannot plant seeds in ground that has not been cultivated and expect an abundant harvest; you might as well be throwing seeds out for the birds (cf. Mt 13:4). The cultivation of a habit of adoring silence in the presence of God is therefore a precondition for the maximum fruitfulness of sacred music. Answering the question "Which is better in the liturgy, music or silence?" Jeremy Holmes eloquently probes this correlativity:

> Silences comes in many shapes. There is a silence of despair; there is the sudden silence at a beautiful sunset; there is a silence of awe; there is a silence of confusion and confuddlement; there is a silence of intimacy and closeness. Of the many shapes of silence, some are appropriate at Mass and some are not.
>
> What defines a silence are the sounds around it, as a frame defines a door. The silence one hears just after a crash and just before a scream is defined by the crash and the scream. The silence that comes after Gregorian chant and before the priest's sacred utterance is defined by the music before it and the words following. At an entertainment Mass with guitars and yodeling music, the silence between the sounds has a definite and nameable character: it is *dead time*. It is the silence we hear between acts.
>
> In the end, one cannot choose between music and silence in the abstract, because music is what defines the silence as *this* kind of silence rather than that. One may as well ask whether we should prefer the silhouette or the white paper around it.
>
> Properly *sacred* music at Mass—Gregorian chant, polyphony, organ instrumentals—acts as a frame around the silence and so defines it as *sacred* silence, densely meaningful, ready to be filled with prayer. Conversely, silence at Mass acts as an internal direction or weight for the music and so keeps it anchored in the eternal stillness, the "Word without a word."[335]

---

[335] Personal correspondence.

Both music and silence are profoundly united in their dependence on each other, and even more, in their inherent trajectory beyond themselves into the heart of the mystery of God.

Saint Benedict of Nursia (c. 480–548) is the father of Western Monasticism and co-patron of Europe. His *Rule* for monasteries came to be so widely accepted and followed over the centuries by such a vast host of culture-preserving and civilization-building monks and nuns that he must be considered one of the chief architects of Christendom and of the great flourishing of the medieval Church. Yet modern Christians are inclined to ask: Can a monk who lived 1,500 years ago have anything relevant to teach us today?

Not only does he have much to teach us, but the very fact that he lived so long ago gives him a special advantage in this regard. For, as C. S. Lewis says in his preface to Saint Athanasius's *On the Incarnation*, moderns—that is, people who all belong to the same current or recent time-period—tend to be imprisoned in a whole set of assumptions about the ways things are or must be or should be, taking them for granted and not even being aware of any alternatives; whereas the ancients, operating by a completely different set of assumptions than ours, are in a position to confront, question, undermine, even shatter our assumptions. He concludes that the more old books we read, the more self-knowledge, self-critique, and self-improvement will become possible for us. The irony is that only old things can make us new, while exclusively new things will make us grow old in our foolish ways.[336]

Saint Benedict understood everything said earlier in this chapter extremely well, as we can gather from his *Rule*, where he speaks in many places about the necessity and importance of silence. Most characteristic are his words about the oratory or chapel: "Let the oratory be what its name implies, and let nothing else be done or kept there. When the Work of God [viz., liturgy] is finished, let all go out in deep silence, and let reverence for God be observed, so that any brother who may wish to pray privately be not

---

[336] See C. S. Lewis, Introduction to St. Athanasius, *On the Incarnation*; also published under the title "On the Reading of Old Books" in *God in the Dock*, 200–207.

hindered by another's misbehaviour."[337] Benedict understands that the liturgy is meant to carve open within us a space for God and a space for silence so that our prayer, the conversation of loving friends, can blossom.

The patriarch of monks also tells us, "Monks ought to be zealous to keep silence at all times."[338] This may seem initially to be an exaggeration when we consider how many hours a day monks devote to corporate chanting of the divine praises at Mass and in the Office, and how much their recreation or their hospitality may call upon them to speak to others. How can the monks be keeping silence "at all times"? The *Rule* wishes us to see vocal prayer and charitable conversation, done in the right spirit, as themselves stemming from and filled with the silence of a heart recollected in God's presence and aspiring to His service. They are, in other words, a translation of that interior silence into chants and words; they share in the peace of God and increase it in one's surroundings.

Benedict insists nevertheless on *literal* silence throughout the night and, whenever possible, during the day. In the richly rewarding chapter 4 of the *Rule*, concerning "the instruments of good works" (which can serve as the basis for an excellent examination of conscience),[339] he provides us with a negative reason based on fallen human nature, and a positive reason based on the lofty aim of the Christian life. The saint of Nursia recognizes that, sinners as we are, we are far too often "given to grumbling," detraction, "evil or depraved speech," excessive talk—and that these things make it difficult for us "to listen with a good will to holy reading" and "to be frequently occupied in prayer." Although he does not mention it, the same difficulty arises from any useless, frivolous, or distracting noise in our environment.

But why should we want to "listen to holy reading" and "be occupied in prayer"? The same chapter establishes the goal: so that we may "become a stranger to worldly deeds," put our hope in God, and "prefer nothing to the love of Christ." For many of us living in the world, these phrases establish a

---

[337] *Rule*, ch. 52, in *The Rule of Saint Benedict in English and Latin*, 119.

[338] *Rule*, ch. 42, following the translation given in the edition published in London by S.P.C.K. in 1931.

[339] See the presentation given in Kwasniewski, "A New Examination of Conscience for Lent."

glowing ideal, always imperfectly realized. Still, one cannot reach a distant destination without taking steps, be they small or great, to reach it.[340] A peaceful, recollected heart, full of silent love, drinking the cup of the Lord's passion and tasting the sweetness of His victory—this is where we want to end up. If we are going to get there, we must begin here, now, today, with carving out more time, more space, for silence in our lives.

---

[340] See Kwasniewski, "The secret to success: prayer at the start of the day."

22

"Where Has God Gone?"
The Pressure of *Horror Vacui*

In a famous passage in *Joyous Wisdom*, "the parable of the madman," Friedrich Nietzsche writes:

> "Where has God gone?" he cried. "I shall tell you. *We have killed him*—you and I. All of us are his murderers. But how have we done this? How were we able to drink up the sea? Who gave us the sponge to wipe away the entire horizon? What did we do when we unchained this earth from its sun? Whither is it moving now? Whither are we moving now? Away from all suns? Are we not perpetually falling? Backward, sideward, forward, in all directions? Is there any up or down left? . . . Do we not hear anything yet of the noise of the gravediggers who are burying God? . . . God is dead. God remains dead. And we have killed him. How shall we, murderers of all murderers, console ourselves?"[341]

"Maybe I'm a babe in the woods," a friend once wrote to me,

but last night I had the shock of my life. I went on YouTube and looked up an Orthodox monastery in Romania that I visited during communism. Some man had apparently been there and taken some pictures, and now he's posted a slide show. He wrote in the description that he'd used "Gregorian music" in the background, and as my dad used to say, I pretty near dropped my teeth. Someone had apparently had people sing Gregorian chant in a studio, added a drum track and a little bit of synthesizer, and had a woman's voice

---

[341] Nietzsche, *The Portable Nietzsche*, 95.

intruding whispering little slogans about peace and other things. The biggest shock to me, though, was that the man who posted this—who was no spring chicken—*actually thought this was Gregorian chant.* There are probably lots of Catholics who think the same thing, but it's Gregorian chant distorted for New Age purposes. I'd never heard anything like that before!

It comes close to one of my universal laws about food: Anything that is beautiful and subtle will eventually have fruit flavoring or corn syrup added. People always feel a compulsion to add something. But they never take anything away.

Recently I had to attend Mass at my neighborhood parish, and I discovered that what is really wrong—besides all the other things that are wrong—is what in art school we were taught to call *horror vacui*, fear of empty space. A typical amateur artist wants to fill every millimeter of space on a canvas with some kind of image, so the whole painting fights with itself. Good artists know how to use empty space. At this parish there's not a second of silence from a half hour before Mass starts until after the crowd leaves. If you want quiet time to prepare for Mass, you have to arrive about two hours early. About ten minutes before Mass starts, the chatter has swelled to the volume of a pavilion at the state fair, and then once Mass starts, the musicians will not leave a second of quiet without twanging. Not even after Communion. When I was a kid, the very same church was solemn and tranquil before Mass. No one breathed a word. Now people confuse church with a meetin' hall and Mass with a TV show. Just the simple fact that the musicians don't see the importance of receding at certain points during the liturgy is bothersome to me as someone with a visual arts background.

This colorful and all-too-true catalog of horrors, of the *horror vacui* sort, again indicates the unfathomable level of cultural regression and religious ignorance at this time in Western history. Apart from particular causes of regression and ignorance, there is a general cause, laid over all like a stifling blanket, that prevents us from recognizing our situation for the abysmal prodigy it is: the arrogance of modern man, who is supposed to be so "advanced" and to have progressed beyond all other ages. In reality, as Pope Pius XII said, "the technical age will accomplish its monstrous masterpiece of transforming man into a giant of the physical world at the expense of his spirit, which is reduced to that of a pygmy in the supernatural and eternal world."[342]

Pope Francis has spoken about the importance of observing moments of silence in the Mass, but he has shown no awareness of two crippling problems.[343] First, silence in the new rite is artificial and barren of ritual significance. It does not arise because the priest is busy doing something else quietly, so that a natural span of silence results for everyone else, nor does it arise from the schola's chanting of the Gradual and Alleluia. Inasmuch as this *novum silentium* is at the beck and call of the celebrant, it becomes a subtle mechanism for enhancing his "presidential status," since he decides when to start and stop it. In that way, it is more like yoga meditation under the direction of a guru than it is Christian liturgical prayer.

Second, silence before, during, and after Mass has been killed, and its assassin is the liturgical reform in every decade of its implementation. For decades, the *GIRM* has been practically a dead letter when it comes to the actual liturgical life of most parishes. The progressives have been only too happy to push along countless practices that go explicitly against the *GIRM*, using the sponge of their hegemony to wipe away the entire horizon and unchain the Mass from the Cross, and no one has seriously attempted to correct them, even after *Redemptionis Sacramentum*,[344] which did little or nothing to reverse the perpetual falling of liturgy "backward, sideward, forward, in all directions."

Cardinal Sarah, like a voice crying in the wilderness, reminds modern Westerners that nothing is more urgent for our spiritual sanity than protecting and promoting silence in our lives—not just in our liturgical worship, but in our personal prayer, even in our leisure and recreation. Without this

---

[342] "L'era tecnica compirà il suo mostruoso capolavoro di trasformare l'uomo in un gigante del mondo fisico a spese del suo spirito ridotto a pigmeo del mondo soprannaturale ed eterno." Radio message of Pius XII to the People of the World, December 24, 1953.

[343] See Brockhaus, "Be intentional about silence during Mass, Pope Francis says." The same superficial notion of liturgical silence is found in the apostolic letter *Desiderio Desideravi*, no. 52.

[344] See Kwasniewski, "Fidelity to Liturgical Law and the Rights of the Faithful."

empty space, there can be no interiority, no contemplation, no actual worship as opposed to "busy work," the sort that substitute teachers give their fidgeting pupils while the real teachers are absent. We seem to be crushed by *horror vacui*, and it is only getting worse with the rapid inundation of all manner of pocketable or wearable devices, which fill every waking moment of our lives with the noise of information and entertainment—"the noise of the gravediggers who are burying God."

At this strange moment in history, the New Liturgical Movement is also going to have to be a movement for natural, normal, face-to-face human interaction without distracting digital demons; for time spent making and repairing things with one's own hands; for the *stabilitas loci* that comes from being quiet in a chair, at a table, in a room, by a window, with a book and nothing else. Such things are the natural analogues of the intimate contact with intangible beauty that comes from singing or hearing plainchant at Mass, smelling the incense, seeing the glittering gold on cope and chalice, becoming aware of one's breathing or heartbeat in the silent Canon.

Élisabeth-Paule Labat, a gifted pianist who gave up her career to become a Benedictine nun, writes: "At first sight, silence appears to be characterised by the absence of sound, and thus to be something negative. Yet on a higher level we sense that there is a positive silence, a silence which indicates not absence but presence, not emptiness but fullness. . . . It is like a transparent veil before the most exalted presence. Within this silence, the course of time seems suspended. The world of earthly realities has not disappeared, but we have left it behind."[345]

"Let us who mystically represent the cherubim and sing the thrice-holy hymn to the life-creating Trinity now set aside all earthly cares" (the Divine Liturgy of Saint John Chrysostom). What are the cultural preconditions—the *personal* prerequisites—for being able to respond from the depths of one's soul to the needs and demands of the liturgy; for recognizing that in liturgy we walk fearfully on holy ground, as we enter a charged space filled with angels; for awakening to the sense of divine *presence* that would infallibly guide us back to our traditional modes of worship, abandoning with a sigh of relief all the modern claptrap that burdens us?

---

[345] Labat, *The Song That I Am*, 112.

I believe we must resolutely push back against a trend that began (inno-
cently enough, perhaps) in the Liturgical Movement, quickly colonized
the schools, and, before long, won over the hierarchy, until it lodged in the
successors of Peter. I refer to the operative assumption that verbal comprehension and interaction is the highest and possibly the only form of
communication—a piece of dubious rationalism at best, and a culturally
destructive tsunami at worst.

Pope Pius XI famously said in his 1928 document *Divini Cultus* that
Catholics should not be "merely detached and silent spectators" at Mass
(*extranei vel muti spectatores*). I am sympathetic to this statement if we
are talking about the value of the faithful's singing of the Ordinary and
responses at a High Mass. There is little reason for them not to do so and
many reasons for them to do so, as explained in chapter 9. But one wonders
if Pius XI, or whoever wrote the text for him, was already under the influence of a certain modern way of thinking, whereby *doing* something external,
or at least seeming to be visibly or audibly involved, is the major point to be
accentuated, the litmus test or punch ticket.[346] This idea grew over the next
forty years into the self-sapping activism of the Novus Ordo era, as I pointed
out elsewhere: "The notion that laity who sit or kneel quietly at Mass and
do not vocally participate are 'detached and silent spectators' is something
of a caricature, and the mantra-like use made of this phrase in subsequent
decades of an increasingly audacious Liturgical Movement culminated in a
heavy-handed enforcement of 'active participation' by authorities (real and
self-appointed), which has numbered among its casualties the interior participation that often thrives on silence and sacred music."[347] Should we not
instead be thinking first about the manner in which one is *entering into* the
liturgy—the way one is assimilating it, relating to it interiorly?

In the old days, it used to be said that Catholics "assisted at" Mass. This
concept is fruitful. Every member of the body assists in (and at) the divine
uplifting of the liturgy, each according to his place, but without thinking
that he has to take on any particular action, other than faith-filled attention.

---

[346] He, doubtless, would not have fallen for so simplistic a version of it. Later figures
like Annibale Bugnini seem to have lost any appreciation for non-rationalistic and
non-externalized participation.

[347] Kwasniewski, *Ministers of Christ*, 142.

It was also common in the old days, in fact for centuries, to say that Catholics went to "hear Mass." We read in the lives of lay saints like Louis IX that "he heard Mass twice a day."

Modern liturgists wince at that expression, for to them it seems to epitomize the worst of the Tridentine (or, let's say, broadly medieval) era: a bunch of laity "doing nothing but" listening while the priest and server spoke all the words of the Mass on their behalf. In their view, only the ones saying or singing the Mass are *doing* it. Indeed, the dialogue Mass, promoted first by the same Pius XI, was intended as an alternative, one might even say a remedy, to move people from hearing to speaking.

But we should pause and think more about hearing. Family counselors often like to make a distinction between hearing and listening—between mere auditory reception and actually absorbing the import of what is being said and responding appropriately. "You heard me, but did you listen to me?" When people are said to "hear Mass," the meaning surely is that they are *listening* intently with the ear of the heart, to use the lovely expression of the *Rule* of Saint Benedict.

Listening is a difficult activity to do well. It is something that requires experience, practice, concentration, receptivity, humility—an openness to being the carved-out space in which a word or sound can dwell and bear fruit. It is not for nothing that the vast majority of works of art that depict Our Lady show her looking at and listening to the Archangel Gabriel rather than talking back to him or taking action. She is pondering the Word of God in her cell; she receives his greeting and wonders within her heart what it means; after the dialogue (usually not depicted), she accepts the Word made flesh. The Virgin Mary assists at the first Mass; she hears the first Mass.

As John Paul II loved to say, the Blessed Virgin Mary reveals to us that *being* is more basic than *doing*, and *receiving* is more fundamental than *giving*—just as our insertion into Christ at baptism, which *happens* to us (we suffer a spiritual death and God raises us up), is more basic to our identity than any particular act we perform on the basis of our baptism.[348] No man makes himself a Christian; he (or his parents on his behalf) consent that he be made a Christian by God.

---

[348] See Kwasniewski, *Resurgent in the Midst of Crisis*, 103–10; *Ministers of Christ*, 83–90.

Modern times are characterized by an unusual degree of noise, busyness, and image saturation. We are always being drawn out of ourselves, out of our deep inner identity as sons of God, into distractions and dissipations. "You were inside and I was outside," as Saint Augustine confessed to God.[349] For this reason, and without for a moment abandoning the importance of the High Mass as the fullest and most beautiful expression of the liturgy, I will say that the quiet Low Mass is *also* more relevant and more needed than ever, as a bulwark against the total extroversion and superficiality of secular life—and of secularized ecclesial life.[350]

One wonders if the forms of meditation offered by Buddhism and other increasingly popular Far Eastern phenomena would ever have made such huge inroads in Western society without the loss of the one omnipresent form of "silent meditation" that we once had in abundance.[351]

There have been many times in my life when I have longed for nothing more than a quiet Low Mass early in the morning. Attending it was like arriving at an oasis in the desert, or stepping through a low wooden door into a secret garden. Assisting at Mass, one can feel the roots sinking deeper into the earth, the branches reaching out higher towards the heavens, the leaves opening to the sun and the buds ripening. It is a time outside of time, a place of holy encounter, leaving one speechless and happy not to speak.

---

[349] See *Confessions* X.27.
[350] See "The Peace of Low Mass and the Glory of High Mass" in Kwasniewski, *Noble Beauty*, 235–55.
[351] See Leong, "Malaysian Ex-Buddhist on the Western Fascination with Buddhism"; Kwasniewski, *Road from Hyperpapalism*, 2:234–40.

23

The Majesty of the Silent Canon

IN AN ESSAY from the 1930s that deserves a second look today, Anglican scholar Charles Harris brings forward an abundance of quotations from the earliest liturgical sources to support his contention that the silent rec-itation of part or all of the Anaphora or Canon of the Eucharistic liturgy became the norm very early on in both East and West. This evidence, and the underlying theology and spirituality to which it points, is a clarion call for Catholics of the Roman rite to continue to work zealously for the resto-ration of the silent Canon, either by the spread of the *usus antiquior* where the custom remains intact, or by the reestablishment of the custom in the *usus recentior*. This ancient and longstanding custom, like the *ad orientem* stance and the exercise of liturgical roles by ordained ministers, expresses the great reverence due to Our Lord Jesus Christ, Eternal High Priest and Sacrament Most Holy.

Harris first talks about the psychology of silence, saying, "The effect of silence (or of subdued or whispered speech) is to lull the outward senses into a receptive condition; to induce tranquility, repose, and inward peace; to relax the tension of the nervous system; and gradually to induce a state of restful waiting upon God, which opens the 'subconscious' or 'unconscious' mind to the influence of grace and religious suggestion."[352]

Those who attend quiet Low Masses are aware of the profound peace and sacred stillness that can reign in the soul as in the church building itself, and as much as I am an ardent advocate of the sung Mass, I recognize, too, that there is a precious devotional value, a mystical-ascetical power, in the *Missa*

---

[352] Harris, "Liturgical Silence," 775. The realization of how far back this practice goes and how widespread it was is yet another incentive for disbelieving the liturgical re-formers' oft-repeated claim to be intent upon restoring ancient practice. They were more in the business of introducing novelty.

lecta or *Missa recitata*. But it has also frequently struck me, as a choirmaster, how much silence there can be even in the midst of a sung Mass, whether it be during the Canon or around the time of the Communion of the priest. The old Roman rite in general has the character of an entering into God's "rest," that mysterious Sabbath rest of the seventh day that anticipates the glory of the everlasting eighth day of heavenly bliss (cf. Heb 4:2–11).

In second place, Harris attempts to locate the origin of the transition from a spoken Anaphora to a partially or completely silent one. "At an early but undetermined date, it gradually became customary, both in the East and in the West, to recite certain of the most solemn Eucharistic prayers, particularly the greater part of the Canon, in a very low or inaudible voice. Such recitation was termed "mystic" (*mystikos*), an epithet which sufficiently indicated its significance.... It evinced just such an overpowering sense, not merely of humility, but even of 'abjection' and 'nothingness,' as befits a creature admitted to the immediate presence of its Creator."[353]

Almost as an aside, Harris dares a general judgment about the character or feel of Catholic worship as compared with Protestant: "It can hardly be denied that the 'mystic' prayer of the celebrant [in the silent recitation of the Canon or Anaphora] has been a prime factor in creating that thrilling atmosphere of rapt adoration which has been the distinctive feature of Catholic worship throughout the ages; and which the more intellectual, instructive, and 'edifying' worship of modern Protestants seems unable to evoke."[354]

Reading these words caused me to cringe when I realized that his description of "Catholic" matched the *usus antiquior* while his description of "Protestant" lined up with the Novus Ordo—intellectual, instructive, and (in the best cases) edifying, as its architects intended it to be, but not typically characterized by a "thrilling atmosphere of rapt adoration." Many Catholics who have fled from the modern to the traditional form of Mass have done so not primarily to escape rampant abuses but to find a spiritual refuge that encourages meditation and adoration. It is a quasi-monastic "flight from the world" in order to find God. If we do not encounter the living God in prayer and go out of ourselves to worship Him in spirit and in truth, we will be hopeless when it comes to living a Christian life in the

---

[353] Harris, 775.
[354] Harris, 776.

workaday world. A certain alternating rhythm of interior recollection and outward engagement is necessary, and perhaps it is the relentless emphasis, in the Novus Ordo context, on the outward, the busy, the active, the evangelistic, that has drained Catholics of their deepest spiritual resources for battling the world, the flesh, and the devil.

Third, Harris argues that the silent or "mystic" recitation of the Anaphora is bound up with an ever more heightened emphasis, in liturgical texts as in preaching, on the awesome reality of the divine mysteries of Christ's Body and Blood entrusted to the Church. Although "even from the beginning of Christianity some degree of awe and dread accompanied the celebration of the Holy Mysteries, as is clear from the language of Saint Paul (1 Cor 11:26–33),"[355] we can trace this awareness most clearly in the three main Eastern liturgies, those of Saint James, Saint John Chrysostom, and Saint Basil.

Harris argues that the Liturgy of Saint James, bearing within itself the early liturgy of Jerusalem, already substantially existed in its present form as early as 348, and places its composition at 330–335 because of its allusions to Nicene Christology. What is more relevant to our purpose here than the date is the description Harris offers: "An atmosphere of mystical awe pervades the whole of this Liturgy. The worshippers are said to be 'full of fear and dread' while they offer 'this fearful and unbloody sacrifice,' which is further described as a 'fearful and awe-inspiring (*phriktēs*) ministration.' After consecration, the elements are spoken of as 'hallowed, precious, celestial, ineffable, stainless, glorious, terrible (*phoberon*), dreadful (*phrikton*), divine (*theon*).'"[356]

Many similar phrases from Saint Cyril of Jerusalem are brought in to confirm the point that this is familiar language for the Christians of this period, the middle of the fourth century.

The Liturgy of Saint Basil, attributed with good reason to the saint (ca. 330–379) himself, is no different: "A sense of 'numinous' awe pervades this Liturgy, which speaks of the Mysteries as not only 'divine, holy, spotless, immortal, heavenly, and quickening'; but also as 'tremendous' or 'fearful' (*phrikton*, literally 'to be shuddered at')."[357]

---

[355] Harris, 776.
[356] Harris, 777.
[357] Harris, 778.

Harris believes that Chrysostom's remarks on 1 Corinthians 14:16 suggest that *parts* of the Anaphora were recited audibly, especially the concluding words "for ever and ever," giving the cue for the people's response of "Amen"—exactly as the Roman rite has the priest say or sing aloud *per omnia saecula saeculorum*, with the same response.

The early Church offers witnesses of this universal practice of silence during the Anaphora. A stunning homily from a Nestorian of the late fifth century, Narsai (d. 502), tells us that after the *Sursum corda* and before the *Sanctus*, "all the ecclesiastical body now observes silence, and all set themselves to pray earnestly in their hearts. The Priests are still, and the deacons stand in silence . . . the whole people is quiet and still, subdued and calm. . . . The Mysteries are set in order, the censers are smoking, the lamps are shining, and the deacons are hovering and brandishing [fans] in likeness of watchers [i.e., angels]. Deep silence and peaceful calm settles on that place: it is filled and overflows with brightness and splendour, beauty and power."[358]

Narsai goes on to note that the priest pronounces the Epiclesis inaudibly, because he is worshipping "with quaking, and fear, and harrowing dread," and yet that the moment of the Epiclesis is proclaimed by a herald to the congregation so that they may be duly moved to reverence and adoration. The herald cries: "In silence and fear be ye standing: peace be with us. Let all the people be in fear at this moment in which the adorable Mysteries are being accomplished by the descent of the Spirit." The advent of the great King is a moment of terrible joy and earnest exultation, as Saint Augustine reminds us in his commentary on Psalm 2:11, *Servite Domino in timore: et exsultate ei cum tremore*, "Serve ye the Lord with fear, and rejoice unto Him with trembling": "Very excellently is *rejoice* added, lest *serve the Lord with fear* should seem to tend to misery. But again, lest this same rejoicing should run on to unrestrained inconsiderateness, there is added *with trembling*, that it might avail for a warning, and for the careful guarding of holiness."[359]

Harris concludes his treatment of oriental liturgies by noting that the practice of the silent or "mystic" recitation of the Anaphora was the established and official use of all rites by the close of the eighth century—in

---

[358] Harris, 779.

[359] St. Augustine, *Exposition of Psalm 2*, no. 9, in *Nicene and Post-Nicene Fathers*, First Series, 8:4.

spite of the emperor Justinian attempting, by an imperial decree in the year 565, to prohibit the practice and require all prayers of the liturgy to be said aloud! Evidence indicates, says Harris, that the same practice of silent recitation obtained in the Roman rite from at least the eighth century.

Lastly, having summarized the Anglican tradition's emphasis on the spoken vernacular word, Harris makes a practical proposal for the Anglican church, with a view to recovering something of the mystical dimension that had been lost. His advice ends up having a strange relevance for Roman Catholics today who seek ways to celebrate the rite of Paul VI by reference to the "gold standard," the traditional Roman rite, its ancestor and exemplar: "An audible voice need not be a loud voice. It is possible to obtain the full 'mystical' effect of silence by reciting the Canon in a very low and subdued voice, fully audible to every careful listener in the church, and yet expressive and suggestive of the deepest religious awe. It is not desirable, for the sake of one or two partially deaf persons, to raise the voice, and thus impede the devotion of the general congregation, which is fostered and augmented by the use of a subdued tone of voice."[360]

While I do not concur with Harris that one obtains the *full* mystical effect of silence by subdued recitation, his advice is sound as far as it goes: a Canon recited more quietly is vastly to be preferred to the radio announcer voice in which the anaphora is typically said by Roman clergy.[361] One is reminded of Cardinal Ratzinger's suggestion that we ought to reexamine whether, in the Novus Ordo, part or all of the Canon should once again be prayed silently, to invite the appropriate response of prayerful reverence, which, ironically, the constant same-tone recitation of familiar texts has a way of diminishing, if not excluding altogether.[362] As he writes in *The Spirit of the Liturgy*, "Anyone who has experienced a church united in the silent

---

[360] Harris, "Liturgical Silence," 782.

[361] A student once confided to me how confused she was as a little child at Mass, watching the priest talking loudly to the congregation in front of him but addressing God. She said it was like someone looking at you but talking at length to someone else. She later realized that the problem had two aspects: the *versus populum* stance and the speaking aloud as if talking to a group. These two aspects are obviously not unconnected; indeed, the one seems to call for the other.

[362] See Olver, "A Note on the Silent Canon in the Missal of Paul VI and Cardinal Ratzinger."

praying of the Canon will know what a really *filled* silence is. It is at once a loud and penetrating cry to God and a Spirit-filled act of prayer. Here everyone does pray the Canon together, albeit in a bond with the special task of the priestly ministry. Here everyone is united, laid hold of by Christ, and led by the Holy Spirit into that common prayer to the Father which is the true sacrifice—the love that reconciles and unites God and the world."[363]

There is a more general lesson in Harris's research: when it comes to the silent or "mystic" recitation of the Canon, we are looking at a custom that goes back to the middle of the first millennium of Christianity. For those who value what is ancient, this is ancient indeed, and since man's needs are fundamentally the same from age to age, the Church, having found early on the liturgical approach that fits best with the reality being celebrated and the persons being saved, preserved that approach jealously for all the centuries thereafter. A modern commentator on the Mass observes:

> The silence [of the Canon] also harmonizes with the mystery of Transubstantiation, in which the material elements of the bread and wine are changed into the Body and Blood of Christ, without the senses perceiving it or the created mind [being] able to comprehend it; the Real Presence and sacrificial life of the Savior under the sacramental species are concealed beyond all discernment. So the holy silence is quite suited to indicate and to recall the concealment and depth, the incomprehensibility and ineffableness of the wonderful mysteries enacted on the altar. "The Lord is in his holy temple; let all the earth keep silence before him!" (Hab 2:20)[364]

For those who think modern man needs something different from the man of every other age, the ancientness of a custom carries no weight. But in order to be fully consistent, the modernist must never shore up his positions by appealing to ancient practices or testimonies; he must fashion his liturgy out of whole cloth from his own head, without reference to the past. Once the criterion of tradition as such is laid aside as inappropriate for modern man, any choice from a past century or millennium will be merely

[363] Ratzinger, *Spirit of the Liturgy* (comm. ed.), Pt. 4, ch. 2, sec. e, 229–30; *Collected Works* 11:136–37.
[364] Jackson, *Nothing Superfluous*, 201.

arbitrary or political. Put simply, the appeal to modernity as a first principle cancels out the appeal to the early Church or to any phase of Christian history. The cancellation of the very possibility of tradition as a norm, when in reality tradition is a constitutive principle of the Catholic Faith, demonstrates that the goal of "modern liturgy for modern man" is false in and of itself.

Everyone who maintains that we ought to worship in continuity with our forefathers can gratefully receive the liturgy from their hands—with its fundamental characteristics that have never changed at all, like the eastward orientation of clergy and people, as well as with those characteristics that received their definitive shape in the Patristic period and were not abandoned until the arrogant experimentation of the 1960s.

Dum medium silentium tenerent omnia, et nox in suo cursu medium iter haberet, omnipotens Sermo tuus, Domine, de caelis a regalibus sedibus venit.[365]

The ancient custom of the silent Canon confirms the intuition that the Word comes to us in the liturgy in a personal mode that transcends the notional presence of the Word obtained by reading individual words from a book.[366] The Introit quoted above strikingly brings together both of these points: the coming of the Word Himself in the midst of silence. As Romano Guardini comments:

> The Christmas liturgy includes these beautiful verses from the eighteenth chapter of the Book of Wisdom: "For while all things were in quiet silence and the night was in the midst of her course, Thy almighty Word leapt down from heaven from Thy royal throne. . . ." The passage, brimming with the mystery of the Incarnation, is wonderfully expressive of the infinite stillness that hovered over Christ's

---

[365] Introit, Sunday within the Octave of Christmas, *Missale Romanum* 1962. Translation below.
[366] See Kwasniewski, "Why 'Mass of the Catechumens' Makes Better Sense Than 'Liturgy of the Word,'" and "Why the 'Word of God' for Catholics is not only the Bible, but more importantly, Jesus Himself."

birth. For the greatest things are accomplished in silence—not in the clamor and display of superficial eventfulness, but in the deep clarity of inner vision; in the almost imperceptible start of decision, in quiet overcoming and hidden sacrifice. Spiritual conception happens when the heart is quickened by love, and the free will stirs to action. The silent forces are the strong forces.[367]

The practice of *lectio divina* (praying with Scripture) is very dear to me as a Benedictine oblate. It is the mainstay of monastic private prayer. The Lord unquestionably speaks to us in and through Sacred Scripture, and we must constantly go to this source to hear Him.[368] But He comes to us more intimately still in Holy Communion. The traditional practice of the priest praying the Canon silently emphasizes that Christ does not come to us in *words* alone but in the one unique Word which HE IS, and which—immanent, transcendent, and infinite as it is—no human tongue can ever express. Once we have absorbed this fact in our life of prayer, the words of Sacred Scripture can penetrate our hearts *more* effectively and have a more than (or other than) Protestant effect on our minds.

What I mean by a "Protestant effect" is the way that Protestants can listen to or look at Scripture again and again—for example, John 6 or 1 Corinthians on the Eucharist, or Matthew 16 on the papacy—and yet their minds remain closed to its obvious Catholic significance. They are like the disciples on the way to Emmaus, who are thoroughly steeped in Scripture but have failed to grasp the central point—namely, the victory of the Messiah over sin and death by His death and resurrection. Jesus *in person* has to explain to them what they already "know" but have never internalized—and Jesus comes to us *in person* in the Real Presence and is internalized in the most radical way when we are permitted a share in His Body, Blood, Soul, and Divinity.

When the "Liturgy of the Word" is vouchsafed a distinct existence as one of the two parts of the Mass, and particularly when this distinctiveness is enhanced by a gargantuan lectionary with often lengthy readings frequently detached from the other prayers and antiphons of the Mass, there arises the impression of a text that is free-floating and self-justifying, the reading and

---

[367] Guardini, *The Lord*, 13.
[368] See Kwasniewski, "*Lectio Divina*," as well as other parts of the series linked there.

preaching of which can become the pastorally central arena, throwing the sacramental essence of the Mass into shadow. How often have we experienced the Liturgy of the Word ballooning to an overwhelming size, out of all proportion with the pulsing heart of the liturgy, the offering of the sacrifice and the ensuing Communion? In many Masses, the time used by the opening greeting, the readings, and the homily is some forty-five minutes, while somehow everything from the presentation of the gifts onwards is crammed into fifteen minutes. In the rush to be done (now that the gregarious and intellectually engaging business of readings and preaching is over), either Eucharistic Prayer II or III is chosen—prayers that are utterly dwarfed by the preceding textual cornucopia, seeming like a pious afterthought. The anaphora and its still point, the consecration, shrink and lose their centrality.

How different is the motion of the traditional liturgy! It is a gradual escalation leading logically, one could even say ecstatically, to the Offertory, the Preface, the Sanctus, the Canon, the prayers after the Canon, and the Communion. Everything prior to this—Prayers at the Foot of the Altar, the Confiteor, the *Aufer a nobis*, the Collects, Epistle, interlectional chants, and Gospel, the Credo—is, and is experienced as, preparatory to something far greater, driving forward with eager longing to reach the fulfillment, the *realization*, of the word *of* God in the one Word which *is* God. The consecration looms at the axis of all.[369]

Accordingly, it makes sense that much of the Order of Mass and the preponderant part of its Proper should be sung or spoken aloud up to the Creed, whereas at the Offertory and again in the Canon a decisive shift is made to silence, to the loving contemplation of the voiceless and eternal *source of meaning* behind the words of Scripture and the Creed. Yet the Holy Spirit led the Church to introduce the wonderfully eloquent elevations of the Host and Chalice, which wordlessly capture all that words could never say about the offering of Christ on the Cross out of love for sinners. This Host is elevated *for us*, for us men and for our salvation, for us to *see* and

---

[369] One could also maintain that the Foremass or Mass of Catechumens in a chanted Mass follows a line of continuous ascendancy from the Introit to the Gospel (with the Creed as our response in faith), while the Mass of the Faithful follows a line that culminates in the consecration (with Communion as our response in charity). For more on the structure of the first part of Mass, see Kwasniewski, "Homogeneity vs. Hierarchy."

worship: "And this is the will of my Father that sent me: that every one who *seeth* the Son, and believeth in him, may have life everlasting" (John 6:40). "And I, if I be lifted up from the earth, will draw all things to myself" (John 12:32). In the midst of the silence of the Canon, suddenly the bells are rung and the priest elevates the High Priest into the sight of all, the Eucharistic God-Man suspended between man and God, the victim whose death reconciles man and God (the significance of a crucifix over the center of the altar takes on its meaning here: the symbol of the death of Christ is "confronted" with its living Reality, the visible image is mystically confronted by its hidden Exemplar). This elevation speaks with a fullness that the silence of the Canon accentuates in the most dramatic manner possible.

This profound silence at the very center of the Mass is just one among a thousand reasons why Christians hungry for the meat and drink of God find the appetite of their souls at once satisfied and provoked by the traditional Latin Mass. It has a word to speak to each of us in its magnificently arranged antiphons, lessons, and prayers, redolent of the weight of ages but fresh in the vigor of their human realism and supernatural savor; more than that, it has the Word without a word to overcome us and comfort us. It touches and stirs obscure depths in us where the Gospel has yet to be preached, transforming us with a gentle and terrible earnestness. To more and more souls, fed up with the stream of verbiage and noise characteristic of modernity (and, sadly, of too many liturgies that echo it), this silence is calling and speaking.

Sacred music is like the sparkling crown jewel placed amidst the colorful gems of good music, artfully set in the gold and silver circlet of silence. The one who wears this artistic, intellectual, and spiritual crown, surmounting the vesture of the virtues, is truly a king or a queen, radiant with a beauty that recalls the hidden but all-pervasive beauty of the Creator, for the sight of whose face we yearn with groans too deep for words (cf. Rom 8:26). These three gifts from God are indispensable in the pursuit of righteousness and in the restoration of our Church and our culture. They are pillars on which the Church's public liturgy as well as the "liturgy" of everyday life triumphantly stand, enabling man's heart to ascend to God and to abide with Him. Good music, sacred music (especially Gregorian chant), and silence are echoes of eternity, intimations of immortality, invitations to the wedding feast of the Lamb. Ensuring their continued and valued existence is one of our noblest missions.

Bibliography

The BIBLIOGRAPHY IS divided into two parts: (I) Sources cited in this book and (II) additional recommendations, including periodicals and websites. For recommendations of particular movies and recordings, see chapter 5. Articles that are listed here with exact dates are to be found on the internet.

SOURCES CITED IN THIS BOOK

Ecclesiastical Documents (Conciliar, Papal, Episcopal)

Benedict XVI. Address to the Italian Episcopal Conference, May 24, 2012.
———. Dedication of Organ in Regensburg Basilica, September 13, 2006.
———. General Audience on St. Romanus the Melodist, May 21, 2008.
———. Meeting with Clergy of the Diocese of Bolzano-Bressanone, August 6, 2008.
———. *Porta Fidei*. Apostolic Letter, October 11, 2011.
———. *Sacramentum Caritatis*. Post-synodal Apostolic Exhortation, February 22, 2007.
Congregation for Divine Worship and the Discipline of the Sacraments. *Redemptionis Sacramentum*. Instruction on certain matters to be observed or to be avoided regarding the Most Holy Eucharist, March 25, 2004.
Council of Trent. *The Canons and Decrees of the Council of Trent*. Translated by H. J. Schroeder. Rockford, IL: TAN Books, 1978.
John Paul II. *Ad Limina Address to the Bishops of Washington, Oregon, Idaho, Montana, and Alaska*, October 9, 1998.
———. Address to the Participants in the International Congress of Sacred Music, January 27, 2001.
———. *Ecclesia de Eucharistia*. Encyclical Letter, April 17, 2003.
———. *Spiritus et Sponsa*. Apostolic Letter, December 4, 2003.
———. *Veritatis Splendor*. Encyclical Letter, August 6, 1993.
Paul VI. Address to the *Associazione Italiana Santa Cecilia*, September 18, 1968. In *Notitiae* 4 (1968): 269–273.
Pius X. *Tra le Sollecitudini*. Instruction on Church Music, November 22, 1903.
Pius XI. *Divini Cultus*. Apostolic Constitution, December 20, 1928.
Pius XII. *Mediator Dei*. Encyclical Letter, November 20, 1947.
———. *Musicae Sacrae*. Encyclical Letter, December 25, 1955.
———. Radio Message to the People of the World, December 24, 1953.
Pontifical Council for Culture. *The «Via Pulchritudinis», Privileged Pathway for Evangelization and Dialogue*. Document of the Plenary Assembly, 2006.
Sacred Congregation of Rites. *De Musica Sacra et Sacra Liturgia*. Instruction on Sacred Music and Sacred Liturgy, September 3, 1958.

————. *Musicam Sacram.* Instruction on Music in the Liturgy, March 5, 1967.

Sample, Alexander K. "Rejoice in the Lord Always." Pastoral Letter on Sacred Music in Divine Worship. Diocese of Marquette, January 21, 2013.

United States Conference of Catholic Bishops. *Sing to the Lord: Music in Divine Worship*, November 14, 2007.

Various. *Papal Legislation on Sacred Music: 95 A.D. to 1977 A.D.* Edited by Robert F. Hayburn. Collegeville, MN: The Liturgical Press, 1979. Reprint, Fort Collins, CO: Roman Catholic Books, 2005.

Vatican II. *Lumen Gentium.* Dogmatic Constitution on the Church, November 21, 1964.

————. *Sacrosanctum Concilium.* Constitution on the Sacred Liturgy, December 4, 1963.

Works by the Author

"A Blast from the Past: The 1926 Eucharistic Congress in Chicago." *New Liturgical Movement*, December 26, 2016.

"A New Examination of Conscience for Lent." *New Liturgical Movement*, February 18, 2015.

"Anton Bruckner, Sacred Tonality, and Parsifal's Redemption: Spiritual Enfleshment and the Musical *Via Positiva.*" *Logos: A Journal of Catholic Thought and Culture* 8, no. 2 (Spring 2005): 17–55.

"Are We Justified in Calling Paul VI's Creation the 'Novus Ordo [Missae]'?" *New Liturgical Movement*, October 17, 2022.

"Are Women Permitted to Sing the Propers of the Mass?" *New Liturgical Movement*, March 8, 2021.

"Arvo Pärt on Gregorian Chant." *The Chant Café*, January 15, 2014.

"Basking in the glow of Epiphany: The wedding feast at Cana." *Rorate Caeli*, January 13, 2018.

"Beyond *Summorum Pontificum*: The Work of Retrieving the Tridentine Heritage." *Rorate Caeli*, July 14, 2021.

"Breaking News: The Communion Hymn is an Optional Add-On." *Views from the Choir Loft*, September 11, 2014.

"The Catholic Choir and Choirmaster: Handmaid of the Liturgy and Guide of the Faithful." *OnePeterFive*, November 16, 2022.

"Celebration vs. Concelebration: Theological Considerations." *New Liturgical Movement*, September 1, 2014.

"Confusion about Graces: A Catholic Critique of the Charismatic Movement." *OnePeterFive*, November 15, 2018.

"The Council Fathers in Support of Latin: Correcting a Narrative Bias." *New Liturgical Movement*, September 13, 2017.

"Daringly Balanced on One Point: The New Papal Letter on Liturgy." *OnePeterFive*, June 29, 2022.

The Ecstasy of Love in the Thought of Thomas Aquinas. Steubenville, OH: Emmaus Academic, 2021.

"Fidelity to Liturgical Law and the Rights of the Faithful." *OnePeterFive*, July 3, 2017.

From Benedict's Peace to Francis's War: Catholics Respond to the Motu Proprio Traditionis Custodes *on the Latin Mass.* Edited by Peter A. Kwasniewski. Brooklyn, NY: Angelico Press, 2021.

"Happy 200th Birthday, 'Silent Night'—and Why Singing Carols Is So Important." *New Liturgical Movement*, December 24, 2018.

"Healthy Food for Grown-Ups." *OnePeterFive*, November 23, 2022.

Holy Bread of Eternal Life: Restoring Eucharistic Reverence in an Age of Impiety. Manchester, NH: Sophia Institute Press, 2020.

"Homogeneity vs. Hierarchy: On the Treatment of Verbal Moments." *New Liturgical Movement*, October 16, 2017.

"Indeterminacy and Optionitis." *New Liturgical Movement*, November 18, 2013.

"Interview with Early Music Composer Elam Rotem." *New Liturgical Movement*, November 19, 2018.

"Is the Laity's Offering of the Mass a Post-Conciliar Re-Discovery?" *New Liturgical Movement*, February 28, 2022.

"It's Time We Stopped the Musical Starvation Diet." In Peter Kwasniewski, *Tradition and Sanity: Conversations and Dialogues of a Postconciliar Exile*, 183–205. Brooklyn, NY: Angelico, 2018.

"John Paul II on Sacred Music." *Sacred Music* 133, no. 2 (Summer 2006): 4–22.

"Karl Rahner and the Unspoken Framework of (Much of) Modern Theology." *OnePeterFive*, July 27, 2022.

"The 'Latin Novus Ordo' Is Not the Solution." *OnePeterFive*, August 24, 2022.

"*Lectio Divina*: Liturgical Proclamation and Personal Reading." *New Liturgical Movement*, March 24, 2014.

"Liberal Arts in Contemporary Education: The American Example." Given at the Classical Education Congress in Warsaw, November 2021. www.thomasaquinas.edu/news/dr-peter-kwasniewski-94-liberal-arts-contemporary-education-american-example.

"The Liturgy as a Temple: God-Made or Man-Made?" *OnePeterFive*, September 13, 2018.

"Ludwig van Beethoven: Celebrating 250 Years of One of the Greatest Musicians of All Time." *OnePeterFive*, December 16, 2020.

Ministers of Christ: Recovering the Roles of Clergy and Laity in an Age of Confusion. Manchester, NH: Crisis Publications, 2021.

"Mythbusting: Why the TLM's Lectionary Is Superior to the New Lectionary." *Rorate Caeli*, March 30, 2022.

Noble Beauty, Transcendent Holiness: Why the Modern Age Needs the Mass of Ages. Kettering, OH: Angelico Press, 2017.

"The Omission of 'Difficult' Psalms and the Spreading-Thin of the Psalter." *Rorate Caeli*, November 15, 2016.

The Once and Future Roman Rite: Returning to the Traditional Latin Liturgy after Seventy Years of Exile. Gastonia, NC: TAN Books, 2022.

"On Discerning Vocations: How to Think about 'States of Life.'" *OnePeterFive*, January 23, 2019.

"On Liturgical Memory." *New Liturgical Movement*, September 4, 2017.

"Poets, Lovers, Children, Madmen—and Worshipers: Why We Repeat Ourselves in the Liturgy." *Rorate Caeli*, February 19, 2019.

Reclaiming Our Roman Catholic Birthright: The Genius and Timeliness of the Traditional Latin Mass. Brooklyn, NY: Angelico Press, 2020.

"'Refuting the Commonplace that 'Liturgy' Means 'Work of the People.'" *New Liturgical Movement*, May 9, 2022.

"The Relationship between Priest and People in the Latin Mass: Space and Time for Divine Intimacy." *Rorate Caeli*, August 23, 2022.

"The Removal of Tabernacles and the Desacrificialization of the Mass." *OnePeterFive*, April 8, 2022.

Resurgent in the Midst of Crisis: Sacred Liturgy, the Traditional Latin Mass, and Renewal in the Church. Kettering, OH: Angelico Press, 2014.

The Road from Hyperpapalism to Catholicism: Rethinking the Papacy in a Time of Ecclesial Disintegration. Volume 2: *Chronological Responses to an Unfolding Pontificate.* Waterloo, ON: Arouca Press, 2022.

"The Sacrificial Nature of the Mass in the *Usus Antiquior*." *OnePeterFive*, March 9, 2022.

"*Sacrosanctum Concilium*: The Ultimate Trojan Horse." *Crisis Magazine*, June 21, 2021.

"The secret to success: prayer at the start of the day." *LifeSiteNews*, October 22, 2018.

Treasuring the Goods of Marriage in a Throwaway Society. Manchester, NH: Sophia Institute Press, 2023.

True Obedience in the Church: A Guide to Discernment in Challenging Times. Manchester, NH: Sophia Institute Press, 2021.

"We, Too, Are the Sacrifice We Offer." *OnePeterFive*, June 17, 2020.

"What a Catholic Hymn Should Be." *New Liturgical Movement*, June 10, 2019.

"What They Requested, What They Expected, and What Happened: Council Fathers on the Latin Roman Canon." *New Liturgical Movement*, August 8, 2022.

"What Vernacular Hymns Can Be: The Case of Old Polish Songs." *New Liturgical Movement*, January 11, 2021.

"Why 'Mass of the Catechumens' Makes Better Sense Than 'Liturgy of the Word.'" *New Liturgical Movement*, December 29, 2014.

"Why Charismatic Catholics Should Love the Traditional Latin Mass." *Rorate Caeli*, October 7, 2020.

"Why Latin Is the Right Language for Roman Catholic Worship." *Rorate Caeli*, June 8, 2022.

"Why the 'Word of God' for Catholics is not only the Bible, but more importantly, Jesus Himself." *LifeSiteNews*, August 29, 2019.

Works by Other Authors

Ahmad, Joseph. "Droning at Mass." *New Liturgical Movement*, January 3, 2020.

———. "Singing Upon the Book: Further Methods of Chant Harmonization." In two parts, *New Liturgical Movement*, October 7 and 8, 2020.

Anonymous. "The Old Liturgy and the New Despisers of the Council." *Rorate Caeli*, July 5, 2022.

Anonymous. "Can Hymns Licitly Replace Propers?" *New Liturgical Movement*, April 23, 2009.

Anonymous. *Laus in Ecclesia: Learning Gregorian Chant.* Hulbert, OK: Abbey Editions, 2017.

Aristotle. *The Complete Works of Aristotle: The Revised Oxford Translation.* Edited by Jonathan Barnes. Princeton, NJ: Princeton University Press, 1984.

———. *De Anima, or About the Soul.* Translated by Glen Coughlin. South Bend, IN: St. Augustine's Press, 2022.

———. *Nicomachean Ethics.* Translated by Robert C. Bartlett and Susan D. Collins. Chicago: The University of Chicago Press, 2011.

———. *Nicomachean Ethics.* Translated by Roger Crisp. New York: Cambridge University Press, 2000.

———. *Physics or Natural Hearing.* Translated by Glen Coughlin. South Bend, IN: St. Augustine's Press, 2005.

Augustine. *Confessions.* 2nd ed. Translated by Frank Sheed. Edited by Michael P. Foley. Indianapolis: Hackett, 2006.

———. *Exposition of the Psalms.* Translated by J. E. Tweed. In *Nicene and Post-Nicene Fathers,* First Series, vol. 8. Grand Rapids, MI: William B. Eerdmans, 1996.

Baroffio, Giacomo. *Re-Tractations: The Spirituality of Gregorian Chant.* Translated by Aurelio Porfiri. Hong Kong: Chorabooks, 2018.

Barr, Robert R. "The Two Cities in Saint Augustine." *Laval théologique et philosophique* 18, no. 2 (1962): 211–29.

Baxter, Jason. "The Shrinking, Post-human Vocabulary of Our Tone-deaf Culture." *Catholic World Report,* September 20, 2022.

Benedict of Nursia. *The Rule of Saint Benedict in English and Latin.* Translated by Justin McCann, OSB. Fort Collins, CO: Roman Catholic Books, n.d.

———. *The Rule of St. Benedict.* Preface by W. K. Lowther Clarke. London: Society for Promoting Christian Knowledge, 1931.

Bennett, Oliver. *Cultural Pessimism: Narratives of Decline in the Postmodern World.* Edinburgh: Edinburgh University Press, 2001.

Benofy, Susan. "The Day the Mass Changed, How it Happened and Why." Published in two parts in the *Adoremus Bulletin,* February and March 2010. Available at *Catholic Culture,* record numbers 9377 and 9378.

———. "Footnotes for a Hermeneutic of Continuity: *Sacrosanctum Concilium's* Vanishing Citations." *Adoremus Bulletin* 21, no. 1 (Spring 2015): 8–9. https://archive.ccwatershed.org/media/pdfs/15/06/03/13-43-26_0.pdf.

———. "*Jubilate Deo* Latin Chants." *Adoremus,* December 31, 2007. https://adoremus.org/2007/12/quotjubilate-deo-latin-chantsquot.

Berquist, Marcus. "Good Music and Bad." In *Learning and Discipleship: The Collected Papers of Marcus R. Berquist.* Edited by Anne S. Forsyth. Santa Paula, CA: Thomas Aquinas College, 2019.

Brockhaus, Hannah. "Be intentional about silence during Mass, Pope Francis says." *Catholic News Agency,* January 10, 2018. www.catholicnewsagency.com/news/37479/be-intentional-about-silence-during-mass-pope-francis-says.

Bruyère, Cécile. *The Spiritual Life and Prayer according to Holy Scripture and Monastic Tradition.* Eugene, OR: Wipf & Stock, 2002.

Bugnini, Annibale. "Per una riforma liturgica generale." *Ephemerides Liturgicae* 63, no. 1 (1949): 166–84. Translation by Carlo Schena, "For a General Reform of the Liturgy." *New Liturgical Movement,* November 16, 17, 18, 21, and 22, 2022.

Carroll, Lucy E. "A Choir Director's Lament on Lyrics for Liturgy." *Adoremus Bulletin* 12, no. 3 (May 2006).

————. "Singing for the Supper or the Sacrifice?" *Adoremus Bulletin* 8, no. 8 (November 2002).

Cavarnos, Constantine. *Guide to Byzantine Iconography*. Belmont, MA: Institute for Byzantine & Modern Greek Studies, 1993.

Childs, Andrew. "The List" [of recommended musical works]. www.angeluson line.org/index.php?section=articles&subsection=print_article&article_id=2807.

Chiron, Yves. *Annibale Bugnini: Reformer of the Liturgy*. Translated by John Pepino. Brooklyn, NY: Angelico Press, 2018.

————. *Paul VI: The Divided Pope*. Translated by James Walther. Brooklyn, NY: Angelico Press, 2022.

————. *Saint Pius X, Restorer of the Church*. Translated by Graham Harrison. Kansas City: Angelus Press, 2002.

Clark, Stephen R. L. *Can We Believe in People? Human Significance in an Interconnected Cosmos*. Brooklyn, NY: Angelico Press, 2020.

Clarke, Vincent. "The Need for an Integral Approach to Music." *The Josias*, December 10, 2020.

Clayton, David. "Using Drones as Harmony—A Simple Way to Add to the Spiritual Effect of Sacred Music." *The Way of Beauty* blog, December 27, 2017. www.thewayofbeauty.org/blog/2017/12/using-drones-as-harmony-a-simple-way-to-add-to-the-spiritual-effect-of-sacred-music.

————. *The Way of Beauty: Liturgy, Education, and Inspiration for Family, School, and College*. Kettering, OH: Angelico Press, 2015.

Cole, Basil. *Music and Morals*. New York: Alba House, 1993.

Conley, James D. "Ever Ancient, Ever New: The Role of Beauty in the Restoration of Catholic Culture." *Crisis Magazine*, October 10, 2013.

Davies, Michael. *Pope John's Council*. Rev. ed. Kansas City, MO: Angelus Press, 2007.

————. *Pope Paul's New Mass*. Kansas City, MO: Angelus Press, 2009.

Day, Thomas. *Why Catholics Can't Sing: Revised and Updated with New Grand Conclusions and Good Advice*. New York: Crossroad Publishing Co., 2013.

de Hemptinne, Pius. *A Benedictine Soul: Biography, Letters, and Spiritual Writings of Dom Pius de Hemptinne*. Translated by Benedictines of Teignmouth. Stamullen, Ireland: Cenacle Press, 2022.

Delalande, D. "Gregorian Chant." In *Introduction to Theology*, edited by A. M. Henry. Translated by William Storey. Chicago: Fides Publishers Association, 1954.

Digges, M. Laurentia. *Transfigured World: Design, Theme and Symbol in Worship*. New York: Farrar, Straus and Cudahy, 1957. Reprint, Waterloo, ON: Arouca Press, 2021.

DiPippo, Gregory. "We Sing of God Alone and for God Alone, Through the Traditional Liturgy." *New Liturgical Movement*, July 23, 2015.

Dubay, Thomas. *Fire Within: St. Teresa of Avila, St. John of the Cross, and the Gospel—on Prayer*. San Francisco: Ignatius Press, 1989.

Eliot, T. S. *Complete Poems and Plays 1909–1950*. New York: Harcourt Brace Jovanovich, 1980.

Esolen, Anthony. *Real Music: A Guide to the Timeless Hymns of the Church*. Charlotte, NC: TAN Books, 2016.

Fiedrowicz, Michael. *The Traditional Latin Mass: History, Form, and Theology of the Classical Roman Rite*. Translated by Rose Pfeifer. Brooklyn, NY: Angelico Press, 2020.

Fiore, Gabriel Mary. "Silence before God in the Life and Writings of Saint Thomas Aquinas." *Nova & Vetera* [English ed.] 19, no. 1 (Winter 2021): 1–19. https:// stpaulcenter.com/01-nv-19-1-fiore.

Friel, David. "Between Universality and Inculturation: Gregorian Chant as a Bridge." *Sacred Music* 149, no. 1 (Spring 2022): 6–27.

Gaebelein, Frank. *The Christian, the Arts, and Truth: Regaining the Vision of Greatness.* Portland, OR: Multnomah Press, 1985.

Gajard, Joseph. *The Solesmes Method: Its Fundamental Principles and Practical Rules of Interpretation.* Translated by R. Cecile Gabain. Collegeville, MN: The Liturgical Press, 1960.

Graber, Linda. "Focus vs. Blur: Multi-Sensory Learning, Motivated Focus, and the Mass." Published in three parts at *OnePeterFive*, January 15, January 25, and February 26, 2016.

Guardini, Romano. *The Lord.* Translated by Elinor Castendyk Briefs. Chicago: Regnery, 1954.

———. *The Spirit of the Liturgy.* Translated by Ada Lane. In the Commemorative Edition of Joseph Ratzinger's *The Spirit of the Liturgy.* San Francisco: Ignatius Press, 2018.

Guéranger, Prosper. *The Traditional Latin Mass Explained.* Brooklyn, NY: Angelico Press, 2017.

Harris, Charles. "Liturgical Silence." In *Liturgy and Worship: A Companion to the Prayer Books of the Anglican Communion*, edited by W. K. Lowther Clarke and Charles Harris, 774–82. London: Society for Promoting Christian Knowledge, 1932.

Hellriegel, Martin B. "'Active Participation' in Chant" (1956). Reprint, *Adoremus*, January 1, 1994. https://adoremus.org/1994/01/active-participation-in-chant.

Hildegard of Bingen. *Mystical Writings.* Edited by Fiona Bowie and Oliver Davies. New York: Crossroad, 1990.

Hillier, Paul. *Arvo Pärt.* New York: Oxford University Press, 1997.

Hourlier, Jacques. *Reflections on the Spirituality of Gregorian Chant.* Translated by Gregory Casprini and Robert Edmonson. Brewster, MA: Paraclete Press, 1995.

Jackson, James W. *Nothing Superfluous: An Explanation of the Symbolism of the Rite of St. Gregory the Great.* Lincoln, NE: Fraternity Publications, 2016.

John Chrysostom. *Exposition of Psalm XLI.* In *Source Readings in Music History from Classical Antiquity through the Romantic Era*, edited by Oliver Strunk. New York: W.W. Norton, 1950.

———. *On Marriage and Family Life.* Crestwood, NY: St. Vladimir's Seminary Press, 1986.

Johner, Dominic. *Chants of the Vatican Gradual.* Collegeville, MN: St. John's Abbey Press, 1940. Reprint, Church Music Association of America, 2007.

Kalinowska, Anna. "The Art of Dress—Problems with Normalcy." *OnePeterFive*, July 12, 2022.

Kalkavage, Peter. "Music and the Idea of a World." *The Imaginative Conservative*, February 9, 2017.

———. "Music: Giving the World a Rhythmic Sway." *The Imaginative Conservative*, May 31, 2016.

———. "The Neglected Muse: Why Music Is an Essential Liberal Art." *The Imaginative Conservative*, July 29, 2021.

Kent, Michael. *The Mass of Brother Michel.* Kettering, OH: Angelico Press, 2017.

Kirby, Marc-Daniel. "Sung Theology: The Liturgical Chant of the Church." In *Beyond the Prosaic: Renewing the Liturgical Movement*, edited by Stratford Caldecott, 127–48. Edinburgh: T&T Clark, 1998.

Kowalska, Maria Faustina. *Diary: Divine Mercy in My Soul*. Stockbridge, MA: Marian Press, 2003.

Kuhner, John Byron. "Rembert Weakland, Proud Vandal." *First Things* online, August 26, 2022.

Labat, Élisabeth-Paule. *The Song That I Am: On the Mystery of Music*. Translated by Erik Varden. Collegeville, MN: Liturgical Press, 2014.

Lang, Uwe Michael. *Signs of the Holy One: Liturgy, Ritual, and Expression of the Sacred*. San Francisco: Ignatius Press, 2015.

Lawrence, Brother. *The Practice of the Presence of God*. Translated by Robert J. Edmonson. Brewster, MA: Paraclete Press, 1985.

Leong, Dickson. "Malaysian Ex-Buddhist on the Western Fascination with Buddhism." *OnePeterFive*, October 19, 2021.

Lewis, C. S. "On the Reading of Old Books." In *God in the Dock: Essays on Theology and Ethics*, edited by Walter Hooper, 200–207. Grand Rapids, MI: William B. Eerdmans, 1970.

———. Introduction to St. Athanasius, *On the Incarnation*. Yonkers, NY: St. Vladimir's Seminary Press, 2011.

Mahrt, William. *The Musical Shape of the Liturgy*. Richmond, VA: Church Music Association of America, 2012.

Marcel, Gabriel. *Being and Having: An Existentialist Diary*. Translated by Katherine Farrer. New York: Harper, 1961.

Marini, Guido, with Maddalena della Somaglia. Interview in *Radici Cristiane* 42 (March 2009). Translated by Shawn Tribe and published as "Msgr. Guido Marini Speaks Again on the Liturgy, Its Forms and Its Importance." *New Liturgical Movement*, February 28, 2009.

———. *Liturgical Reflections of a Papal Master of Ceremonies*. Translated by Nicholas L. Gregoris. Pine Beach, NJ: Newman House Press, 2011.

Maritain, Jacques. *Art and Scholasticism and The Frontiers of Poetry*. Translated by Joseph W. Evans. Notre Dame, IN: University of Notre Dame Press, 1974.

McCabe, Herbert. *God Matters*. London: Continuum, 2005.

McNamara, Edward. "Sounds of Silence." *Zenit*, January 20, 2004. https://zenit.org/2004/01/20/sounds-of-silence.

Merton, Thomas. *The School of Charity: Letters on Religious Renewal and Spiritual Direction*. Edited by Patrick Hart. New York: Farrar, Straus and Giroux, 1990.

———. *The Seven Storey Mountain*. New York: Harcourt, 1999.

Miller, Michael J. "Cardinal Ratzinger on Liturgical Music." *Homiletic & Pastoral Review* (July 2000): 13–20. www.catholicculture.org/culture/library/view.cfm?recnum=4041.

Mirus, Jeff. "So What's Wrong with Rock Music?" *Catholic Culture*, March 15, 2005. www.catholicculture.org/commentary/so-whats-wrong-with-rock-music/.

Mirus, Peter. "Hear No Evil—My Perspective on Rock Music." *Catholic Culture*, February 7, 2005. www.catholicculture.org/commentary/hear-no-evil-my-perspective-on-rock-music/.

Murray, Gerald, with Diane Montagna. "Guarding the Flock: A Canon Lawyer's Advice to Bishops on Latest Vatican Crackdown on Tradition." *The Remnant*, February 15,

2022. https://remnantnewspaper.com/web/index.php/articles/item/5851-the-fu
ture-of-the-latin-mass-a-canon-lawyer-s-take-on-traditionis-custodes.

Murrett, John C. *The Message of the Mass Melodies*. Collegeville, MN: The Liturgical
Press, 1960.

Newman, John Henry. *A Benedictine Education*. Edited by Christopher Fisher. Providence, RI: Cluny, 2020.

———. *Discussions and Arguments*. London: Longmans, Green, and Co., 1907.

———. *Parochial and Plain Sermons*. 8 vols. New York: Longmans, Green, and Co.,
1907–1909.

Nieto, John. "Nature and Art in the Village." In *Integralism and the Common Good*,
vol. 1, *Family, City, State*, edited by P. Edmund Waldstein and Peter Kwasniewski,
151–63. Brooklyn, NY: Angelico Press, 2021.

Nietzsche, Friedrich. *The Portable Nietzsche*. Edited by Walter Kaufmann. N.p.: Viking
Press, 1968.

Olver, Matthew S. C. "A Note on the Silent Canon in the Missal of Paul VI and Cardinal Ratzinger." *Antiphon* 20, no. 1 (2016): 40–51.

Pärt, Arvo. Interview in November 1978. Republished in *Teater, Muusika, Kino* 7
(1988). Retrieved from https://sheetmusiclibrary.website/2022/02/27/arvo-part
-sheet-music/.

Pazat de Lys, Charbel. "Towards a New Liturgical Movement." In *Looking Again at
the Question of the Liturgy with Cardinal Ratzinger*, edited by Alcuin Reid, 98–114.
Farnborough: Saint Michael's Abbey Press, 2003.

Pieper, Josef. *The Four Cardinal Virtues*. Translated by various. Notre Dame, IN: University of Notre Dame Press, 1966.

———. *Only the Lover Sings: Art and Contemplation*. Translated by Lothar Krauth.
San Francisco: Ignatius Press, 1990.

Plato. *The Collected Dialogues of Plato*. Edited by Edith Hamilton and Huntington
Cairns. Princeton, NJ: Princeton University Press, 1961.

———. *The Laws of Plato*. Translated by Thomas L. Pangle. Chicago: The University
of Chicago Press, 1988.

———. *Plato: Complete Works*. Edited by John M. Cooper. Indianapolis: Hackett,
1997.

———. *The Republic of Plato*. Translated by Allan Bloom, 2nd ed. New York: Basic
Books, 1991.

Platt, Michael. "A Different Drummer." www.gw.edu/_elements/userfiles/Platt%20
-%20A%20Different%20Drummer.pdf.

———. "Myth of the Teenager." *Practical Homeschooling* 2 (1993). www.home
-school.com/Articles/myth-of-the-teenager.php.

Rampi, Fulvio. "Gregorian Chant, the Song of the Liturgy." *Altare Dei*, February 28,
2020. www.altaredei.com/2020/02/28/gregorian-chant-the-song-of-the-liturgy.

Ratzinger, Joseph, with Vittorio Messori. *The Ratzinger Report*. Translated by Salvator
Attanasio and Graham Harrison. San Francisco: Ignatius Press, 1985.

Ratzinger, Joseph. *A New Song for the Lord: Faith in Christ and Liturgy Today*. Translated by Martha M. Matesich. New York: Crossroad Herder, 1997.

———. *Christianity and the Crisis of Cultures*. Translated by Brian McNeil. San Francisco: Ignatius Press, 2006.

————. "Conscience and Truth." Presented at the 10th Workshop for Bishops, February 1991, Dallas, Texas. www.catholiceducation.org/en/religion-and-philo sophy/faith-and-reason/conscience-and-truth.html.

————. *Co-workers of the Truth: Meditations for Every Day of the Year.* San Francisco: Ignatius Press, 1992.

————. *The Feast of Faith: Approaches to a Theology of the Liturgy.* Translated by Graham Harrison. San Francisco: Ignatius Press, 1986.

————. *The Spirit of the Liturgy* Commemorative Edition, with Guardini's work of the same title. San Francisco: Ignatius Press, 2018.

————. *The Spirit of the Liturgy.* Translated by John Saward. San Francisco: Ignatius Press, 2000.

————. *Theology of the Liturgy: The Sacramental Foundation of Christian Existence.* Vol. 11 of *Collected Works of Joseph Ratzinger,* edited by Michael J. Miller. San Francisco: Ignatius Press, 2014.

Reid, Alcuin. "Does *Traditionis Custodes* Pass Liturgical History 101?" In *From Benedict's Peace to Francis's War: Catholics Respond to the Motu Proprio* Traditionis Custodes *on the Latin Mass,* edited by Peter Kwasniewski, 252–59. Brooklyn, NY: Angelico Press, 2021.

————. "The Liturgy, Fifty Years after *Sacrosanctum Concilium.*" *Catholic World Report,* December 4, 2013.

————. "*Sacrosanctum concilium* and the Reform of the *Ordo Missae.*" *Antiphon* 10, no. 3 (2006): 277–95.

Reilly, Robert, with Jens F. Laurson. *Surprised by Beauty: A Listener's Guide to the Recovery of Modern Music.* 2nd ed. San Francisco: Ignatius Press, 2016.

Restagno, Enzo, with Leopold Brauneiss, et al. *Arvo Pärt in Conversation.* Translated by Robert Crow. Champaign: Dalkey Archive Press, 2012.

Rivoire, Fr. Réginald-Marie, FSVF. *Does "Traditionis Custodes" Pass the Juridical Rationality Test?* Lincoln, NE: Os Justi Press, 2022.

Rodheudt, Guido. "Pastoral Liturgy and the Church's Mission in Parishes—The Dangerous Hermeneutic of a Concept." In *The Sacred Liturgy: Source and Summit of the Life and Mission of the Church,* edited by Alcuin Reid, 273–89. San Francisco: Ignatius Press, 2014.

Rutherford, Janet E., ed. *Benedict XVI and Beauty in Sacred Music.* Dublin: Four Courts Press, 2012.

Sarah, Robert, with Nicolas Diat. *The Power of Silence Against the Dictatorship of Noise.* Translated by Michael J. Miller. San Francisco: Ignatius Press, 2017.

Saward, John. *The Beauty of Holiness and the Holiness of Beauty: Art, Sanctity, and the Truth of Catholicism.* San Francisco: Ignatius Press, 1997. Reprint, Brooklyn, NY: Angelico Press, 2021.

Schaefer, Edward. *Catholic Music Through the Ages: Balancing the Needs of a Worshipping Church.* Chicago: Hillenbrand Books, 2008.

Schneider, Athanasius. "The Treasure of the Altar: The Ineffable Majesty of Holy Communion." 2015 Lecture at the Angelicum. *Rorate Caeli,* March 24, 2016.

Schweitzer, Albert. *J. S. Bach.* Translated by Ernest Newman. Mineola, NY: Dover Publications, 1966.

Scruton, Roger. *The Aesthetics of Music.* New York: Oxford University Press, 1997.

————. *Music as an Art.* London: Bloomsbury Continuum, 2018.

Shaffern, Robert W. "The Mass According to Vatican II." *The Catholic Thing*, July 10, 2022.

Shaw, Joseph. *How to Attend the Extraordinary Form*. London: Catholic Truth Society, 2020.

———. "St Pius V and the Mass." *Voice of the Family Digest* 24, October 6, 2021. https://voiceofthefamily.com/st-pius-v-and-the-mass.

———. "Vatican II on Liturgical Preservation." *LMS Chairman*, January 17, 2017.

———. "What Sort of Mass Did 'Vatican II' Want?" *LMS Chairman*, May 24, 2016.

Silvestris, Bernard. *The Commentary on Martianus Capella's De Nuptiis Philologiae et Mercurii Attributed to Bernardus Silvestris*. Edited by Haijo Jan Westra. Toronto: Pontifical Institute of Mediaeval Studies, 1986.

Sire, H. J. A. *Phoenix from the Ashes: The Making, Unmaking and Restoration of Catholic Tradition*. Kettering, OH: Angelico Press, 2015.

Smith, Christopher. "Let's Revisit 'Praise and Worship Music is Praise But Not Worship.'" *Chant Café*, September 1, 2015.

———. "Why Praise & Worship Music Is Praise, But Not Worship." *Catholic Education Resource Center*. www.catholiceducation.org/en/culture/music/why-praise-and-worship-music-is-praise-but-not-worship.html.

Sonnen, John Paul. "On Silence in the Liturgy." *Liturgical Arts Journal*, April 10, 2018. www.liturgicalartsjournal.com/2018/04/on-silence-in-liturgy.html.

Spataro, Roberto. *In Praise of the Tridentine Mass and of Latin, Language of the Church*. Translated by Zachary Thomas. Brooklyn, NY: Angelico Press, 2019.

Stickler, Alfons. "Recollections of a Vatican II Peritus." *New Liturgical Movement*, June 29, 2022.

Storck, Thomas. "Mass Culture or Popular Culture?" Available at www.thomasstorck.org/culture or www.ccwatershed.org/media/pdfs/13/09/18/09-31-06_0.pdf.

Swain, Joseph P. *Sacred Treasure: Understanding Catholic Liturgical Music*. Collegeville, MN: Liturgical Press, 2012.

Terry, Richard R. *Catholic Church Music*. London: Greening & Co., 1907.

Thomas Aquinas. *Compendium theologiae*. Translated by Cyril Vollert. St. Louis: B. Herder Book Co., 1947.

———. *On Evil*. Translated by Jean Oesterle. Notre Dame, IN: University of Notre Dame Press, 1995.

———. *Summa theologiae*. Translated by Laurence Shapcote. Edited by The Aquinas Institute. Green Bay, WI: Aquinas Institute and Steubenville, OH: Emmaus Academic, 2012.

Torretta, Gabriel. "The Person in Battle: An Interview Essay with Roger Scruton." *Dominicana* 55, no. 2 (2012): 51–67.

Treacy, Susan. *The Music of Christendom: A History*. San Francisco: Ignatius Press, 2021.

Tribe, Shawn. "Inculturation: Japanese and Chinese Madonnas." *Liturgical Arts Journal*, May 15, 2018.

———. "The Oriental Chasuble of Dom Pierre-Célestin Lou Tseng-Tsiang, OSB." *Liturgical Arts Journal*, October 4, 2017.

———. "The Tradition of the Japanese Madonna." *Liturgical Arts Journal*, February 18, 2021.

Tucker, Jeffrey. *Sing Like a Catholic*. Richmond, VA: Church Music Association of America, 2009.

Ureta, José Antonio. "A Brief Study of Certain Theological Deviations in *Desiderio Desideravi*." Published in five parts at *OnePeterFive*, August 8–12, 2022. Available in its entirety at https://onepeterfive.com/wp-content/uploads/2022/08/Ureta -Complete.pdf.

von Hildebrand, Alice. *Introduction to a Philosophy of Religion*. Chicago: Franciscan Herald Press, 1971.

Vost, Kevin. *Memorize the Stoics!: The Ancient Art of Memory Meets the Timeless Art of Living*. Brooklyn, NY: Angelico Press, 2022.

Warren, David. "Oh Had I Jubal's Lyre." *The Catholic Thing*, May 3, 2014.

Weakland, Rembert. *A Pilgrim in a Pilgrim Church: Memoirs of a Catholic Archbishop*. Grand Rapids, MI: William B. Eerdmans, 2009.

Weber, Samuel. "Sacred Music that Serves the Word of God." www.ewtn.com /catholicism/library/sacred-music-that-serves-the-word-of-god-4984.

Wilson, James Matthew. *The Vision of the Soul: Truth, Goodness, and Beauty in the Western Tradition*. Washington, DC: The Catholic University of America Press, 2017.

Zuckerkandl, Victor. *Man the Musician*. Translated by Norbert Guterman. Princeton, NJ: Princeton University Press, 1973.

Zuhlsdorf, John. "What does *Sacrosanctum Concilium* 116 really say?" *Fr. Z's Blog*, May 23, 2012.

ADDITIONAL RECOMMENDATIONS

Books

Anonymous. *The Doors of Silence: Profound and Brief Meditations by an Anonymous Carthusian Monk*. Edited and translated by Jane Carver. St. Marys, KS: Angelus Press, 2020.

Anonymous. *Silence: A Series of Conferences Given by a Camaldolese Hermit*. Bloomingdale, OH: Ercam Editions, 2011.

Alfeyev, Metropolitan Hilarion. *Orthodox Christianity*, Vol. 4, *The Worship and Liturgical Life of the Orthodox Church*, translated by Andrei Tepper. Yonkers, NY: St. Vladimir's Seminary Press, 2016.

Bergman, Lisa. *Treasure and Tradition: The Ultimate Guide to the Latin Mass*. Homer Glen, IL: St. Augustine Academy Press, 2014.

Biliniewicz, Mariusz. *The Liturgical Vision of Pope Benedict XVI: A Theological Inquiry*. New York: Peter Lang, 2013.

Bouteneff, Peter C. *Arvo Pärt: Out of Silence*. Yonkers, NY: St. Vladimir's Seminary Press, 2015.

Brownsberger, William. "Silence." *Communio* 36, no. 4 (Winter 2009): 586–606.

Cardine, Eugène. *An Overview of Gregorian Chant*. Translated by Gregory Casprini. Brewster, MA: Paraclete Press, 1992.

Chessman, Stuart. *Faith of Our Fathers: A Brief History of Catholic Traditionalism in the United States from Triumph to Traditionis Custodes*. Brooklyn, NY: Angelico Press, 2022.

Copland, Aaron. *What to Listen for in Music*. New York: New American Library, 2009.

Dobszay, László. *The Bugnini-Liturgy and the Reform of the Reform*. Front Royal, VA: Catholic Church Music Associates, 2003.

Fowells, Robert M. *Chant Made Simple*. 2nd ed. Brewster, MA: Paraclete Press, 2007.

Greenberg, Robert. *How to Listen to Great Music: A Guide to Its History, Culture, and Heart*. New York: Plume/Penguin, 2011.

Gribbin, Anselm J. *Pope Benedict XVI and the Liturgy: Understanding Recent Liturgical Developments*. Leominster, UK: Gracewing, 2011.

Hiley, David. *Gregorian Chant*. New York: Cambridge University Press, 2009.

Houghton, Bryan. *Mitre and Crook*. New Rochelle: Arlington House Books, 1979; repr. Brooklyn, NY: Angelico Press, 2019.

Kurek, Michael. *The Sound of Beauty: A Classical Composer on Music in the Spiritual Life*. San Francisco: Ignatius Press, 2019.

Lang, Uwe Michael. *The Voice of the Church at Prayer: Reflections on Liturgy and Language*. San Francisco: Ignatius Press, 2012.

Lartigue, K. T. *Ad Communionem: Antiphons and Psalms*. N.p.: Justitias Books, 2016.

Le Mée, Katharine. *The Benedictine Gift to Music*. Mahwah, NJ: Paulist Press, 2003.

———. *Chant: The Origins, Form, Practice, and Healing Power of Gregorian Chant*. New York: Bell Tower, 1994.

Marier, Theodore. *A Gregorian Chant Master Class*. Bethlehem, CT: Abbey of Regina Laudis, 2008.

Martineau, Jason. *The Elements of Music: Melody, Rhythm, and Harmony*. New York: Walker & Company, 2008.

Mills, B. Andrew. *Psallite Sapienter: A Musician's Practical Guide to the 1962 Roman Missal*. Richmond, VA: Church Music Association of America, 2008.

Mocquereau, André. *A Study of Gregorian Musical Rhythm*. Translated by Aileen Tone. Richmond, VA: Church Music Association of America, 2007.

Mosebach, Martin. *The Heresy of Formlessness: The Roman Liturgy and Its Enemy*. Rev. and expanded ed. Translated by Graham Harrison. Brooklyn, NY: Angelico Press, 2018.

Murray, Paul. *Aquinas at Prayer: The Bible, Mysticism and Poetry*. London: Bloomsbury, 2013.

Newman, John Henry. *John Henry Newman on Worship, Reverence, and Ritual: A Selection of Texts*. Edited by Peter A. Kwasniewski. N.p.: Os Justi Press, 2019.

Nortz, Basil, "The Moral Power of Music." *Catholic Education Resource Center*. www.catholiceducation.org/en/culture/music/the-moral-power-of-music.html.

———. *Music and Morality*. Set of 3 CDs. Lecture 1: Music and Moral Formation. Lecture 2: Historical Perspective. Lecture 3: What is Wrong with Rock Music? Available from https://store-opusangelorum-org.3dcartstores.com/Music-and-Morality_p_59.html.

Nowakowski, Mark. "Listening Like a Catholic: The Discernment of Personal Musical Taste." In two parts. *OnePeterFive*, September 4 and 12, 2014.

———. "Revenge of the Rigid: On Rejecting Grillo, Primitivism, and the Electric Slide." *OnePeterFive*, August 30, 2021.

Porfiri, Aurelio. *Less is More: Selected Writings on Choral Music*. Hong Kong: Chorabooks, 2018.

Rutler, George William. *The Stories of Hymns: The History Behind 100 of Christianity's Greatest Hymns*. Irondale, AL: EWTN Publishing, 2016.

Saulnier, Daniel. *Gregorian Chant: A Guide to the History and Liturgy*. Translated by Mary Berry. Brewster, MA: Paraclete Press, 2009.

Schmitt, Francis P. *Church Music Transgressed: Reflections on "Reform."* New York: The Seabury Press, 1977.

Schneider, Athanasius, with Aurelio Porfiri. *The Catholic Mass: Steps to Restore the Centrality of God in the Liturgy.* Manchester, NH: Sophia Institute Press, 2021.
Shaw, Joseph, ed. *The Case for Liturgical Restoration.* Brooklyn, NY: Angelico Press, 2019.
Treacy, Susan. *A Plain and Easy Introduction to Gregorian Chant.* Charles Town, WV: CanticaNOVA Publications, 2007.
von Hildebrand, Dietrich. *Aesthetics.* Vol. 1. Translated by Brian McNeil. Steubenville, OH: The Hildebrand Project, 2016.
———. *Aesthetics.* Vol. 2. Translated by John F. Crosby, John Henry Crosby, and Brian McNeil. Steubenville, OH: The Hildebrand Project, 2018.
———. *Liturgy and Personality.* Steubenville, OH: The Hildebrand Project, 2016.
Ward, Justine Bayard, and Theodore Marier. *Gregorian Chant Practicum.* Washington, DC: The Catholic University of America, 1990.
Weber, Samuel F. *The Proper of the Mass for Sundays and Solemnities.* San Francisco: Ignatius Press, 2015.
Werner, Eric. *The Sacred Bridge: Liturgical Parallels in Synagogue and Early Church.* New York: Schocken Books, 1970.
Zuckerkandl, Victor. *Sound and Symbol: Music and the External World.* Translated by William R. Trask. Princeton, NJ: Princeton University Press, 1956.

Periodicals

Antiphon, published by the Society for Catholic Liturgy.
The Latin Mass Magazine, published by Keep the Faith.
Sacred Music, published by the Church Music Association of America.

Websites

Benedict XVI Institute (www.benedictinstitute.org)
Benjamin Bloomfield's Psalm Tone Tool (www.bbloomf.github.io/jgabc/psalmtone.html); Readings Tool (www.bbloomf.github.io/jgabc/readings.html); Propers Tool (www.bbloomf.github.io/jgabc/propers.html)
Biretta Books (www.birettabooks.com)
CanticaNOVA (www.canticanova.com)
Catholic Artists Directory (www.catholicartistsdirectory.com)
ChoralWiki/Choral Public Domain Library (www.cpdl.org/wiki)
Church Music Association of America (www.musicasacra.com)
Corpus Christi Watershed (www.ccwatershed.org/) [Explore using the Site Map, as there is an unbelievable amount of music and commentary on this site, and some of it must be dug for]
GregoBase: A Database of Gregorian Scores (www.gregobase.selapa.net)
Gregorian Chant Academy (www.gregorianchantacademy.com)
Institute of Christ the King Sovereign Priest—Sacred Music (www.institute-christ-king.org/resources/sacred-music)
International Music Score Library Project (IMSLP) / Petrucci Music Library (www.imslp.org)
Jennifer Donelson—voice and sacred music instructor (www.jenniferdonelson.com)
Peter Kwasniewski—assorted lectures and sacred music compositions (www.youtube.com/@DrKwasniewski)

Liturgical Arts Journal (www.liturgicalartsjournal.com)
Maternal Heart of Mary (www.maternalheart.org/resources)
New Liturgical Movement (www.newliturgicalmovement.org)
Nicholas Lemme—solfege videos for Propers of the year (www.youtube.com/@nicholas lemme)
Paraclete Press (www.paracletepress.com/collections/chant-resources) [largest selection of Solesmes chant books]
Priestly Fraternity of St. Peter—Sung Mass Guide (www.fsspolgs.org/liturgical-aids /sung-mass-guide/) and Gospels & Epistles (http://www.fsspolgs.org/liturgical -aids/gospels-epistles/)
Sacred Music Library (www.sacredmusiclibrary.com)
Sacred Music US (www.sacredmusicus.wordpress.com) [English chant settings and organ accompaniments by Fr. Samuel F. Weber, OSB]
St. Benedict Tridentine Catholic Community—Chant Sheets for Celebrants (www.windsorlatinmass.org/latin/chant.htm)
The Latin Mass Society of England & Wales—Schola's Guide to Sung Mass (https:// lms.org.uk/scholas-guide-sung-mass)
The Way of Beauty (www.thewayofbeauty.org)
Veronica Brandt (www.youtube.com/@VeronicaBrandt)

Index

Chiron, Yves, 128, 148, 158
choir loft, 155
choirs, xii, xiv–xv, 18, 72–73, 75, 77, 84–85,
91, 96–97, 115, 118–20, 122, 125,
128–35, 143, 145, 149, 154–55, 205,
219–20, 234–35, 256; see schola
Chopin, Frédéric, 42
Choralschola der Wiener Hofburgkapelle,
xiv, 60
"Christian rock," 191
Christmas, 289
Christology, 209, 285
Chrysostom, St. John, vi, xix, 13, 43, 51,
185, 189, 279, 285–86
Church Fathers, 51, 89, 101, 127, 138, 192,
198; see individual names
Church Music Association of America, 132,
155–56
city of God, 248–49
Clark, Stephen R.L., 30
Clarke, Vincent, 34–35, 49
Classical period, 16, 34, 42, 58, 113, 239
Clayton, David, 18, 103, 212–14
Clear Creek Abbey, 132
Clement of Alexandria, St., 104
Cole, Basil, 187
Collect, 122, 291
Columba Marmion, Bd, 7
common good, 85
communication, 10, 70, 79, 256, 264, 280
Communion (chant), 80, 99, 114, 122, 129,
154, 158,
Communion, Holy, 123, 129, 135, 171–72,
181, 202, 236, 254, 263–65, 277, 284,
290–91; in the hand, 112–13; on the
tongue, 219; under both kinds, 150
communion, hierarchical, 122, 124, 128; in
marriage, 173; of St.s, 83
community, overemphasis on, 86, 171, 177,
216, 249
Compline, 144
concelebration, 117, 150
concerto, 13, 33, 56, 58–59, 64
concupiscible passions, 26–31, 46
confirmation, 181, 221
conformism, cultural, 44, 106, 183, 214, 216

congregational singing, 70, 73, 93–94, 102–
5, 117, 119–20, 124–35, 144–45, 148–
49, 153, 161, 205, 235, 262, 280–81
Coniaris, Anthony M., 30
Conley, James D., 172–73
conscience, 48, 167–69, 191, 222–23, 274
consecration, at Mass, 81, 180, 270, 285,
291
consequentialism, 174
consolation, 17, 133, 165, 202
Constantine, emperor, 196
contemplation, xv, 22, 38, 44, 53, 58, 83,
109, 111, 113, 123, 141, 145, 148, 155,
157, 168, 173, 181, 184, 190, 200, 223,
232, 235, 238, 265, 279, 291
contraception, 33, 140–41, 172, 202
contrition, xi, 166, 170, 236
conversion, 19, 51, 61, 75, 106, 108, 157,
165, 197, 211, 214–15, 223, 225, 230,
256
Corelli, Arcangelo, 42
Corpus Christi Watershed, xix, 155
corruption, liturgical, 96, 112–13
Council of Trent, see Trent
countercultural, the need to be, 75, 131, 221,
270
Counter-Reformation, 96, 99, 270
country dances, 48
country music, 195
Credo, 73, 80, 99, 102–3, 115, 120, 122,
129–30, 137, 144, 154, 158, 291
crisis in the Church, 74–75, 160, 202, 247
culture, high, 7, 11, 15–16, 24, 36, 43, 46,
48–49, 54, 58, 77, 84, 160, 163, 186–87,
195, 197, 206, 211
Cyprian of Carthage, St., 189
Cyril of Jerusalem, St., 285

dancing, 11, 14, 25, 27, 30, 34, 43, 47–48,
53, 55–56, 184, 214
Dante, 54
David, king, 5, 43, 89
Davies, Michael, 127
Day, Thomas, 133, 170
de Hemptinne, Pius, 7
De Musica Sacra et Sacra Liturgia (Sacred
Congregation of Rites), 240
de Villiers, Henri Adam, 208

About the Author

PETER A. KWASNIEWSKI holds a BA in Liberal Arts from Thomas Aquinas College and an MA and PhD in Philosophy from the Catholic University of America, with a specialization in the thought of Saint Thomas Aquinas. After teaching at the International Theological Institute in Austria, he joined the founding team of Wyoming Catholic College, where he taught theology, philosophy, music, and art history and directed the choir and schola until 2018. Today, he is a full-time writer and public speaker whose work is seen at websites and in periodicals such as *New Liturgical Movement*, *OnePeterFive*, *Rorate Caeli*, *Catholic Family News*, and *Latin Mass Magazine*. Dr. Kwasniewski has published extensively in academic and popular venues on sacramental and liturgical theology, Catholic Social Teaching, issues in the contemporary Church, and the history and aesthetics of music; he is also a composer whose sacred choral music has been performed around the world. The author or editor of many books, Kwasniewski's writings have been translated into at least eighteen languages. He runs a publishing house, Os Justi Press.

Visit his sites:
www.peterkwasniewski.com
www.CantaboDomino.com
www.osjustipress.com
www.soundcloud.com/drkwasniewski
www.facebook.com/ProfKwasniewski
www.youtube.com/@DrKwasniewski